Through a Bhoys Eyes Part 1

Through a Bhoys Eyes, Volume 1

GARY leckey

Published by GARY leckey, 2024.

THROUGH A BHOYS EYES PART 1

First edition. June 27, 2024.

Copyright © 2024 GARY leckey.

ISBN: 979-8227154293

Written by GARY leckey.

Table of Contents

Through a bhoys eyes
Introduction

The chilly Belfast air carried a weight that Michael had grown accustomed to. It was 1982, and the streets of his beloved city whispered tales of unrest and turmoil. As he walked through the narrow lanes of Falls Road, the biting cold seeped through his thin jacket, making him shiver. The graffiti-covered walls and ever-present murals, vivid in their defiance, served as stark reminders of the divided city he lived in. The scent of smoke from distant fires lingered in the air, mingling with the faint aroma of bread from a nearby bakery, a small comfort amidst the tension. Michael's footsteps echoed on the pavement, the sound a lonely rhythm in the silence that hung heavy with unspoken fears and unending conflict.

Michael's journey to this point was neither simple nor straightforward. Born into a family steeped in the history of Irish nationalism, he had heard stories of struggle and resistance from a young age. His father, a dockworker, would often recount tales of the 1916 Easter Rising, instilling in Michael a deep sense of Irish pride. However, it was the events of Bloody Sunday in 1972, which Michael witnessed as a young boy, that crystallized his resolve. The injustice he felt that day ignited a flame within him, a flame that was now leading him down a path from which there was no return.

As he approached a nondescript house at the end of the street, Michael's heart raced with a mix of anticipation and apprehension. The dull, grey facade of the house betrayed nothing of the significance it held within. This was it – his first official meeting with the IRA. He had been to rallies and protests, but this was different. The weight of the moment pressed down on him, making each step feel heavier than the last.

The narrow street was eerily quiet, the usual background noise of the city replaced by an oppressive silence. Michael's breath formed small clouds in the cold air, and he could feel the sweat trickling down his back despite the chill. This was the moment he would step into the shadows of the struggle, a struggle he believed was for the liberation of his people. The dim light from a nearby streetlamp cast long shadows, adding to the sense of foreboding that clung to him like a shroud.

Inside, the room was dimly lit, the air thick with cigarette smoke and hushed tones. The faint glow from a single bulb cast flickering shadows on the walls, creating an atmosphere heavy with tension. Around the battered wooden table sat figures who Michael had only heard of in whispers. The smoke curled around their faces, obscuring their features, but he recognized some from wanted posters and news broadcasts – they were the leaders of the local IRA brigade.

As he stepped into the room, the floor creaked beneath his feet, drawing the gaze of everyone present. The weight of their scrutiny was palpable. Eyes, full of stories untold and hardened by years of conflict, bore into him. Each pair of eyes seemed to measure his worth, testing his resolve.

When he was introduced, a murmur of acknowledgment rippled through the group, but the atmosphere remained thick with unspoken questions. It was a moment of initiation, a moment of unspoken understanding. The gravity of the occasion settled over Michael, making him acutely aware of the path he was about to tread. He felt a sense of belonging mixed with the daunting realization of the responsibilities and dangers that lay ahead.

The meeting was brief but intense. The low murmur of voices discussing plans, identifying targets, and assigning roles filled the room. The air crackled with the energy of clandestine activity, each word laden with significance. Michael's first mission was to be a courier – a relatively low-risk task, but crucial to the operation at hand.

He leaned forward, his eyes darting from one speaker to another, absorbing every detail, every instruction. The weight of the responsibility settled on his shoulders, but with it came a sense of belonging and purpose. The acrid smell of cigarette smoke mingled with the faint scent of sweat, a testament to the room's charged atmosphere. As he committed the plans to memory, Michael felt a newfound determination solidify within him. This was his path, and he was ready to walk it.

Later that night, as Michael lay in bed, the events of the evening replayed in his mind like a film reel. The dim light from the streetlamp outside cast long shadows on his bedroom walls, flickering with the occasional passing car. He could still smell the lingering traces of cigarette smoke on his clothes and feel the residual tension in his muscles.

He thought about his family – his father's proud stories of the Easter Rising, his mother's quiet strength in the face of adversity. He thought about his city, Belfast, scarred by conflict yet resilient and unyielding. The cause he had now fully embraced consumed his thoughts, filling him with a sense of purpose he had never felt before.

There was fear, undoubtedly, a gnawing anxiety about the dangers and moral quandaries that lay ahead. But this fear was overshadowed by a resolute belief in his actions. Michael understood that the road ahead would be fraught with peril, but he was ready. The flame ignited within him on Bloody Sunday now burned brighter than ever, fueling his determination to fight for what he believed was the right of every Irishman – freedom.

Chapter 1 : The Man, The Myth and what will become the Legend

Michael O'Connor's life began and unfolded in the heart of Belfast, amid the turbulent era that would come to be known as the Troubles. Born in 1964, he grew up in a modest, working-class family deeply rooted in the Catholic community of Falls Road – an area resonant with the struggles and aspirations of Irish republicanism. The narrow streets of Falls Road were a canvas of defiant murals and graffiti, each one telling a story of resistance and hope. The sound of distant clashes and the ever-present hum of military helicopters were the backdrop to his childhood, while the scent of peat fires and the occasional acrid smell of burning barricades filled the air. His home was a sanctuary of warmth and love, where stories of heroism and sacrifice were shared around the dinner table, instilling in Michael a deep sense of pride and purpose.

His father, Patrick O'Connor, was a dock worker, a man of sturdy build and few words, but with a fervent heart for the cause of Irish unity. The lines on his weathered face spoke of years of hard labor and unwavering determination. Patrick's evenings were often spent by the fire, his rough hands holding a cup of tea as he recounted tales of the 1916 Easter Rising and the valor of those who fought for Irish freedom. The flickering flames cast dancing shadows on the walls, creating an almost magical backdrop for his stories. These were not mere bedtime tales for Michael; they were the seeds of a legacy that he would come to inherit, each word embedding a deeper sense of pride and duty within him.

Michael's mother, Aoife, was the quiet yet resilient backbone of the O'Connor family. With her soft-spoken demeanor and gentle smile, she possessed an inner strength that belied her delicate appearance. Her strength lay in her unshakeable faith and her ability to maintain a sense of normalcy amidst the chaos that often surrounded their lives. The comforting aroma of freshly baked bread and the soothing hum of her favorite hymns filled their home, creating a sanctuary of peace and warmth. Aoife instilled in Michael and his siblings values of compassion and resilience, teaching them to hold onto hope even in the most trying times. Her whispered prayers at night and her unwavering support were the anchors that kept the family grounded, no matter how fierce the storm outside.

Growing up in the 70s and early 80s in Belfast, Michael lived in two parallel worlds. One moment he was in the schoolyard, kicking a worn-out soccer ball with his friends, their laughter mingling with the cheers of a game well-played. The next, he would find himself halted at a checkpoint, the cold, scrutinizing eyes of soldiers scanning him, their rifles slung menacingly over their shoulders. The familiar route to school was often interrupted by the sight of armored vehicles rumbling down the streets, the acrid smell of smoke from distant riots lingering in the air. At home, Michael would hear the muffled sounds of explosions and gunfire in the distance as he lay in bed, the tension seeping into his dreams. The Troubles weren't just a backdrop; they intruded into every corner of his existence, shaping his childhood in ways he was only beginning to understand.

At St. Joseph's Secondary School, Michael's education extended far beyond textbooks and exams. In history classes, he sat at wooden desks that bore the carvings of previous students, listening intently as his teacher recounted the centuries of British rule over Ireland.

The tales of rebellion and oppression were not just dates and events; they were living stories that resonated deeply within him, each lesson a spark to the growing flame of nationalism in his heart.

Outside the classroom, the schoolyard was abuzz with fervent discussions. Michael and his friends huddled in tight circles during breaks, their voices low but charged with urgency. They debated the latest IRA operations, dissected the strategies, and speculated on the British military's next move. The air was thick with cigarette smoke and the mingled scents of sweat and anticipation. Occasionally, the distant sound of an explosion or the wail of sirens would punctuate their conversations, a stark reminder of the conflict that surrounded them.

These discussions were not just idle chatter; they were the lifeblood of Michael's burgeoning political consciousness. Each whispered word and exchanged glance deepened his resolve to understand and participate in the struggle for a united Ireland. The realities of his community—checkpoint queues, the ever-present soldiers, and the tension that never seemed to dissipate—were daily reinforcements of the lessons learned in school and the stories shared by his father.

The defining moment that crystallized Michael's path came on a cold January day in 1972. He was only eight years old, but the memory would be seared into his mind forever. As he sat on the worn, plaid couch in his family's living room, the black-and-white television flickered with scenes of chaos and violence. News reports showed British soldiers opening fire on unarmed protesters in Derry, the camera capturing the panicked crowd, the cries of the wounded, and the bodies falling to the ground.

Michael's father, Patrick, stood behind him, his face a mask of anguish and fury. The room was silent except for the somber voice of the news anchor and the occasional gasp from his mother, Aoife, who clutched a rosary in her hands. The scent of her evening stew, usually comforting, now seemed out of place in the heavy atmosphere.

The images of Bloody Sunday struck a deep chord within Michael. The fear and injustice he saw on the screen mirrored the stories his father had told him about past uprisings and struggles for Irish freedom. The blood on the streets of Derry was no different from the sacrifices of those who had fought in the Easter Rising of 1916. The scenes of brave men and women standing up against overwhelming odds filled him with a mix of fear, anger, and a growing sense of purpose.

That night, as he lay in bed, Michael couldn't shake the images from his mind. The sounds of gunfire and screams echoed in his thoughts, blending with the distant real-life explosions that punctuated the silence of Belfast nights. His budding nationalist sentiment, nurtured by his father's tales and the harsh realities of life in Northern Ireland, solidified into a resolute determination. He vowed that one day, he would join the fight for Irish freedom, to stand against the oppression and ensure that the sacrifices of Bloody Sunday were not in vain.

As a teenager, Michael's involvement in the nationalist cause deepened, becoming more than just a topic of conversation or a distant dream. He began attending local meetings and rallies, often held in dimly lit community halls where the air was thick with the scent of tobacco and the murmur of fervent discussion. The walls were adorned with posters of iconic figures like Bobby Sands, their determined gazes inspiring those gathered below.

At these gatherings, Michael listened intently to impassioned speeches about the need for a united Ireland and the injustices faced daily by the Catholic community. The speakers' voices rose and fell with emotion, echoing off the walls and stirring something deep within him. Each meeting left him more convinced of the righteousness of their cause and more determined to play his part.

It was at one such rally, beneath the flickering light of bare bulbs and amidst the sea of earnest faces, that Michael first came into contact with members of the IRA. They moved through the crowd with a quiet authority, their presence both intimidating and reassuring. One of them, a tall man with a scar running down his cheek, took notice of Michael's intense focus and unwavering gaze.

After the speeches, the man approached Michael, engaging him in a conversation that quickly turned to the practicalities of their struggle. They saw in Michael a young man with a combination of intelligence, conviction, and a deep-seated sense of justice – qualities that made him an ideal recruit for their cause. The man's questions were probing, yet respectful, as if he was weighing Michael's readiness for something greater.

Michael felt a thrill of anticipation mixed with a sense of destiny as he spoke with the IRA member. The path he had been contemplating now seemed clearer, more attainable. The words of the speakers, the camaraderie of the crowd, and the direct engagement with those already involved in the struggle solidified his resolve. By the end of the evening, he knew that his future lay with the IRA, fighting for the freedom and justice he had been taught to cherish.

Michael's decision to join the IRA was the culmination of his upbringing, experiences, and deeply held beliefs. It was a choice forged in the crucible of Belfast's turmoil, each moment of his life leading inexorably to this point. The stories of his father, the lessons from his teachers, and the harsh realities of his daily existence had all contributed to this defining moment.

As he stood in his small bedroom, the familiar sounds of the city filtering through the thin walls, Michael reflected on the path that had brought him here. The images of Bloody Sunday still haunted his dreams, the faces of fallen friends and family members a constant reminder of the cost of their struggle. He knew the risks and sacrifices involved in joining the IRA – the threat of imprisonment, injury, or even death. But these dangers were outweighed by his unwavering conviction and the burning desire for justice and freedom.

Joining the IRA was not just a political decision; it was a personal commitment. He felt the weight of his ancestors' sacrifices on his shoulders, the blood and tears they had shed for the dream of a free and united Ireland. Michael's heart swelled with pride and determination as he thought of the legacy he was stepping into. This was more than just a fight for independence; it was a continuation of a centuries-old struggle, a battle that had been passed down through generations.

With a steady hand, Michael reached for the small tricolor flag that hung on his wall, its colors vibrant even in the dim light. He traced the edges with his fingers, feeling the coarse fabric and the history it represented. This symbol of their fight, of their hope, solidified his resolve. He was ready to join the ranks of those who had come before him, to take up the mantle and continue the fight for a free and united Ireland.

Michael took a deep breath, the air heavy with the scent of peat fires and distant rain. He knew that from this moment forward, his life would be irrevocably changed. But he was ready. Ready to face the challenges, the dangers, and the sacrifices. Ready to fight for his people, his family, and his country. As he stepped out into the night, the cold air bracing against his skin, he felt a sense of purpose and destiny that filled him with unwavering resolve.

In 1982, Belfast was a city defined by its divisions. The air was often filled with the relentless thrum of helicopters overhead, their searchlights cutting through the night, and the distant rumble of armored vehicles patrolling the tense streets. The sharp scent of burning rubber from makeshift barricades and the acrid smoke from sporadic clashes lingered in the atmosphere. Streets were lined with vivid murals, each one a powerful depiction of nationalist pride and sorrow, their bold colors standing out against the gray backdrop of the city. These murals were more than just art; they were a visual testament to the community's ongoing struggle, their pain and defiance captured in every brushstroke.

The city was deeply segmented along political and religious lines, with areas like the Falls Road being predominantly Catholic and nationalist. Here, the sense of solidarity was palpable, woven into the fabric of daily life. The Catholic community's determination for a united Ireland was reflected in the conversations overheard in pubs, whispered in church confessions, and shouted from the rooftops during marches and rallies. Meanwhile, just across the invisible but heavily fortified divides, Protestant neighborhoods clung to their own sense of identity and loyalty to the British crown.

As Michael navigated these divided streets, he felt the weight of the city's history pressing down on him. Each step along the Falls Road was a step through a living narrative of resistance and hope, where every mural and every whispered conversation added another layer to the story of his people. The tension was a constant companion, but so too was the sense of purpose that bound his community together in their shared struggle for freedom.

The conflict, known as the Troubles, had been ongoing for over a decade, transforming Belfast into a landscape marked by barricades and military patrols. Makeshift barriers of twisted metal and burning debris frequently blocked the roads, symbols of the community's resistance and defiance. The British Army's presence was especially pronounced in areas like Michael's, where the sight of soldiers patrolling the streets in armored vehicles had become a grimly familiar part of daily life. The echo of their boots on the pavement and the glint of their rifles in the sunlight were constant reminders of the tense occupation.

For Michael and his neighbors, this militarized environment fostered a deep sense of occupation and resistance. The pervasive presence of the army stirred feelings of anger and oppression, while the stories of arrests and raids on homes fueled a simmering resentment. Each checkpoint he passed on his way to school, each search and questioning by soldiers, reinforced his understanding of the conflict. These daily encounters with the stark realities of military control left an indelible mark on his psyche.

The atmosphere of constant vigilance and the ever-present threat of violence shaped Michael's worldview in profound ways. The smell of burning tires, the sight of graffitied slogans demanding freedom, and the sound of protest songs sung defiantly in the streets all contributed to his growing sense of identity and purpose. This was not just a political struggle; it was a personal one, woven into the fabric of his everyday life.

As he navigated the barricaded streets and interacted with his community, Michael's understanding of the conflict deepened. He saw the impact of the Troubles in the weary eyes of his parents, the whispered conversations of fear and hope among neighbors, and the determined faces of those who stood against the occupation. These experiences solidified his resolve to join the fight, to take an active role in the struggle for a united Ireland, and to ensure that the sacrifices of his people were not in vain.

The early 80s were a time of intense political turmoil in Northern Ireland. The hunger strikes of 1981, in which ten Republican prisoners died, reverberated through the nationalist community with profound impact. The death of Bobby Sands, who became a symbol of resistance and martyrdom, ignited a renewed fervor and commitment to the republican cause. Michael, like many others, was deeply moved by the image of Sands' gaunt face and the steadfast determination that shone in his eyes despite his suffering.

The atmosphere was charged with emotion as news of the hunger strikes spread. Michael remembered standing in a sea of mourners at Sands' funeral, the air thick with grief and defiance. The slow, somber beat of the drums, the muted weeping of the crowd, and the sight of countless tricolor flags fluttering in the breeze left an indelible mark on his heart. The community's collective sorrow transformed into a powerful force of solidarity and resistance.

This event, along with the ongoing political and social discrimination against the Catholic community, contributed to a growing sense of injustice and urgency within Michael. The discrimination was evident in the everyday interactions he witnessed and experienced—Catholics being passed over for jobs, harassed by the police, or living in poorer conditions compared to their Protestant neighbors. The bitterness of this inequality fueled his desire for change.

Each day, as he walked through the narrow, graffiti-lined streets of his neighborhood, the murals depicting the hunger strikers reminded him of the sacrifices made. The conversations he overheard in pubs, the impassioned speeches at rallies, and the whispered plans in back rooms all spoke of a community determined to fight back. The spirit of defiance was palpable, infusing Michael with a sense of purpose.

As the injustices piled up, Michael's resolve hardened. He felt a personal connection to the struggle, seeing it as his duty to continue the fight for equality and freedom that Bobby Sands and others had died for. The sense of urgency was ever-present, pushing him to act, to take up the mantle of resistance, and to contribute to the dream of a united and free Ireland.

The path that led Michael to the IRA was both personal and political, a journey shaped by the intertwined forces of family legacy and the turbulent environment of Belfast. The stories of his father, filled with the valor of past uprisings and the unyielding spirit of Irish nationalism, had planted the seeds of resistance in Michael from an early age. The harrowing impact of Bloody Sunday, with its indelible images of brutality and injustice, had ignited a burning desire for retribution and justice within him. The charged atmosphere of Belfast, where every street corner echoed with tension and defiance, further fueled his resolve.

Michael's journey to the IRA began in the shadows, at clandestine meetings held in the back rooms of pubs or the basements of trusted homes. These gatherings were shrouded in secrecy, the participants always wary of informers and surveillance. The air was thick with the smell of tobacco and the low murmur of urgent conversations. Dim lighting cast long shadows, adding to the sense of conspiracy and purpose.

At these meetings, Michael listened intently as seasoned members discussed the political situation, dissecting every move made by the

British authorities and debating the necessity of armed struggle. The leaders spoke with a passion that resonated deeply with Michael, their voices rising and falling with the intensity of their convictions. They painted a vivid picture of the struggle, not just as a fight for territory, but as a battle for the very soul of Ireland.

He absorbed their words, his mind racing with the implications and possibilities. The necessity of armed struggle was not just a distant concept; it was presented as an urgent, inevitable step towards achieving their goals. The arguments were compelling, grounded in the harsh realities of their lives and the historical injustices they had endured.

Each meeting brought Michael closer to the realization that this was his path. The camaraderie, the shared sense of purpose, and the palpable commitment to the cause drew him in. He found himself participating more actively, his voice joining the discussions, his ideas contributing to their strategies. The transition from observer to active participant was seamless, driven by his deepening belief in the righteousness of their cause.

Michael's decision to join the IRA was not made lightly. It was a culmination of years of influence, experience, and introspection. The clandestine meetings crystallized his determination, transforming his simmering discontent into a clear, resolute commitment to the struggle for Irish freedom.

REVISED VERSION WITH Content Enhancement

At these meetings, Michael met IRA members who shared their perspectives on the struggle for Irish freedom. The rooms where they gathered were often dimly lit, with the flicker of candles casting dancing shadows on the walls, creating an atmosphere charged with secrecy and resolve. The air was thick with the scent of tobacco and the low murmur of earnest conversations.

The IRA members spoke passionately about the need for direct action against what they viewed as an oppressive British presence. Their voices, filled with conviction, echoed off the walls, each word a call to arms. They detailed their strategies and shared stories of past operations, their eyes alight with the fierce determination of those who believe in their cause. The discussions were not just about tactics and targets, but about the broader vision of a free and united Ireland.

Michael was particularly influenced by their dedication and the sense of purpose they conveyed. He listened intently, absorbing their words and the intensity behind them. The members' unwavering commitment to their cause resonated deeply with him. He saw in them a reflection of his own desires for justice and freedom for his people. Their stories of sacrifice and their readiness to face danger head-on mirrored the fire that burned within him.

One member, a woman named Ashling, recounted a mission where they had sabotaged a British military convoy. Her eyes, though tired, sparkled with pride as she spoke of the operation's success and the message it sent to their oppressors. Michael could feel the adrenaline and fear she must have experienced, the resolve that had driven her and her comrades to risk everything for their beliefs.

The camaraderie among the IRA members was palpable. They were more than just a group fighting for a common cause; they were a family bound together by shared experiences and mutual respect. Their sense of unity and their belief in the righteousness of their struggle were infectious. Michael felt himself drawn deeper into their world, his own resolve strengthening with each meeting.

As he left these gatherings, the cold night air would hit him, bringing with it the reality of the path he was choosing. The streets of Belfast, with their graffiti-covered walls and the ever-present hum of military patrols, seemed to pulse with the same fervor he felt inside. Michael knew he had found his place among these men and women. Their cause was his cause, their fight his fight.

Michael's initial role in the IRA was relatively low risk, but it was a crucial stepping stone. He started as a courier, tasked with delivering messages and small packages between different members. These assignments took him through the winding streets of Belfast, where he moved quietly and inconspicuously, blending in with the everyday hustle and bustle of the city.

The role allowed Michael to become intimately familiar with the operations of the organization. Each message he carried, each package he delivered, was a thread in the intricate web of the IRA's activities. The weight of the envelopes in his pocket and the furtive glances exchanged during handoffs reinforced the seriousness of his mission. Every interaction, no matter how brief, was charged with a sense of urgency and secrecy.

Michael quickly proved his reliability and commitment to the cause. He learned to navigate the city with a sharp eye, always aware of potential surveillance and the ever-present threat of interception by British forces. The sight of British soldiers patrolling the streets, their eyes scanning for anything out of the ordinary, became a familiar but nerve-wracking backdrop to his clandestine activities. The hum of military helicopters overhead and the distant rumble of armored vehicles served as constant reminders of the stakes involved.

Despite the risks, Michael felt a profound sense of belonging and purpose in these actions. Each successful delivery, each safe exchange, was a small victory in the larger struggle for Irish independence. The whispered words of thanks from his comrades and the occasional nod of approval from senior members of the IRA fueled his resolve. He believed that even these small tasks were vital contributions to the cause, each one bringing them a step closer to their ultimate goal.

The streets of Belfast, with their graffiti-covered walls and the ever-present tension, became a familiar battleground. Michael's heart would race with adrenaline as he approached each rendezvous point, the anticipation of danger sharpening his senses. Yet, amidst the fear, there was also a thrill – a sense of playing a part in something much larger than himself.

Through his role as a courier, Michael began to understand the complex network of the IRA and the dedication of its members. He saw firsthand the sacrifices they made and the unwavering commitment that drove them. This deeper understanding only strengthened his own determination. He knew that his journey had only just begun, and he was ready to take on whatever challenges lay ahead in the fight for Irish freedom.

Michael's choice to join the IRA was not a decision made in haste. It was the culmination of a lifetime of influences and experiences, deeply rooted in his personal history, ideological beliefs, and the tumultuous political climate he grew up in.

From his earliest days, Michael had been steeped in the stories of Irish resistance. His father's passionate recounting of the 1916 Easter Rising, told by the fireside with the flickering flames casting dancing shadows on the walls, had ignited a sense of pride and rebellion in young Michael. The tales of brave men and women fighting against overwhelming odds became part of his identity, shaping his understanding of justice and sacrifice.

The political landscape of Belfast in the 70s and early 80s further solidified his convictions. The city was a battleground, its streets marked by the scars of conflict and the constant presence of armed soldiers. The graffiti on the walls, proclaiming slogans of defiance and freedom, spoke to his growing sense of nationalism. Each encounter with the British military – the checkpoints, the searches, the ever-watchful eyes – added fuel to his simmering anger and determination.

Michael's ideological beliefs were also shaped by his education and the community around him. At St. Joseph's Secondary School, history lessons were not just about dates and events; they were about understanding the long struggle for Irish independence. His teachers, themselves products of the same divided society, taught with a fervor that left a lasting impression. The discussions in the schoolyard, filled with the latest news of IRA operations and British military actions, further ingrained the sense of a continuing battle that he was destined to join.

The turning point came with the events of Bloody Sunday in 1972. The images of unarmed protesters being gunned down by British soldiers were seared into his memory. The fear, chaos, and palpable injustice of that day crystallized his resolve. He could no longer be a passive observer; he felt compelled to act, to stand against the oppression that had plagued his people for generations.

Joining the IRA was a decision born of careful consideration and a deep-seated belief in the cause of Irish freedom. It was a choice that weighed heavily on his shoulders, but one that he embraced with unwavering commitment. The clandestine meetings, the whispered plans, and the solemn vows taken in secret gatherings all led him to this point.

As Michael reflected on his journey, he knew that every step, every experience, had prepared him for this moment. His choice was not just about the present struggle but about honoring the legacy of those who had come before him and securing a future for those who would come after. It was a path fraught with danger and uncertainty, but it was the only path he could see – one that aligned with his deepest convictions and his unwavering desire for justice and freedom.

Michael's family played a pivotal role in his decision. His father's stories of historical uprisings and the sacrifices made by Irish nationalists instilled in him a profound sense of national identity and a deep reverence for those who fought for Ireland's freedom. These stories weren't just tales of the past; they were lessons in resilience and the enduring struggle for justice. This familial connection to Ireland's turbulent history was a guiding force in Michael's decision to join the IRA.

From a young age, Michael would sit at his father's feet, captivated by the rich tapestry of stories that spanned centuries of Irish resistance. His father, Patrick, spoke with a fervor that made the past come alive. By the flickering light of the hearth, he recounted the bravery of the men and women who had risen against British rule, their faces etched in Michael's mind like revered saints in a sacred litany. The smell of peat burning in the fireplace mingled with the earnestness of Patrick's voice, creating an atmosphere charged with reverence and resolve.

Patrick's tales of the 1916 Easter Rising were particularly poignant. He described the rebels' determination and the sacrifices they made, their blood staining the streets of Dublin as they fought for a dream of freedom. Michael could almost hear the echoes of gunfire and the shouts of defiance as his father spoke, his eyes shining with pride and sorrow. These stories were not just about battles and heroics; they were about the unyielding spirit of a people who refused to be broken.

Michael's mother, Aoife, also contributed to this deep-seated sense of identity. Her quiet strength and unwavering support for her husband's convictions provided a stable foundation for Michael's burgeoning nationalism. She would often remind him of the importance of their heritage, weaving tales of their ancestors' resilience into the fabric of their daily lives. The scent of her home-cooked meals, the warmth of her hugs, and her soothing voice were constant reminders of the love and solidarity that bound their family together.

The impact of these familial influences was profound. Michael saw his father's passion and his mother's quiet determination reflected in his own heart. The stories of past uprisings became a lens through which he viewed the current struggles of his community. The injustices faced by the Catholic population in Belfast, the discrimination, and the heavy-handedness of British soldiers were not just contemporary issues; they were continuations of a long history of oppression that his family had taught him to resist.

This deep-rooted connection to Ireland's turbulent history was a guiding force in Michael's decision to join the IRA. It was a decision made with a full understanding of the risks and sacrifices involved, but also with a profound sense of duty and honor. He felt a kinship with the martyrs of the past, a responsibility to carry forward their legacy and to fight for the dream of a free and united Ireland. His family's stories were not just memories; they were a call to action, a beacon lighting the path he knew he had to follow.

Michael's upbringing in Belfast amid the Troubles provided a firsthand view of the conflict's harsh realities. The daily scenes of military patrols, with soldiers clad in full combat gear and armored vehicles rumbling through the streets, were a stark contrast to the innocence of his childhood games. The sounds of distant explosions and the sharp cracks of gunfire were an ever-present soundtrack to his life, punctuating the nights with a grim reminder of the violence that lurked around every corner.

The city bore visible scars of the ongoing struggle. Buildings pockmarked with bullet holes, walls adorned with defiant graffiti, and the remnants of barricades told a story of a community under siege. Michael would often walk past these silent witnesses of conflict, his steps echoing in the eerie quiet that followed each violent episode. The smell of smoke and the sight of rubble-strewn streets were constant, haunting reminders of the price his people paid daily.

The pervasive sense of injustice was palpable. Michael saw it in the eyes of the elderly neighbors who spoke of better times with a mix of nostalgia and sorrow, in the determined faces of young men who joined the resistance, and in the worried glances exchanged by parents as they sent their children off to school under the watchful eyes of armed patrols. The oppressive presence of British forces, the frequent searches, and the arbitrary detentions fostered a simmering resentment that seeped into every aspect of daily life.

Despite the oppression, the community's resilience in the face of adversity deeply affected Michael. He witnessed the solidarity and support that bound his neighbors together. Acts of kindness, like sharing food during shortages or offering shelter during raids, highlighted the strength and unity of his community. The whispered conversations of resistance plans, the secret meetings in back rooms, and the defiant songs sung softly in the night were all testaments to their unyielding spirit.

Witnessing the impact of the conflict on his neighborhood and the people he cared about solidified Michael's resolve to play a part in their struggle. He saw the toll it took on his family, friends, and community, and he felt an overwhelming sense of duty to fight for their freedom. Each day brought new stories of hardship and bravery, further fueling his determination to make a difference.

Michael's resolve was not born out of a desire for glory or revenge, but from a deep-seated belief in justice and the right to self-determination. The sights, sounds, and experiences of his upbringing in Belfast were etched into his soul, guiding him toward a path he felt was his destiny. He knew that joining the IRA was not just a choice, but a necessary step to honor the sacrifices of those before him and to secure a better future for those who would come after.

Michael's decision was also heavily influenced by his ideological beliefs. Over time, he grew to view the IRA's fight not just as a battle for national sovereignty, but as a quest for social justice. The struggle was not merely about drawing borders on a map; it was about dismantling the structures of oppression and creating a fair and just society for all.

As he attended clandestine meetings and listened to impassioned speeches, Michael's understanding of the IRA's mission deepened. He began to see their actions as part of a broader fight against systemic injustice. The voices of the leaders, filled with conviction, painted a picture of a society where equality and freedom reigned. Their words resonated deeply with him, aligning with his own experiences of discrimination and inequality.

To Michael, the IRA's struggle symbolized the fight against oppression in all its forms. He saw parallels between their battle and other global movements for justice and liberation. The stories of civil rights leaders and revolutionaries from around the world inspired him, reinforcing his belief that their fight was part of a universal struggle for human dignity.

His belief in the right to self-determination became a cornerstone of his personal ideology. Michael was convinced that every community had the right to govern itself, free from external control. The idea of a united Ireland, where the people could determine their own future without interference, became a powerful motivator. The vision of an Ireland free from foreign rule, where his people could live in peace and prosperity, fueled his commitment.

Michael's ideological beliefs were further shaped by the injustices he witnessed daily. The sight of his neighbors being harassed by soldiers, the stories of friends who had been unjustly imprisoned, and the pervasive sense of fear and repression all strengthened his resolve. He believed that by joining the IRA, he was taking a stand not only for national sovereignty but for the broader principles of justice and equality.

His conversations with fellow activists reinforced these beliefs. They spoke of a future where the divisions that had plagued their society would be healed, where every individual, regardless of background, could live with dignity and freedom. These discussions were filled with hope and determination, painting a picture of the society they aspired to build.

The vision of a united Ireland, free from foreign rule and built on the principles of justice and equality, became core tenets of Michael's personal ideology. It was a vision that guided his actions and decisions, giving him the strength to face the challenges ahead. He knew that the path he had chosen was fraught with danger, but his commitment to these ideals made every risk worth taking.

Personal experiences of discrimination and witnessing the impact of the conflict on ordinary people reinforced Michael's motivations. Encounters with injustice, whether through stories of family and friends or his own experiences, highlighted the disparities and issues plaguing Northern Irish society. These experiences cemented his belief that joining the IRA was a necessary step in combating these injustices.

From a young age, Michael had seen the harsh realities of discrimination. He remembered the cold stares and muttered insults from those who viewed his Catholic family as second-class citizens. He recalled his father's frustration when denied work opportunities simply because of his faith, and his mother's quiet resilience in the face of daily indignities. These personal encounters with prejudice left a deep impression on him, fueling a sense of anger and a desire for change.

As he grew older, Michael's awareness of these injustices expanded. He heard stories from friends who had been harassed or detained by British soldiers without cause. Their tales of humiliation and fear resonated with him, each one adding another layer to his growing resolve. The sight of families being torn apart by arrests and the oppressive presence of military checkpoints in his neighborhood became a constant reminder of the inequality and repression that defined their lives.

Witnessing the broader impact of the conflict on ordinary people further solidified Michael's motivations. He saw the toll it took on his community – the grief of families who had lost loved ones, the fear etched into the faces of children who had grown up surrounded by violence, and the resilience of those who continued to fight for their rights despite the odds. The graffiti on the walls, the somber murals commemorating fallen heroes, and the whispered conversations about resistance all spoke of a society in turmoil, struggling to reclaim its dignity and freedom.

Michael's own experiences with discrimination also played a crucial role. He vividly remembered the day he was stopped and searched by British soldiers while walking home from school. The rough handling, the accusatory questions, and the sheer helplessness he felt in that moment burned into his memory. It was a stark, personal encounter with the injustice that permeated their lives, reinforcing his belief that action was necessary.

The stories of his family and friends, combined with his own encounters, highlighted the disparities and systemic issues that plagued Northern Irish society. The pervasive sense of injustice and the visible impact of the conflict on those he cared about made it clear that passive acceptance was not an option. Michael felt a growing conviction that joining the IRA was not just a personal choice, but a moral imperative.

He believed that by becoming part of the IRA, he could contribute to the fight against these injustices. It was a way to stand up for his community, to protect the vulnerable, and to challenge the oppressive forces that sought to keep them down. Each experience of discrimination and every story of hardship he heard further cemented his resolve, guiding him toward the path of resistance.

In joining the IRA, Michael saw an opportunity to make a tangible difference. It was a step towards addressing the deep-seated inequalities and fighting for a future where his people could live without fear, in a society that respected their rights and dignity. The injustices he had witnessed and experienced became the driving force behind his commitment to the cause, propelling him forward in the struggle for Irish freedom.

Michael often found himself reflecting on what it meant to be Irish in a land divided by conflict. His sense of national identity was intertwined with the historical narrative of resistance and the contemporary struggle for freedom. This reflection on national identity played a significant role in shaping his decision to join the IRA, seeing it as a way to contribute to defining the future of his country and his people.

During quiet moments, Michael would contemplate the legacy of his ancestors, the stories of rebellion and resilience that had been passed down through generations. He thought about the centuries of British rule, the countless uprisings, and the relentless pursuit of independence. The weight of history pressed upon him, filling him with a sense of pride and responsibility. To be Irish, he realized, was to carry the torch of those who had fought before him, to honor their sacrifices by continuing the struggle.

As he walked through the streets of Belfast, the murals and graffiti that adorned the walls served as constant reminders of this enduring fight. The images of past heroes, their faces painted with a mix of sorrow and defiance, inspired him. The slogans demanding freedom and justice resonated deeply, echoing the sentiments that had been instilled in him since childhood. Each step he took along these streets was a step through a living history, a history he felt compelled to be a part of.

Michael's sense of national identity was further shaped by the contemporary struggle for freedom. The injustices he witnessed daily, the discrimination faced by his community, and the oppressive presence of British forces all reinforced his belief in the need for resistance. He saw the IRA's actions as a continuation of the historical fight for self-determination, a necessary response to the ongoing oppression.

His reflections on national identity often brought him to the realization that the future of Ireland depended on the actions of its people. He believed that by joining the IRA, he could play a part in shaping that future. It was a way to assert his identity, to stand up for his rights, and to fight for a united Ireland where his people could live freely and with dignity.

The decision to join the IRA was not made lightly. It was a culmination of his reflections, his experiences, and his deeply held beliefs. Michael understood the risks involved, but he also recognized the importance of his contribution. He saw it as a way to honor the past, to fight for the present, and to secure the future of his country and his people.

As he stood on the brink of this decision, Michael felt a sense of clarity and purpose. The path ahead was fraught with danger and uncertainty, but it was also filled with the promise of change. By joining the IRA, he was not just joining a militant group; he was joining a movement, a cause that transcended individual actions and aimed at the collective liberation of his nation.

In his heart, Michael knew that this was his way of defining what it meant to be Irish. It was a commitment to the principles of justice and freedom, a dedication to the dream of a united Ireland. His reflection on national identity had led him to this point, guiding his steps towards a future he was determined to help create.

As Michael's involvement in the IRA deepened, so did his understanding of the intricate and often morally ambiguous nature of the armed struggle. This journey brought him face-to-face with realities that tested his convictions and challenged his understanding of the conflict.

The initial excitement of being part of the resistance was soon tempered by the stark realities of their operations. Michael found himself in clandestine meetings where plans were meticulously crafted, every detail weighed with the gravity of its potential consequences. The air was thick with tension and the acrid smell of cigarette smoke, the low murmur of voices discussing strategies that would inevitably lead to violence.

One evening, Michael was assigned to assist in a raid on a British supply convoy. As he crouched in the shadows, the cold metal of his weapon pressing against his side, he could hear the distant rumble of the approaching vehicles. His heart pounded in his chest, the adrenaline mingling with a deep sense of foreboding. When the convoy appeared, the night erupted into chaos – the sharp cracks of gunfire, the shouts of men, and the acrid smell of gunpowder filled the air. Amidst the confusion, Michael saw the face of a young British soldier, no older than himself, eyes wide with fear as he fell. The moment seared into his memory, a stark reminder of the human cost of their struggle.

These experiences forced Michael to grapple with the moral complexities of their fight. He saw comrades captured, tortured, and killed, their sacrifices weighing heavily on his conscience. The lines between right and wrong blurred as he participated in operations that targeted not just military personnel, but sometimes also led to civilian casualties. The guilt and doubt gnawed at him, the faces of innocents caught in the crossfire haunting his dreams.

Michael's understanding of the conflict was further challenged by interactions with those outside his immediate circle. He encountered civilians who supported the cause but were weary of the violence, their eyes pleading for peace. He heard stories from former members who had left the IRA, their voices filled with regret and disillusionment. These perspectives added layers of complexity to his views, forcing him to reconsider the broader impact of their actions.

In quieter moments, Michael would reflect on his journey, the ideals that had driven him to join the IRA, and the harsh realities he now faced. The sense of purpose that had once burned brightly was now shadowed by doubt. Yet, despite the moral ambiguities, he remained committed to the cause, believing that their fight was a necessary evil in the pursuit of a greater good.

His deepening involvement in the IRA also revealed the internal divisions and political maneuvering within the organization. He witnessed power struggles and ideological rifts that threatened to undermine their unity. These internal conflicts added another layer of complexity to his understanding, highlighting the fragile nature of their resistance.

Through it all, Michael's convictions were tested, but his resolve remained. He understood that the path to freedom was fraught with peril and moral quandaries. The journey had changed him, deepened his understanding, and hardened his determination. He knew that the struggle for Irish independence was not black and white, but he believed in the righteousness of their cause and was prepared to face the consequences of his choices.

Michael often found himself in situations where the lines between right and wrong were blurred. Each operation raised questions about the ethics of their actions. He struggled with the knowledge that while their efforts were aimed at British forces, the reality of conflict meant that civilians could inadvertently be caught in the crossfire. The burden of these moral dilemmas weighed heavily on him, leading to many sleepless nights as he wrestled with the justifications of their cause versus the potential for unintended harm.

During one such operation, Michael and his unit were tasked with sabotaging a British military installation. The plan was meticulously detailed, aimed at crippling the enemy's logistical capabilities. As they moved under the cover of darkness, the tension was palpable, each step deliberate and silent. The smell of damp earth and the distant hum of the city were the only accompaniments to their stealthy advance.

The explosion that followed their successful infiltration was deafening, a blinding flash of light followed by a shockwave that rattled the very ground beneath them. As they retreated, Michael's elation was short-lived. The next morning, reports emerged that the blast had also damaged nearby civilian structures, injuring several innocents. The sight of a young mother cradling her wounded child, tears streaming down her face, haunted Michael. The unintended consequences of their actions weighed heavily on his conscience.

These incidents were not isolated. Michael's mind was often besieged by memories of similar operations where the collateral damage was all too real. The image of a market square, once bustling with life, now marred by the scars of an explosion intended for a passing military convoy, remained etched in his memory. The cries of the injured and the bewildered faces of those who had lost everything in an instant echoed in his thoughts long after the operations were over.

Michael struggled with the knowledge that their noble cause came at such a high cost. He spent countless nights staring at the ceiling, the weight of his decisions pressing down on him like a physical burden. The moonlight filtering through his window did little to soothe his troubled mind. He questioned the morality of their tactics, the justification of their actions against the backdrop of innocent suffering.

Conversations with his comrades offered little solace. Some viewed the collateral damage as an unfortunate but necessary part of their struggle, a harsh reality of war. Others, like Michael, were tormented by the moral ambiguities, seeking answers in the grey areas where black-and-white certainties dissolved. The discussions around the campfire, with the flickering flames casting long shadows on their faces, often ended in silence, each man lost in his own thoughts.

In his heart, Michael knew that the fight for freedom was fraught with difficult choices. He understood that their cause was just, but the means to achieve it were often tainted with unintended harm. The faces of those caught in the crossfire, the innocents who paid the price for their struggle, never left him. He wrestled with these moral dilemmas, searching for a way to reconcile his beliefs with the harsh realities of their actions.

Yet, despite the sleepless nights and the burden of his conscience, Michael remained committed. He believed in the righteousness of their cause, in the dream of a free and united Ireland. The journey was complex, filled with ethical quandaries, but he held onto the hope that their struggle would ultimately lead to a better future, one where such sacrifices would no longer be necessary.

REVISED VERSION WITH Content Enhancement

The danger of his involvement was not lost on Michael. He understood that every mission carried the risk of arrest, injury, or death. The thought of his family suffering because of his actions was a constant source of concern. The IRA's struggle was not just his own; it inadvertently involved his loved ones, who were unaware of the full extent of his activities. This duality of his life – the secret IRA member and the family man – was a source of internal conflict.

As Michael prepared for each mission, he was acutely aware of the stakes. The clandestine meetings, the whispered plans in dimly lit rooms, all carried the weight of potential disaster. The cold steel of his weapon, the feel of the rough terrain underfoot during late-night maneuvers, and the ever-present hum of danger created a tense backdrop to his double life. He knew that a single mistake could lead to his capture or worse, and the implications of such an outcome haunted him.

At home, Michael played the role of the dutiful son and brother, concealing his involvement with the IRA from his family. The warmth of his mother's embrace, the innocent laughter of his younger siblings, and the familiar sounds of domestic life provided a stark contrast to the violent world he navigated. The scent of his mother's cooking, the soft hum of the radio playing in the background, and the cozy glow of the family hearth were all reminders of the life he was fighting to protect.

However, this duality of existence was a source of internal conflict. He often found himself torn between the demands of his clandestine activities and the responsibilities to his family. The thought of his mother's worried face if she ever discovered the truth, or his siblings growing up without their brother, weighed heavily on his mind. The fear that his actions could bring harm to those he loved was a constant companion.

One evening, after a particularly harrowing mission, Michael returned home to find his family gathered around the dinner table.

The warmth and normalcy of the scene almost brought him to tears. His father's hearty laughter, his mother's gentle reprimands, and his siblings' playful banter seemed worlds apart from the violence and tension that characterized his secret life. The juxtaposition of these two realities created a deep sense of guilt and unease.

During quiet moments, Michael would retreat to his room, the walls adorned with mementos of a simpler time. He would sit by the window, staring out into the night, the distant sounds of the city a constant reminder of the conflict. The weight of his double life pressed down on him, the internal struggle between duty to his cause and his family's safety tearing at his soul. He knew that his involvement with the IRA was necessary, but the personal cost was steep.

The internal conflict was exacerbated by the secrecy required to protect his loved ones. He couldn't share his fears or burdens with anyone at home, leaving him isolated in his struggles. The late-night whispers, the coded messages, and the constant vigilance took their toll, both physically and emotionally. He longed for a day when he could be honest with his family, when the fight would be over, and the need for secrecy would disappear.

Despite the dangers and the internal turmoil, Michael remained steadfast in his commitment. He believed in the righteousness of their cause and the necessity of their struggle. The hope for a free and united Ireland, where his family and future generations could live in peace, drove him forward. The path was fraught with peril, but it was a path he chose with full awareness of its implications, balancing his love for his family with his dedication to the fight for freedom.

As Michael became more entrenched in the IRA, encounters with violence became more frequent. He witnessed firsthand the aftermath of operations – the chaos, the fear, and sometimes the grief. These experiences left an indelible mark on him, shaping his perspective on the conflict and hardening his resolve. They served as stark reminders of the high stakes involved in their struggle for freedom.

One night, after a particularly intense operation, Michael found himself standing amidst the wreckage of a bombed-out building. The acrid smell of smoke filled the air, mingling with the metallic tang of blood. The wail of sirens and the frantic shouts of rescue workers created a cacophony of urgency. As he moved through the debris, the sight of wounded civilians being tended to by medics and the anguished cries of those who had lost loved ones pierced his heart. The faces of the victims, etched with pain and confusion, haunted him long after the smoke had cleared.

These scenes of devastation were not uncommon. Michael often returned to safe houses with his comrades, their clothes stained with soot and their faces grim. The post-operation debriefings were filled with accounts of their actions, the successes and the inevitable collateral damage. Each story added another layer to the heavy burden he carried. The toll of their fight was visible in the haunted eyes of his comrades, each bearing their own scars from the conflict.

Witnessing the direct consequences of their operations forced Michael to confront the harsh realities of their struggle. He saw the fear in the eyes of civilians caught in the crossfire, the desperate attempts to salvage what little they had left, and the grief-stricken faces of those mourning their dead. These experiences were a brutal reminder of the cost of their fight, the innocent lives shattered by the violence they wrought. Yet, amidst the chaos and destruction, he also saw the resilience of his people, their unyielding spirit in the face of adversity.

These encounters with violence hardened Michael's resolve. The sight of British soldiers patrolling the streets with an air of superiority, the heavy-handed tactics used to control the population, and the systemic injustices that fueled the conflict all reinforced his commitment. Each operation, despite its toll, was a necessary step towards their ultimate goal. The pain and suffering he witnessed were not in vain; they were part of a larger struggle for justice and freedom.

Michael's perspective on the conflict evolved with each experience. He became more attuned to the complexities and moral ambiguities of their fight. The lines between right and wrong, friend and foe, blurred in the fog of war. He grappled with the ethical dilemmas that arose from their actions, the constant battle between his conscience and his commitment to the cause. Yet, these very challenges also strengthened his determination. He knew that their fight was not just for territory, but for the very soul of their nation.

The high stakes involved in their struggle were ever-present in Michael's mind. The knowledge that their actions could bring about both liberation and destruction weighed heavily on him. He understood the immense responsibility that came with each mission, the lives that hung in the balance. This awareness drove him to be more precise, more strategic, and more resolute in his efforts.

As the conflict raged on, Michael's experiences in the IRA forged him into a seasoned fighter, his resolve tempered by the fires of violence and loss. He bore the scars of battle, both seen and unseen, each one a testament to his unwavering commitment. The journey was fraught with peril, but it was a path he had chosen willingly, guided by the hope of a free and united Ireland.

As Michael's involvement with the IRA deepened, so did his comprehension of the complex political landscape that defined the Troubles. His perspective broadened from a focus on immediate operations to understanding their place in the larger struggle for Irish independence.

In the beginning, Michael's thoughts were consumed by the logistics of their missions. The clandestine meetings, the careful planning, the adrenaline-pumping execution – these were his immediate realities. He spent countless hours pouring over maps, memorizing routes, and coordinating with his comrades. The tense moments before a mission, the meticulous preparations, and the high stakes involved occupied his mind.

However, as he spent more time within the organization, he began to see beyond the immediate scope of their actions. Late-night discussions with seasoned members of the IRA, often held in the smoky back rooms of pubs or in hidden safe houses, opened his eyes to the broader political context. The air would be thick with the smell of tobacco and the murmur of voices debating strategy and ideology. These conversations were a window into the larger struggle that their individual actions supported.

Michael started to understand the intricate web of alliances and enmities that characterized the conflict. He learned about the political maneuvering between the British government, the Irish Republic, and various factions within Northern Ireland. He saw how their operations were not just isolated acts of defiance but part of a calculated effort to sway public opinion, apply political pressure, and gain international support. The complexity of the situation was daunting, but it also highlighted the importance of their cause.

One particularly enlightening experience came during a secret meeting with a political strategist from the Republic of Ireland. The strategist explained how the IRA's actions were part of a broader plan to force the British government into negotiations. Michael listened intently, his mind racing with the implications. He realized that their struggle was not just about physical resistance but also about winning hearts and minds, both at home and abroad.

As Michael's comprehension of the political landscape deepened, he began to appreciate the importance of timing and symbolism in their operations. He saw how a well-timed attack could shift the momentum of the conflict, how the martyrdom of key figures could galvanize support, and how propaganda played a crucial role in shaping public perception. The images of past heroes, the carefully crafted messages in their leaflets, and the strategic use of media all contributed to their cause.

This broader understanding did not lessen the dangers he faced but gave his actions a deeper significance. Each mission became more than just a tactical endeavor; it was a piece of a larger puzzle, a step towards their ultimate goal of a united Ireland. The knowledge that their struggle was part of a historical continuum, a long fight for justice and self-determination, reinforced his commitment.

Michael also began to recognize the internal dynamics within the IRA. He saw the ideological debates, the power struggles, and the need for unity in the face of external threats. These insights made him a more thoughtful and strategic member, someone who could navigate the complexities of the organization while staying true to its core mission.

His broadened perspective also brought a new level of responsibility. He understood that his actions, and those of his comrades, had far-reaching consequences. The stakes were not just personal but national and even global. This awareness fueled his dedication and his willingness to make sacrifices for the greater good.

In this journey, Michael transformed from a young man driven by personal grievances and immediate goals into a seasoned fighter with a deep understanding of the political landscape. His resolve was strengthened by this broader comprehension, knowing that their struggle was not in vain but a vital part of the quest for Irish independence.

Michael began to delve deeper into the history of Ireland's struggle for independence. He studied the events leading up to the Troubles, from the partition of Ireland in 1921 to the civil rights movements in the 1960s. This historical perspective helped him understand the long-standing grievances and aspirations of the nationalist community. He saw the IRA's actions as part of a continuum in a centuries-long struggle against British rule.

His evenings were often spent poring over books and historical documents in the dim light of his room. The pages of old volumes, filled with stories of rebellion and resistance, captivated him. The scent of aged paper and the sound of turning pages became a familiar comfort as he immersed himself in the past. He read about the partition of Ireland, the bitter division that had created Northern Ireland and set the stage for decades of conflict. The political machinations, the betrayals, and the agreements that had led to this division were laid bare before him, each fact adding to his growing understanding of the struggle.

The civil rights movements of the 1960s were particularly enlightening. Michael learned about the peaceful protests that had been met with violence, the marches for equality, and the demands for basic human rights. The images of these events, grainy black-and-white photographs of determined faces and raised fists, made a profound impact on him. He saw parallels between the injustices of the past and the present, understanding how these movements had evolved into the violent conflict of the Troubles.

Michael's study sessions were often interrupted by the sounds of Belfast's streets – the distant rumble of armored vehicles, the sporadic bursts of gunfire, and the echoing chants of protests. These sounds, coupled with the historical narratives he was absorbing, created a powerful connection between the past and his present reality. He felt a deep kinship with the figures he read about, from the leaders of the 1916 Easter Rising to the civil rights activists of the 1960s.

This historical perspective helped Michael understand the long-standing grievances of the nationalist community. The stories of land dispossession, economic discrimination, and political marginalization resonated deeply with him. He saw how the seeds of resentment had been sown over centuries, leading to the explosive conflict of his own time. The narrative of struggle and resistance became a lens through which he viewed his own actions and those of his comrades.

Michael saw the IRA's actions as part of a continuum in this centuries-long struggle against British rule. The operations he participated in, the risks he took, and the sacrifices he made were all connected to the broader historical context. Each mission was a link in a long chain of resistance, stretching back through the ages. This realization gave him a profound sense of purpose and continuity, a feeling that he was part of something much larger than himself.

His deeper understanding of history also brought clarity to his motivations. He was not just fighting against the immediate oppression of British forces; he was part of a legacy of resistance, carrying forward the torch of those who had fought before him. The knowledge of past struggles and the enduring spirit of his people reinforced his resolve. He felt a duty to honor the sacrifices of the past by continuing the fight in the present.

As he delved into the history of Ireland's struggle for independence, Michael's perspective broadened and deepened. He came to see the IRA's actions not just as isolated acts of defiance, but as essential steps in a long journey toward justice and self-determination. This historical insight strengthened his commitment, providing him with a sense of direction and an unwavering belief in the righteousness of their cause.

Michael's deeper involvement in the IRA exposed him to the organization's strategic thinking and its role in the broader nationalist movement. He learned about the IRA's connections with other nationalist groups and its efforts to galvanize public support for the cause of a united Ireland. He came to see the IRA not just as a military organization but as a key player in a larger political struggle for self-determination.

As Michael attended more meetings and participated in strategic discussions, he began to understand the intricate web of alliances that underpinned the IRA's operations. These gatherings, often held in secluded basements or remote safe houses, revealed a sophisticated network of cooperation and coordination. The air in these rooms was thick with the intensity of purpose and the smell of tobacco, the dim lighting casting long shadows on the faces of those present. The discussions were far-reaching, covering not just immediate tactical plans but also long-term strategies aimed at achieving their ultimate goal.

One evening, Michael was invited to a meeting that included representatives from various nationalist groups. The atmosphere was charged with a sense of history and camaraderie, the shared goal of a united Ireland uniting diverse factions. He listened intently as leaders discussed the importance of unity and the need to present a cohesive front to the public and international community. The conversations ranged from logistics and funding to propaganda and public relations. Each topic highlighted the multifaceted nature of their struggle, blending military action with political strategy.

Through these interactions, Michael learned about the IRA's efforts to galvanize public support. He saw how carefully crafted messages were disseminated to rally the nationalist community and sway public opinion. Pamphlets, posters, and clandestine radio broadcasts were all tools in their arsenal, each one designed to inspire and mobilize. The importance of winning hearts and minds became clear to him, as did the role of the media in shaping the narrative of their struggle. He witnessed the meticulous planning that went into organizing rallies and protests, understanding that these events were not just expressions of dissent but strategic moves in a larger game.

Michael also became aware of the international dimension of their fight. He learned about the IRA's connections with sympathetic organizations and individuals abroad, efforts to garner support and resources from the global community. These alliances provided not just material aid but also moral support, reinforcing the legitimacy of their cause. The discussions about international solidarity filled him with a sense of global interconnectedness, realizing that their struggle resonated beyond the borders of Ireland.

The realization that the IRA was a key player in a larger political struggle for self-determination deepened Michael's commitment. He understood that their actions were part of a broader movement that sought to rectify historical injustices and achieve lasting peace. The military operations he participated in were not isolated acts of violence but strategic efforts to advance a political agenda. This perspective brought a new level of significance to his involvement, making him feel part of a grand, historical mission.

Through his exposure to the IRA's strategic thinking, Michael saw the organization in a new light. It was not just a militant group fighting against British rule but a vital component of the nationalist movement, working towards a unified and independent Ireland. The blend of military action and political strategy, the connections with other groups, and the efforts to build public support all underscored the complexity and importance of their mission.

As Michael delved deeper into the strategic aspects of the IRA, his role within the organization evolved. He became more involved in planning and decision-making, contributing his insights and ideas to the collective effort. This deeper involvement reinforced his sense of purpose and his belief in the righteousness of their cause. The journey from a young man driven by personal grievances to a key player in a sophisticated political struggle was complete, solidifying his dedication to the fight for Irish independence.

As his understanding grew, so did his recognition of the conflict's complexity. Michael saw that the struggle was not just against a foreign presence but also involved internal divisions within Northern Ireland. He became aware of the varying perspectives within the nationalist community and the challenges of balancing the IRA's military objectives with political strategies.

Michael's deepening involvement in the IRA exposed him to the multifaceted nature of the conflict. He attended meetings where heated debates took place, revealing the ideological rifts and differing priorities within the nationalist community. These gatherings were often intense, the air charged with a mix of passion and tension. The smoke-filled rooms and the clinking of glasses punctuated the fervent discussions, creating an atmosphere of urgency and resolve.

Through these interactions, Michael realized that the struggle for Irish independence was not a monolithic endeavor. There were various factions within the nationalist community, each with its own vision of the future and approach to achieving it. Some groups advocated for more aggressive military actions, while others pushed for diplomatic solutions and political engagement. This diversity of thought presented both opportunities and challenges for the IRA, requiring careful navigation to maintain unity and effectiveness.

One evening, Michael found himself in a spirited debate with a fellow member who questioned the morality and efficacy of their violent tactics. The man, a former civil rights activist, argued for nonviolent resistance and greater emphasis on political processes. Michael listened, his mind racing with the implications of these arguments. The exchange was a stark reminder of the internal divisions they faced and the need to reconcile their military actions with broader political strategies.

These debates highlighted the complexity of balancing the IRA's military objectives with political goals. Michael saw how each operation had to be carefully planned not just for tactical success but also for its political repercussions. A successful mission could bolster their cause, but a misstep could alienate potential allies and fuel internal dissent. The strategic importance of timing, messaging, and public perception became increasingly clear to him.

Michael also became acutely aware of the internal divisions within Northern Ireland itself. He saw the deep-seated sectarian tensions that complicated their struggle. The Protestant loyalist community, fiercely opposed to the nationalist cause, posed a significant challenge. The bitter divide between Catholics and Protestants added another layer of complexity to the conflict, making the pursuit of a united Ireland even more difficult.

As he navigated these challenges, Michael's respect for the IRA's leadership grew. He saw the delicate balancing act they performed, managing military operations while engaging in political dialogue and maintaining cohesion within their ranks. The leaders' ability to strategize, negotiate, and inspire was crucial to their survival and progress. Michael learned to appreciate the nuances of their decisions, understanding that each move was part of a larger, intricate chess game.

This growing awareness of the conflict's complexity reinforced Michael's commitment to the cause. He understood that their struggle required not just bravery and sacrifice, but also wisdom and strategic thinking. The blend of military action and political maneuvering was essential to achieving their goals, and he was determined to contribute to both aspects of the fight.

Michael's journey from a young, impassioned recruit to a seasoned member of the IRA was marked by this deeper understanding. He saw the importance of unity and the need to respect and integrate the varying perspectives within the nationalist community. The path to a united Ireland was fraught with obstacles, both external and internal, but he was prepared to face these challenges head-on.

Through his experiences, Michael realized that the struggle for Irish independence was a complex and multifaceted endeavor. It was a battle fought not just on the streets, but also in the hearts and minds of the people. This recognition deepened his resolve, knowing that their fight was part of a larger, historical continuum that required both strength and subtlety to succeed.

Michael also became aware of the international dimension of the Troubles. He learned about the role of foreign governments, the diaspora, and international opinion in shaping the conflict. This global perspective underscored the importance of public perception and the need for the IRA to consider its actions' broader implications.

Through his deepening involvement with the IRA, Michael began attending strategic meetings where the discussion often turned to the international stage. These sessions were held in hidden safe houses, their locations frequently changed to avoid detection. The dim lighting and low murmur of voices created an atmosphere of intense focus and clandestine urgency. Maps and documents were spread out on tables, detailing not just local targets but also international connections and strategies.

One such meeting featured a guest speaker – an Irish-American activist who had come to share insights on the influence of the Irish diaspora in the United States. The activist spoke passionately about the significant financial and moral support that the diaspora provided, emphasizing how crucial this external backing was for the IRA's operations. Michael listened intently, realizing how interconnected their struggle was with global politics. The speaker's words highlighted the importance of maintaining a positive image abroad and the need to galvanize international support for their cause.

Michael learned about the intricate dance of diplomacy and propaganda that played out on the international stage. The IRA's actions were not just scrutinized by the British and Irish governments but also by foreign entities whose opinions could sway public perception and influence policy. Reports of IRA activities appeared in newspapers across the globe, and these accounts could either garner sympathy or condemnation, depending on their nature and the context in which they were framed.

This understanding brought a new dimension to Michael's view of their struggle. He saw the importance of carefully planned operations that minimized civilian casualties and the necessity of media outreach to convey their message effectively. The public relations aspect of their fight became clear – winning the battle for hearts and minds was as crucial as any military victory. The smell of fresh ink and the rustling of paper became familiar as he helped distribute newsletters and pamphlets designed to sway public opinion and counteract negative press.

Michael also became aware of the role of foreign governments in the conflict. He learned about the complex relationships between the British government and its allies, and the tentative support or condemnation from other nations depending on the political climate. The shifting allegiances and the delicate balance of international diplomacy were factors that could significantly impact their struggle. The IRA had to be mindful of these dynamics, ensuring that their actions did not alienate potential supporters abroad.

His growing awareness of the international dimension also included the strategic importance of building alliances with other liberation movements around the world. Michael read about connections with groups in Palestine, South Africa, and Latin America, understanding how shared experiences of oppression and resistance created bonds of solidarity. These alliances provided not only material support but also a moral framework that legitimized their struggle on a global scale.

The global perspective Michael gained underscored the importance of public perception and the broader implications of the IRA's actions. He realized that their struggle was part of a larger narrative of colonial resistance and the fight for self-determination worldwide. This awareness influenced how he approached his role within the IRA, recognizing that their actions had far-reaching consequences beyond the immediate impact on the ground.

Michael's understanding of the international dimension of the Troubles deepened his commitment to a more strategic and conscientious approach to their operations. He saw the necessity of balancing militant actions with diplomatic efforts and the importance of crafting a narrative that resonated both locally and globally. This broadened perspective enriched his involvement in the IRA, making him not just a soldier in the fight for Irish independence, but also a participant in a global struggle for justice and freedom.

This expanded understanding of the political landscape led Michael to reflect on his role in the conflict. He recognized that each operation he participated in was part of a larger political strategy and that the struggle for Irish independence was multifaceted, involving not just military actions but also political negotiations and public diplomacy.

As Michael's comprehension of the broader context deepened, he began to see his actions in a new light. The realization dawned on him during a quiet evening in a safe house, the air thick with the scent of old books and the flickering glow of a single lamp casting long shadows on the walls. He sat at a worn wooden table, maps and documents spread out before him, the silence only broken by the distant sounds of the city. The complexity of their fight became clearer with each piece of intelligence and strategic plan he examined.

Michael's reflections were often sparked by the debriefings after their operations. Sitting in the dimly lit room, surrounded by his comrades, he would listen to the leaders discuss the outcomes and implications of their actions. The analytical breakdown of each mission, the scrutiny of their successes and failures, and the discussions about the political fallout all contributed to his growing awareness. He understood that their actions on the ground were only one part of a much larger strategy aimed at achieving political leverage and public support.

One particularly enlightening conversation took place after a successful operation. As the group celebrated their victory with a rare moment of camaraderie, the discussion turned to the political repercussions. The leaders spoke about how the operation's success would bolster their negotiating position in upcoming talks with political representatives. Michael listened, the realization sinking in that their military actions were intricately linked to political maneuvers. The clinking of glasses and the laughter of his comrades felt like a brief respite from the heavy weight of their responsibilities.

This expanded understanding made Michael more mindful of the broader implications of their actions. He began to see each mission not just as a tactical endeavor but as a crucial component of their political strategy. The importance of timing, target selection, and minimizing collateral damage became paramount. He realized that their success depended not just on their ability to fight but also on their ability to win the support of the local and international community.

Michael's reflections also extended to the role of public diplomacy. He understood that the narratives they crafted and the messages they conveyed to the media were vital in shaping public perception. He became more involved in the creation and dissemination of propaganda materials, understanding that these efforts were as important as any military victory. The carefully worded leaflets, the clandestine radio broadcasts, and the strategically timed public statements were all tools in their arsenal, designed to sway public opinion and build support for their cause.

The multifaceted nature of the struggle also highlighted the importance of political negotiations. Michael saw that while their armed resistance was necessary, it was equally important to engage in dialogue and diplomacy. He learned about the delicate balance between maintaining a strong militant front and being open to negotiations that could lead to a peaceful resolution. The leaders' ability to navigate these dual paths impressed upon him the need for a comprehensive approach to their struggle.

Michael's reflections on his role in the conflict brought a new sense of purpose and responsibility. He understood that his contributions were part of a larger effort that required both military and political acumen. This realization deepened his commitment to the cause, knowing that their path to independence was not just through the barrel of a gun but also through the power of words and strategic alliances.

As he looked out over the city from his vantage point, the lights of Belfast twinkling in the distance, Michael felt a renewed sense of determination. The struggle for Irish independence was complex and multifaceted, but he was prepared to face the challenges ahead. His role in the IRA was not just as a soldier but as a vital participant in a broader political movement. This understanding enriched his resolve, knowing that every action he took was a step towards their ultimate goal of a free and united Ireland

Michael's evolving understanding brought with it a realization of the need to balance ideals with the realities of political strategy. He grappled with the challenges of aligning the IRA's immediate military objectives with the long-term goal of a peaceful and united Ireland. This balancing act added to the complexity of his involvement but also provided a deeper sense of purpose.

In the quiet moments after operations, Michael found himself lost in thought, reflecting on the broader implications of their actions. The excitement and adrenaline of the mission would fade, leaving behind the heavy weight of contemplation. He would sit in the dim glow of a single lamp, the room silent except for the distant hum of the city, pondering the delicate equilibrium between their violent tactics and the ultimate vision of peace they sought.

One particular evening, after a tense debriefing, Michael engaged in a candid conversation with an older, more experienced member of the IRA named Brendan. They sat in a shadowed corner of a safe house, the air thick with the lingering scent of tobacco and the distant sound of their comrades' voices. Brendan spoke of the importance of strategic thinking, of knowing when to fight and when to negotiate. His words resonated deeply with Michael, illuminating the intricate dance between idealism and pragmatism.

Michael realized that their immediate military objectives had to be carefully weighed against the potential for long-term political solutions. Each operation had to be evaluated not just for its tactical success but for its impact on the broader struggle. The need to win hearts and minds, to maintain public support, and to create opportunities for political dialogue were all critical considerations. The balancing act between militant action and political strategy became a central focus of his thoughts.

The complexities of this balancing act were apparent in the planning of each mission. Michael observed how leaders debated the merits and risks of various targets, considering not just the immediate military gain but also the potential political fallout. The discussions were intense, filled with passionate arguments and strategic calculations. The flickering candlelight cast long shadows on the faces of those present, highlighting the gravity of their decisions. Michael's growing understanding of these dynamics made him a more thoughtful participant in these deliberations.

He also grappled with the ethical implications of their actions. The knowledge that their fight for freedom often resulted in unintended harm to civilians weighed heavily on him. He understood the necessity of their struggle but struggled to reconcile the violence with their ultimate goal of peace. These moral dilemmas added another layer of complexity to his involvement, forcing him to constantly reevaluate his own beliefs and the means by which they pursued their ends.

Despite these challenges, Michael found a deeper sense of purpose in his role. He recognized that achieving a peaceful and united Ireland required more than just force; it required wisdom, patience, and a willingness to engage in dialogue. The leaders' ability to navigate these complexities, to balance military action with political strategy, inspired him. He saw that their struggle was not just about liberation but about building a future where peace and justice could thrive.

Michael's reflections on this balancing act enriched his commitment to the cause. He understood that his actions were part of a larger tapestry, where each thread had to be carefully woven to create a cohesive and sustainable outcome. The awareness of the need for balance gave him a sense of direction and clarity, knowing that their fight was not just for the present but for a future that honored their ideals while acknowledging the realities of their situation.

As he continued his involvement with the IRA, Michael carried this understanding with him. The journey was fraught with challenges, but he was prepared to navigate the complexities with determination and insight. His evolving perspective provided a deeper sense of purpose, guiding his actions and decisions towards the ultimate goal of a peaceful and united Ireland.

Living a life shrouded in secrecy added another layer of complexity to Michael's involvement. The constant need to conceal his activities from friends and loved ones created a barrier of isolation around him. He could share his experiences and fears only with his fellow IRA members, creating a bond forged in secrecy and mutual understanding of the risks they all faced.

Michael's days were a careful balancing act, moving between the normalcy of daily life and the clandestine operations of the IRA. He maintained a facade of ordinary existence, engaging in casual conversations with neighbors, attending family gatherings, and going to work as if nothing was amiss. Yet, beneath this veneer lay a world of covert missions, secret meetings, and the ever-present threat of discovery. The weight of these dual lives bore down on him, a constant reminder of the perilous path he had chosen.

At home, Michael felt the strain of secrecy most acutely. The familiar warmth of his family home, with its comforting smells of his mother's cooking and the sounds of his siblings' laughter, contrasted sharply with the tension he carried inside. Each day, he navigated conversations carefully, deflecting questions and avoiding topics that might reveal his true activities. The innocent queries of his loved ones, who sensed his growing detachment, were like needles pricking at the fabric of his resolve. The fear of bringing danger to their doorstep kept him vigilant, but also distant.

The isolation was profound. Michael could not confide in his childhood friends or share his burdens with his family. His evenings were often spent in solitude, his thoughts a jumble of recent operations, future plans, and the ever-present risks. The loneliness was a constant companion, one that could not be alleviated by the company of those who remained ignorant of his secret life.

It was only among his fellow IRA members that Michael found solace. The bond they shared was unlike any other, born out of mutual trust and the shared experience of living on the edge. In the dimly lit safe houses and hidden meeting spots, they spoke freely, their conversations laced with the language of resistance and camaraderie. The smell of tobacco smoke, the sound of whispered strategies, and the sight of determined faces around him provided a sense of belonging. Here, he could express his fears and doubts without the need for concealment.

One night, after a particularly harrowing mission, Michael sat with his comrades around a makeshift table in a safe house. The room was thick with tension and the lingering smell of explosives. They shared their experiences, the close calls and the moments of triumph, their voices low and earnest. The relief of being understood, of knowing that his fears were shared by others, was palpable. These moments of connection were rare but precious, reinforcing the bonds that held them together.

Despite the camaraderie, the risks they faced were ever-present. Michael knew that each operation could be their last, that the betrayal of a single member could lead to their downfall. The trust they placed in each other was absolute, but it was also a fragile thing, constantly tested by the pressures of their clandestine existence. The knowledge that his life, and the lives of his comrades, depended on their secrecy was a heavy burden, one that they all bore with a mixture of pride and fear.

Living a life shrouded in secrecy was a test of endurance and loyalty. Michael's ability to navigate this dual existence required constant vigilance and emotional resilience. The isolation it brought was profound, but it was also what bound him so closely to his fellow IRA members. Their shared experiences, the understanding of the risks they all faced, and the unspoken agreement to protect each other at all costs created a unique and unbreakable bond.

As Michael continued his journey, the complexities of his secret life deepened his resolve. The isolation and secrecy were prices he was willing to pay for the cause he believed in. His bond with his comrades provided the strength and support he needed to continue, knowing that their collective struggle was worth the personal sacrifices. Together, they faced the challenges of their covert war, united by their shared commitment to the dream of a free and united Ireland.

Despite these challenges and moral quandaries, Michael's commitment to the cause of a united Ireland never wavered. He believed in the necessity of their struggle, viewing it as a just response to years of oppression and injustice. His involvement in the IRA became more than just a duty; it was an integral part of his identity, a commitment to a cause he had grown up believing in and a way to actively contribute to the struggle for Irish freedom.

Michael's resolve was rooted in a deep sense of history and personal conviction. The stories of past rebellions and the enduring fight for independence were etched into his soul, reinforced by the tales his father had told and the injustices he had witnessed firsthand. The oppression faced by his community, the systematic discrimination, and the heavy-handed tactics of the British forces fueled his determination. The dream of a free and united Ireland was not just an abstract ideal; it was a deeply personal mission.

Every operation, despite its risks and moral ambiguities, strengthened Michael's belief in their cause. The adrenaline-fueled moments of danger, the careful planning, and the shared victories with his comrades all reinforced his sense of purpose. He saw their actions as a necessary means to an end, a way to force the world to acknowledge their plight and to push for change. The urgency of their struggle, the immediate need to resist, overshadowed the ethical dilemmas that occasionally gnawed at his conscience.

In the quiet moments between missions, Michael would reflect on the broader significance of their fight. He would sit alone in his room, the dim light casting long shadows, and think about the future they were fighting for. The vision of a peaceful Ireland, where his family and future generations could live free from fear and oppression, was a powerful motivator. This vision was more than just a hope; it was a promise he had made to himself and to those who had sacrificed so much before him.

The camaraderie among his fellow IRA members also played a crucial role in sustaining his commitment. The shared experiences, the trust they placed in one another, and the mutual understanding of the stakes involved created a bond that transcended ordinary friendships. These relationships were forged in the crucible of conflict, their loyalty and dedication to the cause unshakable. In their company, Michael found strength and solidarity, a sense of belonging that reinforced his identity as a freedom fighter.

Michael's commitment to the IRA became an intrinsic part of who he was. It defined his actions, guided his decisions, and gave his life a profound sense of purpose. The struggle for Irish freedom was not just a fight for territory or political power; it was a fight for justice, dignity, and the right to self-determination. Each mission, each act of defiance, was a step towards realizing this dream, a tangible contribution to a cause that had shaped his entire life.

His unwavering dedication was tested time and again, but Michael's belief in the righteousness of their struggle remained steadfast. The personal sacrifices, the risks, and the moral quandaries were all part of a larger narrative of resistance and resilience. He understood that their fight was complex and fraught with challenges, but he also knew that it was necessary. The cause of a united Ireland, free from foreign rule and oppression, was worth every sacrifice.

As he continued his journey, Michael's identity as an IRA member became inseparable from his broader sense of self. The struggle for Irish freedom was not just something he did; it was who he was. This deep-seated commitment provided him with the strength and determination to face the hardships and uncertainties of their fight. It was a commitment born of history, personal experience, and an unyielding belief in the justice of their cause.

In the end, Michael's involvement in the IRA was a testament to his enduring dedication to the dream of a free and united Ireland. It was a commitment that defined his life, shaped his actions, and gave him a profound sense of purpose. Despite the challenges and moral dilemmas, he remained resolute, driven by the belief that their struggle was not only just but essential for the future of his people.

The events of Bloody Sunday in 1972, when Michael was just eight years old, were pivotal in shaping his path. Witnessing the violence and injustice of that day had a profound impact on him, fostering a sense of injustice and a desire to be part of a movement for change. The ongoing conflict of the Troubles further reinforced this sentiment, as Michael witnessed the daily realities of life under what he and his community perceived as an occupation.

On that fateful day, Michael's small hand clutched his father's as they stood in the crowded streets of Derry. The air was thick with tension, the murmur of the crowd filled with a mix of hope and apprehension. The peaceful march, a civil rights demonstration, was intended to protest against internment without trial. The sun was hidden behind a layer of gray clouds, casting a somber light over the scene. As the march progressed, the atmosphere grew increasingly charged.

Suddenly, chaos erupted. The sharp cracks of gunfire shattered the air, followed by screams and the frantic rush of people trying to escape the violence. Michael's father pulled him close, shielding him with his body as they ducked behind a low wall. Peering out, Michael saw soldiers firing into the fleeing crowd, the sight of falling bodies searing into his young mind. The smell of gunpowder and the acrid stench of fear filled his nostrils. The scene was a nightmare, a brutal display of power that left a lasting scar on his psyche.

The aftermath of Bloody Sunday was a blur of grief and anger. Michael's father, normally a stoic man, wept openly for the first time in his life. The community was engulfed in mourning, their sorrow punctuated by a simmering rage. Funerals were held for the victims, and the streets were lined with mourners, their faces etched with pain and defiance. The collective grief of his community, the shared sense of loss and injustice, profoundly impacted Michael. It was in these moments that his nascent sense of injustice began to crystallize into a desire for change.

As Michael grew older, the Troubles became an inescapable part of his daily life. The constant presence of armed soldiers, the checkpoints, and the curfews were a daily reminder of the occupation. The sound of helicopters overhead, the sight of armored vehicles patrolling the streets, and the frequent raids on homes were all part of the harsh reality he and his community endured. The graffiti on the walls, depicting slogans of resistance and solidarity, spoke to the collective yearning for freedom.

Each encounter with the British forces reinforced Michael's resolve. He saw friends and neighbors harassed, detained, and sometimes beaten without cause. The stories of injustice, whispered in hushed tones at family gatherings and in the streets, fueled his anger. The feeling of helplessness, of being subjected to an oppressive regime, festered within him, transforming into a fierce determination to fight back.

The seeds planted on Bloody Sunday grew into a deep-rooted commitment to the nationalist cause. Michael sought out ways to contribute, to be part of the struggle for a united Ireland. The IRA, with its promise of resistance and its commitment to the cause, offered him a path. Joining their ranks was not just a choice but a necessity, a way to honor the memory of those lost and to fight for the future of his people.

The ongoing conflict of the Troubles further solidified Michael's beliefs. Each day under occupation was a testament to the need for change, a reminder of the struggle that defined his community. The resilience and solidarity of his neighbors, their unwavering spirit in the face of adversity, inspired him. The shared goal of freedom and the collective fight against oppression became central to his identity.

Michael's journey from that traumatic day in 1972 to his active involvement in the IRA was marked by a growing understanding of the complexities of their struggle. The violence and injustice he witnessed fueled his desire to be part of a movement for change. The ongoing occupation and the daily realities of the Troubles reinforced his commitment, driving him to take action. His involvement in the IRA became a way to channel his anger and hope, transforming his sense of injustice into a determined fight for a united Ireland.

Michael's ideology was deeply influenced by a blend of nationalism and a desire for social justice. He believed in the right of the Irish people to self-determination and saw the British presence in Northern Ireland as an impediment to this. His involvement in local nationalist groups and rallies exposed him to broader discussions about the political situation in Northern Ireland, further solidifying his belief in the necessity of an armed struggle to achieve a united and independent Ireland.

From an early age, Michael was immersed in the stories and songs of Irish resistance. His father's tales of the Easter Rising and the valor of those who had fought for Irish freedom instilled in him a deep sense of national pride. The walls of their modest home were adorned with portraits of Irish heroes, their stern faces serving as constant reminders of the sacrifices made for their cause. The smell of turf burning in the fireplace and the sound of his father's voice recounting these stories created an atmosphere charged with historical significance.

As a teenager, Michael began attending local nationalist group meetings and rallies. These gatherings were vibrant with passionate discussions and fervent speeches. The crowded halls, filled with the buzz of animated conversations and the smell of cigarette smoke, were places where ideas were exchanged and strategies debated. Michael listened intently to the leaders who spoke with conviction about the need for self-determination and the injustices perpetrated by the British government. The slogans painted on banners and the defiant chants of the crowd stirred something deep within him.

These experiences broadened Michael's understanding of the political landscape. He engaged in late-night discussions with fellow activists, their voices hushed but fervent as they debated the best path forward. The arguments were intense, the air thick with the weight of their shared determination. Through these interactions, Michael's belief in the necessity of armed struggle solidified. He saw it not as a choice but as an imperative, a necessary response to the systemic oppression and violence inflicted upon his community.

Michael's participation in rallies exposed him to the harsh realities of the conflict. He witnessed firsthand the brutal crackdowns by British forces, the batons and tear gas used against peaceful protesters. The sight of bloodied faces and the sound of desperate cries for justice only reinforced his commitment. Each encounter with the authorities, each act of repression, strengthened his resolve to fight back. The streets of Belfast, with their graffiti-covered walls and the ever-present tension, became both a battleground and a symbol of their struggle.

His involvement in local nationalist groups also brought him into contact with seasoned activists and members of the IRA. These individuals, many of whom had spent years in the trenches of the conflict, shared their experiences and insights with Michael. The clandestine meetings, often held in the back rooms of pubs or hidden basements, were charged with an air of secrecy and urgency. The flickering candlelight, the rustle of paper as maps and plans were examined, and the low murmur of voices discussing tactics and targets created an atmosphere of determined resistance.

Through these interactions, Michael came to understand the broader implications of their fight. He saw the connections between their local struggle and the global movements for justice and liberation. The stories of resistance fighters from other parts of the world, their shared experiences of oppression and their victories against seemingly insurmountable odds, inspired him. He realized that their fight was part of a larger tapestry of global resistance, a struggle for justice that transcended borders.

Michael's ideology was thus shaped by a blend of nationalism and a fervent desire for social justice. He believed deeply in the right of the Irish people to determine their own future, free from external interference. The British presence in Northern Ireland was, to him, a manifestation of a broader injustice that needed to be eradicated. His involvement in local nationalist groups and rallies exposed him to the complexities of the political situation, solidifying his belief in the necessity of armed struggle. It was a belief born of history, personal experience, and a profound commitment to the ideals of freedom and justice.

In the end, Michael's journey was marked by a deep-seated conviction that the struggle for a united and independent Ireland was not just a political necessity but a moral imperative. His commitment to this cause, shaped by his experiences and his interactions with fellow nationalists, became the defining feature of his identity. It was a commitment that guided his actions, informed his decisions, and gave his life a profound sense of purpose.

Michael's perspective on the conflict was significantly influenced by his upbringing in a predominantly Catholic and nationalist neighborhood in Belfast. This environment, marked by shared experiences and communal sentiments, profoundly shaped his understanding of the Troubles.

Growing up in the Falls Road area, Michael was surrounded by the sights and sounds of a community deeply entrenched in the struggle for Irish independence. The neighborhood was a patchwork of modest houses, their walls adorned with murals depicting scenes of resistance and solidarity. The narrow streets echoed with the voices of neighbors exchanging news and stories, their conversations often tinged with the tension and resilience that characterized their daily lives. The ever-present smell of peat fires and the distant hum of military helicopters created a backdrop that was both familiar and fraught with underlying conflict.

From an early age, Michael was acutely aware of the division and tension that permeated his community. The stories shared around the dinner table, the whispered conversations among adults, and the hushed tones when discussing British soldiers all conveyed a sense of ongoing struggle. His parents, deeply rooted in the nationalist cause, instilled in him a strong sense of identity and purpose. The walls of their home were filled with symbols of their heritage – Irish flags, portraits of historical figures, and keepsakes from past uprisings.

Michael's education also played a crucial role in shaping his perspective. At St. Joseph's Secondary School, the curriculum included not just standard subjects but also lessons in Irish history and the nationalist narrative. His teachers, many of whom had experienced the Troubles firsthand, taught with a fervor that went beyond textbooks. They shared personal anecdotes, recounted tales of bravery and loss, and emphasized the importance of their cultural heritage. The classroom, filled with the smell of chalk and the sound of fervent discussion, became a place where Michael's understanding of the conflict deepened.

The communal experiences of his neighborhood further solidified Michael's views. He saw firsthand the impact of the British military presence – the frequent patrols, the sudden raids, and the constant surveillance. Checkpoints and barricades were a common sight, their presence a stark reminder of the occupation. The tension was palpable during these encounters, the air thick with mistrust and defiance. Michael often witnessed the harsh treatment of his neighbors, their fear and anger mirroring his own sentiments.

Social gatherings were also imbued with a sense of resistance. Community events, though festive, often turned into discussions about the latest developments in the struggle for independence. The shared meals, the music, and the laughter were interspersed with somber reflections and plans for future actions. These gatherings, filled with the warmth of camaraderie and the resolve of a united cause, reinforced Michael's commitment to the nationalist movement.

The shared experiences of loss and hardship further bonded the community. Michael attended countless funerals for those lost to the conflict, the grief and anger palpable among the mourners. The smell of fresh earth at the gravesites, the sight of tear-streaked faces, and the sound of defiant songs sung in remembrance all left a profound impact on him. These events underscored the sacrifices made and the enduring spirit of resistance that defined his community.

Michael's interactions with his peers also shaped his understanding of the Troubles. His friends, many of whom had similar backgrounds, shared his experiences and perspectives. Their conversations, held in whispered tones in schoolyards and on street corners, often revolved around the conflict and their role in it. The shared sense of purpose and the collective determination to fight for their rights fostered a deep sense of solidarity.

In this environment, Michael's perspective on the conflict was not just shaped by ideology but by the lived experiences of his community. The daily realities of life in a divided city, the stories of past and present struggles, and the communal resolve to achieve independence all played a crucial role in shaping his views. The bonds formed through shared hardship and the collective memory of resistance became integral to his identity.

Michael's upbringing in this predominantly Catholic and nationalist neighborhood in Belfast provided him with a profound understanding of the Troubles. It was an environment that nurtured his sense of justice and fueled his commitment to the cause. The shared experiences and communal sentiments that marked his upbringing became the foundation of his involvement in the struggle for a united and independent Ireland.

Living in a community that faced daily challenges due to political and sectarian divides gave Michael a firsthand view of the conflict's impact on ordinary lives. He grew up in an area where murals commemorating fallen IRA members were as common as graffiti, and where stories of past injustices were passed down like family heirlooms. This constant exposure to the symbols and narratives of resistance deeply ingrained in him a sense of belonging to the nationalist cause.

The streets of Michael's neighborhood were a living tapestry of the ongoing struggle. Vibrant murals depicted the faces of fallen heroes, their eyes painted with a mix of sorrow and defiance. These powerful images were more than just art; they were a testament to the sacrifices made and a call to continue the fight. Walking past these murals daily, Michael couldn't help but feel a profound connection to the men and women who had given their lives for the cause. The smell of fresh paint and the sight of new murals being created were constant reminders of the community's enduring spirit.

Stories of past injustices were woven into the fabric of Michael's upbringing. His grandparents would recount harrowing tales of discrimination and brutality, their voices filled with a mix of anger and resolve. These stories were not just anecdotes; they were lessons in resilience and resistance, passed down like treasured family heirlooms. The sound of his grandmother's voice, recounting the hardships of earlier generations, echoed in his mind long after the stories were told. The warmth of the family hearth, combined with the gravity of these narratives, created an environment steeped in historical consciousness.

Michael's neighborhood was a close-knit community where everyone knew each other's struggles and triumphs. The shared experiences of hardship and resistance forged strong bonds among the residents. The smell of home-cooked meals wafting from open windows, the sound of children playing in the streets, and the sight of neighbors gathering for impromptu meetings all contributed to a sense of solidarity. This collective identity was reinforced by the frequent gatherings where people would discuss the latest news and share their views on the ongoing conflict.

The physical manifestations of the conflict were ever-present. Armored vehicles patrolled the streets, and the distant rumble of military convoys was a constant backdrop to daily life. Checkpoints and barricades were part of the landscape, their presence a stark reminder of the division and tension that permeated the city. Michael often saw the fear and defiance in the eyes of his neighbors as they navigated these obstacles. The palpable sense of oppression fueled his desire to fight back, to stand up for his community's right to self-determination.

Michael's education further solidified his sense of belonging to the nationalist cause. At school, lessons in history were intertwined with the narratives of resistance. His teachers, many of whom were personally affected by the conflict, taught with a fervor that went beyond academic instruction. The classroom discussions, filled with passionate debates and reflections, reinforced his understanding of the historical and political context of their struggle. The sight of his classmates, equally passionate and engaged, created a sense of collective purpose.

Community events also played a significant role in shaping Michael's identity. Celebrations of cultural heritage, commemorations of fallen heroes, and political rallies were all part of the social fabric. The sounds of traditional Irish music, the sight of flags waving in the wind, and the fervent speeches of local leaders all contributed to a vibrant and resilient community spirit. These events were not just social gatherings; they were affirmations of their shared identity and commitment to the cause.

The narratives of resistance and the symbols of the struggle deeply influenced Michael's worldview. The stories of past injustices, the murals honoring fallen fighters, and the daily realities of life in a divided city all contributed to his sense of belonging to the nationalist cause. The community's resilience and solidarity in the face of adversity inspired him to take an active role in the fight for a united Ireland.

Michael's upbringing in this environment gave him a profound understanding of the conflict's impact on ordinary lives. The constant exposure to the symbols and narratives of resistance ingrained in him a deep sense of identity and purpose. It was this background that fueled his commitment to the nationalist cause and his determination to contribute to the struggle for Irish freedom.

Michael witnessed and experienced the discrimination and socio-economic hardships that were prevalent in his community. From unequal employment opportunities to disparities in housing and public services, these daily injustices reinforced his belief that the struggle was not only about national identity but also about fighting for equal rights and opportunities for his community.

Growing up, Michael saw the stark realities of inequality in every aspect of life. His father, a skilled laborer, often spoke of the frustration of being passed over for jobs in favor of less qualified candidates simply because of their Protestant background. The bitterness in his father's voice, the weariness in his eyes, left a deep impression on Michael. The smell of sweat and oil from long days of hard labor, coupled with the scant rewards, underscored the systemic discrimination they faced. The stories shared at the dinner table, filled with accounts of prejudice and exclusion, were not just tales of misfortune but lessons in the harsh truths of their existence.

Housing was another glaring area of disparity. Michael's family lived in a cramped, run-down apartment, one of many in a dilapidated building that had seen better days. The peeling paint, the leaky roof, and the cold drafts that seeped through the thin walls were constant reminders of their second-class status. In contrast, he saw well-maintained homes in Protestant neighborhoods, their tidy facades a stark contrast to the neglect in his own community. The inequality was evident in every brick and beam, a physical manifestation of the broader social divide.

Public services, too, were skewed against his community. Schools in Catholic areas were often underfunded, their facilities lacking compared to those in Protestant neighborhoods. Michael remembered the worn-out textbooks, the overcrowded classrooms, and the makeshift repairs that barely held the buildings together. The sound of dripping water from a leaky ceiling during a history lesson, the chill in the air from an inefficient heating system, and the sight of broken desks and chairs were daily reminders of the neglect they endured. These conditions fueled his determination to fight for better opportunities and a fairer system for future generations.

Access to healthcare was another area of inequality. Michael's mother often had to wait hours in overcrowded clinics to receive basic medical attention. The long lines, the overworked staff, and the limited resources highlighted the disparities in public services. The smell of antiseptic and the sight of weary faces in the waiting room were ingrained in his memory, symbols of a system that seemed indifferent to their needs. These experiences reinforced his belief that the struggle was not just about national identity but about achieving equal rights and opportunities for all.

The economic hardships faced by his community were compounded by the constant threat of violence and intimidation. British soldiers patrolled their streets, their presence a daily reminder of the oppressive system they lived under. Michael often witnessed friends and neighbors being harassed or detained without cause, their rights trampled under the guise of maintaining order. The sound of boots on the pavement, the barked commands, and the sight of armored vehicles were constant reminders of the occupation. These injustices strengthened his resolve to fight back and seek justice for his community.

Michael's involvement in local nationalist groups provided him with a platform to channel his anger and frustration into action. The meetings were filled with passionate debates and discussions about how to address these socio-economic issues. The energy in the room, the sense of shared purpose, and the collective determination to make a difference inspired him. The smell of burning candles, the rustle of paper as plans were made, and the fervent voices of his comrades created an atmosphere of hope and defiance.

Through his activism, Michael came to understand that their struggle was multifaceted. It was about reclaiming their national identity, but it was also about addressing the systemic inequalities that plagued their daily lives. The fight for Irish independence was intertwined with the fight for social justice, and both were essential to achieving true freedom. The belief that they could create a fairer, more just society for future generations drove him to continue his efforts despite the challenges and dangers involved.

Michael's experiences of discrimination and socio-economic hardships deeply influenced his perspective on the conflict. They reinforced his belief that their struggle was not only about national identity but also about fighting for equal rights and opportunities for his community. This understanding added a layer of urgency and righteousness to his commitment, making his involvement in the IRA not just a political stance but a personal mission for justice and equality.

Community gatherings, whether for commemorations, marches, or simply at local pubs, often turned into informal forums where residents shared stories of their experiences with British forces or discussed the latest political developments. These gatherings were instrumental in shaping Michael's understanding of the collective struggle and the shared aspirations for a better future.

The pubs in Michael's neighborhood were more than just places to enjoy a pint; they were the heartbeats of the community. The warm, dimly lit interiors, filled with the scent of spilled beer and the sound of traditional Irish music, provided a haven where residents could come together and share their lives. Conversations flowed as freely as the drinks, with each corner of the room hosting debates about the latest news or recollections of past events. Michael often found himself listening intently, absorbing the wisdom and experiences of the older generations.

During commemorations and marches, the streets came alive with a sense of purpose and unity. The air was thick with the smell of burning candles and the sound of solemn hymns. These events honored those who had sacrificed their lives for the cause, and the emotional speeches given by community leaders left a lasting impact on Michael. The sight of banners waving in the wind, each one bearing a message of defiance and hope, filled him with a sense of pride and determination. These gatherings reinforced the importance of their struggle and the collective memory that bound them together.

At these events, Michael would often hear firsthand accounts of interactions with British forces. Neighbors would recount their experiences with raids, arrests, and daily harassment. The raw emotion in their voices, the anger, and the sadness were palpable. These stories were not just tales of woe but were shared with a sense of resilience and defiance. The sight of elderly men and women, their faces etched with lines of hardship, passionately discussing their encounters served as a powerful reminder of the enduring spirit of his community.

The local pubs also served as informal meeting places for political discussions. In these smoky, bustling environments, Michael participated in animated debates about the future of their community and the broader political landscape. The clinking of glasses and the murmur of background conversations created a lively atmosphere where ideas could be exchanged freely. Here, Michael learned about the intricacies of political strategy, the importance of solidarity, and the need for a multifaceted approach to their struggle. The sight of his fellow community members, united in their resolve, inspired him to contribute actively to their cause.

These gatherings were instrumental in shaping Michael's understanding of the collective struggle. He realized that their fight was not just about immediate resistance but also about building a better future for their children. The aspirations for a united Ireland, free from oppression, were shared by all who attended these gatherings. The sense of unity and shared purpose was palpable, and Michael felt a deep connection to the people around him.

The shared laughter, the impassioned arguments, and the collective mourning for those lost all contributed to a strong communal bond.

Through these interactions, Michael's understanding of the conflict deepened. He came to see the broader implications of their struggle, recognizing that it was not just about fighting British forces but also about preserving their cultural identity and securing a future where justice and equality prevailed. The stories shared at these gatherings painted a vivid picture of the daily realities of life under occupation, fueling his determination to fight for change.

Michael's involvement in these community forums also allowed him to develop his own voice. He began to speak up, sharing his thoughts and ideas, and contributing to the collective discourse. The encouragement and support he received from his peers bolstered his confidence and reinforced his commitment. The knowledge that he was part of a larger movement, that his actions and words could make a difference, gave him a profound sense of purpose.

Community gatherings, whether solemn commemorations or lively debates at the local pub, were crucial in shaping Michael's understanding of their collective struggle and aspirations for a better future. These events provided a platform for sharing experiences, building solidarity, and nurturing the shared dream of a free and united Ireland. They were a testament to the resilience and unity of his community, and they played an essential role in guiding Michael's journey within the nationalist movement.

The visible presence of the British military in his neighborhood, with frequent patrols and checkpoints, served as a constant reminder of the conflict. The interactions between the community and the soldiers, often marked by tension and hostility, underscored for Michael the reality of living in a contested space. These experiences fueled his belief in the need for a robust response to what was perceived as an occupation.

Every day, Michael encountered the harsh realities of military presence. The streets he walked were lined with barbed wire and fortified checkpoints, their stark structures disrupting the otherwise familiar landscape of his neighborhood. The rumble of armored vehicles, the sharp bark of orders from soldiers, and the ever-watchful eyes of surveillance cameras were inescapable parts of his daily life. The smell of diesel from the military trucks mixed with the usual scents of the city, a constant reminder of the tension that permeated the air.

Patrols were a regular occurrence, their presence a source of anxiety and resentment. Michael often watched as soldiers, clad in full combat gear, moved through the streets with an air of authority. The sight of them stopping residents, demanding identification, and conducting searches created an atmosphere of fear and oppression. The tension was palpable during these encounters, the air thick with the potential for confrontation. The cold, impersonal manner of the soldiers, coupled with their intimidating presence, left a lasting impression on him.

The interactions between the community and the soldiers were frequently hostile. Michael witnessed numerous altercations, where frustrated residents clashed with the heavily armed patrols. Shouts and insults were exchanged, the situation often escalating into physical confrontations. The sight of friends and neighbors being pushed around, handcuffed, or even beaten for minor infractions or perceived defiance stoked a deep anger within him. The injustices he saw daily reinforced his belief in the need to resist and fight back against what he perceived as an oppressive force.

Checkpoints were another source of daily humiliation and frustration. Michael experienced firsthand the indignity of being stopped, questioned, and searched while simply trying to go about his day. The intrusive nature of these searches, the condescending attitudes of the soldiers, and the constant delays were a daily affront to his dignity. The sight of long lines of residents, waiting patiently to pass through these checkpoints, highlighted the control the military exerted over their lives. The sense of powerlessness in these moments was overwhelming, fueling his desire for liberation.

These experiences were not just his alone; they were shared by his entire community. Conversations in the local pub, murmured in low tones, often revolved around the latest incident of military aggression. Stories of harassment, arbitrary detentions, and violence at the hands of the soldiers circulated widely, each one adding to the collective anger and resolve. The communal sense of grievance and the shared experiences of oppression created a strong bond among the residents, uniting them in their opposition to the British presence.

Michael's belief in the need for a robust response was further reinforced by the visible symbols of resistance around him. The graffiti on the walls, the murals honoring fallen fighters, and the posters calling for resistance were daily affirmations of their struggle. These symbols served as constant reminders of the collective determination to fight back and reclaim their rights. The sight of these symbols, coupled with the daily indignities imposed by the military, solidified his commitment to the nationalist cause.

Living in this contested space, where the lines between occupier and occupied were starkly drawn, shaped Michael's worldview. The visible presence of the British military, the daily encounters marked by tension and hostility, and the pervasive sense of injustice all underscored the reality of their situation. These experiences left no room for complacency; they demanded action. Michael's belief in the need for a robust response was not just a theoretical stance but a deeply felt necessity, born out of the lived experiences of oppression and resistance.

These daily interactions with the British military fueled Michael's determination to fight for his community's rights and freedoms. The visible and oppressive presence of the soldiers in his neighborhood underscored the reality of living in a contested space, where every day was a struggle for dignity and justice. This environment, marked by tension and hostility, reinforced his conviction that a strong, organized response was essential to achieving their goal of a free and united Ireland.

Michael's encounters with local IRA members, who were often respected figures in the community, also played a crucial role in shaping his views. Their narratives about the struggle, combined with their commitment to the cause, were influential in portraying the IRA as defenders of the community's rights and freedoms.

Growing up in Belfast, Michael frequently encountered men and women who were quietly revered within his neighborhood. These individuals were often seen as pillars of the community – reliable, strong, and deeply committed to the well-being of their people. The aura of respect surrounding them was palpable, and their words carried significant weight. The sight of these figures at local events, their presence commanding respect and admiration, left a lasting impression on Michael.

One of the most influential figures in Michael's life was Seamus, a local shopkeeper known for his involvement with the IRA. Seamus's shop was more than just a place to buy daily necessities; it was a hub of community activity. The smell of fresh bread and the sound of lively conversations filled the air as neighbors gathered to share news and discuss the latest developments. Seamus often spoke about the ongoing struggle with a conviction that was both inspiring and reassuring. His stories of bravery, sacrifice, and resistance painted a picture of the IRA as protectors of the community.

During quiet moments in the back of Seamus's shop, Michael listened intently to the older man's tales. Seamus would recount operations with a mix of pride and solemnity, his voice steady and his eyes reflecting the weight of his experiences. The atmosphere was charged with a sense of history and purpose, the faint smell of tobacco smoke and the sound of creaking floorboards adding to the gravity of their conversations. These narratives provided Michael with a deeper understanding of the complexities of their struggle and the necessity of their actions.

Another key figure was Brigid, a nurse who had become a local legend for her efforts in providing medical aid to those injured in clashes with British forces. Brigid's commitment to the cause was unwavering, and her compassionate nature earned her the love and respect of many. The sight of her moving quickly through the streets, her medical bag in hand, was a common one. She often spoke at community gatherings, her voice filled with passion and resolve. The stories she shared of tending to the wounded and standing up to the soldiers were both harrowing and inspiring, reinforcing the image of the IRA as defenders of their people.

Michael also encountered young men like Liam, who had recently joined the IRA and were full of fervor and idealism. Liam's enthusiasm was infectious, his tales of training and operations filled with a sense of adventure and purpose. The two would often meet at the local pub, the warm glow of the lights and the sound of traditional music creating a backdrop for their intense discussions. Liam's commitment to the cause, despite the risks involved, served as a powerful motivator for Michael. The bond they shared, forged in their mutual desire for justice, strengthened his resolve to join the fight.

These encounters with local IRA members provided Michael with a personal connection to the broader nationalist movement. The respect and admiration these individuals commanded were not just due to their actions but also their unwavering commitment to the community's welfare. Their stories, filled with personal sacrifices and collective victories, portrayed the IRA not merely as a militant organization but as a crucial defender of their rights and freedoms.

The narratives shared by these respected figures were instrumental in shaping Michael's views. They offered him a perspective that highlighted the legitimacy and necessity of their struggle. The personal accounts of resistance, the visible scars of their battles, and the unwavering dedication to their cause made a profound impact on him. These stories were more than just tales of defiance; they were lessons in courage, loyalty, and the enduring fight for justice.

The commitment of these IRA members to the cause, despite the immense personal risks, deeply influenced Michael. He saw in them the embodiment of the principles he believed in – the fight for self-determination, the protection of their community, and the pursuit of a fair and just society. Their example provided him with a clear path, reinforcing his belief that joining the IRA was not just a choice but a duty.

In this environment, where respected figures of the community were also key members of the IRA, Michael's understanding of the organization was profoundly shaped. He came to see the IRA as not just a group of militants but as integral to the community's defense and future. This perspective solidified his commitment to the cause, making his involvement in the IRA a defining aspect of his identity and his fight for a united and independent Ireland.

Personal relationships within the community further solidified Michael's commitment to the nationalist cause. Friends and family members who had suffered due to the conflict, stories of lost loved ones, and the collective mourning for those who had died fighting for the cause, all contributed to his emotional connection to the struggle.

Michael's family was at the heart of his understanding of the conflict. His father, a stoic man with a quiet strength, often shared stories of friends and relatives who had fought and died in the earlier phases of the struggle. The living room, dimly lit by the soft glow of a single lamp, would become a space of remembrance as his father recounted these tales. The scent of his father's pipe smoke mingled with the warmth of the fire, creating an intimate atmosphere for these deeply personal stories. Each tale was a reminder of the sacrifices made and the enduring spirit of resistance that defined their family.

The loss of his uncle Sean was particularly poignant for Michael. Sean had been a charismatic figure, full of life and a fervent supporter of the nationalist cause. His death in a skirmish with British forces left a void in the family that was never filled. The memory of Sean's laughter, his impassioned speeches at family gatherings, and the day they received the news of his death were seared into Michael's mind. The funeral, attended by a sea of mourners, was a powerful moment of collective grief and solidarity. The sight of his uncle's casket, draped in the Irish flag, and the sound of solemn hymns being sung by the community, left a lasting impact on him.

Friends, too, played a crucial role in shaping Michael's commitment. His best friend, Danny, had been beaten by British soldiers during a protest. The memory of seeing Danny's bruised and bloodied face, the anger and helplessness he felt, was a catalyst for Michael's deepening involvement in the struggle. They would sit together in the evenings, their conversations filled with plans for the future and discussions about how they could contribute to the cause. The camaraderie they shared, the whispered hopes and fears, strengthened their bond and their resolve.

The neighborhood itself was a constant source of inspiration and motivation. Michael's neighbors, many of whom had lost loved ones or suffered at the hands of British forces, shared their stories with a mix of sorrow and determination. The communal gatherings, whether at funerals, commemorations, or informal meetings in the local pub, were spaces where these experiences were shared and collective resolve was forged. The smell of candles at vigils, the sight of tear-streaked faces at memorials, and the sound of defiant songs sung in unison, all contributed to a sense of shared purpose.

The death of young Aisling, a local girl caught in the crossfire during a raid, was another heart-wrenching event that reinforced Michael's commitment. The image of her lifeless body, the grief of her parents, and the community's outrage were powerful reminders of the cost of the conflict. The makeshift memorial, with flowers, candles, and notes of remembrance, became a place of mourning and reflection. Michael spent hours there, contemplating the innocence lost and the urgent need for justice and change.

The stories of personal suffering and loss were not just tales of tragedy; they were narratives of resilience and defiance. Each story, each shared experience, added layers to Michael's understanding of the conflict and deepened his emotional connection to the struggle. The collective mourning for those who had died, the shared anger and grief, and the community's unwavering spirit of resistance became integral parts of his identity.

These personal relationships and experiences cemented Michael's commitment to the nationalist cause. They provided him with a deeply emotional and personal connection to the struggle, transforming his involvement from a political stance to a profound personal mission. The faces of friends and family, the memories of lost loved ones, and the shared aspirations for a better future were powerful motivators that guided his actions and strengthened his resolve.

Michael's journey was shaped by the bonds he shared with those around him. The pain and suffering experienced by his loved ones, the stories of loss and sacrifice, and the collective mourning of his community fueled his determination to fight for their rights and freedoms. This emotional connection to the struggle made his commitment to the nationalist cause not just a matter of ideology, but a deeply personal mission for justice and equality.

Michael's early tasks within the IRA were foundational, aimed at building trust and demonstrating his commitment. He was tasked with distributing informational pamphlets and assisting in low-risk logistical operations. These activities, while not front-line engagements, were crucial in maintaining the IRA's communication and operational networks. They provided Michael with a deeper understanding of the organization's structure and strategy.

Michael's initiation into the IRA began with tasks that seemed mundane but were essential to the movement's infrastructure. His first assignment was distributing informational pamphlets throughout his neighborhood. These pamphlets, filled with nationalist rhetoric and updates on the struggle, were designed to inform and rally the local community. Michael would receive bundles of these leaflets in a dimly lit back room of a local pub, the smell of ink still fresh and the paper slightly warm from the press.

The distribution process was both strategic and stealthy. Michael would move through the streets at dusk, slipping pamphlets into mailboxes, under doors, and onto car windshields. The twilight hour provided a cloak of anonymity, the fading light casting long shadows that he used to his advantage. The rustle of paper and the sound of his footsteps were the only noises in the otherwise quiet streets. Each leaflet he delivered was a small act of resistance, a way to keep the community informed and engaged.

Assisting in logistical operations was another critical aspect of his early involvement. Michael helped organize and transport supplies, ensuring that safe houses were stocked with essentials. These operations required careful planning and execution. He would often meet with his contacts in secluded locations, the air filled with the scent of damp earth and the quiet hum of nature as they discussed routes and schedules. The meticulous nature of these tasks taught him the importance of precision and reliability in their struggle.

One of Michael's regular assignments involved transporting messages between different IRA cells. In an era before widespread digital communication, these messages were often handwritten notes or coded letters. He would receive these missives from a trusted courier, the exchange happening in a crowded marketplace or a busy street to avoid suspicion. The weight of these small pieces of paper, often tucked inside his jacket pocket, felt immense. He knew that each message was a vital link in the chain of their operations, containing plans, updates, and instructions.

Michael's tasks also included helping to organize community events and rallies. These gatherings were crucial for maintaining morale and unity among the local population. He would assist in setting up venues, distributing flyers, and coordinating with speakers. The energy at these events was palpable, the air buzzing with anticipation and resolve. The sight of flags waving, the sound of passionate speeches, and the collective chants of the crowd reinforced his belief in their cause.

These early tasks were foundational in building trust within the IRA. Michael's reliability and dedication did not go unnoticed. He proved himself to be a dependable and committed member, willing to undertake any task to support the cause. The leaders and senior members of the IRA began to recognize his potential, gradually entrusting him with more responsibilities.

Through these activities, Michael gained a deeper understanding of the IRA's structure and strategy. He saw how each task, no matter how small, played a critical role in the larger framework of their operations. The network of safe houses, the distribution of information, the coordination of supplies – all these elements were meticulously organized to sustain their struggle. Michael learned about the importance of discretion, the value of thorough planning, and the necessity of maintaining strong communication channels.

These foundational tasks also provided Michael with valuable insights into the broader strategy of the IRA. He understood that their fight was not just about direct confrontations but also about building and maintaining a resilient support network. The logistical operations, the dissemination of information, and the organization of community events were all part of a comprehensive approach to their struggle. This holistic understanding of their strategy deepened his commitment and shaped his approach to his role within the organization.

Michael's early experiences within the IRA were instrumental in shaping his perspective and honing his skills. These tasks, while not as glamorous as front-line engagements, were critical to the success of their operations. They taught him the importance of every role within the movement, fostering a sense of solidarity and shared purpose. Through these foundational activities, Michael's commitment to the nationalist cause was solidified, preparing him for the more significant challenges that lay ahead.

Alongside these tasks, Michael received basic training in various skills essential for his role in the IRA. This included learning secure communication methods, basic surveillance techniques, and understanding the organizational hierarchy. Additionally, Michael was exposed to the ideological teachings of the IRA, which helped solidify his understanding of the group's goals and methods. This period of learning and acclimatization was crucial for Michael, shaping his perspective on the armed struggle and his role within it.

The training sessions were held in various clandestine locations to avoid detection. One of the most common venues was an old farmhouse on the outskirts of Belfast, its secluded setting providing the perfect cover for their activities. The smell of damp wood and earth greeted Michael as he entered the dimly lit rooms, the flickering light of oil lamps casting long shadows on the walls. The atmosphere was charged with a mix of anticipation and seriousness as he joined other recruits, each eager to learn and prove their commitment.

Secure communication methods were among the first skills Michael mastered. He learned how to use coded language and clandestine messaging techniques to avoid interception by British forces. These lessons were often practical, with Michael practicing sending and receiving coded messages under the watchful eyes of experienced operatives. The sound of pens scratching on paper, the rustle of notes being folded and exchanged, and the intense focus on their tasks created an environment of meticulous discipline. The importance of precision and secrecy was drilled into him, reinforcing the critical nature of secure communications in their operations.

Basic surveillance techniques were another key component of his training. Michael was taught how to observe and gather intelligence without attracting attention. These sessions often took place in urban settings, where he learned to blend into crowds and use his surroundings to his advantage. The city streets became his classroom, the bustling markets, and busy intersections providing ample opportunities for practice. The smell of street food, the clamor of vendors, and the constant movement of people created a dynamic backdrop for his lessons. He learned to notice the subtle details – a car parked too long, a stranger lingering near a meeting point, the patterns of movement that might indicate surveillance.

Understanding the organizational hierarchy of the IRA was crucial for Michael's integration into the group. He attended meetings where senior members explained the structure and function of various cells and units within the organization. The hierarchy was designed to maintain operational security and efficiency, with each member knowing only what was necessary for their role. These sessions were often held in the basement of the farmhouse, where maps and diagrams were pinned to the walls. The musty smell of old paper and the low hum of voices discussing strategy created an atmosphere of focused learning. Michael came to understand the importance of discipline and loyalty within this structure, recognizing how each part contributed to the effectiveness of the whole.

Ideological training was also a significant part of Michael's education. He attended lectures and discussions led by senior IRA members who delved into the history of the struggle, the political goals of the movement, and the moral justifications for their actions. These sessions were intense and thought-provoking, often held around a large wooden table in the farmhouse's main room. The scent of burning peat from the fireplace, the crackling of the flames, and the earnest voices of his mentors created a setting reminiscent of historical revolutionary gatherings. Michael listened intently as they spoke about the legacy of colonialism, the fight for self-determination, and the vision of a united Ireland. These teachings resonated deeply with him, solidifying his belief in the righteousness of their cause.

This period of training and acclimatization was crucial for Michael. It provided him with the practical skills needed for his role in the IRA and a deeper understanding of the ideological framework that underpinned their struggle. He learned to see the broader picture, understanding how their actions fit into the larger goal of achieving independence and justice for their people. The combination of practical training and ideological education gave him a well-rounded perspective on the armed struggle.

Michael's instructors emphasized the importance of commitment and resilience. They spoke of the sacrifices required and the unwavering dedication needed to achieve their goals. The stories of past victories and the lessons learned from previous struggles were shared with reverence, creating a sense of continuity and purpose.

Michael's respect for his mentors grew, their experiences and wisdom guiding him as he navigated his own path within the organization.

Through this period of intensive learning, Michael's perspective on the armed struggle and his role within it was profoundly shaped. He gained not only the skills necessary for effective participation but also a deeper conviction in the justice of their cause. This foundational training was instrumental in preparing him for the challenges ahead, forging a sense of duty and purpose that would guide his actions in the years to come.

The community's tacit support and his family's history played a significant role in Michael's continued involvement. The stories of his father and the collective experiences of his neighborhood reinforced his belief in the IRA's cause. This sense of community and belonging further deepened Michael's commitment to the movement.

Michael's father, Patrick, was a well-respected figure in their neighborhood, known for his quiet strength and unwavering dedication to the nationalist cause. Evenings in the O'Connor household often turned into informal history lessons, with Patrick recounting tales of past rebellions and the sacrifices made by those who came before them. The living room, with its worn furniture and the soft glow of a single lamp, was a sanctuary of sorts where these stories came to life. The smell of peat burning in the fireplace mingled with the faint scent of his father's pipe tobacco, creating a comforting backdrop to the tales of valor and resilience.

Patrick's stories were not just about distant events; they were deeply personal. He spoke of friends and family members who had fought and died for the cause, their names etched into the collective memory of the community. Michael listened with rapt attention, his father's voice a steady guide through the tumultuous history of their struggle. These narratives instilled in him a profound sense of duty and continuity, a feeling that he was part of a larger, ongoing fight for justice and freedom.

The neighborhood itself was a tapestry of shared experiences and quiet defiance. Murals commemorating fallen heroes adorned the walls, their faces a constant reminder of the price of their resistance. The vibrant colors of the murals stood in stark contrast to the grayness of their daily lives, symbolizing hope and resilience. The narrow streets, with their familiar sights and sounds, were filled with the whispers of past and present struggles. The sense of community was palpable, reinforced by the shared hardships and the collective desire for a better future.

Community gatherings played a crucial role in maintaining this sense of solidarity. Whether at local pubs, during commemorations, or at marches, these events were where stories were shared and bonds were strengthened. The pubs, with their warm, dimly lit interiors and the comforting hum of conversation, were places where Michael felt the collective heartbeat of his neighborhood. The smell of spilled beer and the sound of traditional Irish music created an atmosphere of camaraderie and unity. These gatherings were informal forums where the latest political developments were discussed, and the community's resolve was renewed.

At commemorations and marches, the air was charged with emotion and purpose. The smell of burning candles and the sight of flags waving in the wind were ever-present. Speeches from local leaders stirred the crowd, their words echoing the collective sentiments of grief, anger, and determination. Michael stood among the crowd, feeling a profound connection to those around him. The shared tears for lost loved ones and the defiant chants for freedom reinforced his belief in the righteousness of their cause.

The community's tacit support was evident in the subtle ways people contributed to the cause. Neighbors would offer their homes as safe houses, provide meals for volunteers, or simply lend a sympathetic ear. These acts of quiet resistance and solidarity were the backbone of their struggle, creating an unspoken network of support that bolstered the IRA's efforts. Michael saw this support firsthand, feeling the strength of a community united in its desire for liberation.

The collective experiences of his neighborhood, combined with his family's history, reinforced Michael's belief in the IRA's cause. The stories of past sacrifices, the daily realities of oppression, and the unwavering spirit of his community deepened his commitment. He understood that his involvement in the IRA was not just a personal choice but a continuation of a legacy of resistance and resilience.

This sense of community and belonging was integral to Michael's identity. It provided him with a sense of purpose and a connection to something larger than himself. The bonds forged through shared experiences and the collective memory of struggle were powerful motivators. They fueled his determination to fight for the rights and freedoms of his people, reinforcing his belief that their cause was just and necessary.

Michael's commitment to the IRA was thus deeply rooted in the community that surrounded him. The support of his neighbors, the stories of his father, and the collective experiences of his neighborhood all played crucial roles in shaping his perspective and strengthening his resolve. This sense of belonging and the shared aspiration for a better future were central to his continued involvement in the movement, guiding his actions and sustaining his dedication to the cause of a united and independent Ireland.

Raised in a family where Irish history and the struggle for independence were often discussed, Michael grew up with a strong sense of national identity. His father's stories about the Easter Rising and other rebellions instilled in him a deep respect for those who fought for Irish freedom. These tales were not just historical accounts; they were personal narratives that connected Michael to Ireland's long-standing fight against British rule.

In the O'Connor household, evenings often turned into sessions of storytelling and reflection. Patrick O'Connor, Michael's father, was a man of few words but when he spoke of Ireland's past, his voice was filled with reverence and passion. The living room, with its well-worn armchairs and the soft, golden glow of the fireplace, became a stage where history came alive. The smell of burning peat, the warmth of the fire, and the quiet of the night created a setting that was both intimate and solemn.

Patrick's stories were vivid and filled with detail. He spoke of the Easter Rising of 1916, describing the courage of the men and women who took a stand against British rule. The images of Patrick Pearse and James Connolly, leaders of the rebellion, were etched into Michael's mind. His father's eyes would shine with pride as he recounted the bravery of these figures, their speeches, and their ultimate sacrifice. The crackling of the fire provided a poignant backdrop to these tales of heroism and loss.

These stories were more than just lessons in history; they were personal connections to a legacy of resistance. Patrick often recounted how their own family had been touched by these struggles. He spoke of ancestors who had fought in the Irish War of Independence and the Civil War that followed. The narratives were filled with names of relatives who had been imprisoned, those who had gone on hunger strikes, and those who had perished in the fight. The family's old photo albums, with their black-and-white images of stern-faced men in uniform, served as tangible reminders of this heritage. The smell of aging paper and the feel of the fragile pages in his hands made these connections real for Michael.

The tales of rebellion and resistance were not confined to the past. Patrick drew parallels between the historical struggles and the contemporary fight against British presence in Northern Ireland. He spoke of the civil rights marches, the Bloody Sunday massacre, and the ongoing efforts of the IRA. The discussions often grew heated, the air thick with the intensity of their convictions. Michael felt a deep sense of anger and injustice as his father spoke of the continued oppression faced by their community.

These stories instilled in Michael a profound respect for those who fought for Irish freedom. He saw them not as distant figures but as part of his own heritage, warriors in a cause that was still very much alive. The accounts of their bravery and sacrifice became a guiding light for him, shaping his values and his understanding of his place in the world.

Michael's education also reinforced this sense of national identity. At school, the history lessons were infused with the same spirit of resistance that he found at home. His teachers, many of whom had experienced the Troubles firsthand, taught with a fervor that went beyond the textbooks. The smell of chalk dust, the sound of fervent discussions, and the sight of his classmates, equally engaged and impassioned, created an environment where national identity was not just taught but lived.

Community gatherings, whether in the form of commemorations or informal meetings, further deepened Michael's connection to the struggle. The local pub, a central hub of social life, often hosted discussions about Ireland's past and future. The smell of ale and the lively hum of conversation provided a backdrop for these impromptu history lessons. Older men and women, their voices filled with pride and sorrow, shared their personal experiences and the stories of those who had fought before them. Michael listened, his heart swelling with a mix of pride and determination.

The collective memory of his community, passed down through stories and commemorations, was a powerful force in Michael's life. It connected him to a broader narrative of resistance and resilience, one that spanned generations. The murals on the walls of his neighborhood, depicting scenes of past rebellions and honoring fallen heroes, were daily reminders of this legacy. The vibrant colors and poignant imagery reinforced the stories he had heard, turning his everyday surroundings into a living testament to their cause.

These personal narratives were instrumental in shaping Michael's understanding of the struggle for Irish freedom. They instilled in him a sense of duty and a desire to contribute to the ongoing fight against British rule. The respect he felt for those who had come before him, combined with the injustices he witnessed in his own life, fueled his commitment to the nationalist cause. His father's stories, filled with personal connections and historical significance, were the foundation of his identity and his unwavering dedication to the fight for a united and independent Ireland.

As Michael matured, he developed a more nuanced understanding of the political landscape in Northern Ireland. His ideological beliefs aligned closely with the IRA's vision of a united Ireland, free from British rule. He saw the IRA not just as a militant organization, but as a necessary force in the struggle for national liberation and the rights of the Irish people.

Michael's deepening political awareness was shaped by his direct experiences and the ongoing education he received from his family and community. As he grew older, his perspective on the conflict broadened, encompassing not only the immediate struggles of his neighborhood but also the historical and political context of the entire island.

The discussions with his father became more complex, moving beyond the recounting of historical events to include analyses of current political dynamics. Patrick O'Connor, with his wealth of knowledge and experience, guided Michael through the intricacies of the political situation. The living room, with its familiar warmth and the smell of peat from the fireplace, continued to be a place of learning. The conversations now included debates on the strategies and tactics of the IRA, the role of political parties, and the impact of international opinion on their struggle.

Michael began to read extensively, seeking out books and articles that provided deeper insights into the conflict. His father's modest library, filled with works on Irish history and politics, became a treasure trove of knowledge. The scent of old books and the quiet solitude of the small study room provided the perfect environment for his intellectual growth. He absorbed the writings of prominent figures in the nationalist movement, as well as those of international liberation leaders, drawing parallels between their struggles and his own.

His involvement in the community also evolved. Michael started attending more formal political meetings and discussions, often held in hidden basements or secluded back rooms of pubs. The air was thick with the smell of smoke and the low murmur of voices discussing strategy and ideology. Here, he interacted with local leaders and activists, listening to their debates and contributing his own thoughts. These gatherings were intense and filled with fervor, reinforcing his belief in the legitimacy and necessity of their cause.

Michael's ideological beliefs crystallized around the concept of a united Ireland, where all Irish people could live free from British rule and discrimination. He saw the British presence as an ongoing form of colonialism that denied his people their basic rights and freedoms. The stories of economic hardship, social injustice, and political oppression that he heard daily only strengthened his resolve. He believed passionately in the right to self-determination and viewed the IRA's fight as a continuation of the historical struggle for Irish independence.

He came to understand the IRA not just as a group of militants, but as a multifaceted organization that played a critical role in the broader struggle. The IRA's efforts to protect communities, provide social services, and engage in political dialogue were all part of a comprehensive approach to achieving their goals. Michael appreciated the strategic balance the IRA maintained between armed resistance and political engagement. This dual approach was essential in their fight against a well-equipped and powerful adversary.

Michael's participation in IRA activities deepened his appreciation for the organization's strategic and ideological framework. His early tasks had already given him a glimpse into the operational side of the movement. Now, his growing responsibilities included planning and executing more complex operations. Each mission, each strategic meeting, reinforced his belief in the necessity of their actions. He saw firsthand the impact of their efforts, from the protection they provided to their communities to the political pressure they exerted on the British government.

The ideological teachings he received during his training also played a crucial role in shaping his beliefs. Senior IRA members provided historical context, explaining how their current struggle was part of a long continuum of resistance against British rule. They discussed the moral and ethical justifications for their actions, framing their fight as a legitimate struggle for liberation. These teachings resonated deeply with Michael, aligning perfectly with the values and beliefs instilled in him from a young age.

As Michael's understanding of the political landscape matured, so did his commitment to the IRA's vision of a united Ireland. He saw the organization as an essential force for change, one that was both a protector and a liberator. The combination of his personal experiences, the stories and teachings of his family, and his own intellectual journey solidified his belief in the righteousness of their cause.

Michael's ideological alignment with the IRA was not just a matter of political conviction but a deeply personal commitment. He believed in the necessity of their struggle, not only for the liberation of their nation but also for the protection and advancement of the rights of the Irish people. This belief drove him to continue his involvement with unwavering dedication, viewing each action he took as a step towards a free and united Ireland.

Michael's decision to join the IRA also stemmed from a strong personal conviction about the legitimacy of armed struggle in certain contexts. He wrestled with the moral implications of this path but ultimately felt that the political situation in Northern Ireland justified such measures. For Michael, joining the IRA was a way to actively engage in shaping the future of his country and to stand up against what he viewed as an oppressive foreign occupation.

Michael's internal struggle with the moral implications of armed resistance was a significant part of his journey. The decision to take up arms was not made lightly. It was the result of deep contemplation and a growing conviction that peaceful methods alone were insufficient to achieve their goals. The stories of past struggles and current injustices weighed heavily on him, reinforcing his belief that more direct action was necessary.

Late at night, Michael would sit by the window of his small bedroom, looking out at the quiet, darkened streets of his neighborhood. The distant sounds of the city, the occasional bark of a dog, and the faint hum of traffic were the only noises that broke the silence. These moments of solitude provided him with the space to reflect on the path he was about to take. The smell of the night air, cool and slightly damp, seemed to carry with it the weight of history and the voices of those who had fought before him.

He often thought about the stories his father had told him – tales of bravery and sacrifice, of men and women who had faced insurmountable odds in the fight for Irish freedom. These narratives were not just historical accounts; they were lessons in resilience and justice. Michael understood that the current political situation in Northern Ireland was a continuation of this struggle. The daily experiences of discrimination, violence, and occupation underscored the need for a robust response.

The moral dilemma was a constant companion. Michael knew that the decision to engage in armed struggle carried significant risks, not only for himself but for his community. He grappled with the potential for loss and the ethical implications of violence. The faces of innocent civilians caught in the crossfire haunted his thoughts. Yet, he also saw the suffering of his people under British rule –

the systemic injustices, the brutality of the security forces, and the erosion of their rights and dignity. The balance of these considerations was a heavy burden.

Discussions with trusted friends and mentors helped him navigate this moral landscape. In the dimly lit back rooms of pubs, where the smell of stale beer mingled with the smoke of hand-rolled cigarettes, Michael engaged in intense conversations about the ethics of armed resistance. The voices around him, filled with passion and conviction, provided different perspectives. Some argued for the necessity of violence in achieving their goals, while others emphasized the importance of minimizing harm and protecting civilians. These debates were instrumental in helping Michael clarify his own beliefs.

Ultimately, Michael concluded that the political situation in Northern Ireland justified armed struggle. He believed that the British presence represented an illegitimate occupation that could not be ended through peaceful means alone. The history of failed negotiations and broken promises reinforced his conviction that direct action was necessary to force change. He saw the IRA as a legitimate force for liberation, one that could challenge the British state and inspire international support for their cause.

Joining the IRA was, for Michael, a way to actively engage in shaping the future of his country. He wanted to be more than a passive observer of history; he wanted to be a participant, a catalyst for change. The sense of urgency he felt was palpable – a combination of anger at the injustices he witnessed daily and a deep-seated desire for a free and united Ireland. This urgency drove him to take up arms, to stand with his comrades in the fight against oppression.

Michael's decision was also deeply personal. It was about defending his community, protecting his family, and honoring the legacy of those who had fought before him. The sight of British soldiers patrolling his streets, the sound of raids in the night, and the stories of friends and neighbors who had suffered at the hands of the security forces all fueled his determination. He wanted to ensure that future generations would not have to endure the same hardships and indignities.

The commitment to the armed struggle was both a burden and a source of strength. It required him to confront his fears and doubts, to reconcile the use of violence with his desire for peace and justice. But it also provided him with a clear sense of purpose and a tangible way to contribute to the liberation of his people. Michael's involvement in the IRA became a defining aspect of his identity, shaping his actions and guiding his decisions.

In the end, Michael's decision to join the IRA was a reflection of his deeply held beliefs about justice, freedom, and the right to self-determination. It was a path fraught with moral complexities and personal risks, but one that he felt was necessary to achieve the goals of a united and independent Ireland. His choice was driven by a profound commitment to his community and a steadfast belief in the legitimacy of their struggle.

These factors combined to solidify Michael's decision to join the IRA. It was a choice that reflected his deep-seated beliefs about justice, freedom, and the right of the Irish people to self-determination.

Michael's journey to this decision was a confluence of personal, historical, and ideological influences. His upbringing in a family deeply rooted in the history of Irish resistance had instilled in him a profound respect for those who fought for freedom. The stories his father shared, filled with the valor and sacrifices of past generations, created a foundation upon which his beliefs were built. These tales were not just relics of the past but living narratives that shaped his identity and convictions.

The ongoing conflict in Northern Ireland was a constant reminder of the unfinished struggle. The daily encounters with British soldiers, the oppressive presence of military checkpoints, and the pervasive sense of surveillance and control fueled Michael's sense of injustice. The tension and hostility that marked interactions between the community and the military underscored the reality of living in a contested space. These experiences were not abstract political points but lived realities that demanded a response.

Michael's involvement in the community further reinforced his commitment to the nationalist cause. The gatherings at local pubs, the commemorations, and the marches were more than social events; they were acts of resistance and solidarity. The stories shared at these events, the collective mourning for lost loved ones, and the shared aspirations for a better future deepened his emotional connection to the struggle. The sights and sounds of these gatherings – the defiant chants, the waving flags, the solemn hymns – all contributed to a sense of unity and purpose.

The ideological training he received within the IRA provided a framework for understanding the broader context of their fight. The discussions about the legitimacy of armed struggle, the moral and ethical considerations, and the historical justifications for their actions helped Michael navigate his own moral dilemmas. He came to see the IRA not just as a militant group but as a necessary force in the pursuit of national liberation and justice. The balance between armed resistance and political strategy that the IRA maintained resonated with his belief in a multifaceted approach to achieving their goals.

The personal connections he made within the IRA also played a crucial role. The camaraderie and trust he developed with fellow members created a sense of belonging and mutual support. The shared risks and sacrifices, the long nights spent planning and strategizing, and the collective commitment to their cause solidified his resolve. These relationships were forged in the crucible of conflict, creating bonds that were as much about personal loyalty as they were about political commitment.

Michael's decision to join the IRA was ultimately a reflection of his deeply held beliefs about justice and freedom. He believed passionately in the right of the Irish people to self-determination, free from foreign rule. The systemic injustices he witnessed, the economic and social disparities, and the violence inflicted on his community all reinforced his conviction that direct action was necessary. The history of failed negotiations and the persistent oppression faced by his people convinced him that armed struggle was a legitimate and necessary path.

In making this choice, Michael understood the risks and the moral complexities involved. He grappled with the potential consequences, not only for himself but for his family and community. Yet, he also recognized the importance of standing up against oppression and actively contributing to the fight for a better future. His decision was not taken lightly but was the culmination of a lifetime of influences and experiences that had shaped his beliefs and identity.

Joining the IRA was for Michael both a personal and political act. It was a way to honor the legacy of those who had fought before him and to actively participate in the ongoing struggle for

Irish independence. His commitment to the cause was unwavering, driven by a profound sense of duty and a deep-seated belief in the justice of their fight. The factors that led him to this decision were complex and multifaceted, but together they created a clear path that Michael was determined to follow.

Michael's decision was also heavily influenced by the community and environment in which he lived. Growing up in Belfast during the Troubles, he was immersed in a society deeply impacted by political and sectarian conflict. The solidarity and resilience shown by his community in the face of adversity further fueled his desire to be part of the struggle. Witnessing the daily challenges and injustices faced by his neighbors and friends, Michael felt a growing responsibility to contribute to their fight for a better future.

Belfast during the Troubles was a city marked by division and strife. The stark contrast between the Catholic and Protestant neighborhoods was evident in the physical barriers, the murals, and the pervasive presence of armed soldiers. Michael's neighborhood was a close-knit Catholic community that bore the brunt of the conflict's harsh realities. The streets he walked every day were filled with reminders of their struggle – graffiti calling for freedom, posters of missing persons, and memorials for those who had been killed.

The community's resilience in the face of adversity left a lasting impression on Michael. He saw how neighbors supported each other through the toughest times, sharing resources, offering words of comfort, and standing together against external threats. The local shops, pubs, and churches became hubs of solidarity, where people gathered to share news, plan actions, and maintain a sense of normalcy amidst the chaos. The familiar smells of fresh bread from the bakery, the sound of children playing in the streets, and the warmth of friendly greetings all contributed to a sense of unity and defiance.

Michael's family played a central role in fostering his commitment to the nationalist cause. His father's stories of past rebellions and the sacrifices made by previous generations were more than just historical accounts; they were lessons in resilience and the importance of fighting for justice. The living room, with its flickering fireplace and the smell of his mother's cooking, was a place where these stories were shared and where Michael's sense of identity and purpose was shaped.

The collective experiences of his community were a powerful motivator. Michael witnessed the daily injustices faced by his neighbors – from random searches and arrests to the economic hardships imposed by systemic discrimination. He saw friends being harassed by soldiers, families torn apart by violence, and the constant fear that permeated their lives. These experiences were not isolated incidents but part of a broader pattern of oppression that demanded a response.

The community gatherings, whether formal meetings or spontaneous discussions at the local pub, were crucial in shaping Michael's perspective. The pubs, filled with the murmur of conversation and the clink of glasses, were places where strategies were discussed, and solidarity was strengthened. The smell of ale, the warmth of the crowded rooms, and the shared laughter and anger created an atmosphere of collective resolve. Here, Michael heard firsthand accounts of resistance, debated tactics, and felt the collective pulse of a community determined to fight for their rights.

Michael's interactions with key figures in the community also influenced his decision. He met local IRA members who were respected for their courage and commitment. These individuals, who lived among them and faced the same dangers, were seen as protectors and leaders. Their stories of sacrifice, their strategic insights, and their unwavering dedication inspired Michael. He saw in them a reflection of his own desires for justice and freedom.

The environment of Belfast during the Troubles was one of constant tension and danger, but it was also one of solidarity and resistance. Michael felt a growing sense of responsibility to contribute to the fight for a better future. He understood that the struggle was not just about abstract political goals but about the real lives of his friends, family, and neighbors. Their daily challenges and the resilience they showed in the face of adversity deepened his commitment.

Michael's decision to join the IRA was a culmination of these influences. It was a choice driven by a profound sense of duty to his community and a belief in the legitimacy of their struggle. The solidarity and resilience he witnessed around him reinforced his desire to actively participate in shaping their future. He believed that by joining the IRA, he could make a tangible difference in the fight against oppression and contribute to the dream of a free and united Ireland.

This sense of responsibility and commitment to his community was a defining aspect of Michael's identity. It provided him with the strength and determination needed to face the challenges ahead. His decision was not made lightly but was the result of a deep connection to his community and a steadfast belief in the justice of their cause. For Michael, joining the IRA was not just a political act but a personal commitment to stand with his people in their struggle for a better future.

Personal experiences of discrimination and the tangible effects of the conflict on his life played a significant role in Michael's decision. Encounters with British soldiers, witnessing the impact of raids and arrests on his community, and experiencing the reality of living in a divided society made the conflict deeply personal for him. These experiences moved the struggle from a historical and ideological concept to a tangible reality that he lived every day.

Michael's encounters with British soldiers were frequent and often fraught with tension. The sight of heavily armed troops patrolling his neighborhood was a daily reminder of the occupation. The sound of boots on pavement, the smell of exhaust from military vehicles, and the cold, impersonal stares of the soldiers created an atmosphere of fear and hostility. Michael experienced the humiliation of random searches, the anxiety of watching friends and neighbors being questioned or detained, and the constant surveillance that invaded their privacy. These encounters were not just inconveniences; they were violations that left deep scars on his psyche.

One evening, as Michael was returning home from the local pub, he was stopped at a checkpoint. The memory of that night was vivid: the harsh glare of floodlights, the aggressive bark of orders, and the rough handling as soldiers searched him. The smell of sweat and fear hung in the air as he stood with his hands raised, feeling the invasive pat-downs and the cold metal of weapons pressed against his back. The incident left him feeling violated and powerless, fueling his anger and deepening his resolve to resist.

The impact of raids and arrests on his community was another powerful influence. Michael often woke to the sound of doors being smashed in the early hours of the morning, the cries of frightened children, and the shouts of soldiers. These raids were a brutal disruption of their lives, leaving homes ransacked and families traumatized. The sight of friends and neighbors being dragged away, their faces etched with fear and defiance, was a stark reminder of the cost of the conflict. The smell of dust and debris, the sight of upturned furniture, and the lingering tension after a raid made the violence of the occupation a constant presence in their lives.

One particularly harrowing memory was the arrest of his childhood friend, Liam. Michael had grown up with Liam, and they had shared countless adventures and dreams. Seeing Liam handcuffed and thrown into the back of a military vehicle was a moment of profound helplessness and rage. The image of Liam's terrified eyes, the sound of his mother's anguished cries, and the feeling of cold fury that gripped Michael's heart solidified his commitment to the cause. He knew that the struggle was not just about abstract principles but about the very real lives of those he loved.

Living in a divided society, the sectarian lines were drawn sharply in every aspect of daily life. Schools, businesses, and even social gatherings were segregated, creating an environment of constant tension and mistrust. The physical barriers, like the peace walls that separated Catholic and Protestant neighborhoods, were a tangible manifestation of this division. Michael often walked along these walls, the towering structures casting long shadows over his path, their surfaces covered in graffiti and political messages. The smell of fresh paint and the feel of the rough concrete under his fingers were reminders of the divisions that shaped his world.

The discrimination faced by his community was systemic and pervasive. Michael saw how Catholics were denied equal opportunities in employment and housing, how they were treated as second-class citizens in their own land. The frustration and anger of his parents, who struggled to provide for their family in the face of such discrimination, left a lasting impact on him. The stories of missed opportunities, of dreams deferred and denied, were common topics at the dinner table, where the smell of his mother's cooking did little to mask the bitterness of their discussions.

These personal experiences made the conflict deeply personal for Michael. The injustices he witnessed and experienced were not just theoretical grievances but everyday realities that affected him and his loved ones. The sense of helplessness and anger he felt in the face of these injustices fueled his desire to fight back. The struggle was no longer just a historical or ideological concept but a tangible reality that demanded action.

Michael's decision to join the IRA was thus a response to the immediate and pressing realities of his life. It was a way to reclaim a sense of agency and to stand up against the oppression that he and his community faced daily. The personal experiences of discrimination, the impact of raids and arrests, and the reality of living in a divided society all combined to solidify his commitment to the nationalist cause. Joining the IRA was not just a political statement but a deeply personal act of resistance against an oppressive system that had shaped his entire life.

For Michael, joining the IRA was also about finding a voice and agency in a situation where he often felt powerless. It was a means to take control and actively participate in shaping the narrative of his country's future. He saw it as a way to contribute to a cause that he believed was just and necessary, a cause that was larger than himself.

Michael's life in Belfast during the Troubles was defined by a constant feeling of powerlessness. The oppressive presence of

British soldiers, the pervasive sense of surveillance, and the systemic discrimination his community faced all contributed to this sense of helplessness. Each day brought new challenges and indignities, from the random searches and aggressive raids to the economic hardships and social exclusion imposed by the conflict. These experiences fostered a deep desire within Michael to take control of his destiny and fight back against the forces that sought to oppress him and his people.

Joining the IRA offered Michael a way to reclaim his agency. It provided him with a sense of purpose and the means to actively participate in the struggle for Irish independence. The decision was not made lightly; it was the culmination of a lifetime of witnessing injustice and experiencing the impact of the conflict firsthand. The smell of gunpowder, the sound of whispered plans in darkened rooms, and the feel of cold metal in his hands were all part of his new reality, one where he could contribute directly to the fight for freedom.

The process of joining the IRA was both rigorous and clandestine. Michael met with senior members in hidden locations, often under the cover of night. The meetings were tense and filled with a sense of urgency. In the dim light of a secluded basement, surrounded by the smell of damp earth and the quiet hum of whispered conversations, Michael was initiated into the organization. The commitment required was immense, but it was a path he was determined to follow. The IRA's network of safe houses, secret routes, and underground communications became his new environment, offering him a role in a larger, coordinated effort.

For Michael, this newfound role was empowering. He felt a sense of camaraderie and solidarity with his fellow members, who shared his commitment and determination. The shared experiences of training, planning, and executing operations created a bond that was both personal and ideological. The sight of comrades, their faces set with resolve, and the sound of their voices, firm and unwavering, reinforced his belief in their cause. Together, they were part of a movement that aimed to challenge the status quo and fight for a united Ireland.

The training Michael received further equipped him with the skills needed to contribute effectively to the IRA's operations. He learned secure communication methods, surveillance techniques, and tactical planning. Each lesson, whether conducted in the quiet of a hidden safe house or the rugged terrain of a remote training camp, added to his sense of capability and control. The smell of fresh earth during outdoor drills, the feel of coded messages in his hands, and the intense focus required for surveillance exercises all contributed to his growing confidence and sense of purpose.

Participating in the IRA's activities also gave Michael a platform to voice his beliefs and contribute to the strategic direction of their struggle. He was no longer a passive observer but an active participant in shaping the future of his country. The discussions and debates with fellow members, often held in the secrecy of underground meetings, allowed him to share his insights and ideas. The atmosphere was charged with intellectual fervor and a shared commitment to their cause. The flickering candlelight, the rustle of maps and plans, and the intense, hushed conversations were all part of the environment where decisions were made and strategies were forged.

Michael's involvement in the IRA was also a way to honor the legacy of those who had fought before him. He saw himself as part of a continuum of resistance, carrying forward the fight for freedom and justice. The stories of past rebellions, the faces of fallen heroes on the murals of his neighborhood, and the collective memory of his community's struggles were all sources of inspiration. The smell of burning candles at vigils, the sight of Irish flags waving defiantly, and the sound of solemn songs of resistance filled him with a deep sense of connection to his heritage and purpose.

Ultimately, joining the IRA was Michael's way of finding a voice in a world that often sought to silence him. It was a means to take control of his destiny and actively participate in the fight for a just and necessary cause. The sense of empowerment and agency he gained through his involvement was transformative, shaping his identity and guiding his actions. For Michael, the struggle for a united Ireland was not just a political movement but a deeply personal mission, one that gave his life meaning and direction.

In the IRA, Michael found a way to contribute to a cause that was larger than himself. It was a commitment to fight for the rights and freedoms of his people, to stand against oppression, and to work towards a future where justice and equality prevailed. This sense of purpose and the empowerment it brought were the driving forces behind his decision to join the IRA, solidifying his role in the ongoing struggle for Irish independence.

The amalgamation of these personal, social, and ideological factors culminated in Michael's resolute decision to join the IRA. It was a decision that reflected not just his desire for Irish unity but also his deep-seated need to fight for justice and equality. Michael's journey into the IRA was thus a path chosen with full consciousness of its implications, driven by a profound belief in the righteousness of his cause and a deep commitment to the struggle for a free and united Ireland.

Michael's decision to join the IRA was the result of a complex interplay of personal experiences, community influence, and ideological convictions. The daily realities of living in Belfast during the Troubles, with its pervasive atmosphere of tension and conflict, shaped his worldview in profound ways. The sight of British soldiers patrolling the streets, the sounds of raids and arrests, and the stories of discrimination and hardship faced by his friends and neighbors all contributed to his sense of urgency and resolve.

Personal experiences of discrimination were a powerful motivator. Michael had seen firsthand the impact of systemic inequality and oppression on his community. The random searches, the aggressive raids, and the economic hardships imposed by the occupation were daily reminders of the injustices they faced. The smell of tear gas during protests, the sight of boarded-up shops and homes, and the feeling of fear and anger during military encounters were all etched into his memory. These experiences moved the struggle from an abstract concept to a tangible reality that demanded action.

The social environment in which Michael grew up was another significant influence. His family, friends, and community played crucial roles in shaping his beliefs and commitments. The stories of past rebellions and sacrifices shared by his father, the solidarity and resilience shown by his neighbors, and the collective mourning and defiance at community gatherings all reinforced his sense of belonging and purpose. The familiar faces at the local pub, the warm greetings from neighbors, and the shared laughter and sorrow during commemorations created a strong sense of unity and determination.

Ideologically, Michael was deeply aligned with the goals of the IRA. He believed in the right of the Irish people to self-determination and viewed the British presence as an illegitimate occupation. The teachings he received during his training, the historical context provided by senior IRA members, and the strategic discussions he participated in all solidified his belief in the legitimacy and necessity of their struggle. The intellectual debates held in dimly lit basements, the intense focus during tactical planning sessions, and the earnest conversations about the future of Ireland all contributed to his ideological commitment.

Michael's journey into the IRA was marked by a conscious understanding of its implications. He knew the risks involved – the potential for arrest, injury, or even death. He was aware of the moral complexities and the difficult choices he would have to make. Yet, his conviction in the righteousness of their cause outweighed these concerns. He saw his involvement not just as a duty but as a vital contribution to a larger, just cause. The sense of empowerment and agency he gained through his participation was transformative, giving his life a clear sense of direction and purpose.

Joining the IRA was a decision made with full awareness of its gravity. It was a path chosen after deep reflection and driven by a combination of personal experiences, social influences, and ideological beliefs. For Michael, the fight for a free and united Ireland was more than a political struggle; it was a deeply personal mission for justice and equality. The commitment to this cause was unwavering, rooted in a profound belief in the rights and dignity of his people.

Michael's involvement in the IRA was thus not just an act of rebellion but a declaration of his identity and values. It was a testament to his deep-seated need to fight against oppression and to stand up for the principles of justice and equality. The amalgamation of his personal, social, and ideological influences created a resolute determination to contribute to the struggle for Irish independence.

In the end, Michael's decision to join the IRA was a reflection of his profound commitment to the cause. It was a choice that encapsulated his desire for Irish unity, his need to combat injustice, and his belief in the legitimacy of their struggle. This journey was a defining aspect of his life, guiding his actions and shaping his identity. Through his involvement, Michael found a way to actively participate in shaping the future of his country, driven by a deep commitment to the principles of freedom and equality.

Michael's journey within the IRA was marked by a gradual process of gaining trust and forging relationships with fellow members, a critical aspect of his involvement in the organization.

Upon joining the IRA, Michael was acutely aware that trust was not given lightly. The organization operated in an environment of constant surveillance and infiltration by British forces, making discretion and reliability paramount. Michael's initial tasks were foundational, aimed at building this trust. Distributing pamphlets and handling logistical operations were not glamorous, but they were crucial. The smell of ink from freshly printed pamphlets, the weight of packages in his hands, and the quiet satisfaction of completing these tasks without detection were all part of his early experiences.

As Michael proved his reliability and dedication, he began to interact more closely with senior members. These interactions were often conducted in secrecy, in the back rooms of pubs or the basements of safe houses. The atmosphere was always charged with a mix of tension and camaraderie. The dim lighting, the murmurs of hushed conversations, and the constant vigilance created an environment where trust had to be earned through consistent actions.

One of Michael's most significant relationships was with Seamus, a seasoned IRA operative known for his strategic mind and unwavering commitment. Seamus took Michael under his wing, guiding him through the complexities of the organization. The bond they formed was built on mutual respect and shared experiences. Late-night discussions in the quiet corners of their hideouts, with the smell of tobacco smoke lingering in the air and the soft glow of a single lamp illuminating their maps and plans, were times when Michael absorbed invaluable lessons. Seamus's stories of past missions, his tactical advice, and his philosophical reflections on their struggle deeply influenced Michael's understanding of their cause.

Another important figure in Michael's journey was Brigid, a nurse and logistician within the IRA who was instrumental in organizing medical supplies and safe houses. Brigid's calm demeanor and meticulous planning were crucial in ensuring the safety and efficiency of their operations. Michael often assisted her, learning the importance of logistics and the unseen work that sustained their efforts. The smell of antiseptic and the sight of well-organized supplies in Brigid's makeshift medical stations were reminders of the critical support roles within the IRA. Through their collaboration, Michael came to appreciate the diverse skills and contributions necessary for their collective success.

Forging relationships with his peers was equally important. Michael's fellow recruits, many of whom came from similar backgrounds, shared his passion and determination. The bonds they formed were forged in the crucible of shared risk and commitment. Training sessions in secluded rural areas, with the sounds of the countryside punctuated by the crack of gunfire and the shouts of instructors, were physically demanding but essential for building teamwork. The camaraderie that developed during these sessions, the shared meals around campfires, and the whispered conversations in the dark strengthened their trust in each other.

Michael's growing responsibilities within the IRA required him to work closely with various cells and units. Each group had its dynamics and challenges, but Michael's ability to navigate these relationships was crucial. He learned to balance the need for operational secrecy with the necessity of clear communication. The intricate web of contacts, the coded messages, and the clandestine meetings were all part of the trust-based network that enabled the IRA to function effectively. Michael's role in coordinating these efforts, ensuring that information and resources flowed smoothly, became increasingly vital.

The trust Michael earned was not solely based on his reliability and skills but also on his unwavering commitment to their shared cause. His willingness to take on dangerous assignments, his resilience in the face of adversity, and his loyalty to his comrades solidified his place within the organization. The sense of belonging he felt, the knowledge that he was part of a collective effort to fight for their rights and freedom, reinforced his dedication.

Michael's journey within the IRA was marked by this gradual process of gaining trust and forging relationships. Each task completed, each mission undertaken, and each relationship built was a step towards deeper integration into the organization. The respect and camaraderie he earned were vital for his role in the IRA, providing him with the support and resources needed to contribute effectively to their struggle.

Through these relationships, Michael found not only comrades but also mentors and friends who shared his vision and commitment. The collective experiences, the shared risks, and the mutual trust forged in the heat of their struggle became the foundation of his involvement in the IRA. Michael's journey was not just about individual actions but about being part of a larger, interconnected effort to achieve their goals. This network of trust and relationships was critical to his success and to the effectiveness of the IRA's operations.

AS MICHAEL'S RESPONSIBILITIES grew, he began participating in joint operations, providing him the opportunity to work closely with other IRA members. These operations, often fraught with risk, required a high degree of coordination and trust among the team. Successfully completing these missions together served as a bonding experience, strengthening the ties between Michael and his comrades.

Michael's first joint operation was a nerve-wracking experience that tested his skills and resolve. The operation was a coordinated raid on a British supply depot, a mission critical to disrupting the enemy's logistics. The planning phase was intense, held in the dimly lit basement of a safe house. The room was filled with the smell of damp earth and the low hum of whispered conversations as maps and blueprints were spread across a wooden table. Michael, alongside his fellow operatives, listened intently to the briefing. The flickering candlelight cast long shadows on the walls, adding to the gravity of the situation.

The night of the operation, the team moved silently through the narrow streets of Belfast. The air was thick with tension, each member acutely aware of the dangers that lay ahead. The sound of their footsteps was barely audible over the distant hum of the city. Michael could feel the weight of his equipment and the cold metal of his weapon, both reassuring and a reminder of the stakes. The smell of the city at night – a mix of exhaust fumes, distant fires, and the occasional whiff of the river – heightened his senses.

Coordination and trust were paramount. Each team member had a specific role, and any mistake could jeopardize the entire operation. Michael's task was to secure the perimeter, ensuring that no unexpected patrols would interfere. As he crouched behind a low wall, his heart pounding, he listened to the coded clicks of the radio, signaling that the team was in position. The night was dark and still, the only sound being the occasional rustle of leaves or the distant bark of a dog.

The operation unfolded with precision. The team breached the depot's defenses, moving quickly and efficiently. The sounds of whispered commands, the soft thud of boots on gravel, and the occasional metallic clink as they dismantled security systems filled the air. Michael's vigilance paid off when he spotted a late-night patrol approaching. A quick, silent signal to his comrades ensured that the team could withdraw without detection. The adrenaline rush of the successful raid was exhilarating, a stark contrast to the quiet tension of the approach.

Back at the safe house, the team celebrated their success. The basement was filled with laughter and the clinking of glasses, the smell of sweat and adrenaline slowly giving way to the comforting aroma of shared food and drink. These moments of camaraderie were vital, reinforcing the bonds forged in the heat of action. Michael felt a deep sense of belonging, knowing that he was part of a group that trusted him and relied on his abilities.

As Michael participated in more joint operations, the bonds with his comrades grew stronger. Each mission presented new challenges and dangers, but also opportunities to prove their mettle and deepen their trust. The shared experiences of planning, executing, and reflecting on these operations created a sense of unity and mutual respect. Michael learned to read his teammates' unspoken signals, to anticipate their actions, and to work seamlessly as part of a cohesive unit.

One particularly challenging operation involved sabotaging a key transport route used by British forces. The team had to work under the cover of darkness, using the rugged terrain to their advantage. The operation required meticulous planning and precise execution. The cold night air, the rough feel of the rocky ground underfoot, and the constant awareness of potential threats heightened their focus. The sound of distant water, the rustle of wind through the trees, and the occasional call of a nocturnal animal were the only background to their tense, silent work.

Successfully completing such high-stakes missions together served as powerful bonding experiences. The sense of accomplishment and relief after a successful operation was shared by all, creating a profound sense of unity. These experiences were not just about achieving strategic objectives but also about building and reinforcing the trust and camaraderie essential for their continued efforts.

The trust developed during these operations was invaluable. It ensured that each member could rely on the others, knowing that their safety and success depended on mutual support. The shared risks and rewards of their missions created a strong sense of loyalty and dedication to one another. Michael's relationships with his comrades deepened, their shared experiences in the face of danger creating bonds that were as unbreakable as they were necessary.

Through these joint operations, Michael's involvement in the IRA became more than just a role; it became a defining part of his identity. The high degree of coordination and trust required for these missions, and the sense of shared purpose and solidarity that emerged from them, solidified his commitment to the cause and his comrades. The bonds forged in the crucible of their struggle were instrumental in shaping Michael's journey and his unwavering dedication to the fight for a free and united Ireland.

Beyond the operational aspect, Michael found common ground with fellow IRA members through shared experiences and ideals. Conversations during downtime or in safe houses often revolved around their personal journeys to the IRA, discussions on the political situation, and reflections on the aspirations for a united Ireland. These interactions deepened his understanding of the diverse motivations and backgrounds of the members, enriching his own perspective on the struggle.

In the quiet moments between operations, Michael and his comrades often gathered in the safe houses scattered throughout Belfast and the surrounding countryside. These locations, though often modest and bare, provided a sanctuary where they could rest, plan, and bond. The familiar smells of worn furniture, the occasional waft of a home-cooked meal, and the sounds of hushed conversations created a comforting backdrop to their shared experiences.

One evening, as the team gathered in a small farmhouse hidden deep in the countryside, the atmosphere was one of relaxed camaraderie. The faint smell of peat smoke from the hearth mixed with the scent of tea brewing on the stove. The soft glow of the fire cast warm shadows on the walls, creating a cozy environment where stories flowed freely. Michael listened intently as Seamus, the seasoned operative who had become a mentor to him, recounted his early days in the movement. The sound of Seamus's steady voice, the crackling fire, and the occasional clink of teacups provided a serene setting for their conversation.

Seamus's story was one of hardship and determination. He spoke of growing up in a Belfast torn apart by sectarian violence, of losing friends and family to the conflict, and of the moment he decided to join the IRA. His narrative was filled with vivid details – the rough feel of the cobblestones under his feet during marches, the cold steel of the handcuffs when he was first arrested, and the fierce pride in his heart as he took the oath of allegiance to the IRA. Michael felt a deep sense of respect and admiration for Seamus, whose experiences mirrored his own in many ways.

Brigid, the nurse and logistician, shared her perspective from a different angle. Her involvement had started as a desire to provide medical aid to those injured in the conflict, but it had grown into a deeper commitment to the cause. She spoke of the countless nights spent tending to wounded comrades, the improvised medical stations in basements and attics, and the unyielding spirit of those she helped. The smell of antiseptic and the sight of blood-stained bandages were constant reminders of the human cost of their struggle. Brigid's compassion and dedication added a poignant dimension to Michael's understanding of their fight.

Liam, a younger recruit who had joined around the same time as Michael, brought a fresh and passionate perspective. His enthusiasm was infectious, his voice animated as he discussed his hopes for a united Ireland. Liam's tales of participating in protests, the adrenaline rush of evading capture, and his deep belief in the rightness of their cause resonated with Michael. The energy and optimism of the younger recruits injected a sense of urgency and hope into their conversations, reinforcing the idea that their struggle was not just about resistance but about building a better future.

These shared stories and discussions extended beyond their personal journeys to broader political debates. The team often found themselves engrossed in conversations about the state of the conflict, the strategies of the British government, and the international response to their cause. The air was thick with the smell of tobacco and the sound of passionate voices as they dissected news reports, analyzed political statements, and debated the best course of action. These intellectual exchanges were as intense as any operation, requiring them to think critically and strategically.

Michael found that these interactions enriched his own perspective on the struggle. He learned to appreciate the diverse motivations and backgrounds of his fellow members, understanding that their fight was united by a common goal but driven by a variety of personal experiences and ideals. The conversations revealed the complexities and nuances of their cause, highlighting the different ways each member contributed to the larger effort.

The safe houses became places of learning and reflection, where Michael absorbed the collective wisdom of his comrades. The smell of old books and the sound of pages turning as they shared readings on political theory and history added an academic dimension to their discussions. The warmth of the fire, the taste of simple but hearty meals, and the shared silence as they contemplated their future provided moments of respite and bonding.

Through these interactions, Michael's commitment to the IRA and the cause of a united Ireland deepened. He realized that their struggle was not just about armed resistance but about preserving their heritage, protecting their community, and fighting for a just and equitable society. The shared experiences and ideals forged a strong sense of solidarity and purpose, reinforcing his belief in the righteousness of their cause.

The bonds formed during these moments of downtime were crucial to the team's cohesion and effectiveness. The trust and understanding built through these conversations translated into better coordination and support during operations. Michael knew that he could rely on his comrades, not just because of their shared training but because of the deep personal connections they had forged.

In the end, it was these shared experiences and ideals that sustained Michael through the challenges of their struggle. The knowledge that he was part of a community bound by a common cause, enriched by diverse perspectives and united by a shared vision for the future, gave him the strength and determination to continue. Michael's journey within the IRA was marked by these moments of connection and understanding, which were as vital to their success as any tactical operation.

Trust within the IRA was not only built through shared tasks but also forged in moments of adversity. Experiences such as evading capture during operations, providing mutual support during challenging times, and navigating the uncertainties of the conflict served to cement the bonds between Michael and other members. The shared experience of facing danger and the reliance on each other for safety and success created a strong sense of camaraderie.

One of the most harrowing experiences that tested Michael's resolve and solidified his bonds with his comrades was during a raid on a British patrol station. The operation required precision and stealth, as they aimed to disrupt communications and gather intelligence. As they approached the station under the cover of darkness, the tension was palpable. The air was cool and still, the only sounds were their careful footsteps and the distant hum of the city.

The team moved silently, each member knowing their role. Michael's task was to disable the alarm system, a crucial step to ensure their success. As he worked quickly and efficiently, the smell of freshly cut grass and the faint scent of oil from the machinery inside the station filled his nostrils. Suddenly, the quiet night was shattered by the sound of an approaching vehicle. A British patrol was returning earlier than expected.

The team had to think fast. Seamus, with his calm and decisive leadership, signaled for an immediate retreat. The adrenaline surged through Michael's veins as they scattered into the surrounding fields. The sound of heavy boots on gravel, the sharp commands of the British soldiers, and the blinding searchlights sweeping the area made the escape treacherous. Michael's heart pounded in his chest as he crouched behind a stone wall, the rough texture of the stones pressing into his back, praying he wouldn't be discovered.

In that moment of peril, the importance of trust and mutual support became painfully clear. Michael relied on his comrades to watch his back, just as they relied on him to stay calm and quiet. The smell of damp earth and the chill of the night air heightened his senses, every rustle and movement around him a potential threat. The minutes stretched into an eternity until the patrol finally moved on, allowing the team to slip away undetected.

Back at the safe house, the atmosphere was tense but relieved. The smell of sweat and the faint odor of smoke from the fire mixed as they recounted the night's events. The experience had been a close call, but it had also cemented their trust in one another. The shared danger and the reliance on each other for survival created a bond that was unbreakable. The camaraderie forged in those moments of adversity was as strong as any blood tie.

Michael also found that mutual support during personal challenges strengthened these bonds. During a particularly intense period of crackdowns, when many IRA members were being arrested or killed, the emotional toll was heavy. Michael struggled with the fear of losing his comrades and the constant threat of capture. The safe house, usually a place of planning and strategy, became a refuge where they supported each other through the psychological strain.

Brigid, with her nurturing spirit, played a key role in these times. She provided not only medical care but also emotional support, her presence a comforting constant. The soft light of the safe house, the smell of antiseptic, and the quiet murmur of reassuring words created an environment of care and solidarity. Michael and his comrades shared their fears and hopes, their laughter and tears, finding strength in their unity.

The shared experience of facing danger was not limited to operations. Navigating the uncertainties of the conflict required constant vigilance and adaptability. Whether it was avoiding surveillance, creating safe routes through the city, or dealing with the aftermath of a failed mission, these experiences were fraught with risk. The team's ability to stay united and support each other through these challenges was crucial to their success and survival.

One night, after a particularly grueling operation that had resulted in several casualties, Michael and his team gathered in a dimly lit room of a safe house. The air was heavy with the smell of blood and sweat, and the low murmurs of conversation were punctuated by the occasional sob. Seamus, his voice steady despite the exhaustion etched on his face, spoke of resilience and unity. His words, combined with the shared silence of those who had faced death together, were a powerful reminder of their shared commitment and strength.

The reliance on each other for safety and success created a bond of camaraderie that was integral to their operations. Each mission undertaken, each close call, and each shared moment of vulnerability added layers to their trust and solidarity. Michael knew that in the face of adversity, his comrades would stand by him, just as he would stand by them. This unbreakable bond was a testament to their collective resilience and dedication to their cause.

Through these experiences, Michael's journey within the IRA was defined by a profound sense of camaraderie and mutual trust. The shared dangers and the reliance on each other forged relationships that were essential to their struggle. These bonds, built in the crucible of conflict and adversity, were a cornerstone of their effectiveness and their unwavering commitment to a free and united Ireland.

Michael also benefited from the mentorship of more experienced members. Figures like Brendan, who had taken him under his wing, played a significant role in his development within the organization. This mentorship went beyond teaching skills; it was also about imparting the values, history, and vision of the IRA, further integrating Michael into the fabric of the organization.

Brendan was a seasoned veteran of the IRA, known for his strategic acumen and deep understanding of their cause. From the moment Michael joined, Brendan saw potential in him and took it upon himself to guide the young recruit. The mentorship began with practical training but soon evolved into a comprehensive education in the ethos of their struggle.

In the early days, Brendan focused on honing Michael's tactical skills. They spent countless hours in secluded training grounds, the sounds of nature punctuated by the sharp cracks of gunfire and the muffled thud of boots on soft earth. The smell of gunpowder and the feel of the cold metal of weapons became familiar to Michael. Under Brendan's watchful eye, he learned how to handle firearms, navigate difficult terrain, and execute covert operations with precision.

Beyond the physical training, Brendan imparted the strategic and psychological aspects of their fight. In quiet moments, often late at night around the flickering light of a campfire, Brendan would share stories of past missions, both successes and failures. The smell of burning wood and the warmth of the fire created an atmosphere conducive to reflection and learning. Brendan's tales were rich with detail, painting vivid pictures of the challenges they faced and the ingenuity required to overcome them.

However, Brendan's mentorship extended far beyond practical skills. He was deeply committed to instilling in Michael the values and history that underpinned the IRA's mission. In the safe house, a room filled with the musty scent of old books and the soft rustle of turning pages, Brendan would delve into the rich history of Ireland's struggle for independence. He would read aloud from historical texts, recounting the sacrifices of those who had come before them and the long lineage of resistance they were part of.

One evening, as they sat in a dimly lit room, Brendan began to recount the events of the Easter Rising of 1916. His voice, steady and filled with reverence, brought to life the courage and determination of the rebels. The flickering candlelight cast long shadows on the walls, creating a solemn ambiance. Michael listened intently, the stories resonating deeply with him. The names and faces of the past revolutionaries became more than just historical figures; they became part of his own narrative, his own reason for fighting.

Brendan also emphasized the importance of understanding the broader political landscape. He taught Michael to analyze news reports, to read between the lines of political statements, and to understand the international implications of their actions. These lessons often took place in the safe house's main room, where maps and newspapers covered the wooden table. The smell of ink and paper mixed with the faint aroma of tea brewing on the stove, creating an environment of focused intellectual engagement.

Through these discussions, Michael gained a deeper appreciation for the complexities of their struggle. He learned that their fight was not just about immediate military objectives but also about winning hearts and minds, both locally and internationally. Brendan's insights helped him see the larger picture, understanding how their actions fit into the grander scheme of achieving a united Ireland.

The mentorship was also deeply personal. Brendan shared his own journey, the sacrifices he had made, and the personal costs of the struggle. He spoke of friends lost, of family members who disapproved of his involvement, and of the constant fear and uncertainty that came with being a member of the IRA. These candid conversations, filled with the raw emotion of lived experience, were some of the most impactful for Michael. The smell of strong Irish whiskey, often shared during these late-night talks, added a bitter-sweet note to Brendan's stories, highlighting the blend of pride and sorrow that defined their fight.

Brendan's mentorship fostered a sense of belonging and purpose in Michael. He felt more deeply connected to the IRA, not just as an organization but as a living, breathing embodiment of a centuries-old struggle for justice and freedom. The values of courage, resilience, and unwavering commitment to their cause were instilled in him, guiding his actions and decisions.

Michael's integration into the IRA was thus not just about learning to fight but about becoming part of a larger narrative. Brendan's guidance helped him internalize the vision of a united Ireland, free from oppression, and his role in achieving that vision. The mentorship provided a foundation of knowledge, skills, and values that were essential for his development as a committed member of the IRA.

Through Brendan's mentorship, Michael's journey within the IRA was enriched and deepened. The blend of practical training, historical education, and personal support created a comprehensive framework for his involvement. Michael emerged from this mentorship not only as a skilled operative but as a fully integrated member of the IRA, ready to contribute to their cause with a clear understanding of its significance and a deep commitment to its success

***

AS HE PROVED HIS WORTH and commitment, Michael gained not only trust but also respect within the IRA. His opinions and insights began to be valued in planning sessions, and he found himself being included in more strategic discussions. This recognition was a testament to the relationships he had built and the trust he had earned.

Michael's journey within the IRA had been marked by gradual steps towards deeper involvement and greater responsibility. His consistent reliability in executing missions, coupled with his growing tactical acumen, had not gone unnoticed by his superiors. The respect he garnered was evident in the way senior members began to seek his input during crucial planning meetings.

One evening, Michael was called to a strategic planning session held in a secluded farmhouse. The air outside was crisp, and the sky clear, revealing a blanket of stars that provided a serene contrast to the intensity of the discussions inside. The farmhouse, dimly lit and filled with the scent of burning peat, was a hive of activity. Maps and documents covered the large wooden table at the center of the room, illuminated by the flickering light of a few oil lamps.

As Michael entered, he was greeted with nods of acknowledgment from senior operatives. Brendan motioned for him to join them at the table. The sense of respect was palpable, and Michael felt a mix of pride and responsibility as he took his seat. The discussions were intense, focusing on an upcoming operation that required careful coordination and precise execution.

Michael listened intently as the team laid out the objectives and potential challenges. The smell of tobacco smoke mingled with the earthy aroma of the peat fire, creating a familiar and comforting atmosphere despite the gravity of their task. When Brendan turned to Michael and asked for his thoughts, it was a moment of validation. Michael's heart pounded slightly as he gathered his thoughts, aware that his words carried weight.

He spoke clearly and confidently, offering insights based on his experiences in the field. He suggested modifications to their approach, highlighting potential risks and proposing alternative strategies to mitigate them. As he spoke, he could see nods of agreement and thoughtful expressions from the others. The respect in their eyes was evident, a silent acknowledgment of his growing expertise.

This inclusion in strategic discussions was a significant milestone for Michael. It was not just about having a voice but about contributing meaningfully to their collective efforts. The respect he had earned was a reflection of the trust and relationships he had built within the organization. His comrades valued his judgment, knowing that his insights were grounded in practical experience and a deep understanding of their cause.

These planning sessions became a regular part of Michael's involvement in the IRA. Each meeting was an opportunity to learn and to contribute. The farmhouse, with its cozy interior and the soft sounds of the countryside outside, became a place of strategic importance. The shared meals, the long nights of discussion, and the quiet moments of reflection by the fire were all part of the process of planning their actions and ensuring their success.

The recognition of his peers and superiors also brought new responsibilities. Michael found himself coordinating smaller units, overseeing the execution of complex operations, and mentoring newer recruits. The transition from being a follower to a leader was both challenging and rewarding. He drew on the mentorship he had received from Brendan and others, striving to provide the same guidance and support to those under his charge.

In these leadership roles, Michael's respect for the IRA's structure and his understanding of its values deepened. He saw firsthand the importance of trust, communication, and mutual support. Each operation, whether successful or fraught with difficulties, reinforced the bonds between him and his comrades. The shared experiences of planning, execution, and debriefing after each mission created a strong sense of unity and purpose.

One particularly challenging mission involved coordinating multiple teams for a large-scale operation aimed at disrupting British supply lines. The planning took weeks, with countless hours spent in the farmhouse, refining their strategy. Michael's role was crucial, as he was responsible for ensuring that all units were synchronized and prepared. The night before the operation, the farmhouse was a hub of activity, the air filled with anticipation and the smell of strong coffee as they made final preparations.

The operation was a success, a testament to their meticulous planning and the trust they had in each other. As they regrouped in the safe house afterward, the sense of accomplishment was palpable. The shared laughter, the clinking of glasses, and the relieved smiles were all indicators of a job well done. Michael's leadership had been instrumental, and the respect and gratitude of his comrades were evident in their expressions and words.

Through these experiences, Michael's integration into the IRA reached a new level. The trust and respect he had earned were not just personal achievements but reflections of his commitment to their cause and his ability to contribute effectively to their collective efforts. The relationships he had built, the strategic insights he provided, and the leadership roles he assumed were all part of his journey within the organization.

Michael's respect within the IRA was a testament to his dedication, skills, and the trust he had earned. It was also a recognition of his ability to see the bigger picture, to understand the nuances of their struggle, and to lead with both conviction and compassion. His journey from a new recruit to a respected leader was marked by the relationships he forged and the trust he built, solidifying his place within the fabric of the organization and its mission for a united Ireland.

The relationships Michael formed within the IRA became a crucial part of his identity. He no longer saw himself as just an individual fighting for a cause but as a member of a collective, united by a shared purpose. These bonds transcended the professional realm, becoming a defining aspect of his life and commitment to the struggle.

Michael's integration into the IRA was marked by the deep personal connections he developed with his comrades. These relationships went beyond the scope of their operations, embedding themselves into the very fabric of his life. The sense of unity and shared purpose was not just a professional necessity but a source of personal strength and identity.

The safe houses and training grounds where they spent countless hours planning and executing operations became second homes to Michael. The familiar sounds of strategizing whispers, the rustle of maps, and the clinking of equipment were the backdrop to his daily life. The smell of wood smoke and the taste of simple, communal meals created an environment where camaraderie flourished. These spaces were where Michael's bonds with his fellow IRA members deepened and evolved.

One evening, after a particularly grueling day of training, Michael and his comrades gathered around a fire outside their safe house. The sky was clear, the stars bright against the dark canvas, and the cool night air was filled with the comforting sounds of crackling flames and low murmurs of conversation. The warmth of the fire, the smell of burning wood, and the shared sense of accomplishment created a moment of reflection and connection.

Brendan, his mentor, began to speak about the importance of unity and trust within their ranks. His voice, steady and filled with conviction, carried the weight of experience and wisdom. He spoke of the collective strength they drew from each other, emphasizing that their success depended not only on their individual skills but on their ability to work together seamlessly. Michael listened intently, feeling a deep sense of belonging and pride in being part of such a committed and resilient group.

These moments of bonding were crucial in transforming the professional relationships into profound personal connections. Michael found himself sharing his thoughts and fears with his comrades, understanding that they, too, grappled with similar emotions. The conversations often extended late into the night, with stories of past experiences, hopes for the future, and the shared commitment to their cause. The smell of tobacco and the taste of whiskey during these late-night talks added a layer of intimacy and trust.

The sense of unity extended beyond the strategic and tactical aspects of their operations. It permeated their daily lives, influencing how they interacted and supported each other. During times of personal hardship, the support of his comrades was invaluable to Michael. The loss of a fellow member or the news of a loved one's suffering was a shared burden, met with collective mourning and resolve. The safe house, usually a place of planning and action, transformed into a haven of solidarity and comfort during such times.

Michael's relationship with Brigid, the nurse and logistician, exemplified this personal connection. Brigid's role went beyond her logistical and medical expertise; she was a source of emotional support and wisdom. Her calm presence and nurturing spirit were a balm during the most stressful moments. The smell of antiseptic and the quiet efficiency of her movements as she tended to wounds created an environment of care and trust. Her stories of resilience and compassion reinforced Michael's own commitment to the cause, reminding him of the human element at the heart of their struggle.

The camaraderie extended to the younger recruits as well. Michael took on a mentorship role, guided by the example set by Brendan. He found fulfillment in sharing his knowledge and experiences, helping new members navigate the complexities of their involvement. The training sessions, filled with the sounds of drills and the encouraging words of instructors, became opportunities to forge new bonds and strengthen the team's unity.

These relationships became a defining aspect of Michael's identity. He no longer saw himself as just an individual fighting for a cause but as an integral part of a collective effort. The shared experiences, the mutual trust, and the unwavering commitment to their mission created a powerful sense of belonging. The IRA was not just an organization; it was a family united by a common purpose.

The sense of being part of something larger than himself was a source of immense strength for Michael. It gave his actions meaning and his sacrifices purpose. The bonds he formed with his comrades were a constant reminder that he was not alone in his struggle. Their shared vision for a united Ireland and their collective determination to achieve it provided the motivation and resilience needed to face the challenges ahead.

The relationships Michael built within the IRA transcended the professional realm. They were deeply personal connections that shaped his identity and reinforced his commitment to the struggle. The camaraderie, trust, and shared purpose became the cornerstone of his involvement, guiding his actions and sustaining his dedication. Through these relationships, Michael found a sense of belonging and a deeper understanding of the collective strength that defined their fight for a free and united Ireland.

Michael's involvement gradually increased in complexity. He received training in more advanced tasks, including basic weapon handling, surveillance techniques, and understanding the strategic objectives of the IRA. This period of training was critical for Michael, as it equipped him with the skills necessary for more significant roles and helped deepen his understanding of the IRA's methods and goals.

The training sessions took place in various secluded locations, each chosen for its remoteness and security. The settings ranged from dense forests to abandoned farmhouses, each providing the privacy necessary for their clandestine activities. The air was often filled with the sounds of nature – birds singing, leaves rustling in the wind, and the distant murmur of streams – a stark contrast to the intense focus and discipline required during the training exercises.

One of the most significant aspects of Michael's training was learning basic weapon handling. Under the guidance of experienced operatives like Brendan, Michael became proficient in using various firearms. The weight of a gun in his hands, the smell of gun oil, and the sharp crack of gunfire became familiar sensations. The training was rigorous, involving hours of practice to ensure precision and safety. Each session ended with a thorough debriefing, where the smell of burnt gunpowder still lingered in the air, and the group would discuss techniques and improvements.

Surveillance techniques were another crucial component of Michael's advanced training. He learned how to observe and gather intelligence without being detected, a skill essential for planning and executing operations. Training often involved shadowing mock targets through urban and rural settings, honing his ability to blend into the environment. The feel of a camera in his hands, the quiet click of the shutter, and the tense moments of waiting in hidden spots became routine. Michael learned to notice the smallest details, from the pattern of footsteps to the subtle changes in a person's behavior, all while maintaining his cover.

Understanding the strategic objectives of the IRA was perhaps the most intellectually demanding part of his training. Senior members held detailed briefings, often in dimly lit rooms with maps and documents spread out on wooden tables. The smell of old paper and the sight of red pins marking significant locations created an atmosphere of serious contemplation. These sessions were more than just tactical discussions; they were lessons in the political and historical context of their struggle.

Michael learned about the IRA's long-term goals, the importance of public perception, and the necessity of aligning their actions with broader political strategies. These discussions were intense, filled with passionate debates and careful analysis. The flickering candlelight, the quiet hum of voices, and the occasional thud of a fist on the table underscored the gravity of their mission. Michael's insights and questions during these sessions reflected his growing understanding and commitment, earning him further respect from his peers.

One memorable training session involved a simulated operation to disrupt a British military supply line. The exercise required the team to apply all the skills they had learned – weapon handling, surveillance, and strategic planning. The setting was a rugged, forested area, chosen for its challenging terrain. The air was crisp and filled with the earthy scent of pine needles and moss. The team moved silently, communicating through hand signals and hushed whispers. The operation was a success, and the debriefing afterward was filled with a sense of accomplishment and camaraderie.

During this period, Michael also received training in basic first aid and field medicine. Brigid, with her extensive medical knowledge, taught him how to treat wounds, perform emergency procedures, and manage stress injuries. The smell of antiseptic, the feel of bandages, and the calm precision of Brigid's instructions were integral to these lessons. Michael understood that these skills were not just about survival but about ensuring the safety and well-being of his comrades during operations.

As Michael's training progressed, he found himself taking on more significant roles within the IRA. He began leading small units, coordinating logistics, and contributing to strategic planning. The trust and respect he had earned through his dedication and growing expertise were evident in the responsibilities he was given. Each new task was a step forward in his journey, deepening his involvement and commitment to their cause.

The training period was transformative for Michael. It equipped him with the skills and knowledge necessary for more complex and impactful roles. The hands-on experience, the intellectual rigor of strategic discussions, and the personal mentorship he received all contributed to his development as a capable and trusted member of the IRA. The bonds he formed with his trainers and fellow operatives, forged through shared challenges and mutual respect, further integrated him into the organization.

Michael's deepened understanding of the IRA's methods and goals reinforced his belief in the righteousness of their struggle. He saw himself not just as a participant but as an essential part of a collective effort to achieve a united Ireland. The skills and insights he gained during this critical period of training prepared him for the significant roles he would play in their ongoing fight, solidifying his identity as a committed and respected member of the IRA.

As Michael's involvement deepened, so did his ideological commitment to the IRA's cause. The training sessions, interactions with senior members, and participation in planning meetings reinforced his belief in the necessity of armed struggle. This ideological solidification was accompanied by a growing sense of identity as a member of the IRA, seeing himself as an integral part of the movement for Irish independence.

The more Michael trained, the more he absorbed the ethos and values that underpinned the IRA's mission. Each session was not merely a practical exercise but a lesson in the philosophy and history of their struggle. The rigorous physical training, the detailed briefings, and the intense discussions all contributed to his deepening ideological commitment.

In one memorable session, held in an old stone barn nestled in the hills, Brendan gave an impassioned lecture on the history of Ireland's fight for independence. The barn was cool and dim, the walls lined with crates and equipment. The smell of hay and the distant sound of sheep bleating outside created a rustic, almost timeless atmosphere. Brendan's voice echoed slightly in the spacious room as he recounted the stories of past heroes, their sacrifices, and the long lineage of resistance against British rule.

Michael felt a surge of pride and purpose, understanding that he was part of a continuum of struggle that spanned generations.

Interactions with senior members like Brendan were crucial in shaping Michael's ideological perspective. These veterans shared not just their tactical knowledge but also their deep-seated beliefs about justice, freedom, and the right to self-determination. During one of their frequent late-night discussions, Michael and Brendan sat by the fire, the smell of burning peat mingling with the aroma of strong Irish whiskey. Brendan spoke of the moral imperatives that drove their actions, the ethical considerations of armed struggle, and the vision of a free and united Ireland. These conversations were profound, leaving Michael with a reinforced conviction in the righteousness of their cause.

Participating in planning meetings also played a significant role in solidifying Michael's ideological commitment. These meetings were often held in hidden rooms, where the flickering light of oil lamps cast shadows on maps and documents spread out on wooden tables. The air was thick with the smell of tobacco smoke and the quiet intensity of focused discussion. Michael listened as senior operatives discussed strategy, weighed the risks and benefits of various actions, and debated the best ways to achieve their goals. The seriousness and dedication with which these discussions were conducted left a lasting impression on him.

Michael's growing sense of identity as a member of the IRA was further reinforced by the camaraderie and mutual respect he shared with his comrades. The bonds formed through shared experiences, both in training and in operations, created a strong sense of unity and purpose. He felt a profound connection to his fellow operatives, knowing that they were all driven by the same ideals and aspirations. The sense of belonging was palpable, especially during moments of collective reflection and celebration.

One such moment occurred after a successful operation where Michael had played a key role. The team gathered in a safe house, the air filled with the sounds of laughter and the clinking of glasses. The sense of accomplishment and unity was overwhelming. Michael looked around at his comrades, feeling a deep sense of pride and solidarity. The shared struggles, the risks they took, and the goals they pursued together forged a bond that transcended individual interests.

As Michael's responsibilities grew, so did his understanding of the broader implications of their actions. He began to see the strategic importance of each operation, how it fit into the larger picture of their fight for independence. The ideological teachings he received from senior members and his own experiences in the field coalesced into a coherent and compelling belief system. He saw the IRA not just as a militant organization but as a vital force for justice and liberation.

This ideological commitment was also a source of personal strength for Michael. It provided him with a clear sense of purpose and direction, guiding his actions and decisions. The knowledge that he was contributing to a noble and just cause gave him the resilience to face the dangers and challenges inherent in their struggle. The sense of identity he derived from being a member of the IRA was integral to his self-conception, shaping his values, priorities, and aspirations.

Michael's ideological solidification was evident in his speeches and actions. During one strategic meeting, he passionately argued for a bold operation that, while risky, had the potential to significantly impact British military logistics. His argument was based not only on tactical considerations but also on a deep belief in the moral righteousness of their cause. His words resonated with his comrades, many of whom nodded in agreement, their faces reflecting the same determination and conviction.

Through these experiences, Michael's commitment to the IRA's cause deepened, and his identity as a member of the organization solidified. He saw himself not just as an individual fighting for a cause but as an integral part of a larger movement for Irish independence. The training sessions, the mentorship of senior members, and the camaraderie of his comrades all contributed to his ideological development and personal growth.

Michael's journey within the IRA was thus marked by a profound ideological transformation. His belief in the necessity of armed struggle was reinforced by his experiences and the teachings he received. The relationships he formed and the respect he earned further integrated him into the fabric of the organization, making him a dedicated and respected member of the IRA, committed to the struggle for a free and united Ireland.

Michael's early involvement in the IRA was marked by a combination of learning, relationship-building, and ideological reinforcement. As he embraced this path, he became more aware of the risks and sacrifices involved. Yet, his commitment to the cause of Irish freedom remained unwavering, driven by personal and ideological motivations.

From the outset, Michael was thrust into a world of intense learning and rapid adaptation. His days were filled with training sessions designed to equip him with the skills necessary for the IRA's operations. These sessions took place in various hidden locations, each chosen for its seclusion and safety. The smell of damp earth in underground bunkers, the feel of cold steel as he learned to handle weapons, and the focused silence of surveillance exercises all became integral parts of his daily routine.

During these early days, Michael's interactions with senior members like Brendan were instrumental in shaping his understanding of their cause. Brendan's guidance went beyond tactical training; it was a deep dive into the ethos of the IRA. In the dim light of their safe house, surrounded by the smell of burning peat and the sound of whispered conversations, Brendan would share stories of past struggles and the principles that guided their fight. These lessons were profound, embedding in Michael a strong sense of duty and purpose.

Relationship-building was another crucial aspect of Michael's early involvement. The bonds he formed with his fellow operatives were built on trust and mutual respect. These relationships were forged through shared experiences, both in training and in the field. The camaraderie developed during late-night planning sessions, where the smell of strong coffee and the sight of maps illuminated by oil lamps created an atmosphere of unity and focus. These bonds were not just professional; they were deeply personal, rooted in their collective commitment to the cause.

One evening, after a long day of training, Michael and his comrades gathered around a fire outside their safe house. The night was cool, the stars bright against the dark sky, and the air filled with the comforting sounds of crackling flames and low murmurs of conversation. This was a time for relaxation and reflection. Michael listened as his peers shared their personal journeys to the IRA, their hopes for the future, and their fears. The smell of smoke, the warmth of the fire, and the shared stories created a sense of belonging and solidarity.

As Michael's involvement deepened, so did his ideological commitment. The training sessions, strategic meetings, and personal interactions all reinforced his belief in the necessity of their struggle. He became more aware of the risks and sacrifices involved. The danger of arrest, injury, or even death was a constant presence. Yet, these risks only solidified his resolve. He understood that their fight was not just about immediate gains but about a long-term vision for a free and united Ireland.

One particularly challenging operation brought home the realities of these risks. The mission was to disrupt a British military convoy, a task fraught with danger. The planning was meticulous, held in a secluded farmhouse where the smell of old wood and the sight of detailed maps set the scene for serious discussion. The night of the operation was tense, the air filled with anticipation and the faint sounds of distant wildlife. As they moved into position, the weight of his weapon and the quiet communication through hand signals underscored the gravity of their task.

The operation was successful, but not without close calls. The adrenaline rush of narrowly avoiding detection, the sound of gunfire, and the sight of the convoy halted in its tracks were stark reminders of the stakes involved. Back at the safe house, the debriefing was intense, the air filled with the smell of sweat and the relieved laughter of comrades who had faced danger together. These experiences reinforced Michael's commitment, showing him the tangible impact of their actions and the importance of their mission.

Despite the constant danger, Michael's commitment to the cause of Irish freedom remained unwavering. His personal motivations were deeply intertwined with his ideological beliefs. The stories of past heroes, the teachings of senior members, and the shared experiences with his comrades all contributed to a profound sense of purpose. The smell of burning candles during vigils, the sight of Irish flags waving defiantly, and the sound of solemn songs of resistance filled him with a deep sense of connection to his heritage and mission.

Michael's early involvement in the IRA was a period of intense growth and solidification. The learning experiences, the relationships he built, and the ideological reinforcement he received all played crucial roles in shaping his journey. He emerged from this period with a clear understanding of the risks and sacrifices involved, yet his commitment to their cause was stronger than ever. Driven by personal and ideological motivations, Michael saw himself as an integral part of the movement for Irish independence, ready to face whatever challenges lay ahead in their fight for freedom.

Michael's first direct encounter with the IRA in a leadership role was a defining moment in his journey, marking his transition from a dedicated member to a key player in their operations. Reflecting on that day, Michael vividly remembered the anticipation and gravity that filled the air.

The Setting

The meeting took place in a nondescript house on a quiet street, far from the prying eyes of the authorities. Michael had been led there by a contact he had made through his involvement in nationalist rallies. The house, with its faded exterior and small, unkempt garden, appeared ordinary to any passerby. Yet, as Michael approached, he could feel the weight of its significance. Inside, this seemingly ordinary house was a hive of secretive activity, serving as a hidden nerve center for local IRA operations.

The Atmosphere

Upon entering, Michael was immediately struck by the atmosphere. There was a palpable sense of urgency and seriousness. The room was dimly lit, with the only illumination coming from a few flickering candles and an old, dusty lamp in the corner. The air was thick with the smell of tobacco smoke, mingling with the faint aroma of brewed tea. Maps, documents, and photographs were scattered across a large wooden table, their edges curling from frequent handling and the occasional coffee stain. A sense of purpose hung in the air, a sharp contrast to the everyday life outside on the streets.

The Characters

At the meeting, Michael was introduced to several key members of the IRA. Among them was Seán, a seasoned veteran known for his strategic acumen and calm demeanor. His presence was commanding, and the respect he garnered from others was evident in the way they listened when he spoke. Another key figure was Aisling, a woman in her thirties who played a crucial role in logistics and communication. Her sharp eyes missed nothing, and her voice carried a tone of authority. Then there was Brendan, a young man about Michael's age, who had quickly risen through the ranks due to his dedication and bravery. Brendan's energy and enthusiasm were contagious, and he exuded a sense of determination that Michael found inspiring.

Initial Impressions

Michael was initially overwhelmed by the experience. He was in the presence of individuals he had only heard about in hushed tones. There was a mix of admiration and apprehension as he listened to them discuss plans and strategies. The reality of what he was getting involved in began to set in, and he felt both a sense of excitement and a weight of responsibility. The sight of these seasoned fighters, their faces etched with determination and experience, made the gravity of his choice all too real.

The Conversation at the Meeting

Michael's first IRA meeting as a leader was a profound learning experience, characterized by an intense and focused conversation that revealed the depth and seriousness of the organization's approach to the conflict. Seán began the meeting, outlining the current state of affairs. His voice was steady and deliberate, each word chosen with care. "We've had successes, but challenges remain. The British forces are tightening their grip. We need to be more strategic, more calculated," he said, his eyes locking onto Michael's for a brief moment, as if assessing his readiness.

Aisling took over, discussing logistics for an upcoming operation. Her meticulous planning was evident as she reviewed supply routes, communication protocols, and contingency plans. "Timing is crucial. One misstep, and we risk exposure," she said, her voice calm but firm. The room was silent, everyone absorbing the critical information.

Brendan added his insights, speaking passionately about the importance of unity and morale among the ranks. "We need to remember why we're here. Each action we take should bring us one step closer to our goal," he said, his enthusiasm infectious.

Planning Future Operations

Attention then shifted to planning future operations. The members laid out proposed targets and objectives, carefully considering the potential risks and rewards of each. They discussed logistics, timing, and resource allocation, ensuring that each plan was feasible and aligned with the broader goals of the IRA. Michael observed how each member brought unique insights to the table. Some focused on the tactical aspects, analyzing the best approaches for execution, while others considered the political implications, ensuring that their actions would align with the IRA's strategic objectives.

Debate on Strategies and Tactics

A significant portion of the meeting involved robust debate on various strategies and tactics. One topic of discussion was the balance between armed operations and political efforts. Some members argued for more aggressive military action to apply pressure on the British government, while others advocated for a more measured approach that would garner public support and avoid alienating the community. Michael listened intently as the debate unfolded, noting the passion and conviction in each argument. The discussion was not just about tactics but also about the philosophy and ethics underlying the IRA's approach to the conflict.

The Depth of Planning

What impressed Michael most was the depth of thought and planning that went into each decision. The members considered a range of factors: the potential impact on civilian populations, the response from British forces, media portrayal, and the implications for future peace negotiations. It was evident that the IRA's actions were not impulsive but the result of careful deliberation and strategic planning. Each decision was weighed meticulously, reflecting a commitment to their cause that went beyond mere militancy.

Inclusion of Diverse Perspectives

The meeting also highlighted the diversity of perspectives within the IRA. Members came from different backgrounds and had varied experiences, which they brought to the table. This diversity enriched the conversation, allowing for a comprehensive approach to planning and strategy. Michael appreciated the range of insights, from Seán's seasoned perspective to Aisling's logistical expertise and Brendan's youthful enthusiasm.

Michael's Growing Understanding

As the meeting progressed, Michael's understanding of the complexity and gravity of the IRA's operations deepened. He began to appreciate the challenges of coordinating a resistance movement under constant threat of infiltration and suppression. The conversation at the meeting was not just an exchange of ideas but a reflection of the collective wisdom and experience of the group, guiding their struggle for Irish independence.

Involvement and Expectations

Towards the end of the meeting, the conversation turned to Michael. Seán, who had taken a lead in the discussion, addressed him directly, asking about his motivations and his understanding of the struggle. Michael spoke honestly about his reasons for being there, his family background, and his desire to contribute to the cause. The members listened intently, nodding in approval. It was clear they were assessing his potential as a member of the organization.

As the meeting progressed, Michael was gradually drawn into the discussions. He listened intently as the members debated tactics and shared updates on recent activities. The conversation was a mix of practical discussions about logistics and deeper ideological debates about the direction of the struggle.

Understanding the Role of Each Member

Michael observed how each member brought unique skills and perspectives to the table. Seán, with his years of experience, provided strategic oversight. Aisling's expertise in logistics and communications was evident as she discussed supply routes and message encryption. Brendan, full of youthful zeal, shared insights from recent operations on the ground.

Michael's Engagement in the Discussion

Encouraged by the open atmosphere, Michael cautiously began to contribute to the conversation. He shared his observations from the neighborhood and his thoughts on the public perception of the IRA's activities. His comments were received with interest, and he felt a growing sense of acceptance among the group.

Emphasizing Caution and Commitment

The meeting took a serious turn when Seán emphasized the importance of caution and commitment. He spoke about the dangers they all faced, including surveillance by British forces and the constant threat of infiltration. Seán's words were a sobering reminder of the stakes involved in their struggle.

Assigning Michael's First Tasks

As the meeting drew to a close, Michael was assigned his first tasks. They were designed to test his commitment and reliability. His initial role involved logistical support, such as transporting materials and delivering messages to contacts within the city. While these tasks were low-key, they were crucial for maintaining the IRA's operational capabilities.

The Meeting's Impact on Michael

As Michael left the meeting, he felt a complex mix of emotions. He was exhilarated by the trust placed in him but also sobered by the realization of the serious path he had chosen. The meeting was a pivotal moment in Michael's life, marking the beginning of his active involvement in the IRA and the armed struggle for Irish independence.

Walking back through the quiet streets, Michael felt the cool night air on his face. The distant sounds of the city were a reminder of the world outside their struggle. The smell of damp pavement and the sight of the occasional passerby brought him back to reality. He knew that his life had changed irrevocably. The camaraderie he had witnessed, the strategic depth of their discussions, and the shared commitment to Irish freedom had left an indelible mark on him.

In the days following the meeting, Michael immersed himself in his new responsibilities. The relationships he had begun to forge at that first meeting deepened, and he found himself increasingly integrated into the fabric of the IRA. Each mission, each strategy session, and each shared hardship strengthened his resolve and his identity as a leader within the organization.

Michael's journey had truly begun, and there was no turning back. The lessons learned and the bonds formed during that first leadership meeting would guide him through the many challenges ahead, fueling his unwavering commitment to the cause of Irish independence.

Michael's first mission with the IRA was a significant step in his journey, marking his transition from a passive supporter to an active participant in the armed struggle. As he sat alone in his room after the meeting, Michael found himself lost in thought, reflecting on the gravity of what lay ahead.

The room was dimly lit, a single lamp casting a soft, yellow glow that barely reached the corners. The air was cool, and the faint hum of distant traffic seeped through the window, blending with the occasional creak of the old house settling. Michael sat on the edge of his bed, elbows on his knees, his hands clasped together tightly. His mind raced, the weight of the evening's briefing settling heavily on his shoulders.

He thought about the maps spread out on the table, the intricate plans and strategies they had discussed. Each detail had been meticulously considered—timing, logistics, the risks involved. Michael could still hear Seán's steady voice echoing in his mind, outlining the mission with a calm authority that both reassured and intimidated him.

The reality of his involvement struck him hard. No longer was he a mere supporter, attending rallies and meetings; he was now a critical part of the operation. The responsibility felt immense, almost overwhelming. He had always known the stakes, but tonight it felt more real than ever. The lives that depended on the success of their mission, the potential for failure, the personal risks—everything loomed large in his thoughts.

Michael's gaze drifted to a small photograph on his bedside table, a picture of his family. He wondered what they would think if they knew the full extent of his involvement. Would they understand? Would they support him, or would they be consumed by fear for his safety? The thought of his mother's worried face and his father's stern disapproval weighed heavily on his heart. He felt a pang of guilt but also a steely resolve. This was his path, his choice, and he believed deeply in the cause.

He took a deep breath, trying to steady his nerves. The smell of old wood and the faint trace of tobacco from his clothes lingered in the air. The flickering light cast shadows that danced on the walls, mimicking the turmoil within him. He knew that the road ahead would be fraught with danger and uncertainty. Each mission would bring new challenges, new moral dilemmas. He thought about the possible encounters with British forces, the split-second decisions that could mean life or death, and the constant threat of betrayal or capture.

Despite the fear gnawing at the edges of his resolve, there was also a sense of determination. Michael had chosen this path, not out of a desire for violence, but from a deep-seated belief in the fight for freedom. He remembered the stories of past heroes, the sacrifices made by those who had come before him. Their legacy was now his to carry forward.

As he sat there, Michael tried to visualize the mission ahead. He imagined the streets they would navigate, the sounds of the city at night, the feel of the cold metal of the weapon he would carry. He pictured the faces of his comrades, their shared resolve, the unspoken bond that united them in their struggle. Each thought solidified his commitment, pushing the fear to the background and bringing his purpose into sharper focus.

Finally, he stood up and moved to the window, looking out into the darkened street. The world outside seemed so calm, so unaware of the turmoil within him. He knew that by morning, he would need to present a composed, confident front to his comrades. But for now, in the solitude of his room, he allowed himself a moment of vulnerability. He let the gravity of his situation wash over him, grounding himself in the reality of what was to come.

Michael took one last deep breath, feeling the cool night air fill his lungs. As he exhaled, he released some of the tension, embracing the challenge ahead. He was ready to step into his role, to lead with conviction and courage. Tomorrow would bring the first mission, the first true test of his resolve. Tonight, he allowed himself to prepare mentally, to accept the fears and uncertainties, and to reaffirm his commitment to the cause he believed in so deeply.

The next day after the meeting, the gang gathered in their usual spot, an old, dimly lit room at the back of a safe house. The air was thick with the smell of tobacco smoke and the faint aroma of brewed tea. Michael sat among them, the weight of the previous night's briefing still heavy on his mind.

Aisling took charge of the conversation, her tone authoritative yet reassuring. "Let's go over the mission details one more time," she began, her eyes scanning the group before settling on Michael. "You'll need to blend in with the environment. Avoid anything that makes you stand out. Remember, the key here is not to be noticed. You're a ghost, Michael. Be observant but be discreet."

She handed Michael a small notebook and a pen. "Take detailed notes but do it subtly. If you need to write something down, don't do it in the open. Memorize what you can and write it down later."

Brendan, sitting next to Michael, nodded in agreement. "Blend in, mate. Act like you belong there, no matter where you are. The less they notice you, the better."

Aisling continued, shifting to the practical aspects of the mission. "Be aware of your surroundings at all times. If you feel like you're attracting attention or if the situation gets risky, abort the mission. There's no shame in pulling back to avoid capture. We need you back here with the information, not in a British holding cell."

The room fell silent for a moment, the gravity of her words sinking in. Michael felt a mixture of apprehension and determination. He knew the importance of the mission and the risks involved.

Aisling paused, looking directly at Michael. "I know this is your first field operation, and it's normal to feel nervous. Use that adrenaline to stay sharp but stay calm. Panic is your worst enemy out there."

Michael took a deep breath, feeling the weight of her gaze. "I'll stay calm. I'll do my best."

Brendan leaned in, offering a reassuring smile. "We've got your back, Michael. Remember, you're not alone in this."

Aisling nodded. "Exactly. Brendan will be your point of contact. He'll be in the vicinity on standby in case you need backup. But remember, direct communication during the operation is risky. Use it only if absolutely necessary."

Michael looked at Brendan, who gave him a confident nod. "I'll be close by. If things go south, just give the signal."

The room was filled with a tense but supportive atmosphere. Each member of the group knew the stakes and the importance of Michael's mission. They all shared a silent understanding of the dangers and the trust placed in each other.

Aisling's voice softened as she addressed the group. "We all know what we're up against. Let's stay focused and watch each other's backs. We're in this together."

Michael felt a surge of resolve. Surrounded by his comrades, he knew he was part of something bigger than himself. The mission ahead was daunting, but he felt ready. He looked around the room, seeing the determination in their eyes, and felt a renewed sense of purpose.

"Alright then," Aisling concluded, "let's get to it. Stay sharp, stay safe."

The group dispersed, each member preparing for their respective roles. Michael stayed behind for a moment, absorbing the last bits of advice and support from his friends. He knew the path ahead would be challenging, but with his comrades by his side, he felt ready to face whatever came his way.

In the days leading up to the mission, Michael immersed himself in preparation, understanding that his success depended on his attention to detail and thoroughness. The gravity of the task ahead weighed on him, but he channeled his anxiety into meticulous planning and mental readiness.

Michael spent countless hours reviewing maps and documents in the dimly lit safe house. The room smelled of old paper and tobacco, a constant reminder of the serious nature of their work. He traced the routes repeatedly, committing every turn and landmark to memory. The sound of the occasional floorboard creaking under his feet as he paced added to the intensity of his focus.

Aisling's words echoed in his mind: "You'll need to blend in with the environment. Avoid anything that makes you stand out. Remember, the key here is not to be noticed." Michael practiced this art of invisibility in his mind, visualizing himself moving through the streets, blending with the crowd, and remaining unnoticed. He spent time in front of the small mirror in his room, adjusting his posture and demeanor to appear as ordinary as possible.

He carried the small notebook Aisling had given him, writing notes discreetly, practicing how to jot down information without drawing attention. Each note was a potential piece of the puzzle that could make or break the mission. He practiced memorizing details quickly and accurately, only writing them down when he was sure he was alone.

The safe house was a hub of activity, but Michael found pockets of solitude to mentally prepare himself. He would sit quietly, eyes closed, visualizing the mission from start to finish. He imagined every possible scenario, planning his reactions to unforeseen events. The smell of the old wood and the distant hum of the city seeped into his consciousness, grounding him in the reality of his task.

Brendan provided practical advice, sharing tips from his own experiences. "Always have an exit plan," he would say, leaning in with a serious expression. "Know your surroundings like the back of your hand. And if things go south, don't hesitate to get out. Your safety is paramount." Michael absorbed these lessons, grateful for Brendan's guidance and the camaraderie they shared.

Aisling's voice was a constant in his preparation, reminding him to stay calm and use his adrenaline to stay sharp. "Panic is your worst enemy out there," she had told him, her gaze steady and reassuring. Michael practiced calming techniques, breathing deeply to center himself, ready to face the unknown with a clear mind.

Michael also familiarized himself with the tools of his trade. He spent hours learning to handle the equipment he would carry, ensuring he knew it inside out. The feel of the cold metal in his hands, the sound of the mechanisms clicking into place, all became second nature to him. He knew that proficiency with his gear could be the difference between success and failure.

The nights were the hardest. Alone in his small room, Michael wrestled with his thoughts. The flickering candlelight cast long shadows on the walls, creating a dance of light and dark that mirrored his internal struggle. He thought about his family, their faces flashing before him, and the future he hoped to secure for them. The distant sounds of the city at night, the occasional car passing by, and the rustling of leaves in the wind were his only companions in these quiet moments.

Despite the fear and uncertainty, Michael's resolve never wavered. He believed deeply in the cause, in the fight for freedom and justice. The stories of past heroes, the sacrifices made by those who had come before him, filled him with a sense of purpose. He knew that his actions, no matter how small, were part of a larger struggle for the future of his people.

As the day of the mission approached, Michael felt a mixture of nervous anticipation and calm readiness. He had prepared as thoroughly as he could, and now it was time to put that preparation to the test. He took one last look at the maps, the notes, and his gear, feeling a sense of completeness. The next steps would define his path, and he was ready to face whatever lay ahead with courage and determination.

In the days leading up to the mission, Michael immersed himself in preparation, understanding that his success depended on his attention to detail and thoroughness. Reflecting on the skills and knowledge he had acquired, he used everything he had learned to plan and execute the mission as a leader.

Studying the Map

Michael spent hours studying the map provided by Aisling. The map, spread out on the wooden table in the dimly lit room, became his focus. He memorized every street, alleyway, and landmark in the designated area, tracing his fingers over the routes repeatedly. Using information from previous observations shared by the IRA, he carefully noted the usual timings and routes of the British army patrols. He visualized multiple scenarios, planning his positions and movements to maintain an optimal vantage point while remaining inconspicuous. The flickering candlelight cast shadows on the map, making the details seem alive as he committed them to memory.

Learning from Brendan

Brendan, who had more experience in field operations, took on the role of Michael's mentor. They spent long hours together, Brendan teaching Michael the basics of surveillance. "It's about seeing without being seen," Brendan emphasized during one of their sessions. "You're not just looking; you're analyzing movements, patterns, anything out of the ordinary." Michael practiced these skills under Brendan's watchful eye, learning how to observe without being obvious, finding the right spots for observation, and tracking movements without losing focus. Brendan's guidance was invaluable, and Michael absorbed every lesson, knowing that these skills would be crucial in the field.

Blending In

Understanding the importance of blending in, Michael carefully chose his attire for the mission. He picked clothes that were common and nondescript, ensuring that he would not stand out in the crowd. Brendan's advice on how to behave in public resonated with him. "The best way to hide is in plain sight. Act like you belong there, like you're just another person going about their day." Michael practiced this too, walking through busy streets, blending into the flow of people, and mastering the art of invisibility.

Mental and Emotional Preparation

Michael also prepared mentally and emotionally. He knew that staying calm and focused was crucial. He practiced deep breathing exercises to control his nerves and spent time visualizing the mission going successfully. Each night, he would sit quietly, eyes closed, breathing deeply to steady his mind. He imagined every step of the mission, from the initial approach to the final retreat, visualizing a smooth execution. This mental preparation was as important as the physical and technical aspects of his preparation.

Final Preparations

On the eve of the mission, Michael reviewed all his plans and preparations one last time. He sat in his small room, the quiet of the night amplifying his thoughts. The smell of the old wood and the distant hum of the city grounded him. He took out the small notebook Aisling had given him and reviewed his notes, ensuring he had everything memorized. The flickering candlelight cast long shadows, creating a dance of light and dark that mirrored his internal state.

Michael felt the weight of responsibility, but also a sense of readiness. He had studied the map meticulously, absorbed Brendan's teachings, chosen his attire wisely, and prepared his mind and body for the task ahead. The thought of his comrades, the trust they placed in him, and the cause they fought for fueled his resolve. He knew that his actions could make a significant difference, and he was determined to succeed.

As he lay down to sleep, Michael felt a calm resolve settle over him. He was as prepared as he could be, and now it was time to put his plans into action. The mission ahead was daunting, but he felt ready to face whatever challenges came his way. He closed his eyes, taking one last deep breath, and let sleep take him, knowing that tomorrow would be a defining day in his journey.

As darkness fell on the evening of the mission, Michael felt a complex mix of emotions. The adrenaline coursing through his veins was a stark reminder of the reality and risks of what he was about to undertake. The city, cloaked in the shadows of night, seemed both eerily quiet and fraught with unseen dangers. Michael stood at the edge of his room, looking out into the darkened street, the distant glow of streetlights casting a dim halo over the cobblestones.

The fear of potential arrest or even violent confrontation loomed large in his mind. He could hear the echo of footsteps from passersby, each sound amplifying his sense of urgency and caution. His heart pounded in his chest, each beat resonating with the gravity of the mission. The weight of the small notebook in his pocket, filled with crucial notes, felt heavier than ever.

Despite these fears, Michael's belief in the cause provided him with a sense of resolve. He took a deep breath, the cool night air filling his lungs and momentarily calming his racing heart. He thought of his family, his friends, and the countless others who had suffered and struggled for their freedom. Their faces flashed before him, their stories of courage and sacrifice fortifying his determination.

Michael's mind flashed back to the meticulous preparations he had made in the days leading up to this moment. The hours spent studying maps, memorizing routes, and learning from Brendan's seasoned advice. "You're a ghost, Michael. Be observant but be discreet," Brendan had told him. These words echoed in his mind, grounding him in the task ahead.

He adjusted his nondescript clothes, ensuring that he would blend into the background. He took one last look at himself in the small, cracked mirror, practicing the calm, composed demeanor he needed to maintain. The importance of blending in, of acting like he belonged, was now more critical than ever.

As he prepared to leave, Michael practiced the deep breathing exercises he had learned, each breath steadying his nerves. The mixture of fear and adrenaline sharpened his senses, making him acutely aware of every sound, every movement. He knew that staying calm and focused was crucial; panic was his worst enemy.

Michael's belief in the cause, in the fight for a free and united Ireland, filled him with a sense of purpose. The fear and uncertainty were real, but they were eclipsed by his commitment to the mission. He was ready to face whatever challenges lay ahead, driven by a deep-seated conviction that this was the path he was meant to walk.

With one final breath, Michael stepped out into the night, the cool air brushing against his skin. The city lay before him, a labyrinth of shadows and light, and he moved forward with resolve, ready to carry out the mission that awaited him.

Michael and his team set out under the cover of night, blending into the shadows of Belfast's streets. The city's familiar landmarks took on an eerie quality in the darkness, the dim streetlights casting long, wavering shadows. The quiet of the night was punctuated by distant sounds of the city – a dog barking, the hum of a car engine, the occasional murmur of voices.

He moved with purpose but without haste, keenly aware of the need to appear casual to any onlookers. Each step was measured, his movements deliberate yet unhurried. The chill in the air bit at his skin, but he welcomed it, letting the sensation keep him alert. His clothes, nondescript and common, helped him blend seamlessly into the backdrop of the night.

The route to his observation point was carefully planned to avoid known areas of heavy surveillance and potential checkpoints. Michael had memorized every turn, every alleyway, every obscure path that would keep them away from prying eyes. The map Aisling had provided was etched into his mind, each detail scrutinized and rehearsed.

As they walked, Michael's senses were heightened. He listened intently for any sign of trouble, the faintest hint of a disturbance. The distant rumble of an armored vehicle sent a ripple of tension through him, but he stayed focused, reminding himself of Brendan's advice. "Blend in, act like you belong," he had said. Michael adopted a casual demeanor, glancing around occasionally as if merely on an evening stroll.

His team followed suit, each member playing their part in the delicate dance of invisibility. They moved as one, a silent, coordinated unit, their footsteps muffled against the cobblestones. The camaraderie and trust they shared were palpable, a silent assurance that they had each other's backs.

As they approached the designated area, Michael's mind went over the plan once more. The observation point was chosen for its strategic vantage, offering a clear view of the target area while providing ample cover. The memories of their last briefing flashed through his mind, each instruction and piece of advice playing back with clarity.

Arriving at the observation point, Michael signaled his team to take their positions. The spot was an abandoned building, its darkened windows offering a perfect cover. They moved with practiced efficiency, settling into their roles without a word. Michael took his place, peering through a crack in the boarded-up window, his eyes scanning the street below.

The familiar landmarks and routes looked different under the cover of night. The usual hustle and bustle of Belfast were replaced with an uneasy stillness. The glow from the streetlights provided just enough illumination to see movement but not enough to give away their position.

Michael felt a surge of adrenaline, mixed with a sense of calm determination. This was what they had prepared for, what they had trained for. His heart beat steadily, the fear and uncertainty replaced by a focused resolve. The mission had begun, and there was no turning back.

Every sound, every movement in the streets below was scrutinized. The patterns of the British patrols, the timing of their routes – all had been carefully studied and were now being observed in real-time. Michael's mind was a whirl of activity, analyzing, assessing, planning.

Despite the tension, he felt a sense of purpose and clarity. The fear that had once threatened to overwhelm him was now a driving force, sharpening his senses and fueling his determination. The cause they fought for, the dream of a free and united Ireland, was worth every risk, every moment of danger.

As the night wore on, Michael remained vigilant. His team, positioned around him, shared the silent understanding of the stakes involved. They were more than just comrades; they were a family bound by a common cause.

In the stillness of the night, Michael's resolve solidified. This mission, like many before it, was a step towards a greater goal. With every passing moment, he felt the weight of responsibility but also the strength of conviction. They would see this through, no matter the cost.

Arriving at his designated location, a spot he had chosen during his preparations for its clear view of the expected patrol route, Michael and the gang settled into a discreet position. The night was calm, the silence only broken by the occasional distant noise of the city.

Michael chose a shadowed alcove, which provided both a good vantage point and cover. The alcove was nestled between two buildings, the walls close enough to provide a sense of enclosure but open enough to allow a clear line of sight. From here, he could observe the patrol without being easily seen. The cold brick against his back served as a stark reminder of the reality of their mission, grounding him in the moment.

He crouched down, his eyes scanning the street before him. The dim glow of the streetlights cast long shadows, creating a play of light and dark that could either conceal or reveal his position. Michael adjusted his stance, ensuring he remained within the shadows, his figure blending into the darkened backdrop.

His team followed suit, each member finding their own positions, carefully chosen to cover different angles while maintaining a low profile. The sound of their quiet movements was barely audible, a testament to their practiced stealth. Michael felt a sense of pride and reassurance in their coordination; they were a well-oiled machine, each person knowing their role.

The minutes stretched out, each one heavy with anticipation. Michael's heart beat steadily, the initial rush of adrenaline giving way to a focused calm. He replayed Brendan's advice in his mind, "It's about seeing without being seen. You're not just looking; you're analyzing movements, patterns, anything out of the ordinary." He let his eyes roam the street, noting the positions of the streetlights, the layout of the buildings, and any potential hiding spots.

He heard the faintest sound of footsteps approaching, a rhythmic pattern that contrasted with the stillness of the night. Michael tensed slightly, every sense on high alert. The patrol was nearing, just as they had anticipated. He leaned slightly forward, ensuring he had a clear view while remaining concealed in the shadows.

The patrol came into view, a small group of soldiers moving with a deliberate pace. Michael watched their movements closely, noting their formation and the way they scanned their surroundings. He could see the weariness in their steps, the cautious vigilance in their eyes. These were men accustomed to danger, just as he was.

Michael's breathing slowed, his focus sharpening. He mentally recorded every detail, from the soldiers' uniforms to their weapons and the way they communicated with each other. His small notebook lay ready in his pocket, but he knew better than to take it out now. Instead, he committed everything to memory, planning to write it down later when it was safe.

The patrol passed by, their footsteps gradually fading into the distance. Michael remained still, giving it a few more minutes to ensure they were truly gone. The night seemed to grow quieter, the tension easing slightly as the immediate threat passed.

He glanced at his team, each one still in their positions, eyes alert and watching. A silent nod passed between them, a confirmation that the first part of their mission had gone as planned. Michael allowed himself a brief moment of relief, but he knew there was still much to do.

As he settled back into the alcove, the reality of their situation settled over him once more. They were in enemy territory, every moment a potential risk. But Michael felt ready, his resolve strengthened by the successful observation. He knew that every detail they gathered tonight would be crucial for their future plans.

The night stretched on, and Michael remained vigilant, his mind and body attuned to the tasks at hand. The shadows of Belfast provided both cover and challenge, but he was prepared to navigate them. For the cause, for his comrades, and for the dream of a united Ireland, he would see this mission through.

Time seemed to slow down as Michael awaited the arrival of the British army patrol. The cold night air seemed to sharpen his senses, each breath a reminder of the gravity of the moment. His heart rate increased, the steady thump resonating in his ears as he anticipated their approach. Years of conflict had made the presence of the army in these streets a common sight, but tonight, for Michael, it felt different – tonight, they were not just a symbol of occupation but a direct risk to his mission and safety.

As the first signs of the patrol appeared, Michael's training took over. He stilled his body, conscious of making no sudden movements. His muscles tensed and then relaxed as he found his position, melding into the shadows. He knew the importance of remaining a silent observer, a ghost in the night. His focus was absolute, every sense attuned to the task at hand. The distant murmur of the city faded away, leaving only the immediate sounds of the patrol approaching.

The flicker of flashlight beams danced across the buildings, the crunch of boots on gravel growing louder. When the patrol finally came into view, Michael's preparation proved invaluable. He noted their numbers, the weapons they carried, their formation, and any distinguishing features. His observation was methodical, his note-taking discreet. Every detail could be crucial, and he missed nothing.

The soldiers moved with a practiced precision, their eyes scanning the surroundings with wary vigilance. Michael watched the leader, a sergeant by the look of his stripes, directing his men with silent hand signals. The tension in the air was palpable, a silent acknowledgment of the ever-present danger.

Michael's heart pounded in rhythm with the soldiers' steps. He focused on his breathing, keeping it slow and steady, ensuring no fog of breath would give away his position. The shadows provided cover, but he knew he must not rely on them alone. Every movement had to be deliberate and controlled.

The patrol paused briefly, the soldiers exchanging low murmurs that Michael strained to hear. He caught fragments of their conversation, enough to piece together their route and timing. The sergeant's voice was low and authoritative, a contrast to the younger, more nervous tones of the newer recruits.

Michael's eyes flicked over the patrol, noting the way they carried their rifles, the positions they took, and the subtle body language that spoke of their alertness and fatigue. He recorded mental snapshots of their faces, the insignias on their uniforms, and any unique characteristics that could identify them later.

One soldier, in particular, caught his attention – a tall man with a distinctive limp. Michael watched as he adjusted his position frequently, the discomfort clear on his face. It was a small detail, but one that could prove significant in future encounters.

As the patrol continued on, Michael remained motionless, his senses still heightened. He waited until the last soldier had disappeared around the corner before allowing himself to exhale fully. The immediate danger had passed, but the night's mission was far from over.

Michael's training had served him well, but he knew that each encounter carried new risks and challenges. The weight of the small notebook in his pocket was a comforting reminder of his role, a silent affirmation of his purpose. He carefully wrote down the observations he had memorized, each note precise and concise.

The tension in his body began to ease, replaced by a steely determination. He had successfully navigated this first test, but he knew there would be more to come. The streets of Belfast were both familiar and perilous, and he would need all his wits and training to complete the mission.

Michael looked at his team, each of them emerging from their positions, silent and focused. A shared nod passed between them, a silent acknowledgment of their success so far. They were a unit, bound by a common cause and a shared understanding of the risks they faced.

As they moved to their next position, Michael felt a renewed sense of purpose. The mission was unfolding as planned, but he remained vigilant. Every shadow, every sound could signal a new threat. Yet, despite the ever-present danger, he felt a deep conviction in his actions.

The night was far from over, and Michael was ready to face whatever came next. His training, his preparation, and his unwavering belief in the cause would guide him through. With a final glance at the darkened street behind him, he led his team forward, the mission ever clear in his mind.

The intensity of the moment was a profound experience for Michael. It was more than just observing a military patrol; it was the realization of his commitment to a cause, the embodiment of the path he had chosen. The night of his first mission would be a defining moment in his journey with the IRA, a step deeper into the heart of the conflict and the struggle for Irish freedom.

As Michael lay in wait, the silence of the night was eventually broken by the distant sound of the British army patrol with the new weapons they were transporting coming into view. The clatter of military boots on pavement and the low murmur of voices grew steadily louder, signaling their approach.

From his hidden vantage point, Michael watched as the soldiers came into view. His heart pounded in his chest, a mix of fear and exhilaration. He counted the soldiers – there were six in total, moving in a tight formation, their rifles held at the ready. He noted the time on his watch; it was crucial to track the exact timing of their patrols.

Each second felt elongated, the sounds of the patrol amplifying in the stillness. Michael's breathing was shallow, his senses heightened. He could see the glint of the new weapons under the dim streetlights, their presence a stark reminder of the ongoing conflict. The soldiers moved with practiced precision, their eyes scanning the surroundings for any signs of threat.

Michael focused on the details, noting the soldiers' formation and the way they carried their rifles. The leader, a sergeant, directed the group with subtle hand signals, his authority evident in his movements. The new weapons, slung across their backs, added a new layer of threat to the already tense situation.

The soldiers' footsteps echoed off the buildings, a rhythmic cadence that seemed to sync with Michael's heartbeat. He remained perfectly still, every muscle tensed yet controlled. His training took over, guiding his observations and ensuring he missed nothing.

As the patrol passed by his position, Michael made mental notes of any distinguishing features – a tall soldier with a slight limp, another with a noticeable scar across his cheek. These details could be crucial for future missions. He committed them to memory, knowing the importance of every piece of information.

The patrol moved on, their figures gradually disappearing into the darkness, the sounds of their presence fading into the night. Michael waited, ensuring they were truly gone before he allowed himself to relax slightly. The immediate threat had passed, but the mission was far from over.

He took a moment to jot down his observations in the small notebook Aisling had given him, each note precise and concise. The act of writing grounded him, reaffirming his purpose and the importance of his role. The weight of the notebook in his pocket was a comforting reminder of his commitment to the cause.

Michael's heart rate began to steady, the initial rush of adrenaline giving way to a focused calm. He had successfully navigated this first test, but he knew there would be more to come. The streets of Belfast, shrouded in darkness, held both danger and opportunity.

As he looked at his watch again, noting the exact time of the patrol's passage, Michael felt a surge of resolve. This mission, with all its risks and challenges, was a crucial step in the larger struggle for Irish freedom. The night air felt colder now, the reality of his actions settling over him.

He signaled to his team, who emerged from their positions, silent and vigilant. A shared nod passed between them, a silent acknowledgment of their success so far. They were more than just comrades; they were a unit bound by a common cause and a shared understanding of the stakes involved.

As they moved to their next position, Michael felt a renewed sense of purpose. The mission was unfolding as planned, but he remained vigilant. Every shadow, every sound could signal a new threat. Yet, despite the ever-present danger, he felt a deep conviction in his actions.

The night was far from over, and Michael was ready to face whatever came next. His training, his preparation, and his unwavering belief in the cause would guide him through. With a final glance at the darkened street behind him, he led his team forward, the mission ever clear in his mind.

Michael observed the patrol closely, paying attention to details that could be of strategic importance. From his concealed position, he had a clear view of the soldiers as they moved methodically through the streets. The dim streetlights cast long shadows, but the soldiers' figures were sharply defined in his keen gaze.

He noticed the insignias on their uniforms, each one indicating rank and unit. The leader, identifiable by his sergeant stripes, walked with an air of authority, his head constantly turning as he surveyed the area. Michael memorized the insignias, knowing they could provide valuable information about the unit's structure and hierarchy.

The type of weapons they carried also caught his attention. The new rifles glinted under the streetlights, their sleek, modern design a stark contrast to the older models he had seen before. He noted the way the soldiers handled their weapons – some with a casual familiarity, others with a more rigid grip that suggested less experience.

Michael's eyes flicked over each soldier, assessing their demeanor. Some seemed relaxed, chatting quietly among themselves. Their laughter, though subdued, punctuated the silence of the night, creating an eerie juxtaposition against the tension of the mission. These soldiers moved with a certain ease, their body language indicating a level of comfort and routine.

In contrast, other soldiers appeared more vigilant, their eyes constantly scanning the surroundings. Their movements were sharper, more deliberate, as if expecting an ambush at any moment. Michael could see the strain in their faces, the way their hands occasionally tightened on their rifles. These were the ones to watch closely – their heightened awareness made them more unpredictable and dangerous.

As the patrol moved past, Michael took mental notes of everything he observed. The height and build of each soldier, any distinguishing features, the way they interacted with each other – all these details could be crucial. He noted a soldier with a noticeable limp, another with a scar running down his cheek. These observations, seemingly minor, could make a significant difference in planning future operations.

Michael's focus was intense, his senses heightened by the adrenaline coursing through his veins. He was acutely aware of the stakes – one wrong move, one overlooked detail, could jeopardize the entire mission. The sounds of the soldiers' boots on the pavement, the low murmur of their voices, even the occasional clink of metal against metal – all these auditory cues were cataloged in his mind.

The patrol continued on its route, the soldiers gradually disappearing into the distance. Michael waited, his muscles taut, until he was certain they were out of sight. Only then did he allow himself a brief moment of relief, the tension easing slightly from his body.

He carefully wrote down his observations in the small notebook, each note precise and detailed. The act of writing helped to solidify his thoughts, ensuring he would remember every important aspect. The notebook was a vital tool, a repository of the intelligence they needed to succeed.

Michael's heart rate began to slow, the immediate danger passing but the mission far from complete. He glanced at his watch again, confirming the timing of the patrol's passage. The exactness of this information was critical for their future plans.

As he signaled to his team to regroup, Michael felt a renewed sense of purpose. The successful observation of the patrol was a small but significant victory. It reinforced his belief in the cause and his commitment to seeing the mission through.

With the patrol behind them, Michael and his team moved quietly to their next position. The night was still young, and there was much more to do. Every step was taken with care, every sound analyzed for potential threats. Michael led the way, his mind focused on the task ahead, his resolve unshaken.

The streets of Belfast, with their familiar yet foreboding aura, would continue to test him. But Michael was ready. He had prepared for this, trained for this, and believed deeply in the fight for freedom. Each moment, each observation, brought him closer to that goal.

With the British army patrol now out of sight, Michael remained in his concealed spot for a few extra moments, ensuring they were truly gone and that it was safe to emerge. The darkness of the night enveloped him, providing a cloak of safety as he listened intently for any lingering sounds of the soldiers. The distant hum of the city seemed to grow louder in the absence of the patrol's footsteps, filling the silence that had once been charged with tension.

The adrenaline of the moment was still coursing through his veins as he began to process the success of his first mission. His heart, which had been pounding furiously, now began to steady, the rhythm slowing as the immediate danger passed. He took a deep breath, the cool night air filling his lungs and helping to clear his mind.

Michael's muscles, tense and ready for action, gradually relaxed. He carefully scanned the area once more, his eyes adjusting to the darkness, ensuring there were no hidden threats. The shadows, which had seemed so menacing earlier, now felt like familiar allies, part of the landscape he had successfully navigated.

He mentally replayed the events of the patrol's passage, reaffirming the details he had observed. The number of soldiers, their formation, the new weapons, the distinguishing features – all of these were now etched into his memory, vital pieces of intelligence for the IRA. He felt a sense of pride in his meticulous observation and the calm he had maintained under pressure.

The significance of the moment began to sink in. This was more than just a successful mission; it was a personal victory, a testament to his resolve and capability. Michael had proven to himself and his comrades that he could handle the responsibilities and dangers of active participation in the struggle for Irish freedom.

As he slowly emerged from his hiding spot, he did so with the cautious grace of someone who had learned the importance of every movement. Each step was deliberate, his senses still heightened, ready to react if needed. The sounds of the night – the distant sirens, the occasional bark of a dog, the rustle of leaves in the wind – seemed to welcome him back into the fold of the city.

He signaled to his team, who had also remained hidden, their figures gradually materializing from the shadows. A silent exchange of nods and glances conveyed their mutual acknowledgment of the mission's success. They moved with practiced stealth, regrouping without a word, each member aware of their next steps.

Michael took another deep breath, the lingering tension giving way to a quiet confidence. He knew there would be many more nights like this, filled with risk and uncertainty. But tonight had been a crucial first step, a baptism by fire that had solidified his commitment to the cause.

As they made their way back to the safe house, Michael allowed himself a brief moment of reflection. The faces of his family and friends, the stories of past struggles, and the vision of a free Ireland all played through his mind. This mission, though small in the grand scheme of things, was a part of that larger journey.

The success of this first mission filled him with a renewed sense of purpose. He felt more connected to his comrades, more integrated into the fabric of the IRA. The adrenaline that had fueled him was now replaced by a steady determination, a clear-eyed focus on the road ahead.

Michael's mind shifted back to the practicalities of their next steps. There would be debriefings, more planning, and continued vigilance. But for now, he allowed himself a moment of quiet satisfaction. They had achieved their goal, and he had proven his worth.

As they disappeared into the night, Michael knew that this was just the beginning. The path ahead would be fraught with challenges, but he felt ready to face them. The experience of this night had strengthened his resolve, deepened his understanding of the conflict, and affirmed his place in the struggle for freedom.

Michael carefully pulled out his notebook, his hands slightly trembling from the intensity of the experience. The cold night air bit at his fingers as he opened the small, worn notebook, the pages already filled with notes from previous observations and plans. The soft light from a distant streetlamp provided just enough illumination for him to see what he was writing.

He methodically transcribed the detailed notes he had memorized, ensuring that every piece of information was accurately captured. Each line he wrote felt like a step further into his commitment to the cause, each word a testament to the night's success. His handwriting, normally steady, wavered slightly from the residual adrenaline coursing through his veins.

Michael's mind was focused, replaying the events of the patrol with crystal clarity. He wrote down the number of soldiers first – six in total. Next, he described their formation, noting how they moved in a tight, cohesive unit. He included the exact time of their patrol, checking his watch once more to confirm.

The type and condition of their equipment was detailed next. He described the new rifles, their sleek design, and how the soldiers handled them. These observations were crucial, as the IRA needed to understand the capabilities and readiness of the British forces. Michael took care to note any visible wear on the equipment, indicating the level of use and possible weaknesses.

Their demeanor was another critical aspect. Michael wrote about the mix of relaxed and vigilant soldiers, capturing the contrasts within the patrol. He described the casual conversations and laughter among some, juxtaposed with the intense, watchful eyes of others. This information could help predict their behavior in future encounters, adding a layer of strategic insight.

As he wrote, Michael felt the weight of his responsibility. This information was crucial and could prove invaluable for the IRA's strategic planning. Every detail he recorded had the potential to impact their operations, to make the difference between success and failure.

He paused occasionally, listening intently to ensure no one approached, then resumed his meticulous note-taking. The notebook filled with his observations was more than just a record; it was a tool for their fight, a piece of the larger puzzle in their struggle for freedom.

Michael's hands steadied as he continued to write, the act of transcribing the details bringing a sense of calm and order to his thoughts. The process of turning his mental notes into written ones felt like solidifying the night's events into something tangible, something that could be used to further their cause.

When he finished, he closed the notebook and tucked it back into his pocket, feeling a sense of accomplishment. The trembling in his hands had subsided, replaced by a steady resolve. The night's mission had been a success, and he had played his part well.

Michael looked around at his team, who were also busy with their own tasks, each contributing to the mission in their way. He felt a strong sense of camaraderie, a bond forged in the shared dangers and goals. They were not just a group of individuals; they were a unit, a team working towards a common purpose.

As they prepared to move on, Michael took one last moment to review the notes in his mind, ensuring nothing was forgotten. Satisfied with his work, he signaled to his team, and they began to make their way back, moving with the same careful stealth that had brought them there.

The night was far from over, and there would be more missions, more challenges ahead. But for now, Michael felt a deep sense of fulfillment. He had proven his worth, contributed valuable information, and taken a significant step on his journey with the IRA.

As they disappeared into the shadows, Michael's thoughts were already on the next steps, the future missions, and the ongoing struggle. Each success, each piece of information, brought them closer to their goal. And he was ready to face whatever came next, driven by a cause he believed in and a determination that only grew stronger with each passing day.

As he recorded the last of his observations, a sense of accomplishment washed over Michael. He had successfully completed his first mission, a task of significant importance. The cool night air, once sharp and biting, now felt invigorating, a reminder of the life pulsing through him and the success he had just achieved.

Michael felt a surge of pride, knowing that his actions would contribute to the broader goals of the IRA. The detailed notes he had meticulously transcribed were more than just observations; they were pieces of a larger strategy, tools that could be used to advance their cause. He closed his notebook with a satisfying snap, the weight of it a comforting reminder of the night's achievements.

The adrenaline that had fueled his vigilance now transformed into a warm, steady confidence. He had faced the inherent dangers of the mission with composure and had emerged successful. This was a validation of his training, his resolve, and his place within the IRA. Each detail he had captured was a testament to his commitment and his ability to contribute meaningfully to their struggle.

Michael glanced at his team, each member busy with their own post-mission routines. The silent nods and brief smiles exchanged spoke volumes. They all understood the significance of the night's work, and there was a shared sense of triumph in the air. His comrades' trust and support further amplified his sense of pride and belonging.

Reflecting on the night's events, Michael felt a deep connection to the history and the cause that had brought him here. He thought of the stories his father had told him, the legacy of resistance, and the sacrifices made by those who had come before him. Tonight, he had added his own chapter to that story, and it was a moment he would carry with him always.

The path ahead was still fraught with challenges, and Michael knew that there would be many more missions, each with its own risks and rewards. But the success of this first mission had fortified his determination. He felt ready to face whatever came next, armed with the knowledge that he could meet the demands of their cause.

As they prepared to move on, Michael took a final, deep breath, savoring the cool night air and the sense of accomplishment that filled him. The city of Belfast, with its familiar yet formidable streets, felt a little different now. It was a battleground, yes, but also a place where he had proven his worth and strengthened his resolve.

With a renewed sense of purpose, Michael signaled to his team. They moved with practiced stealth, their footsteps barely audible on the pavement. The night's mission was complete, but their journey was far from over. Each step they took was a step towards their shared goal, and Michael felt an unshakable conviction in the righteousness of their cause.

As they disappeared into the shadows, Michael's mind was already on the future. He knew that this was just the beginning, and that there would be many more nights like this one. But he also knew that he was ready, that he had the skills, the support, and the unwavering belief in their fight for freedom.

The sense of accomplishment stayed with him, a powerful reminder of what they were fighting for and what they could achieve together. It was a feeling he would hold onto, driving him forward in the struggle for a free and united Ireland.

But with this success also came a profound realization. Michael understood that his life had irrevocably changed. He was no longer an observer or a mere supporter of the cause; he had become a leader in the conflict. This mission marked his transition into a role that carried significant weight and responsibility.

As the night's events replayed in his mind, Michael felt the gravity of his new position settle over him. The quiet streets of Belfast, now draped in the shadows of early morning, seemed to echo with the magnitude of this shift. He was not just a participant in the struggle for Irish freedom; he was now one of its leaders.

The realization was both empowering and daunting. Michael felt a surge of pride in his ability to contribute effectively, but also a weighty awareness of the responsibility that came with leadership. He had proven himself capable, but he also knew that this success brought higher expectations and greater risks.

His thoughts drifted to the faces of his comrades, the trust they had placed in him, and the collective hope they all shared. He understood that his actions would now carry more weight, that his decisions could impact not only the success of their missions but the lives of those he led.

Michael's mind raced with the implications of his new role. He thought of the strategic planning, the coordination, the need for careful execution of each operation. He would have to be more vigilant, more prepared, and more decisive. The stakes were higher, and the margin for error was slimmer.

The transformation felt like a rite of passage, a stepping stone to a deeper commitment. Michael's journey with the IRA had entered a new phase, one that required not only bravery but also wisdom and foresight. He would need to lead by example, to inspire confidence and maintain the morale of his team even in the face of adversity.

Standing in the quiet aftermath of their successful mission, Michael felt a mix of emotions – pride, determination, and a sober recognition of the challenges ahead. The streets, now quiet and seemingly peaceful, masked the ongoing conflict and the struggle that would continue to unfold.

Michael took a moment to center himself, to embrace the reality of his new role. He knew that there would be no turning back, that his path was now irrevocably intertwined with the fight for Irish independence. He felt a deep sense of duty, a calling to rise to the occasion and lead with integrity and courage.

He looked around at his team, their figures moving with quiet efficiency as they prepared for their next steps. They were counting on him, and he would not let them down. The success of this mission was just the beginning, a foundation upon which they would build their future efforts.

Michael's heart swelled with resolve. He was ready to face the challenges that lay ahead, to lead his team with the same dedication and commitment that had brought them this far. The realization of his new role was profound, but it was also a source of strength and motivation.

As they moved through the shadows, back towards the safety of their hideout, Michael felt the weight of leadership settle comfortably on his shoulders. He was not alone in this journey; he had the support of his comrades and the unwavering belief in their cause.

The night had been a turning point, a defining moment in his journey. Michael embraced his new role with a sense of purpose and determination. He was a leader now, and he would carry this responsibility with honor and resolve.

As they disappeared into the darkness, Michael knew that the path ahead would be challenging, but he was ready. The success of this mission had marked a new beginning, one that would see him leading the charge in the struggle for freedom. And he would face it with unwavering courage and steadfast conviction.

As he made his way back to the safe house, Michael's mind was a whirlwind of thoughts and emotions. The streets that he had walked countless times before now held a different meaning for him. Each step he took seemed heavier, laden with the weight of his newfound responsibilities and the significance of his actions.

The familiar alleys and corners of Belfast, bathed in the dim glow of streetlights, appeared transformed. He saw them not just as the backdrop of his daily life, but as the stage for a larger, more consequential struggle. The graffiti-covered walls, the faded posters of lost comrades, and the murals of resistance – all seemed to whisper the stories of those who had fought and fallen before him.

He was part of something much larger than himself, a struggle that had defined the lives of so many in his community. This realization filled him with a profound sense of purpose. The echoes of past heroes, the sacrifices of those who had come before, and the hopes of those who looked to the future all converged in his thoughts.

Michael's emotions were a complex mix of pride, fear, and determination. He felt pride in his successful mission, in the role he was playing in the fight for Irish freedom. The fear of what lay ahead, of the dangers and sacrifices required, was ever-present but now accompanied by a steely resolve.

As he passed by the landmarks of his youth, each one seemed imbued with new meaning. The schoolyard where he once played football was now a symbol of the normalcy they were fighting to protect. The local pub, a place of camaraderie and shared stories, represented the community's resilience and unity.

The faces of his family and friends flashed through his mind. He thought of his father, who had instilled in him the stories of Irish resistance, and his mother, whose quiet strength had been a constant support. Their expectations and hopes were now intertwined with his actions and decisions.

The safe house came into view, a seemingly ordinary building that housed their extraordinary efforts. Michael felt a sense of relief as he approached, but also a heightened awareness of the importance of this sanctuary. It was a place where plans were made, where strategies were discussed, and where they found brief respite from the ongoing conflict.

Entering the safe house, Michael was greeted by the familiar faces of his comrades. Their nods and brief smiles conveyed a shared understanding of the night's significance. The sense of camaraderie and mutual trust was palpable, reinforcing his commitment to the cause and to each other.

As he settled in, Michael's mind continued to process the night's events. The success of the mission was a testament to their collective effort, but it also marked the beginning of a new chapter in his journey. He was now more deeply embedded in the struggle, with greater responsibilities and higher stakes.

The safe house, with its dim lighting and the quiet hum of activity, felt like a haven. Yet, it was also a reminder of the constant vigilance required, the endless planning and preparation that defined their lives. Michael knew that this moment of reflection was brief; soon, they would be back to planning the next mission, the next step in their relentless pursuit of freedom.

Michael took a deep breath, grounding himself in the reality of his situation. The streets of Belfast, the struggle of his community, and the faces of his comrades all fused into a single, resolute purpose. He was ready to continue this journey, to lead with courage and to face the challenges ahead with unwavering determination.

As the night deepened, Michael's resolve hardened. He was part of something much larger than himself, a pivotal player in a historic struggle. The path was fraught with peril, but he was ready to walk it, driven by the hope of a free and united Ireland.

Upon his safe return, Michael was ready to report his findings to the leadership, commanders, and other high-profile IRA members. The success of his first mission was a crucial step in his journey with the IRA, one that would lead to more significant roles and deeper involvement in the days to come.

The safe house was abuzz with quiet activity. Shadows flitted across the dimly lit room as members moved purposefully, engaged in hushed conversations. The familiar scent of damp wood and old paper filled the air, grounding Michael as he prepared to present his report.

Taking a moment to steady himself, Michael gathered his notes and approached the area where the leadership convened. The room was sparsely furnished, a stark reminder of the austere circumstances under which they operated. A worn table stood at the center, surrounded by serious faces illuminated by the soft glow of a single lamp.

As he stepped forward, Michael felt the weight of their gazes upon him. The leadership included seasoned veterans whose experiences and strategies had shaped the course of their struggle. Among them was Seán, with his sharp, calculating eyes; Aisling, whose logistical expertise was unparalleled; and Brendan, whose encouragement had been invaluable.

Michael cleared his throat, the sound barely audible above the low murmur of the room. "I have completed the mission and gathered the necessary observations," he began, his voice steady but carrying the weight of the night's events.

He methodically detailed the patrol's composition, their formation, the exact timing of their movements, and the new weapons they carried. Each piece of information was presented with precision, his earlier nervousness replaced by a calm, authoritative tone. He described the demeanor of the soldiers, the mix of vigilance and casualness, and noted any distinguishing features.

As Michael spoke, he saw the subtle nods of approval from the leadership. They listened intently, absorbing the details that would inform their strategic decisions. His meticulous observations were not just data; they were insights that could shape their next moves.

When he finished, there was a brief silence as the leaders processed his report. Seán was the first to speak, his voice carrying a tone of both approval and expectation. "Your observations are thorough, Michael. This information will be invaluable for our planning. Well done."

Aisling added, "Your attention to detail is impressive. It's clear you were well-prepared and executed the mission with precision. This is exactly the kind of intelligence we need."

Brendan, with a proud smile, simply said, "I knew you had it in you."

Michael felt a swell of pride but also a deeper understanding of the responsibilities that came with his role. The success of this mission was a stepping stone, a demonstration of his capability and reliability. It was an affirmation that he was ready for more significant roles and deeper involvement in the days to come.

The leadership began to discuss the implications of Michael's findings, planning their next steps based on the intelligence he had provided. Michael listened, absorbing their strategies and learning from their experience. He realized that each mission, each piece of information, was a part of a larger puzzle, one that required careful assembly and execution.

As the meeting concluded, Seán addressed him directly. "Prepare for your next assignment, Michael. Your success tonight has proven your value to our cause. There will be more tasks, each more critical than the last. Stay vigilant, and continue to operate with the same diligence and commitment."

Michael nodded, the weight of his new responsibilities settling comfortably on his shoulders. He was ready to face whatever challenges lay ahead, driven by a sense of duty and an unwavering belief in their cause. The night's success had not only solidified his place within the IRA but also deepened his resolve to contribute meaningfully to their struggle.

Leaving the meeting, Michael felt a renewed sense of purpose. The streets of Belfast, once again bathed in darkness, seemed to welcome him back, a silent ally in their fight. He knew that the path ahead would be fraught with danger, but he was prepared to walk it with determination and courage.

The success of his first mission was just the beginning. With each step he took, Michael became more entwined with the struggle for Irish freedom, his role growing more significant with each passing day. And he embraced it fully, ready to lead, ready to fight, ready to make a difference.

There was a distinct sense of pride that washed over Michael as he considered his involvement. He had been accepted into an organization that stood for something much larger than himself – a symbol of resistance and the fight for Irish freedom. This pride stemmed not just from being part of the IRA but from the trust and responsibility that had been bestowed upon him. He felt a deep connection to the cause, one that resonated with his beliefs and the narrative of struggle that he had grown up with.

However, this pride was tempered by a sobering awareness of the risks and responsibilities inherent in his role. The discussions during the meeting had made it clear that every operation carried potential dangers, and the weight of this reality sat heavily on him. Michael understood that his actions could have significant consequences, not only for himself but also for his family and the wider community.

As he left the safe house and walked through the dimly lit streets, the gravity of his commitment settled over him. He knew that the path he had chosen was fraught with peril – arrests, injuries, and the ever-present threat of lethal encounters. Each step echoed with the silent knowledge of the sacrifices that might be required.

Michael's mind wandered back to the faces of his family. He thought of his father, whose stories of resistance had planted the seeds of his own beliefs, and his mother, whose quiet strength had been a constant source of support. He knew that his involvement with the IRA placed them in a vulnerable position. The thought of his actions bringing harm to his loved ones was a burden he carried with a heavy heart.

The streets of Belfast, familiar yet ominous, seemed to reflect his internal conflict. The graffiti and murals that decorated the walls spoke of defiance and resilience, but also of loss and sorrow. Michael's gaze lingered on a mural commemorating fallen comrades, the painted faces staring back at him as a stark reminder of the cost of their struggle.

He felt a knot of tension in his chest, the adrenaline from the night's mission mingling with the weight of his reflections. The sense of pride he felt was real, but it was accompanied by a profound understanding of the stakes involved. His role in the IRA was not just a position of honor but one of immense responsibility.

The conversations he had overheard during the meeting replayed in his mind. The leaders' discussions of strategy, the meticulous planning, and the acknowledgment of potential risks underscored the seriousness of their cause. Michael knew that every decision, every action, had to be weighed carefully against the potential consequences.

Despite the risks, there was no doubt in Michael's mind about the necessity of their struggle. The fight for Irish freedom was not just a political battle but a deeply personal one, rooted in the history and identity of his people. The legacy of resistance, passed down through generations, was a part of who he was.

As he continued his journey back, Michael resolved to carry the weight of his responsibilities with honor. He would lead with integrity, making decisions that reflected not only the strategic needs of the IRA but also the ethical considerations of their cause. He knew that this balance would be difficult to maintain, but it was essential for the legitimacy of their struggle.

The night air grew colder, a chill that seemed to seep into his bones. Yet, within him burned a steady flame of determination. Michael understood that the path he had chosen was a dangerous one, but it was also a path of purpose and conviction.

The quiet streets offered a moment of solitude, a chance for Michael to reflect on his journey. He was part of something much larger than himself, a movement that sought to reshape the future of Ireland. The pride he felt was tempered by the knowledge of the risks, but it was this very awareness that made his commitment all the more meaningful.

As he neared his destination, Michael felt a renewed sense of resolve. He was ready to face the challenges ahead, to lead with courage and to bear the weight of his responsibilities with strength. The fight for Irish freedom demanded no less, and he was prepared to give his all.

The success of his first mission had marked the beginning of a deeper involvement, a step further into the heart of the conflict. Michael embraced the duality of his emotions – the pride and the fear, the honor and the burden. It was this complex blend that defined his role and fueled his determination to continue the struggle.

Michael recognized that this meeting and his first mission were just the beginning of a long and challenging journey. The road ahead would be filled with obstacles and tough decisions. He anticipated moments of doubt and moral quandary, understanding that the struggle for freedom was complex and often messy.

As he walked the streets of Belfast, now tinged with the first light of dawn, the enormity of what lay ahead weighed on him. He could almost see the future stretching out before him, a path lined with trials and tribulations. The realization that this journey would test his resolve in ways he could not yet imagine was both daunting and invigorating.

Despite these challenges, Michael's commitment to the cause remained unshakeable. His belief in the righteousness of the fight for a united Ireland, free from British rule, was a driving force behind his actions. The stories of his forebears, their sacrifices and unyielding spirit, were etched into his heart, providing a wellspring of motivation. He felt a sense of duty to continue the struggle that generations before him had waged, inspired by their sacrifices and the hope of a better future for his country.

The memories of his father's tales and the passionate speeches at rallies reverberated in his mind. These were not just words; they were the echoes of a long and painful history, one that demanded justice and reparation. Michael's heart swelled with pride at the thought of being part of this legacy, each step he took a tribute to those who had walked the path before him.

The trust placed in him by his comrades in the IRA was a significant motivator for Michael. It was not just about proving himself worthy of their trust but also about living up to the ideals of the organization. The camaraderie he felt with his fellow members was a bond forged in shared purpose and peril. Every mission, every action was a step towards earning and reaffirming that trust.

He felt a deep sense of responsibility to contribute effectively and honorably to the IRA's efforts, driven by a desire to make a meaningful difference in the fight for Irish independence. The faces of his comrades, their whispered words of encouragement and steadfast belief in their cause, were constant reminders of the collective effort they all contributed to. Each one of them relied on the others to do their part, and Michael was determined not to let them down.

Michael's thoughts wandered to the future, to the plans they would make and the operations they would execute. He knew that his decisions would have far-reaching consequences, that the weight of his actions extended beyond his immediate circle. The lives of his family, his friends, and even those he had never met would be affected by the choices he made. This realization did not deter him; rather, it steeled his resolve.

He was acutely aware of the moral complexities that lay ahead. The fight for freedom was not black and white; it was filled with shades of grey. He anticipated moments where he would question the rightness of their methods, where the line between justice and vengeance might blur. These moments of doubt would test his moral compass, but he was prepared to face them with honesty and integrity.

Michael's journey was just beginning, but already he felt the weight of its significance. The path he had chosen was fraught with danger, yet it was also illuminated by the hope of a brighter future for Ireland. He walked with a sense of purpose, each step a commitment to the cause and to the people who had placed their trust in him.

As the sun began to rise, casting a new light on the familiar streets, Michael felt a renewed sense of determination. The beginning of his journey was marked by a successful mission, but he knew there was much more to come. The road ahead would be long and arduous, but he was ready to face it with courage and conviction.

In the quiet moments before the city fully awakened, Michael made a silent vow. He would honor the legacy of those who had come before him, fight for the future of those who would come after, and lead with the integrity and resilience that the cause demanded. The struggle for Irish independence was his to carry forward, and he embraced it with all his heart.

Chapter 2: Belfast- A City Under Siege

In the dim light of early morning, Michael sat alone in his small room, the pale glow from the single bulb casting long shadows on the peeling wallpaper. The cool air was still, filled with the faint scent of damp and the lingering aroma of last night's supper. His mind replayed the events of his first mission with the IRA, a whirlwind of images and emotions that refused to settle.

The successful surveillance of the British patrol brought a mix of satisfaction and introspection. He could still hear the rhythmic crunch of gravel under their boots, the low murmur of their voices as they passed by, oblivious to his presence. Hidden in the shadows, Michael had noted every detail – the precise timing of their rounds, the casual yet alert demeanor of the soldiers, the way they paused at certain points, scanning their surroundings with practiced eyes.

He thought about the critical information he had gathered, realizing its potential impact on the IRA's future strategies. Each detail about the patrol's routine and behavior was a valuable piece of a larger puzzle that could shape upcoming operations. The methodical way the lead soldier checked his watch, the casual flick of a cigarette butt into the gutter, the brief moments of relaxed conversation – all these seemingly mundane actions held the key to understanding their patterns and weaknesses.

The adrenaline that had coursed through his veins during the mission now gave way to a profound sense of purpose. Michael's mind raced with the implications of his findings. He could almost hear the distant echoes of future plans being laid out, the murmurs of his comrades as they poured over his notes, strategizing the next move. The potential to outmaneuver their oppressors, to strike when least expected, filled him with a fierce determination.

As the first light of dawn crept through the tattered curtains, Michael felt a surge of pride mixed with the weight of responsibility. This mission had been a small but crucial step in a long and arduous journey. The image of the British patrol, so confident and unguarded, lingered in his mind, a reminder of both the challenge and the opportunity that lay ahead.

Each piece of information he had painstakingly recorded was a weapon in its own right, capable of turning the tide in their favor. The knowledge that he had contributed to this effort, that his vigilance and courage had not been in vain, brought a rare smile to his lips. In the quiet solitude of his room, Michael embraced the silence, allowing himself a moment of reflection before the day's inevitable demands pulled him back into the relentless struggle for freedom.

As dawn's first light filtered through the thin curtains, casting a soft, golden hue across his room, Michael's thoughts shifted to the broader implications of his actions. The early morning silence, broken only by the distant chirping of birds, gave him space to ponder the weight of his contribution.

He understood that the intelligence he provided could escalate IRA activities, potentially intensifying the conflict with British forces. The detailed patterns he had observed – the timing of the patrols, the soldiers' routines, their vulnerabilities – were not just tactical advantages; they were catalysts for action. Each piece of information was a potential trigger for a future operation, a step closer to striking at their oppressors with precision and effect.

This escalation meant not just increased danger for himself but also for his community. The thought of his neighbors, those familiar faces he saw every day, living under the looming threat of intensified conflict gnawed at him. He could imagine the increased military presence, the frequent raids, and the harsh scrutiny that would inevitably follow any successful IRA operation. The sound of armored vehicles rumbling through the narrow streets, the abrupt knocks on doors in the dead of night, and the fearful eyes of children peering out from behind their parents' legs – these were the realities that weighed heavily on his conscience.

Michael knew that his actions, while driven by a righteous cause, carried a profound responsibility. The intelligence he provided could indeed turn the tide in their favor, but it would also draw the iron gaze of the British forces ever more closely upon Falls Road and its inhabitants. The delicate balance between resistance and the safety of his community was a tightrope he walked with every mission.

He thought about his family, his mother's quiet strength and his father's proud tales of Irish defiance, and how their lives could be impacted. The idea of bringing more danger to their doorstep was a bitter pill to swallow. Yet, he also knew that inaction was not an option. The fight for freedom came with sacrifices, and the resolve to face these sacrifices head-on was what separated the determined from the defeated.

As the sunlight grew stronger, casting sharper shadows in the room, Michael steeled himself for the days ahead. He could feel the weight of his dual roles – as a protector and a fighter. The path he had chosen was fraught with peril, but it was a path he believed in with every fiber of his being. The intelligence he had gathered was a testament to his commitment, a tool to be used wisely and with consideration for the greater good.

In the quiet of the early morning, with the city slowly coming to life outside his window, Michael embraced the gravity of his actions. He was not just a cog in the machinery of rebellion; he was a guardian of his people's hopes and dreams. The risks were real, and the dangers ever-present, but so too was the unyielding spirit that drove him and his comrades forward in their quest for a free and united Ireland.

Michael's role had changed from a passive observer to an active leader, a transformation that was both empowering and overwhelming. The early morning light, filtering softly through the worn curtains, seemed to illuminate the significance of this shift. No longer was he merely watching from the shadows; he was now a pivotal part of the strategic engine driving the resistance. This newfound position imbued him with a sense of purpose, but it also brought with it an almost palpable weight of responsibility.

He felt the weight of his new responsibilities pressing down on his shoulders, a constant reminder of the stakes involved. Each decision he made, each piece of intelligence he provided, was now a thread in the complex tapestry of their struggle. The lives of his comrades, and the fate of his community, were intertwined with his actions. The power to influence the course of the conflict was in his hands, a fact that both empowered and daunted him.

Sitting in his small room, the stillness of the morning offering a brief respite from the chaos outside, Michael's mind was a whirlpool of thoughts. He reflected on the path that had brought him here, the small, seemingly insignificant steps that had gradually built into this moment of transformation. The transition from a curious boy listening to his father's tales of heroism, to a determined young man gathering intelligence in the shadows, and now to a leader whose decisions could alter the course of their fight for freedom.

The empowerment he felt was tempered by the enormity of the tasks ahead. He knew that leadership within the IRA was not just about making plans and giving orders; it was about embodying the spirit of their cause, inspiring others with his resolve, and making sacrifices for the greater good. The stakes were higher now, and the margin for error slimmer. Every move he made would be scrutinized, every action carrying the potential for significant consequences.

Michael's thoughts drifted to his comrades, the men and women who looked to him for guidance and support. He thought about the trust they placed in him, the expectations they had, and the silent promises he had made to them. The camaraderie they shared, built on shared risks and common goals, was a source of strength. Yet, it also underscored the gravity of his role – their fates were, in part, his to shape.

Preparing himself for the challenges ahead, Michael took a deep breath, feeling the cool morning air fill his lungs. He knew that his journey with the IRA was just beginning, and that the road ahead would be fraught with peril and uncertainty. But he was ready to face whatever came his way. The transformation from observer to leader had solidified his commitment, turning his resolve into a sharpened weapon.

Fully aware of the responsibilities that lay before him, Michael embraced the mantle of leadership. The path he walked was steeped in history and sacrifice, a continuation of the struggle that had defined his people for generations. He was a part of this legacy now, a bearer of its torch, leading his people through the darkness toward the promise of freedom and unity.

The streets of Belfast buzzed with a myriad of reactions to the IRA's recent activities, including the covert operation carried out by Michael. The early morning sun bathed the city in a soft, golden light, casting long shadows that seemed to whisper the secrets of the night.

In the heart of the nationalist neighborhood, groups of locals gathered, their faces animated with a mix of emotions. The aroma of fresh bread wafted through the air from the nearby bakery, mingling with the sharper scent of burning coal from the chimneys. Children played hopscotch on the pavement, their laughter a stark contrast to the serious discussions happening around them.

Near the corner pub, a cluster of elderly men stood in a tight circle, their voices low but intense. "Did you hear about the latest move? Michael's crew managed to get some crucial intel," one said, his eyes gleaming with a mix of pride and concern. His companions nodded, the lines on their faces deepening as they considered the implications.

Further down the street, a group of women exchanged hushed whispers while hanging laundry on sagging clotheslines. The colorful garments flapped in the breeze, punctuating their quiet conversation. "I just worry about the children," one woman murmured, her hands busy with a clothespin. "With the soldiers patrolling more frequently, it's only a matter of time before things get even more dangerous."

In a small courtyard, teenagers huddled together, their eyes wide with excitement and fear. They spoke in rapid bursts, their words overlapping in a rush of enthusiasm. "Michael's a hero," one boy declared, his fist pumping the air. "He's doing what needs to be done." Another boy, quieter and more reserved, glanced around nervously. "But what if they find out? What if they come here?"

The local priest, Father O'Connell, moved from group to group, offering words of comfort and caution. His presence was a steadying influence, his calm demeanor a balm to the anxious community. He paused to speak with a young mother, her baby cradled in her arms. "We must stay strong and united," he said softly, his hand resting gently on her shoulder. "But we must also be careful. Our actions have consequences, and we must always consider the greater good."

Michael, observing from a distance, felt the weight of their expectations and fears. The mosaic of reactions mirrored his own inner turmoil – the pride in their support, the concern for their safety, and the apprehension about what lay ahead. Each conversation, each whispered word, was a reminder of the delicate balance he had to maintain.

As he walked through the streets, the familiar sights and sounds of his neighborhood filled him with a renewed sense of purpose. The echo of his footsteps on the cobblestones, the distant hum of a radio playing an old Irish tune, and the fleeting smiles of the children at play – all these anchored him in the reality of what he was fighting for.

Michael knew that the path he had chosen was fraught with danger, not just for himself but for everyone he cared about. The support of his community was both a blessing and a burden, fueling his determination while amplifying the risks. But as he watched the sunrise over the rooftops of Belfast, he felt a surge of resolve. This was his home, and he would do whatever it took to protect it.

In the corners of smoky pubs and in the privacy of living rooms, there were words of quiet approval. The low murmur of conversations blended with the clinking of glasses and the faint strains of traditional Irish music playing from an old jukebox. The scent of stout and whiskey hung in the air, mingling with the sharp tang of cigarette smoke.

Inside McCarthy's Pub, a small group of regulars huddled around a battered wooden table, their faces illuminated by the warm glow of a flickering candle. "Michael and his lot, they're making a real difference," one man said, his voice barely above a whisper. He took a long drag from his cigarette, exhaling a cloud of smoke that lingered in the air. "It's about time someone stood up to them."

His companion nodded, his eyes reflecting a mix of determination and weariness. "Aye, it's dangerous, but what's the alternative? Sit back and do nothing?" He took a sip from his pint, the amber liquid catching the light. "We all want the same thing – freedom, dignity. They're fighting for all of us."

Across the room, an elderly woman leaned over the bar, speaking in hushed tones with the bartender. Her eyes sparkled with pride as she recounted the latest whispers of the IRA's exploits. "They're brave lads, every one of them," she said, her voice filled with emotion. "Standing up against those who'd keep us down. Makes me proud to be Irish."

In the privacy of living rooms, families gathered around crackling fireplaces, their discussions carrying a similar fervor. The warm glow of the fire cast dancing shadows on the walls, creating an atmosphere of intimacy and solidarity. "Michael's doing what needs to be done," a father said, his arm around his wife's shoulders. "He's risking everything for our future."

His teenage son, eyes wide with admiration, listened intently. "I want to be like him someday," he said quietly, almost to himself. The mother, her expression a mix of pride and worry, reached out to ruffle her son's hair. "We all have our part to play," she said softly, her voice steady. "But we must be careful. We can't afford to lose any more."

These residents spoke of the IRA with a sense of hope, their discussions tinged with a fierce pride. They saw the actions of Michael and his comrades as a necessary stand against oppression, a vital push for the freedom and rights they all yearned for. The solidarity in their voices was palpable, a bond forged from shared aspirations and the collective dream of a better future.

In these quiet, private moments, the spirit of resistance was alive and well. The words of approval, the nods of agreement, the passionate discussions – all were testament to a community united in its desire for change. The pride in their heritage, the determination to fight for their rights, and the hope for a brighter tomorrow infused every conversation, every whispered word of support.

Michael, though not present in these rooms, could feel the ripple effects of their support. It strengthened his resolve, knowing that his actions were not in vain, that they resonated deeply with those he fought to protect. The quiet approval of his community was a powerful motivator, a reminder that he was part of something much larger than himself.

But not all voices echoed this sentiment. In the marketplaces and on the sidewalks, there were murmurs of dissent. The bustling streets of Belfast, alive with the sounds of daily commerce, provided a stark backdrop to the quiet undercurrent of fear and apprehension.

At the corner market, the aroma of fresh produce mingled with the salty tang of the nearby sea. Vendors called out their wares, their voices punctuating the air with cheerful shouts, but beneath the surface lay a tension that was hard to ignore. A group of women, their faces lined with worry, huddled near a fruit stand, their voices low and urgent.

"I'm scared for my children," one woman confessed, her hand clutching a worn shopping bag. "Every time I hear a loud noise, I fear the worst." Her friend nodded, her expression mirroring the anxiety etched in her companion's eyes. "The violence is getting worse. What if the British soldiers start targeting our homes? We can't live like this."

A man passing by with his young daughter overheard their conversation and paused. "We all want freedom, but at what cost?" he interjected, his voice heavy with concern. "I just want my family to be safe. Is that too much to ask?" The little girl clung to his hand, her wide eyes filled with confusion, sensing the unease in the adults' voices.

On the sidewalks, clusters of people gathered, their conversations marked by an underlying sense of dread. "Michael and the others are brave, no doubt," an older man said, leaning on his cane. "But this can't go on forever. The British will retaliate, and it's us who will suffer." His companion, a younger man with a serious demeanor, sighed deeply. "We need peace. This cycle of violence is tearing us apart."

At a small café, the chatter was similarly mixed. Patrons sipped their tea and coffee, the clink of cups and the hum of conversation creating a soothing ambiance that belied the serious discussions taking place. "I lost my brother last year," a woman said quietly, her gaze distant. "I can't bear to lose anyone else. This fighting...it has to stop." Her friend reached out, placing a comforting hand on her arm. "We need to find another way, a way that doesn't involve more bloodshed."

These voices yearned for peace, tired of the endless cycle of conflict. The fear of escalating violence and the potential backlash from British forces loomed large in their minds. They worried about the safety of their families and the future of their community, their hearts heavy with the desire for a life free from the constant threat of violence.

Michael, moving through these spaces, could sense the undercurrent of dissent. The murmurings of fear and longing for peace were inescapable. They weighed on him, a reminder of the complex reality of their struggle. The support he received was powerful, but the doubts and fears of his community were equally impactful. It was a delicate balance, this fight for freedom, fraught with the hopes and fears of the people he fought to protect.

As the sun set over Belfast, casting long shadows across the city, Michael knew that the path ahead was uncertain. The voices of dissent, echoing through the marketplaces and along the sidewalks, were a poignant reminder of the human cost of their struggle. The yearning for peace, the fatigue of conflict, and the desperate hope for a better future – these were the realities he carried with him as he continued his journey, determined to find a way forward for himself and his community.

Among families, the divide was even more palpable. The late afternoon light filtered through the lace curtains of a modest home, casting intricate patterns on the worn wooden floors. In the cozy warmth of the living room, a family sat around the dinner table, the aroma of home-cooked stew filling the air. The atmosphere, however, was thick with tension.

Parents grappled with mixed emotions, torn between protecting their children and supporting the cause. "I don't want you involved in this," a mother said, her voice trembling as she spoke to her teenage son. Her eyes, usually filled with warmth, now brimmed with worry. "We've already lost too much."

The son, his face a mixture of defiance and passion, leaned forward. "But, Mum, we can't just sit back and do nothing. Michael and the others are fighting for our freedom. I want to help." His youthful idealism clashed with the harsh realities his parents had lived through.

In another home, a father sat by the fire, staring into the flickering flames. His young daughter played with her dolls at his feet, unaware of the gravity of the conversation between her parents. "If we don't support the cause, we're betraying our own people," he said, his voice low and filled with conflict. "But what if something happens to the kids? How do we live with that?"

His wife, sitting across from him, nodded slowly. "I understand, but I can't bear the thought of our children growing up in this violence. We need to think about their future, about giving them a chance at a normal life." Her hands twisted a piece of cloth, her knuckles white with tension.

Younger generations were caught in the turmoil, drawn to the romanticism of the struggle yet anxious about the uncertainty of their futures. In a dimly lit bedroom, two brothers whispered late into the night, their voices barely audible over the creaking of the old house. "Imagine being part of something so important," the older brother said, his eyes shining with excitement. "We could make a real difference."

The younger brother, though, was more hesitant. "But what about school? What about our dreams? I want to become a teacher, not spend my life fighting." His words hung in the air, a stark reminder of the futures at stake.

In the schoolyard, groups of teenagers clustered together, their conversations a mix of bravado and anxiety. "Michael's a hero," one girl said, her tone filled with admiration. "He's standing up for what's right." Her friend, however, glanced around nervously. "But it's dangerous. What if we get hurt? What if things never get better?"

The divide within families mirrored the broader community's struggle. Parents worriedly glanced at their children, their hearts torn between fear and pride. They wanted to protect their loved ones from the harshness of the conflict, yet they couldn't ignore the deep-seated desire for freedom and justice that resonated within their homes.

Michael, aware of these divides, felt the weight of their struggles. He knew the romanticism that drew the younger generation, the allure of being part of something greater. Yet, he also understood the fears of the parents, the uncertainty that clouded their hopes for the future. These were the very lives he was fighting for, each family a microcosm of the larger battle for peace and freedom.

As the evening settled over Belfast, the city's lights twinkling like stars against the encroaching darkness, Michael resolved to honor both the aspirations and the apprehensions of his community. The path was fraught with challenges, but he believed that through unity and resilience, they could forge a future where the next generation could live free from the shadows of conflict.

In Belfast's bustling neighborhoods, local businesses found themselves at the heart of the conflict's economic impact. The narrow streets were alive with activity, the air filled with the sounds of vendors calling out their wares and the chatter of customers haggling over prices. Amidst this daily hustle, the subtle undercurrents of the ongoing struggle were ever-present.

Some shop owners, whose families had weathered decades of political upheaval, extended quiet support to the IRA. These shopkeepers, bound by personal and historical ties to the nationalist cause, discreetly offered assistance. In a small grocery store on Falls Road, the bell above the door jingled as customers came and went, the scent of fresh produce mingling with the earthy aroma of potatoes and onions. Behind the counter, Mrs. O'Leary, a woman with kind eyes and a steady demeanor, conducted her business with a practiced ease. Yet, beneath her calm exterior lay a network of clandestine activities.

The hidden room behind her unassuming storefront, accessible through a narrow passage concealed by a shelf of canned goods, served as a venue for secret meetings. The space, modest and dimly lit, was furnished with a simple table and chairs, the walls adorned with old photographs and newspaper clippings that whispered tales of resistance. Here, in the quiet hours of the evening, trusted members of the IRA gathered to discuss their plans, their voices hushed and serious.

In a nearby pub, McCarthy's, the regular patrons were more than just customers. They were trusted messengers, their everyday interactions serving as a cover for covert communications. The bartender, a burly man with a jovial demeanor, wiped down the counter while keeping an ear out for coded phrases that signaled the need for a private word. "Got any fresh shipments in?" a customer might ask, their eyes meeting the bartender's briefly. The bartender would nod subtly, indicating that a message would be passed along.

Across the street, a small print shop run by Mr. Gallagher, an elderly man with a penchant for storytelling, operated under a similar guise. While he busied himself with printing flyers and posters for local events, he also produced pamphlets and leaflets for the IRA. The rhythmic hum of the printing press provided a comforting background noise, masking the whispered conversations and the passing of folded notes.

The trusted messengers moved through the city with practiced nonchalance. A young delivery boy, his cap pulled low over his eyes, cycled through the streets, a satchel slung over his shoulder. To the untrained eye, he was just another worker going about his day. But within the satchel, hidden among innocuous parcels, were messages and instructions crucial to the IRA's operations. As he made his rounds, he exchanged brief, knowing glances with shopkeepers and patrons, each interaction a seamless blend of the ordinary and the extraordinary.

These businesses, small and unassuming, were the lifeblood of the community's covert resistance. The owners and workers, motivated by a deep sense of duty and a shared history of struggle, played their parts with quiet determination. The economic impact of the conflict was keenly felt, but so too was the unwavering resolve to support the cause in whatever way they could.

Michael, moving through these neighborhoods, was acutely aware of the intricate web of support that surrounded him. The discreet nods, the subtle exchanges, and the hidden rooms were all part of a larger, collective effort to stand against oppression. The quiet bravery of these local businesses, their willingness to risk everything for the sake of freedom, reinforced his own commitment to the cause.

As the sun set over Belfast, casting a warm glow over the bustling streets, the city's heartbeat was a testament to its resilience. In the shadows of the storefronts and the whispers of the marketplaces, the spirit of resistance lived on, fueled by the unwavering support of those who dared to dream of a better future.

In stark contrast, other business owners watched with growing unease as the conflict's toll on the local economy became increasingly apparent. The vibrant pulse of Belfast's neighborhoods seemed to falter under the strain, the once bustling streets now marked by a palpable tension that hung in the air like a heavy fog.

At O'Connell's Bakery, the scent of freshly baked bread wafted into the street, mingling with the less pleasant odor of exhaust from military vehicles. The cheerful bell above the door rang less frequently these days, its cheerful chime a lonely echo in the otherwise quiet shop. Mrs. O'Connell, her apron dusted with flour, glanced anxiously at the empty tables where customers once sat, enjoying their morning pastries. The regulars had become scarce, scared away by the frequent military patrols that rumbled ominously through the streets.

Across the road at Thompson's Hardware Store, Mr. Thompson stood behind his counter, his brow furrowed as he examined the dwindling inventory on his shelves. "The supply lines are a mess," he muttered to his wife, who was busy dusting the already spotless counters. "We can't get half the stock we need, and what we do get is delayed or overpriced." His voice carried a mix of frustration and resignation, the weight of the ongoing conflict pressing heavily on his shoulders.

In the small grocer's, Mr. Patel carefully arranged cans on a shelf, his movements deliberate but heavy with worry. He watched the street through the front window, the usual parade of shoppers reduced to a trickle. The occasional bursts of laughter from children playing in the distance were now overshadowed by the ever-present hum of military helicopters. "It's bad for business," he confided to a customer, a regular who still braved the tension to buy his weekly groceries. "People are afraid. They don't want to come out unless they have to."

Further down the street, the once lively McAllister's Pub now hosted a few patrons who huddled over their drinks, their conversations subdued. The owner, Mr. McAllister, wiped down the bar with a rag, his eyes scanning the nearly empty room. "This place used to be packed every night," he said to a friend nursing a pint. "Now look at it. People are too scared to come out for a pint, and who can blame them? It's like a ghost town after dark."

Some business owners, whose families had weathered decades of political upheaval, extended quiet support to the IRA. These shopkeepers, bound by personal and historical ties to the nationalist cause, discreetly offered assistance. Hidden rooms behind unassuming storefronts became venues for clandestine meetings. Trusted messengers relayed information, their everyday interactions serving as a cover for covert communications.

Meanwhile, others lamented the disruption of supply lines. Mr. Huang, who ran a small import shop, shook his head as he unpacked a shipment that had arrived days late. "This used to be so simple," he sighed, frustration evident in his voice. "Now, every delivery is a gamble. Half the time, things don't show up at all." He arranged the goods on his shelves, hoping against hope that his customers would return before the supplies ran out.

The economic impact of the conflict was evident in every corner of Belfast. Shops that once bustled with activity now stood quiet, their owners watching the streets with a mix of hope and apprehension. The fear of escalating violence and the reality of disrupted commerce cast long shadows over their livelihoods, each day bringing new challenges and uncertainties.

Michael, walking these same streets, felt the weight of their collective anxiety. The struggle for freedom was more than just a political battle; it was a fight that touched every aspect of life, from the bustling markets to the quiet corners of family homes. The resolve to persevere was palpable, but so too was the fear of what lay ahead.

As night fell over the city, the flickering lights of the businesses still open cast a warm glow, a testament to their endurance. Despite the hardships, these business owners, whether in support of or in quiet opposition to the IRA's methods, embodied the resilience of a community striving to survive and find hope amidst the turmoil.

Crucial for their businesses, now interrupted by roadblocks and security checks, their conversations were filled with concerns about the future. In O'Connor's Butcher Shop, the usual hum of activity was replaced by anxious murmurs. "The roadblocks are killing us," Mr. O'Connor said to a fellow shopkeeper, his hands gripping the counter tightly. "Deliveries are late, if they come at all. How are we supposed to keep our doors open?"

His friend nodded in agreement, their faces marked by shared worry. "It's the same for us. Every security check, every delay, it's a blow to our business. And the customers, they don't want to deal with the hassle, so they stay away."

In the corner of a small café, a group of business owners gathered, their voices low and filled with concern. "We need stability," one woman said, her hands wrapped around a cup of tea. "This constant unrest, it's tearing our community apart. If things don't change, I don't know how much longer we can hold on."

Their discussions reflected a deep desire for peace and stability. They feared that continued unrest would not only threaten their livelihoods but also erode the very fabric of the community they served. As they spoke, their eyes frequently darted to the windows, watching for any sign of trouble, the fear of escalating violence ever-present.

Michael, listening to these conversations, understood the gravity of their concerns. The businesses were more than just sources of income; they were the lifeblood of the community, places where people gathered, shared stories, and supported one another. The potential collapse of these establishments symbolized a deeper threat to the social fabric of Belfast.

As he moved through the city, the mix of hope and apprehension in the voices of the business owners stayed with him. The path to freedom was fraught with challenges, but he believed that through unity and resilience, they could forge a future where peace and stability reigned. The dream of a better tomorrow, free from the shadows of conflict, was worth fighting for, not just for himself but for the entire community.

The division among the business community painted a vivid picture of a society torn between supporting a deeply rooted cause and yearning for normalcy. The bustling streets of Belfast, with their mix of thriving and struggling businesses, told a story of resilience and tension. Each storefront, each corner shop, carried the weight of its owner's choices and fears.

At O'Connell's Bakery, Mrs. O'Connell stood behind the counter, her smile warm yet strained. The scent of fresh bread filled the air, a comforting reminder of simpler times. Yet, her eyes darted to the window every time a military vehicle rumbled by. "We stand with them," she murmured to a customer, handing over a loaf of bread. "But it's hard, you know? Every day feels like a gamble."

Across the road, at Thompson's Hardware Store, Mr. Thompson rearranged his dwindling stock with a furrowed brow. The shelves, once brimming with supplies, now looked sparse. He sighed heavily as he glanced at the latest invoice, the costs inflated due to disrupted supply lines. "We need peace," he confided to a fellow shopkeeper who had stopped by. "I support the cause, but my business can't survive like this."

In the dim light of McAllister's Pub, a small group of regulars huddled over their drinks. The conversations were subdued, filled with a mix of support and fear. Mr. McAllister wiped down the bar, his thoughts heavy. "We're all for freedom," he said quietly to an old friend, "but what about our livelihoods? The constant unrest is driving people away."

The small grocer's, run by Mr. Patel, echoed similar sentiments. He stood behind the counter, watching the sparse flow of customers. "It's not just about business," he said to a loyal customer. "It's about our community. We're caught in the middle, trying to support the cause but also needing to keep our doors open."

In contrast, Mrs. O'Leary's hidden room behind her grocery store was bustling with activity. The modest space, accessed through a secret door, hosted clandestine meetings for the IRA. The flickering candlelight cast shadows on the faces of those gathered, their voices low and determined. "Every bit of help counts," she said, passing around a plate of biscuits. "We do what we can, even if it's risky."

The streets themselves seemed to reflect this division. On one corner, a group of young men, inspired by the romanticism of the struggle, talked passionately about their next moves. On another, older men and women discussed the pressing need for stability, their voices tinged with worry. The frequent roadblocks and security checks had become a part of daily life, disrupting routines and instilling a constant sense of unease.

In O'Connor's Butcher Shop, the usual hum of activity was replaced by anxious murmurs. "The roadblocks are killing us," Mr. O'Connor said to a fellow shopkeeper, his hands gripping the counter tightly. "Deliveries are late, if they come at all. How are we supposed to keep our doors open?"

These divergent responses underscored the complex interplay of politics and daily life, revealing the multifaceted impact of the Troubles on Belfast's economic and social landscape. The community was a tapestry of interconnected lives, each thread representing a different stance, a different fear, a different hope.

Michael, walking through these neighborhoods, felt the weight of this division. The support and the dissent, the hope and the fear, all mingled together, creating a rich, complex narrative of a city in turmoil. The path to freedom was not just a political struggle; it was a fight that touched every aspect of life, weaving through the heart of the community.

As the evening shadows lengthened over Belfast, Michael's resolve hardened. The dream of a better tomorrow, free from the shadows of conflict, was worth fighting for. He carried with him the voices of the business owners, the families, and the children, each one a reminder of what was at stake. Through unity and resilience, he believed they could forge a future where peace and stability reigned, a future where the complex tapestry of Belfast's community could thrive.

Belfast's streets were alive with whispers and rumors, creating a palpable undercurrent of anticipation and anxiety. The city hummed with the collective tension, each corner, each alleyway, alive with speculation. In the shadow of the ongoing conflict, speculations about the IRA's next move and the potential response from British forces were rampant.

In the bustling market square, vendors chatted with their customers in hushed tones. The aroma of fresh produce and baked goods mingled with the sharper scent of tension in the air. Mrs. Flanagan, a fruit seller with a keen ear for gossip, leaned over her stall, her voice barely above a whisper. "They say the IRA is planning something big, something that'll shake the city to its core," she confided to a regular customer, her eyes darting around to ensure no one else was listening. "But who knows if it's true?"

At a nearby newsstand, Mr. Byrne arranged his newspapers, his hands moving methodically even as his mind raced with the latest rumors. A group of men stood nearby, their conversation a blend of curiosity and concern. "I heard they're gearing up for a large-scale operation," one man said, his voice tinged with both excitement and fear. "Something that'll draw a massive response from the British."

His companion, a man with a more skeptical demeanor, shook his head. "Or it could be nothing but talk," he countered. "Rumors are like wildfire in this city – they spread fast and often burn out just as quickly."

In the dimly lit corners of McAllister's Pub, patrons huddled over their drinks, their voices low and conspiratorial. The usual chatter was replaced with a more serious tone as they speculated on the possible outcomes of the latest developments. "Word is, there might be peace talks," one man suggested, his tone hopeful. "If that's true, maybe there's a chance this can all end without more bloodshed."

Across the room, another group of men dismissed the idea with a wave of their hands. "Peace talks? In this climate?" one of them scoffed, taking a swig of his pint. "More likely, we'll see an escalation before anything else. The Brits won't just sit back and let the IRA dictate terms."

On the school playground, teenagers exchanged their own versions of the rumors, their youthful enthusiasm clashing with the grim reality of their surroundings. "Michael's involved in something big," one boy said with a mix of admiration and apprehension. "They say he's planning a move that'll put him on the map for good."

His friend, more cautious by nature, furrowed his brow. "I hope he knows what he's doing," he murmured. "One wrong step and the whole community could pay the price."

Even in the quiet corners of family homes, the whispers persisted. Parents discussed the latest speculations after tucking their children into bed, their voices tinged with worry. "Do you think there's any truth to the rumors about the peace talks?" a mother asked her husband, her eyes reflecting both hope and fear. "It would be a blessing if it were true."

The father, his face lined with worry, shook his head slowly. "It's hard to say. Every rumor seems to carry a grain of truth, but finding that grain is the challenge."

Michael, moving through the city, felt the weight of these whispers. The anticipation and anxiety were almost tangible, pressing down on him as he navigated the familiar streets. The rumors, whether of grand operations or potential peace talks, highlighted the city's desperate desire for resolution – one way or another.

As night fell and the city lights flickered on, the whispers continued, weaving through the fabric of Belfast's streets. The undercurrent of anticipation and anxiety created an atmosphere thick with uncertainty, each rumor adding another layer to the complex tapestry of the city's struggle. Michael knew that the path forward was fraught with challenges, but the collective hope and fear of the people fueled his resolve. The future of Belfast hung in the balance, and he was determined to play his part in shaping it.

In cafes and on street corners, conversations were laced with guesses and half-truths, each person adding their spin to the stories. The clinking of cups and the murmur of voices in the local cafes seemed to form a symphony of speculation. This atmosphere of uncertainty fed into the community's collective psyche, heightening feelings of apprehension about the future.

At a small café near the city center, the smell of freshly brewed coffee mingled with the soft chatter of patrons. Mrs. Murphy, the owner, moved between tables, refilling cups and listening to snippets of conversation. "I heard Michael's planning something big," one man said, leaning in close to his friend. "They're saying it'll change the course of things, for better or worse."

His friend, stirring his coffee absentmindedly, nodded. "But have you heard about the possible peace talks? Some folks think it's a sign that this might all end soon." The uncertainty in his voice mirrored the cautious hope that seemed to flutter through the café.

Outside, on the bustling street corners, groups of people gathered, their voices a mix of excitement and trepidation. "They say the British forces are preparing for a major crackdown," a woman whispered to her neighbor, her eyes wide with worry. "If it's true, we're all in for a rough time."

Nearby, a young man, his hands shoved deep into his pockets, added his own take. "Or it could just be another false alarm," he said, trying to sound nonchalant. "Rumors like these pop up all the time. We've learned to take them with a grain of salt."

At the bus stop, an elderly man shook his head as he listened to the latest speculations. "It's all guesswork," he said to anyone who would listen. "But these whispers, they get to you. You start to wonder what's real and what's not."

In a cozy bookstore, the atmosphere was no different. Customers browsed the shelves, but their minds were clearly elsewhere. "Do you think there's any truth to the peace talks?" a young woman asked the shopkeeper, her voice tinged with both hope and skepticism. "Or is it just another story to keep us calm?"

The shopkeeper, a wise old man with a twinkle in his eye, shrugged. "Hard to say, lass. Every story has some truth to it, but it's buried deep under layers of speculation and fear."

The whispers and rumors flowed like an invisible current through the city, touching every corner of Belfast. They crept into the minds of the people, feeding their anxieties and shaping their perceptions of the future. Each person, from the café patrons to the street corner gatherers, contributed to the collective narrative, weaving a tapestry of uncertainty and hope.

Michael, navigating these streets, could feel the tension in the air. The guesses and half-truths, the whispered conversations, all painted a picture of a community on edge. The anticipation and anxiety were almost tangible, pressing down on him as he moved through the familiar streets. He knew that these rumors, whether of impending operations or potential peace talks, were more than just idle gossip – they were a reflection of the city's desperate desire for resolution.

As the sun set over Belfast, casting long shadows across the streets, the whispers continued. The collective psyche of the community was a fragile thing, easily swayed by the tide of speculation. Michael understood that the path forward was fraught with challenges, but the hopes and fears of the people fueled his resolve. In this atmosphere of uncertainty, he remained steadfast, determined to navigate the complexities of the conflict and help guide his city toward a brighter future.

The community stood at a pivotal juncture, reflecting the harsh realities of life in a conflict zone. The streets of Belfast were a maze of intertwined fates, where political convictions often clashed with the practicalities of daily survival. This created a complex tapestry of hope, fear, and resilience that colored every aspect of life.

In the heart of the city, an elderly man sold newspapers at a corner stand, his weathered face a testament to years of witnessing the city's turmoil. "Have you heard the latest?" he asked a passerby, his voice low and gravelly. "They say the IRA's next move could be the turning point." The customer nodded, the lines of worry etched deep into his brow, reflecting a shared understanding of the stakes involved.

At the local grocery, Mrs. Thompson arranged cans on the shelf, her hands moving automatically while her mind raced with the latest whispers. "People talk about peace talks like they're just around the corner," she said to a regular customer, her voice tinged with skepticism. "But who really knows? Every day brings something new, something uncertain."

The practicalities of daily survival often clashed with these political convictions. Mr. Patel, at his small grocer's, looked over his dwindling stock with a sigh. "We're trying to keep our heads above water," he confided to a neighbor. "But every new rumor, every new bit of news, it shakes things up. People don't know whether to prepare for the worst or hope for the best."

In a small workshop, a group of craftsmen worked in near silence, the usual banter replaced by somber reflections. "My brother thinks it's all going to blow over soon," one of them said, breaking the silence. "But I'm not so sure. Every day, it feels like we're standing on the edge of something big, something we can't see coming."

The rumors and speculations were more than just idle talk; they were the manifestation of a society trying to make sense of its turbulent reality. In the quiet moments of the evening, families gathered around dinner tables, their conversations a mix of cautious optimism and deep-seated fear. "Do you think it'll ever end?" a young girl asked her father, her wide eyes searching for reassurance. He paused, his fork hovering over his plate. "I hope so, love. I really do. But it's hard to say. We just have to keep going, keep hoping."

The resilience of the community shone through in these small, everyday interactions. Despite the ever-present fear, there was a persistent thread of hope, a belief that things could and would get better. Michael, moving through these scenes, felt this resilience deeply. The rumors, the whispers, the speculative conversations – they were all part of a larger narrative, one that spoke of a community striving to find its footing amidst the chaos.

As night fell, the lights in the homes and businesses of Belfast flickered on, casting a warm glow against the encroaching darkness. The city was alive with the pulse of its people, each one navigating the complex interplay of politics and survival. Michael knew that the path forward was fraught with challenges, but he also saw the strength and determination in the faces around him.

The community's hopes and fears were intertwined, creating a rich tapestry that reflected their collective struggle and resilience. Michael carried these emotions with him, understanding that his role was not just to fight but to help guide his city toward a future where hope could prevail over fear. In the end, it was this shared sense of purpose that would see them through the darkest days.

In the aftermath of escalated IRA activities, Belfast underwent a profound transformation. The vibrant streets, once a hub of local life, now echoed with the grim reminders of a city under siege. The British forces, determined to quash any further IRA actions, ramped up their presence significantly.

The lively markets and bustling cafes that once defined the city's heartbeat were overshadowed by the imposing sight of armored vehicles and patrols of soldiers. The hum of everyday life was now punctuated by the rumble of military trucks and the clipped commands of officers. The smell of fresh bread from local bakeries mingled with the acrid scent of diesel and metal.

Mrs. O'Connell's bakery, which used to draw crowds with its warm, inviting aroma, now saw fewer customers. The bell above the door rang occasionally, a lonely sound against the backdrop of a city in lockdown. She glanced nervously at the street, watching as a convoy of armored vehicles rolled past, the ground vibrating under their weight. "It's like living in a war zone," she murmured to a loyal customer. "Every day feels more uncertain than the last."

Thompson's Hardware Store, a cornerstone of the community, stood in stark contrast to its former self. Mr. Thompson watched from behind his counter, his eyes following the soldiers patrolling outside. The sound of boots on pavement, a constant reminder of the tension that gripped the city. "They're everywhere now," he said to his wife, who was organizing the dwindling stock. "It's hard to remember what peace felt like."

In the narrow alleyways and corners of Belfast, children who once played freely now stayed close to home, their games interrupted by the presence of military patrols. The laughter of youth was replaced by the distant sounds of drills and the mechanical whir of surveillance equipment. In a small courtyard, Michael watched as a group of teenagers gathered, their usual chatter subdued. "We used to play football here," one of them said, kicking a pebble. "Now we just watch the soldiers."

The local pub, McAllister's, where the community once gathered to share stories and laughter, now held a different kind of meeting. Patrons huddled in small groups, their conversations tinged with fear and defiance. "We can't let this be our new normal," Mr. McAllister said, his voice low but firm. "We have to find a way to keep our spirits up, even with them watching our every move."

The transformation was stark and unsettling. The streets of Belfast, lined with barbed wire and checkpoints, bore little resemblance to the lively, communal spaces they once were. The British forces' presence was a constant, oppressive shadow, a reminder of the escalating conflict. The soldiers, with their rigid postures and watchful eyes, seemed to drain the city of its vibrancy, replacing it with an atmosphere of suspicion and fear.

Michael walked these changed streets, the weight of the city's transformation heavy on his shoulders. He saw the fear in the eyes of shopkeepers, the worry etched into the faces of parents, and the lost innocence in the gaze of children. The impact of the escalated IRA activities was palpable, a living, breathing force that reshaped Belfast's identity.

As he moved through the city, Michael's resolve only hardened. The transformation of Belfast was a stark reminder of the stakes involved, the urgent need for action, and the profound consequences of the struggle. The city, now a militarized zone, was a testament to both the resilience of its people and the overwhelming challenges they faced. Despite the oppressive presence of the British forces, the spirit of Belfast's community remained unbroken, a flickering flame in the face of adversity.

Checkpoints sprung up across Belfast, disrupting the daily flow of life. The once seamless movement through the city was now punctuated by barriers and armed guards. These checkpoints, often leading to invasive searches and interrogations, heightened the sense of unease among residents.

In the early morning, as the sun cast long shadows over the cobblestone streets, Mrs. Flanagan left her home for the market. She approached a newly erected checkpoint, her steps hesitant. The sight of soldiers, their faces impassive behind helmets and visors, was intimidating. As she reached the barrier, a soldier motioned for her to stop. "Identification, please," he demanded, his tone brisk. Mrs. Flanagan fumbled with her bag, her hands trembling slightly as she handed over her papers. The search that followed was thorough and invasive, leaving her feeling exposed and humiliated. "Just doing our job," the soldier said as he finally waved her through, but the experience lingered, a stark reminder of the city's changed reality.

Children on their way to school now had to navigate these checkpoints as well. Young Danny, a boy of ten, clutched his schoolbag tighter as he and his friends approached the soldiers. The usual chatter and laughter were replaced by nervous whispers. "Do you think they'll search us again?" one of his friends asked. Danny shrugged, trying to appear brave, but the fear was evident in his eyes. The sound of their school shoes on the pavement, once a comforting rhythm, now seemed loud and out of place against the backdrop of military machinery and the occasional barked orders from soldiers.

Shopkeepers like Mr. Patel faced constant interruptions as deliveries were delayed or stopped altogether at the checkpoints. He stood outside his grocery store, watching as a delivery truck was pulled over. Soldiers rifled through the goods, their stern faces betraying no emotion. "Every day, it's the same thing," Mr. Patel muttered to a fellow shopkeeper. "They're looking for something, anything, to justify their presence." The delay meant spoiled produce and frustrated customers, further straining his already tenuous business.

In the evenings, the once familiar sounds of Belfast – children playing, music spilling from pubs, the hum of conversation – were drowned out by the rumble of armored vehicles and the measured tread of soldiers on patrol. Mr. McAllister's pub, a place that once buzzed with life, now held a subdued crowd. Patrons glanced nervously towards the windows, the tension palpable. "It's like we're living in a prison," one regular said, his voice low. "We can't even enjoy a pint without feeling watched."

People who were once familiar with moving freely through their city now faced constant scrutiny and suspicion. Mrs. O'Connell, making her way home after closing her bakery, felt the eyes of the soldiers on her back. She quickened her pace, the weight of their gaze heavy. "It wasn't always like this," she thought, recalling a time when the streets were filled with neighbors and friends, not checkpoints and soldiers.

The sound of military machinery – the whirring of helicopters overhead, the clatter of armored vehicles on the streets – and the sight of armed soldiers patrolling became the new normal. The familiar sights and sounds of everyday city life, the vendors calling out in the market, children's laughter, and the chatter of friends meeting on street corners, were replaced by the oppressive presence of the military.

Michael, moving through these transformed streets, felt the tension in every interaction, every sideways glance. The checkpoints were not just physical barriers but symbols of a city under siege. Each search, each interrogation, frayed the fabric of trust and community that once held Belfast together. The resilience of the people was being tested daily, their spirits weighed down by the constant threat of scrutiny.

As night fell, casting long shadows across the city, the reality of the new normal settled over Belfast like a shroud. The community's determination remained, but the constant presence of checkpoints and soldiers was a stark reminder of the struggle ahead. Michael knew that behind every weary face was a story of resilience and a desire for a return to normalcy. The path to freedom was fraught with challenges, but the spirit of Belfast's people remained unbroken, even in the face of relentless scrutiny.

This increased military presence not only altered the physical landscape of Belfast but also had a profound psychological impact on its residents. The once familiar streets, now dotted with checkpoints and patrolled by soldiers, seemed to close in on the people who had called them home for generations.

The sense of being constantly watched was inescapable. Mrs. Flanagan, while arranging the fruit on her market stall, felt the weight of unseen eyes on her every move. The cheerful greetings she used to exchange with passersby had been replaced by wary nods. "It's like living in a fishbowl," she whispered to a fellow vendor, her voice laced with anxiety. "You never know who's watching or what they're thinking."

The disruption to daily routines was felt keenly. Mr. Thompson, who prided himself on opening his hardware store at the crack of dawn, now faced delays and inspections that ate into his business hours. "Every morning it's the same," he grumbled to his wife, who tried to console him with a cup of tea. "Lines of people waiting, soldiers checking everything. It's exhausting." The rhythm of life had been thrown off balance, leaving a trail of frustration and unease.

Children, once free to roam and play, were now confined by invisible barriers of fear. Young Danny, who used to race his friends to school, now walked with his head down, his steps cautious. "Why are they here, Mum?" he asked one evening, his innocent eyes filled with confusion. His mother, struggling to find the right words, simply held him close. "It's complicated, love," she whispered, her heart heavy with the knowledge that his childhood was being overshadowed by conflict.

The pervasive atmosphere of tension deeply affected the community's morale. At McAllister's Pub, the laughter that once filled the room was a distant memory. Patrons spoke in hushed tones, their conversations punctuated by anxious glances towards the door. "We used to come here to forget our troubles," one man said to his friend, his voice barely above a whisper. "Now it feels like they follow us everywhere."

Residents found their sense of safety and freedom significantly diminished. Mrs. O'Connell, walking home from her bakery, felt a constant knot of fear in her stomach. The streets she had once navigated with ease now seemed fraught with danger. "It's like the city's turned against us," she confided to her sister. "I don't feel safe anymore, not even in my own home."

The psychological toll was evident in the small, everyday interactions. Mr. Patel, usually a source of cheer at his grocery store, now wore a perpetual frown. He watched the soldiers outside with a mix of fear and defiance. "They think they can break us," he said to a customer, his voice trembling with emotion. "But we won't let them."

Michael, observing these changes, felt the weight of his community's despair. The city he loved had transformed into a landscape marked by surveillance and uncertainty. The once vibrant streets, filled with the sounds of daily life, now echoed with the heavy footsteps of soldiers and the hum of military vehicles. The psychological impact was undeniable, eroding the spirit of resilience that had always defined Belfast.

Yet, amid the fear and tension, there remained a flicker of hope. The community, though battered, was not broken. In whispered conversations and quiet acts of defiance, the spirit of Belfast endured. Michael knew that this resilience was their greatest strength, a beacon of hope in the darkest of times.

As he walked the transformed streets, Michael's resolve hardened. The psychological scars left by the increased military presence were deep, but they were not insurmountable. The fight for freedom was as much about preserving the spirit of the people as it was about winning battles. In the face of surveillance and uncertainty, the community's unwavering determination would light the way forward.

The once vibrant and bustling streets of Belfast, known for their lively markets, friendly conversations, and community gatherings, were now corridors of surveillance, echoing with the ominous sounds of military presence. The clatter of armored vehicles and the measured tread of soldiers' boots replaced the familiar sounds of street vendors and children playing, casting a long shadow over the city's spirit.

In the heart of the city, the lively markets where Mrs. Flanagan sold her fruits had turned somber. The cheerful banter with customers had been replaced by cautious whispers. She arranged her apples and pears with a heavy heart, her eyes constantly flicking towards the patrols. "It's like they've taken the soul out of the place," she murmured to her neighbor, who nodded in agreement, his own stall equally subdued.

The oppressive environment deeply impacted the mood of the community. Mr. Thompson's hardware store, once a hub of friendly advice and neighborly chat, felt like a fortress under siege. Customers entered quickly, conducted their business, and left without lingering. The sense of camaraderie was eroding. "It's hard to remember the last time someone stayed for a chat," Mr. Thompson remarked to his wife, the weariness evident in his voice. "Everyone's just trying to get by without attracting attention."

Friendly conversations that once flowed freely in places like McAllister's Pub were now stifled by the ever-present fear of being overheard. The pub's atmosphere had shifted from warm and inviting to tense and wary. Patrons huddled in corners, their voices low and guarded. "We used to laugh and sing here," Mr. McAllister reminisced to a regular, his eyes scanning the room. "Now it feels like we're all holding our breath."

Community gatherings, a staple of Belfast's social life, were disrupted. Church halls that once hosted vibrant meetings and social events now stood empty or filled with hushed, anxious discussions. Mrs. O'Connell, who had always been active in organizing neighborhood events, felt the weight of the changed times. "People are scared to gather," she told Father O'Donnell, the parish priest. "They worry about what might happen if they're seen together."

The constant surveillance altered the community's perception of safety and freedom. Mrs. Patel, a mother of two, no longer felt comfortable letting her children play outside. The familiar streets where she had grown up now seemed threatening. "I used to feel safe here," she confided to a friend. "Now I can't shake the feeling that we're always being watched."

Even the simplest of errands were fraught with tension. Young Danny, on his way to buy milk, walked quickly and kept his head down, avoiding eye contact with the soldiers he passed. The carefree spirit of youth had been replaced with a premature understanding of danger and caution. "Be careful," his mother would remind him, her voice tight with worry. "Don't draw attention."

The once vibrant essence of life in Belfast was overshadowed by an omnipresent sense of oppression. The community's morale suffered as the friendly, open atmosphere gave way to suspicion and fear. The sounds of daily life – laughter, conversation, the bustle of activity – were drowned out by the mechanical hum of military patrols and the barked orders of soldiers.

Michael, moving through these altered streets, felt the profound shift in the city's character. The transformation was stark and unsettling, a testament to the heavy toll of the conflict. Yet, he also saw glimpses of resilience in the eyes of the people, a determination to endure despite the oppressive environment.

As night fell, the streets of Belfast were bathed in the harsh glow of searchlights, the once comforting darkness now filled with a sense of foreboding. The community, though deeply affected, held on to a thread of hope. Michael knew that this spirit, though battered, was not broken. The fight for Belfast's heart and soul was far from over, and he was determined to see it through.

The very essence of life in Belfast had changed, but within the corridors of surveillance and the echoes of military presence, the flicker of community resilience remained. Michael resolved to nurture this flicker into a flame, guiding his city through the darkest times towards a future where the streets could once again bustle with the vibrant life they once knew.

The transformation of Belfast's streets, once vibrant and bustling, into an environment dominated by military surveillance continued to unfold. The ever-present hum of surveillance helicopters overhead and the frequent rumbling of armored vehicles through the streets added to the growing sense of a city under siege.

In the early morning, Mrs. Flanagan opened her market stall, the usual morning chatter replaced by the distant thump of helicopter blades. She glanced upwards, squinting at the shadow that passed overhead, her heart sinking with each pass. "It's like they're always watching," she murmured to her neighbor, who nodded, his eyes similarly drawn to the sky.

The community, accustomed to a certain freedom and neighborliness, now navigated their daily lives with a heightened sense of caution and wariness. Mr. Thompson, preparing to open his hardware store, paused as an armored vehicle rumbled past, the ground vibrating beneath his feet. He exchanged a grim look with Mrs. O'Connell, who was unlocking her bakery across the street. "Feels like we're living in a war zone," he said, shaking his head. "Every day, it gets harder to remember what normal was."

Children, once free to roam and play, now walked to school in tight-knit groups, their eyes wide with apprehension. Young Danny clutched his schoolbag, walking briskly beside his friends. "Stay close," his mother had warned him that morning, her voice filled with an urgency that was new and unsettling. The sight of soldiers on every corner, their rifles slung over their shoulders, was a stark contrast to the familiar backdrop of their daily walk.

The once familiar rhythms of city life were disrupted, replaced by a cautious uncertainty. In McAllister's Pub, the lively conversations and laughter had given way to hushed, wary tones. Patrons sipped their drinks, casting furtive glances at the door. "You never know who might walk in," Mr. McAllister muttered to a regular. "Or what they might be looking for."

Neighborhood gatherings, once a staple of Belfast's community spirit, were rare and subdued. In the small park where families used to picnic and children played, only a few people lingered, speaking in low voices. "Everything feels different," one woman said to her friend, watching her child play close by. "Like we're waiting for something to happen."

The residents of Belfast adapted to this new reality shaped by conflict and surveillance. Mrs. Patel, who had always taken pride in her grocery store being a community hub, now found herself watching the door with a mix of dread and determination. "We've had to change the way we do everything," she told a customer. "But we're still here. We're not going anywhere."

Michael, moving through these transformed streets, felt the weight of the city's new reality pressing down on him. The hum of helicopters and the rumble of armored vehicles were constant reminders of the conflict that had reshaped their lives. He saw the cautious steps, the quick, nervous glances, and the subdued conversations that had become the norm.

Despite the oppressive atmosphere, there was a thread of resilience woven through the fabric of the community. The people of Belfast, though wary and cautious, continued to go about their lives, finding new ways to connect and support one another. The spirit of neighborliness had not been extinguished; it had simply adapted to the harsh new conditions.

As night fell, the streets were bathed in the harsh glow of searchlights, casting long, stark shadows. The familiar comfort of the evening was replaced by a vigilant watchfulness. Michael knew that the path ahead was fraught with challenges, but he also saw the strength in his people's eyes. The transformation of Belfast's streets was profound, but the essence of the community, its resilience and determination, remained unbroken.

In this new reality of conflict and surveillance, the residents of Belfast navigated their lives with a careful balance of caution and hope. The ever-present military presence had altered the city's landscape, but it had not crushed the spirit of its people. Michael resolved to hold onto that spirit, to nurture it, and to lead his city toward a future where the streets could once again echo with the vibrant life they once knew.

The streets, once bustling with the lively chatter of locals, now echoed with the heavy tread of military boots. The familiar sounds of laughter and conversation were replaced by the relentless march of soldiers. Patrols became more frequent, and armored vehicles became a common sight, their presence disrupting the rhythm of everyday activities.

In the early hours of the morning, Mrs. Flanagan opened her market stall, the usual cheerful greetings from neighbors now replaced by tense nods. The rumble of an armored vehicle passing by shook the ground, rattling the apples neatly arranged on her stand. "Every day, it's something new," she whispered to her neighbor, who was busy setting up his own stall. "It's like living in a different city."

Checkpoints were set up at key intersections, leading to long lines and invasive searches that frayed the nerves of the residents. Mr. Thompson, carrying a box of tools for his hardware store, approached a checkpoint with a sense of dread. The soldiers, their faces stern and impassive, motioned for him to stop. "Papers," one of them barked, extending a gloved hand. Mr. Thompson handed over his identification, his heart pounding as the soldier scrutinized it, then waved him through with a curt nod. The once simple walk to work had become an ordeal.

Children on their way to school faced similar disruptions. Young Danny clutched his schoolbag tightly, the line at the checkpoint moving agonizingly slow. He glanced nervously at the soldiers, their rifles slung over their shoulders, and whispered to his friend, "Do you think they'll search us today?" His friend shrugged, eyes wide with fear. The carefree days of racing to school felt like a distant memory.

In McAllister's Pub, the atmosphere was heavy with unease. Regulars huddled in small groups, their conversations punctuated by anxious glances towards the door. The sound of military boots outside sent a ripple of tension through the room. "We used to come here to forget our troubles," one patron murmured to his companion. "Now it feels like they're always just around the corner."

The frequent patrols and armored vehicles disrupted the everyday rhythm of the city. Mrs. O'Connell, carrying a tray of freshly baked bread, paused as a convoy of military trucks passed by. The smell of warm bread, once a comforting aroma, seemed out of place in the oppressive atmosphere. "It's hard to keep the business going with all this," she confided to a customer. "People are scared to come out."

Residents queued at checkpoints, the lines stretching down the block. The invasive searches left people feeling exposed and vulnerable. Mr. Patel, waiting in line with a delivery for his grocery store, watched as a woman ahead of him was searched. Her face flushed with embarrassment as a soldier rifled through her bag. "It's degrading," Mr. Patel muttered to the man behind him. "We're treated like criminals in our own city."

The once vibrant streets of Belfast, filled with the sounds of daily life, had transformed into corridors of control and surveillance. The heavy tread of military boots, the rumble of armored vehicles, and the stern faces at checkpoints were constant reminders of the city's new reality.

Michael, walking these streets, felt the weight of the community's unease. The transformation was stark and deeply unsettling. The checkpoints, the patrols, the constant presence of soldiers – all these changes had frayed the nerves of the residents, altering their perception of safety and freedom. The once familiar rhythms of city life were disrupted, replaced by a cautious uncertainty.

Yet, amid the tension, Michael saw flashes of resilience. The determination in Mrs. Flanagan's eyes as she set up her stall, the quiet defiance of Mr. Thompson as he carried on with his work, and the whispered words of encouragement among neighbors – all these were signs that the spirit of Belfast had not been broken.

As night fell, the city was bathed in the harsh glow of searchlights, the streets quiet but for the hum of military machinery. The transformation was profound, but so too was the enduring strength of the community. Michael knew that the path forward would be difficult, but the resilience and determination of the people gave him hope. In the face of disruption and surveillance, the essence of Belfast – its spirit of community and defiance – remained unyielding.

The eyes of surveillance cameras felt more intrusive than ever, leaving a lingering sense of being constantly watched. The mechanical whir as they panned the streets, the occasional flash of their lenses in the sunlight, and the persistent hum of their operation added to the feeling of an omnipresent observer. The community's sense of privacy dwindled, replaced by a growing unease.

In the market square, where Mrs. Flanagan once engaged in lively banter with her customers, she now found herself glancing warily at the cameras mounted on nearby buildings. She adjusted the display of her fruits, feeling the invisible eyes on her back. "It's like they're always there," she whispered to a customer, her voice low. "Watching every move we make."

Conversations became more guarded. Mr. Thompson, chatting with a neighbor outside his hardware store, kept his voice low and his sentences short. "You never know who's listening," he said, his eyes darting to the camera perched above the streetlight. The neighbor nodded, understanding the unspoken need for caution. Their discussions, once filled with animated debate and laughter, now felt stilted and uneasy.

Public gatherings grew less frequent. The park, where children used to play and families picnicked, was now sparsely populated. Mrs. O'Connell walked her dog along the path, her steps slow and her eyes scanning the area for signs of surveillance. She spotted a camera nestled in the branches of a tree, its lens reflecting the afternoon sun. "Even here, we're not alone," she thought, pulling her coat tighter around her.

In McAllister's Pub, the change was palpable. The once vibrant atmosphere, filled with laughter and camaraderie, had turned somber. Patrons sat closer together, their conversations hushed. Mr. McAllister cleaned glasses behind the bar, his eyes occasionally flicking to the camera installed near the entrance. "They've taken our freedom," he said quietly to a regular. "And now, they're taking our spirit too."

The community's sense of privacy had all but vanished. Mr. Patel, discussing a delivery with his supplier, spoke in a near whisper. The camera on the corner of his shop seemed to loom larger every day, a silent sentinel that recorded every transaction, every word. "We can't even talk freely," he lamented to his supplier. "It's like we're prisoners in our own homes."

Gatherings in public spaces became rare events. The community center, once a bustling hub of activity, now stood largely empty. When people did gather, their eyes were always on the lookout for the nearest camera, their voices tinged with apprehension. "We used to come here to feel safe," a woman said to her friend as they stood by the entrance. "Now, it feels like there's no escape from their eyes."

Michael, observing the changes, felt the weight of the community's unease. The constant surveillance had eroded the trust and openness that once defined Belfast. The cameras, with their unblinking eyes, had created an atmosphere of suspicion and fear, replacing the warmth of neighborly interactions with a cold, calculated watchfulness.

The once familiar rhythms of city life were disrupted. The laughter of children, the chatter of friends, the casual greetings between neighbors – all had been replaced by cautious glances and whispered conversations. The community's sense of freedom had been compromised, and with it, the very essence of life in Belfast had changed.

Yet, even in this climate of surveillance and unease, Michael saw sparks of resilience. The quiet defiance in Mrs. Flanagan's eyes, the determined whispers of Mr. Thompson, and the furtive gatherings of neighbors – all spoke of a community that, though battered, was not broken. The cameras could watch, the soldiers could patrol, but the spirit of Belfast, its core of resilience and solidarity, remained unyielding.

As night fell and the city lights cast long shadows on the streets, Michael knew that the fight for Belfast's heart was far from over. The sense of being constantly watched had altered the community, but it had also forged a deeper resolve. In the face of oppression, the people of Belfast would find new ways to connect, to resist, and to keep their spirit alive.

The increased military presence not only heightened the sense of oppression among the nationalist community but also served as a stark reminder of the ever-present conflict. The tension was not just in the streets but had seeped into homes and businesses, affecting every aspect of life in Belfast.

In the early morning, as the city began to stir, the rumble of armored vehicles echoed through the narrow streets. Mrs. Flanagan, opening her market stall, glanced nervously at the patrol passing by. The soldiers, with their impassive faces and imposing rifles, were a constant reminder of the fraught atmosphere. "It's hard to feel free with them around," she whispered to a fellow vendor. The usual buzz of morning greetings had been replaced by a subdued silence, as if the very air was heavy with unspoken fears.

Homes, once sanctuaries of peace, now felt the strain of constant surveillance. Mr. Thompson sat at his kitchen table, his morning coffee growing cold as he listened to the distant hum of a helicopter. His wife, normally cheerful, moved about the kitchen with a worried frown. "Even here, we can't escape it," he said, looking out the window at the street below. The sense of security that had once been a given in their own home was now a fragile illusion.

Businesses, too, felt the weight of the military's presence. In his hardware store, Mr. Thompson noticed fewer customers each day. The once-familiar faces of his regulars now bore expressions of anxiety and fatigue. "It's not just the checkpoints," he told a colleague. "People are scared to be seen. They're scared of what might happen if they linger too long." The friendly banter that had once filled the store was now a series of hushed exchanges.

At McAllister's Pub, the atmosphere had shifted dramatically. The lively discussions and laughter that used to fill the room were replaced by tense, whispered conversations. Patrons huddled together, their eyes darting towards the windows at every noise from outside. "We can't even enjoy a pint in peace," one man muttered, his hands gripping his glass tightly. The pub, once a refuge from the outside world, now felt like another point of surveillance.

The tension was palpable in every corner of the city. Children, who should have been playing carefree, now moved in tight groups, their eyes wide with a mix of curiosity and fear. Young Danny, walking home from school, quickened his pace as he passed a group of soldiers. The once-familiar route now felt like a gauntlet. "Stay close," his mother had warned him that morning, her voice edged with concern. The innocence of childhood was overshadowed by the constant reminder of conflict.

In the quiet of the evening, families gathered around their dinner tables, the weight of the day's events hanging heavy in the air. Mrs. O'Connell tried to keep the conversation light, but the tension was inescapable. "I saw another patrol today," her husband said, breaking the silence. "They're everywhere." The children, sensing their parents' unease, ate quietly, the usual chatter of the evening meal replaced by a heavy silence.

Michael, walking through the transformed streets of Belfast, felt the pervasive impact of the increased military presence. It wasn't just about the visible changes – the checkpoints, the patrols, the surveillance cameras – it was about the invisible ones. The way people spoke, the way they moved, the way they interacted with each other – all had been altered. The tension seeped into every aspect of life, an uninvited guest in homes, businesses, and hearts.

The ever-present conflict had woven itself into the fabric of daily life. The sense of oppression was a constant companion, shadowing every step and every word. Yet, amidst this, Michael saw the glimmers of resilience. The quiet determination in Mrs. Flanagan's eyes as she set up her stall, the whispered words of encouragement between neighbors, the defiant gatherings in McAllister's Pub – all were signs that the spirit of Belfast, though strained, was not broken.

As night fell, casting long shadows over the city, Michael knew that the struggle was not just on the streets but within the hearts of the people. The increased military presence was a stark reminder of the conflict, but it also highlighted the enduring strength of the community. In the face of oppression, the people of Belfast continued to find ways to connect, to resist, and to hold on to their sense of identity. The path ahead was fraught with challenges, but the spirit of Belfast remained unyielding, a beacon of hope in the darkest of times.

Amidst this heightened surveillance and tension, the resolve of some community members was strengthened, viewing the British forces' actions as further justification for the IRA's cause. For others, it deepened the desire for peace and a return to normalcy. The atmosphere in Belfast had shifted, marking a new chapter in the city's long history of conflict.

In the shadows of St. George's Market, a group of young men gathered, their faces set with determination. Michael stood among them, his voice low but firm. "We can't let them crush our spirit," he said, glancing around at the attentive faces. "Every checkpoint, every patrol – it only proves why we need to fight." The nods of agreement around him were subtle but resolute. The increased military presence, with its oppressive surveillance, had only solidified their commitment to the cause.

At the same time, in a modest living room, Mrs. O'Connell and her husband sat in quiet conversation. The news played softly in the background, images of armored vehicles and soldiers filling the screen. "I just want it to end," she said, her voice weary. "I want our children to grow up without this fear." Her husband nodded, his hand reaching across the table to grasp hers. "We all do," he replied. "We need to find a way back to peace." Their longing for normalcy, for a life free from conflict, was a quiet but powerful force.

The resolve of the community was a tapestry of differing desires and motivations. In McAllister's Pub, where the atmosphere had grown heavy with tension, discussions took on a sharper edge. "We have to stand strong," one man argued, his fist clenched around his pint. "They're trying to break us, but we won't let them." Across the table, another patron shook his head. "We need to find a way to talk," he said softly. "This can't go on forever. Our kids deserve better."

Children, sensing the shift, adapted in their own ways. Young Danny, who once played freely in the streets, now spent more time indoors, drawing pictures of a peaceful Belfast. His mother watched him, her heart aching for the innocence lost. "What are you drawing, love?" she asked gently. Danny looked up, his eyes bright. "A city without soldiers," he replied simply. His words hung in the air, a poignant reminder of the deeper desire for peace that many held.

In the marketplaces and streets, the atmosphere had undeniably shifted. Vendors who once called out their wares with cheerful banter now spoke in hushed tones, their eyes scanning for any signs of trouble. Mrs. Flanagan, arranging her fruits, exchanged a glance with Mr. Patel. "It's different now," she said quietly. "Everyone's more cautious." Mr. Patel nodded, his expression somber. "But we keep going. We have to."

Michael, moving through these spaces, felt the weight of the city's new chapter. The heightened surveillance and tension were inescapable, but so too were the signs of resilience and resolve. For some, the presence of the British forces was a rallying cry, a justification for continued resistance. For others, it was a desperate call for peace, a yearning for the simple joys of a life without conflict.

The streets of Belfast, now marked by the presence of soldiers and surveillance cameras, echoed with the whispers of these conflicting desires. The community, though strained, continued to find ways to adapt and endure. Michael knew that this chapter in Belfast's history was pivotal. The choices made now, the paths taken, would shape the future for generations to come.

As night fell, the city's lights cast long shadows, and the hum of military machinery persisted. Yet, amidst the darkness, the spirit of Belfast remained. The resolve of its people, whether fueled by a desire for resistance or a longing for peace, was a testament to their enduring strength. Michael walked these streets with a renewed sense of purpose, knowing that the fight for Belfast's future was far from over. The atmosphere had shifted, but the heart of the city beat on, resilient and unbroken.

In the quiet of his room, away from the eyes of his comrades, Michael found himself wrestling with an internal conflict that gnawed at his conscience. The room was dimly lit, shadows dancing on the walls from the flickering candle on his desk. He sat there, hunched over, his hands clasped tightly as if seeking comfort from their own grip. The realization of the real-world implications of his actions with the IRA had begun to sink in, heavier than he had ever anticipated.

He stared at a worn photograph of his family, their faces smiling up at him from a happier time. His mother's gentle eyes, his father's proud stance, his siblings' carefree grins—all seemed to haunt him now. The thought that his involvement could bring danger to their doorstep was a source of deep torment. He closed his eyes, but the images remained, vivid and accusing.

The weight of his decisions pressed down on him. Each mission, each piece of intelligence gathered, had felt like a step towards a noble cause. But now, in the solitude of his room, the noble cause seemed intertwined with threads of fear and regret. He remembered the look on his mother's face the last time they had spoken, her eyes filled with a mix of pride and worry. "Be careful, Michael," she had said, her voice trembling slightly. "Promise me you'll stay safe." He had nodded, unable to fully meet her gaze.

The faces of his family flashed before him in the dim light, each one a reminder of what he stood to lose. His younger brother, who looked up to him with a mixture of admiration and awe, unaware of the full gravity of Michael's choices. His sister, who still believed in the simple joys of life, not yet tainted by the harsh realities of their world. The thought of them being caught in the crossfire, of soldiers barging into their home, filled him with a dread that was hard to shake.

Michael ran a hand through his hair, frustration and fear mingling in his mind. The silent room seemed to echo his turmoil, the shadows on the wall morphing into shapes of uncertainty. He had always believed in the cause, in the fight for freedom and justice. But the stark reality that his actions could bring harm to those he loved was a bitter pill to swallow.

He stood up, pacing the small room, trying to dispel the gnawing anxiety. The wooden floor creaked under his weight, the familiar sound oddly comforting. He approached the window, looking out at the darkened streets of Belfast. The city, under heavy surveillance and military presence, seemed to mirror his internal conflict. The tension, the fear, the constant watchfulness—it was all there, outside and within.

Michael knew he had to find a balance, a way to reconcile his commitment to the cause with his duty to protect his family. The idea that his involvement could bring danger to their doorstep was a torment he could not ignore. He pressed his forehead against the cool glass of the window, closing his eyes. "What am I doing?" he whispered to himself, the question hanging in the air, unanswered.

The quiet of his room offered no solace, only a stark reflection of his inner turmoil. He understood the stakes, the necessity of their fight, but the cost seemed to grow heavier each day. The faces of his family, the potential consequences of his actions, weighed on him like never before. Michael took a deep breath, steeling himself. He needed to find a way to protect those he loved while continuing the fight he believed in.

As the night deepened, Michael sat back down at his desk, the flickering candle casting long shadows. He pulled out a piece of paper and began to write, hoping to find clarity in his own words. The path ahead was uncertain, but he knew he had to navigate it carefully. The safety of his family, the future of Belfast, depended on it. The internal conflict gnawing at his conscience was a battle he had to face, one step at a time.

He lay in bed, staring at the ceiling, as scenes from his childhood played in his mind – a time of innocence, far removed from the harsh realities of his current life. The soft glow of the moon filtered through the window, casting pale patterns on the ceiling above. Michael's thoughts drifted back to simpler days, when the world seemed full of promise and his biggest concerns were childish misadventures.

He remembered the warm, comforting embrace of his mother's kitchen, the smell of freshly baked bread filling the air. Her gentle admonitions to always choose the path of right echoed in his mind. "Be a good boy, Michael," she would say, her eyes full of love and hope. "Always do what's right." Those words, so simple then, now felt like a heavy burden, a reminder of the moral compass he was struggling to follow.

His father's proud tales of Irish resilience were another constant in his memories. Sitting by the fire, his father would recount stories of past struggles, of heroes who stood firm against oppression. "We are a strong people, Michael," he would say, his voice filled with pride. "Never forget where you come from." Michael had listened with wide-eyed admiration, dreaming of one day being part of that legacy. But now, those tales felt like a distant dream, overshadowed by the grim reality of his current existence.

These memories formed a stark contrast to the life he was living – a life shrouded in secrecy and fraught with danger. The innocent boy who once played freely in the fields, who looked up to his parents with unwavering trust, had grown into a man entangled in a complex web of resistance and conflict. The ideals he had cherished as a child now seemed muddied by the harsh choices he had to make.

He could almost hear his mother's voice, soft and soothing, guiding him towards the light. But the path of right seemed increasingly elusive, buried under layers of secrecy and violence. The proud, reassuring words of his father seemed hollow against the backdrop of the ever-present threat that loomed over his family and his city.

The ceiling above, a blank canvas in the moonlight, became a screen for his thoughts. He saw himself running through the fields, laughing with his siblings, his mother's voice calling them in for dinner. He saw his father, standing tall and proud, a symbol of strength and integrity. These scenes played out in sharp relief, a painful reminder of what he had lost and what he was fighting to protect.

Michael's heart ached with the weight of these memories. The life he had once known, filled with warmth and certainty, had been replaced by a cold, unyielding reality. The contrast was almost too much to bear. He felt a tear slide down his cheek, a rare release of the emotions he kept tightly bottled up.

He thought about his comrades, the shared sense of purpose that bound them together. Yet, in the quiet of his room, the camaraderie felt distant. It was his family, their faces vivid in his mind, that grounded him. The thought of his actions bringing danger to their doorstep filled him with dread.

As he lay there, the silence of the night pressing in, Michael made a silent promise to himself. He would find a way to navigate this treacherous path, to honor his mother's teachings and his father's legacy while protecting those he loved. The road ahead was fraught with peril, but he would face it with the same resilience that had been passed down to him.

The memories of his childhood, of a time of innocence and clarity, would be his guide. They were a beacon of hope, a reminder of what he was fighting for. As the night wore on and sleep finally began to claim him, Michael clung to those memories, finding solace in the past even as he steeled himself for the future.

Michael's thoughts drifted to the streets of Belfast, to the faces of his neighbors, and the increased military presence. The weight of responsibility for their safety pressed heavily on him. Each decision he made, every action he took, no longer affected just him but rippled through the lives of those around him.

Lying in the quiet darkness of his room, Michael envisioned the bustling streets he knew so well, now shadowed by armored vehicles and patrolled by stern-faced soldiers. He saw Mrs. Flanagan at her market stall, her warm smile replaced by a wary glance over her shoulder. The usual banter with customers had turned into tense, hurried exchanges. "How can I protect them?" he thought, the question echoing in the silence.

The faces of his neighbors, etched with lines of worry and fatigue, filled his mind. Mr. Thompson, once the cornerstone of friendly advice at his hardware store, now moved with a subdued caution. The frequent checkpoints and invasive searches had drained the cheer from his interactions, leaving only a shadow of the camaraderie that once defined the community. "Every choice I make," Michael reflected, "puts them at risk or offers them hope."

The increased military presence was a constant, oppressive reminder of the stakes involved. The sound of boots on pavement, the low hum of helicopters overhead, the ever-watchful surveillance cameras—all these elements were part of the new normal that had seeped into the fabric of daily life. Michael could feel the eyes of his comrades, his family, and his neighbors upon him, expecting him to lead, to make the right choices in this labyrinth of danger and duty.

His thoughts turned to the children, who navigated their way to school through a landscape fraught with tension. Young Danny, clutching his schoolbag, trying to avoid the intimidating gaze of soldiers at the checkpoints. The innocence of his childhood was being overshadowed by a reality far too harsh for his years. "Their futures depend on our actions today," Michael mused, feeling the weight of that truth settle heavily on his chest.

In the evenings, the atmosphere in McAllister's Pub had transformed. The lively laughter and music that once spilled out onto the streets were now muted, replaced by guarded conversations and furtive glances. The patrons, though resolute, carried a palpable tension with them, a collective unease that seemed to deepen with each passing day. "They look to us for strength," Michael thought, "and we cannot afford to let them down."

The responsibility for their safety pressed down on him like a physical weight. Each mission, each strategic decision, had far-reaching implications. A successful operation could bolster their cause, bring a step closer to freedom. But a misstep could invite retaliation, endangering the very people he sought to protect. "Every action ripples," he reminded himself, "through the lives of everyone around us."

As he lay there, staring at the ceiling, Michael knew that his role was not just that of a fighter, but a protector and a guide. The lives intertwined with his were not just names and faces—they were his community, his family. The pressure to navigate this path without causing harm was immense, yet it was a burden he knew he had to bear.

The streets of Belfast, the faces of his neighbors, and the looming military presence were all part of the complex tapestry he was now a part of. The choices he made would define not just his fate, but the fate of an entire community. In the stillness of his room, he resolved to carry this weight with the same strength and resilience that had been instilled in him from a young age.

Michael took a deep breath, grounding himself in the memories of his childhood and the values his parents had taught him. The path ahead was fraught with uncertainty, but he would navigate it with a steadfast heart, driven by the duty to protect and the hope for a better future. As sleep finally began to claim him, he held onto this resolve, knowing that each new day brought both challenges and the opportunity to make a difference.

As dawn broke, Michael's resolve faced a test. The first light of morning crept through the gaps in his curtains, casting long, faint shadows across the room. He lay in bed, the quiet of the early hour amplifying the turmoil within him. His commitment to the cause of Irish freedom – a cause that had defined so much of his life – now battled with the growing fear of the personal cost it demanded.

Rising slowly, Michael walked to the small window and looked out at the awakening city. Belfast, shrouded in the soft morning mist, seemed deceptively peaceful. But he knew better. The streets below, now lit by the first rays of sunlight, were the very same where he had seen armored vehicles patrolling and soldiers standing guard. The familiar landmarks of his childhood had transformed into a landscape marked by conflict and tension.

His thoughts drifted back to the faces of his comrades, the men and women who shared his commitment to the cause. Each one of them carried their own burdens, their own fears and hopes. He had seen their courage, felt their determination, but also sensed their doubts. It was a shared struggle, yet in the quiet moments, it felt intensely personal. The realization that every action he took could ripple through their lives weighed heavily on him.

Michael's mind turned to his family once more. The image of his mother, her gentle eyes filled with both love and worry, flashed before him. "Stay safe," her voice echoed in his memory. The promise he had made to her felt fragile now, a thin thread stretched taut by the demands of his commitment. His father's proud tales of resilience, once a source of inspiration, now seemed to carry a heavier weight. Could he live up to those expectations without losing himself in the process?

The struggle was no longer just external; it had become a deeply personal battle, fought in the silent hours of introspection. Michael ran a hand through his hair, feeling the weariness seep into his bones. The dawn light revealed the signs of his inner conflict – the lines of worry on his face, the tension in his posture. The man he saw in the reflection of the window was both a fighter and a protector, roles that increasingly felt at odds with one another.

Walking to his desk, Michael picked up a small, worn notebook. Its pages were filled with plans, observations, and the occasional note of encouragement from his comrades. Flipping through it, he came across a sketch he had made of the city, marking key locations for their operations. It was a stark reminder of the reality they faced, yet it also brought a sense of clarity. He traced a line on the map with his finger, the familiar route to one of their safe houses, and felt a renewed sense of purpose.

But alongside this purpose, the fear lingered. The fear of what his actions might bring to those he loved, the fear of failing his community, and the fear of losing himself in the process. It was a fear that gnawed at him, relentless and insistent. Michael knew he had to confront it, to find a way to balance his commitment to the cause with the personal cost it demanded.

As the first light of dawn continued to spread, Michael made a silent vow. He would carry the weight of these fears, but he would not let them paralyze him. The struggle for Irish freedom was a path fraught with danger and uncertainty, but it was also a path that demanded courage and resilience. He would honor the sacrifices of those who had come before him and protect the future of those who would follow.

In the stillness of the morning, with the city slowly coming to life around him, Michael felt a shift within himself. The internal battle was far from over, but he had found a new resolve. He would face the dawn, and the days to come, with a steadfast heart, committed to the cause and mindful of the personal cost it demanded. The light of dawn was a reminder that each new day brought both challenges and opportunities, and he was determined to meet them with unwavering resolve.

In response to the heightened tension and surveillance, Michael found himself in a series of intense meetings with other IRA members. They gathered in a nondescript location, away from prying eyes, to discuss the fallout from their recent operations.

The meeting place was a small, dimly lit room in the back of an old warehouse, its walls lined with shelves of forgotten tools and dusty boxes. The air was thick with the smell of oil and damp wood, a stark contrast to the clean, cold scent of the streets outside. Michael arrived early, his footsteps echoing softly in the quiet space as he took a seat at the rough wooden table that dominated the center of the room.

One by one, his comrades filtered in, their faces etched with concern and determination. Seamus, a burly man with a weathered face, nodded grimly as he took his place. Next came Fiona, her sharp eyes scanning the room as she settled into her chair, followed by Liam, whose normally cheerful demeanor was replaced by a somber intensity.

The discussions began in hushed tones, the weight of their situation palpable. Michael leaned forward, his elbows resting on the table, listening intently as Seamus spoke first. "Our last operation has put us under even more scrutiny," he said, his voice low and gravelly. "We need to be more careful, more precise."

Fiona nodded in agreement, her brow furrowed in concentration. "The British forces are increasing their patrols and checkpoints," she added. "We can't afford any mistakes. One slip, and it could cost us everything."

The atmosphere in the room was tense, each member acutely aware of the stakes. Michael's mind raced as he considered the recent events, the increased military presence, and the ever-present surveillance. The eyes of the community, his family, and his comrades were on him, expecting him to lead with both courage and caution.

"We need to adapt," Michael said, his voice steady but filled with conviction. "We must stay one step ahead. Our operations need to be smarter, more calculated. We can't let them crush our spirit."

The room fell silent as his words hung in the air. Each person there understood the gravity of their situation. They were not just fighting a physical battle; they were fighting a psychological one as well. The constant pressure, the fear of being watched, the need to protect their loved ones—all these elements weighed heavily on their shoulders.

Liam broke the silence, his voice soft but resolute. "We need to gather more intel, find out their patterns, their weaknesses. If we know what they're planning, we can counteract it."

Fiona leaned forward, her eyes glinting with determination. "I can reach out to our contacts," she said. "We need to rebuild our network, ensure our communications are secure."

As the discussions continued, Michael felt a renewed sense of purpose. Despite the heightened tension and surveillance, despite the fear and uncertainty, there was a shared commitment in the room. They were united by a common cause, driven by a shared vision of freedom and justice.

The meeting went on for hours, plans forming and evolving as they brainstormed and debated. By the time they finally dispersed, the sun was beginning to rise, casting a pale light through the grimy windows of the warehouse. Michael stood for a moment, watching as his comrades left, each one disappearing into the early morning mist, blending back into the fabric of the city.

He took a deep breath, the cold air filling his lungs, and felt a sense of clarity. The path ahead was fraught with danger, but he was not alone. They were a community, a family, bound together by their shared struggle. And together, they would find a way to navigate the challenges that lay ahead.

As he stepped out into the street, the city waking up around him, Michael's resolve hardened. The meetings, the plans, the discussions—they were all steps towards a greater goal. The fight for freedom was not just about grand gestures, but about the quiet, determined steps they took each day. And he was ready to take those steps, no matter the cost.

These planning sessions were a crucible of ideas, with each member bringing their perspective to the table. The room buzzed with a tense energy as the members of the IRA gathered around the worn wooden table, their faces illuminated by the dim overhead light. The air was thick with the scent of dust and determination.

Michael sat at the head of the table, his eyes scanning the room, taking in the expressions of his comrades. Each face told a story of sacrifice and resolve, each perspective shaped by personal experiences and convictions. He listened carefully, his mind working to weigh the different viewpoints and understand the delicate balance between aggression and restraint.

Seamus leaned forward, his voice a low rumble. "We need to hit them hard, make them feel the cost of their occupation," he argued, his fists clenched on the table. "A show of strength will remind them that we won't back down."

Fiona, ever the strategist, shook her head. "Strength is important, but so is precision," she countered, her tone measured and calm. "We can't afford unnecessary risks. Every action must be calculated to avoid collateral damage. We need the support of our community, not their fear."

Liam, who had a knack for gathering intel, chimed in. "Our intelligence must be solid. We need to know their movements, their plans, so we can act decisively and minimize our exposure. A single mistake could unravel everything we've worked for."

Michael absorbed their words, feeling the weight of their arguments. The debates were intense, each member passionately defending their position, but there was also a mutual respect in the room. These discussions were not just about forming immediate plans; they were about understanding the broader implications of their struggle.

The conversations ebbed and flowed, each point carefully considered. Michael watched as ideas were dissected, reformed, and polished. The dynamic interplay of aggression and restraint was a constant theme. They needed to strike a balance that would keep their cause alive without alienating the very people they sought to liberate.

"We need a unified strategy," Michael said finally, his voice cutting through the heated debate. "We must be bold, but we must also be wise. Every move we make reflects on our cause and impacts our community. We cannot afford to act rashly."

He could see the understanding in their eyes, the recognition of the complexities they faced. These planning sessions were shaping not only their tactics but also their collective understanding of the struggle they were engaged in. The nuances of their fight were becoming clearer, the lines between right and wrong more defined yet more challenging to navigate.

Fiona nodded, a hint of a smile playing on her lips. "Agreed. We need to be smart about this. Let's outline our next steps with precision and care."

The group bent over their maps and notes, their voices a mix of urgency and determination. They discussed potential targets, analyzed intelligence, and refined their strategies. Each idea was scrutinized, each plan meticulously crafted.

Through these sessions, Michael's understanding of their struggle deepened. He saw the broader picture, the interplay of political, social, and personal factors that shaped their fight. The responsibility he felt was immense, but so was his resolve.

As the meeting drew to a close, Michael looked around the room, feeling a renewed sense of purpose. The planning sessions had been a crucible of ideas, forging a stronger, more cohesive strategy. They had emerged with a clearer vision, united by their commitment to their cause and to each other.

Walking out of the meeting, the early morning air crisp and cool, Michael felt a profound sense of clarity. The struggle they were engaged in was complex, fraught with danger and uncertainty, but it was also driven by a deep and abiding hope. Each planning session, each debate, was a step forward, a testament to their resilience and their unwavering belief in a better future.

The path ahead was still fraught with challenges, but Michael knew they were not alone. Together, they would navigate the delicate balance between aggression and restraint, fighting for their cause with both strength and wisdom. And in doing so, they would honor the spirit of Belfast and the enduring resilience of its people.

In the ongoing discussions, the tension was palpable as IRA members grappled with the changing dynamics of their struggle. The small room, dimly lit and filled with the quiet hum of nervous energy, served as a battleground for their conflicting perspectives. Michael sat at the head of the table, feeling the weight of their collective uncertainty.

Seamus, his face etched with years of hardship, spoke first, his voice rough and impassioned. "We need to hit them hard," he declared, slamming his fist on the table. "A stronger response will show them we're not backing down. Every time they tighten their grip, we need to break free with more force. It's the only way they'll respect our resolve."

Across the table, Fiona folded her arms, her gaze steady and calm. "And what happens when they retaliate?" she asked, her voice cool but firm. "We're not just talking about soldiers in uniform. We're talking about our families, our neighbors. Every action we take has repercussions. We need to think about the bigger picture."

The room fell into a tense silence, the air thick with unspoken fears and unresolved conflicts. Michael watched as the others absorbed Fiona's words. She had a point, and they all knew it. The line between aggression and recklessness was thin, and crossing it could mean devastating consequences for the very people they sought to protect.

Liam, ever the voice of reason, leaned forward, his hands clasped together on the table. "Intelligence gathering is key," he said. "We need to know their moves before they make them. This isn't just about brute force; it's about outsmarting them. We build our network, gain the community's trust, and use that information to strike strategically."

A murmur of agreement rippled through the room, but the tension remained. The stakes were high, and every decision felt like a step into the unknown. Michael could see the weariness in their eyes, the scars of a prolonged struggle etched deeply into their expressions. They were tired, but they were also determined.

"We can't ignore the community," Fiona added, her voice softer now but no less resolute. "Their support is our strength. If we lose them, we lose everything."

Seamus shook his head, frustration evident in his stance. "I'm not saying we forget the community. But if we keep playing it safe, they'll see us as weak. We need to show them we're still in this fight, that we're willing to make the hard choices."

The debate continued, each argument revealing the deep-rooted convictions and fears within the group. Michael listened carefully, weighing the different viewpoints, understanding that finding a balance was crucial. They needed to be strong, but they also needed to be smart.

"We must remember why we're here," Michael said, breaking the silence that had settled over the room. "Our goal is freedom, but freedom comes at a cost. We need to be strategic in our actions, mindful of the impact on our community, but also resolute in our fight. It's not an easy path, but it's the only way forward."

The room grew quiet, the members reflecting on his words. They were united by a common cause, but the way forward was fraught with complexity. The tension, though heavy, was a testament to their commitment to finding the best path forward.

As the discussions drew to a close, Michael felt a renewed sense of purpose. The debates had not just shaped their immediate plans but had deepened his understanding of the complexities of their struggle. The balance between aggression and restraint was delicate, but it was a balance they had to find.

Leaving the meeting, the cool night air hit him, a stark contrast to the heated debates inside. Michael looked up at the sky, the stars barely visible through the haze. He took a deep breath, steeling himself for the challenges ahead. The path was uncertain, but the resolve within their group was strong. They would navigate this together, each decision carefully weighed, each step taken with the goal of a brighter future for Belfast.

In the quiet of the night, as the city around him settled into a tense stillness, Michael knew that their struggle was far from over. But he also knew that with each debate, each plan, and each action, they were forging a path forward, guided by the strength of their convictions and the resilience of their community.

Michael, caught in the middle of this ideological divide, found himself reflecting on the values that had drawn him to the IRA. The principles of freedom, justice, and resilience that had been instilled in him from a young age now faced the harsh realities of their struggle. His voice became crucial in these debates, as he sought to bridge the gap between the two perspectives.

In the dimly lit room, the discussions grew more heated, each side fervently defending their stance. Michael leaned back in his chair, his mind racing with thoughts and memories. He remembered his father's tales of Irish resilience, the pride in his voice when he spoke of their ancestors' struggles. He thought of his mother's gentle admonitions to always choose the path of right. These values were the foundation of his commitment, and they guided him now as he listened to the impassioned arguments around him.

Seamus was in the midst of another fiery speech, his fists clenched as he spoke. "We can't keep hiding in the shadows, waiting for the perfect moment," he argued. "We need to show them that we're still here, still fighting. A stronger response will make them think twice about their next move."

Fiona countered with her usual calm demeanor. "And what about the backlash, Seamus? What about the innocent lives caught in the crossfire? We need to be smart, not just strong. Our actions have consequences, and we can't afford to lose the support of our community."

The room fell silent as Michael leaned forward, his gaze steady and thoughtful. "We need a strategy that honors both perspectives," he began, his voice clear and measured. "We can't afford to act recklessly, but we also can't be paralyzed by fear. We need to balance cautious planning with decisive action."

He paused, letting his words sink in. The eyes of his comrades were fixed on him, the weight of their expectations pressing heavily. "Here's what I propose," he continued. "We gather as much intelligence as we can, identify key targets that will have a significant impact, and plan our actions meticulously. When we strike, we do so with precision and purpose, minimizing the risk to civilians. We show our strength through smart, strategic moves, not just brute force."

Seamus looked skeptical but intrigued. "And what if we get it wrong? What if our cautious approach gives them time to strengthen their defenses?"

Michael nodded, acknowledging the concern. "That's a risk, but it's one we can mitigate with thorough planning and solid intelligence. We need to be adaptable, ready to shift our tactics as the situation evolves. Our goal is to make each action count, to demonstrate our resolve without causing unnecessary harm."

Fiona smiled slightly, a glimmer of hope in her eyes. "It's a delicate balance, but I think it's possible. If we combine our strengths—Seamus's determination, Liam's intelligence work, and the community support we've been building—we can create a strategy that works."

The tension in the room began to ease as the members considered Michael's proposal. It was a middle ground, a path that respected the need for action while recognizing the importance of caution. The debates that had seemed insurmountable began to transform into a collaborative effort to refine their approach.

Liam nodded thoughtfully. "I can double down on our intelligence efforts, make sure we have the best possible information before we act. With solid intel, we can strike effectively and efficiently."

Seamus, though still visibly concerned, seemed to soften. "Alright, Michael. I see where you're coming from. If we can hit them hard and smart, I'm in. But we need to be ready to adapt if things go sideways."

The room filled with a renewed sense of purpose as the members began to outline the specifics of their new strategy. Maps were spread out, notes were taken, and roles were assigned. Michael watched as his comrades worked together, their collective energy directed towards a common goal.

As the meeting drew to a close, Michael felt a sense of accomplishment. He had managed to bridge the ideological divide, guiding the group towards a strategy that balanced aggression with caution. The path ahead was still fraught with challenges, but they now had a clearer direction, a plan that honored their values and addressed the complexities of their struggle.

Leaving the meeting, Michael stepped into the cool night air, his heart filled with a renewed resolve. The discussions had been intense, but they had also been productive. He knew that the balance they sought would not be easy to maintain, but with careful planning and unwavering commitment, they could navigate the difficult terrain ahead.

The city around him was quiet, the tension still palpable but now tinged with a sense of hope. Michael walked through the streets of Belfast, determined to lead his comrades with both strength and wisdom. The struggle for freedom was far from over, but they were ready to face whatever came next, united by their shared vision and their unyielding spirit.

The meetings often went on for hours, with passionate discussions and strategic planning. The air in the small, dimly lit room was thick with the intensity of their debates, the walls echoing with the fervent voices of men and women committed to their cause. Michael's involvement in these sessions marked a significant development in his role within the IRA. He was no longer just a participant in operations but was now actively shaping the organization's response to the challenges they faced.

Each meeting was a crucible of ideas and emotions, with members bringing their experiences and perspectives to the table. Seamus, with his fiery determination, often pushed for aggressive actions, his voice rising as he emphasized the need to show strength. Fiona, calm and strategic, countered with arguments for caution and precision, her words carefully chosen to advocate for a smarter approach.

Michael sat at the head of the table, his presence commanding respect. He listened intently to each speaker, his mind processing the flood of information and viewpoints. His eyes scanned the room, noting the expressions of his comrades – the furrowed brows, the clenched fists, the thoughtful nods. He knew that each voice mattered, that finding a balance was crucial.

One night, as the discussions stretched into the early hours, Michael found himself leading the charge. "We need to find a middle ground," he began, his voice steady and clear. "Aggression alone won't win this fight, but neither will inaction. We must combine our strengths – Seamus's resolve and Fiona's strategic thinking – to craft a response that is both bold and calculated."

The room fell silent as he continued. "Our recent operations have put us under intense scrutiny. The increased military presence means we need to be more careful, but it also offers opportunities if we act wisely. We must gather intelligence, understand their patterns, and strike when the moment is right."

Liam, ever the pragmatist, nodded in agreement. "Intelligence is our greatest weapon," he said. "If we know their moves, we can anticipate their actions and respond effectively. We need to build a network of informants, strengthen our communication channels, and ensure that every decision is based on solid information."

Fiona leaned forward, her eyes locking with Michael's. "And we need to keep the community on our side," she added. "Their support is our lifeline. If we lose them, we lose everything."

The group nodded, the tension easing as a plan began to take shape. They worked together, their discussions transforming into actionable steps. Maps were spread out, notes were scribbled, and strategies were debated and refined. The hours flew by, but the energy in the room never waned.

Michael's role had evolved. He was no longer just another voice in the crowd but a leader who could bridge the ideological divides and guide the group toward a cohesive strategy. His ability to listen, to weigh different perspectives, and to articulate a balanced approach had earned him the respect of his comrades.

As dawn approached and the meeting drew to a close, Michael felt a profound sense of accomplishment. They had crafted a plan that balanced aggression with caution, a strategy that honored their commitment to the cause while protecting the community they served. The challenges ahead were daunting, but they were prepared to face them with a united front.

Leaving the meeting, Michael stepped into the crisp morning air, the weight of his new responsibilities settling on his shoulders. The city around him was still and quiet, the first light of day breaking over the rooftops. He walked through the empty streets, his mind filled with the discussions and decisions of the night.

The journey ahead was fraught with uncertainty, but Michael knew that they were stronger together. His role within the IRA had changed, but his commitment to their cause remained unwavering. He would continue to lead with both strength and wisdom, guiding his comrades through the complexities of their struggle.

As he reached his home, the resolve in his heart solidified. The meetings, the debates, and the plans were all part of a larger mission – a mission to achieve freedom and justice for Belfast. Michael was ready to face whatever came next, confident in the knowledge that he was not alone in this fight. Together, they would navigate the challenges, united by their shared vision and their unyielding spirit.

As each meeting adjourned, Michael left with a sense of the weighty responsibilities that came with his increased involvement. The intense discussions and debates not only prepared him for the challenges ahead but also reinforced his commitment to the cause, despite the personal struggles he faced.

The room, once buzzing with fervent dialogue and strategic planning, gradually emptied as members departed one by one. The air, still thick with the echoes of their impassioned voices, seemed to hum with the residual energy of their resolve. Michael lingered for a moment, taking a deep breath and letting the weight of his new role settle on his shoulders.

He walked out into the night, the cool breeze offering a momentary respite from the intensity of the meetings. The streets of Belfast, quiet and dimly lit, stretched out before him like a labyrinth of uncertainty and promise. Each step he took was measured, the gravity of his decisions resonating with every footfall.

Michael's mind replayed the scenes from the meetings. Seamus's fervent calls for bold action, Fiona's calm and calculated arguments, and Liam's pragmatic insights – all these perspectives had woven together to form a complex tapestry of strategy and resolve. As he reflected on the discussions, he felt a deepened understanding of the delicate balance they needed to maintain.

The debates had been fierce, but they had also been enlightening. Michael had seen the fire in his comrades' eyes, the unwavering determination that drove them forward. He knew that their strength lay not just in their numbers, but in their ability to listen, adapt, and unite around a common goal. The commitment to their cause was palpable, and it fueled his own resolve.

Walking through the familiar streets, Michael couldn't help but think of his family. The faces of his parents and siblings floated before him, their expressions a mix of pride and concern. His mother's gentle admonitions and his father's tales of resilience echoed in his mind, reminding him of the values that had shaped his path. The personal struggles he faced were real, but so was the duty he felt to honor their legacy.

He paused at a street corner, the distant hum of the city enveloping him in a contemplative silence. The responsibilities of his role weighed heavily, but they also brought a clarity of purpose. Michael understood that every decision he made, every strategy he crafted, had far-reaching implications. It was not just about fighting; it was about protecting, leading, and ensuring that their actions aligned with their principles.

The meetings had become a crucible, forging not just plans but also fortifying his commitment. The path ahead was fraught with danger and uncertainty, but it was also illuminated by the shared vision of his comrades. They were not just fighting for freedom; they were fighting to preserve the essence of their community, their way of life.

As dawn approached, painting the sky with hues of orange and pink, Michael felt a renewed sense of determination. The personal struggles he faced – the fears, the doubts, the constant worry for his family – were all part of the larger tapestry of their struggle. Each challenge was a test of his resolve, a step towards a future he believed in with all his heart.

He resumed his walk, the morning light casting long shadows on the pavement. The city was waking up, and with it, the relentless push towards their goal. Michael knew that the road ahead would be arduous, but he was ready to face it with unwavering courage. The weighty responsibilities of his role were a testament to his growth, his evolving understanding of leadership and sacrifice.

Arriving home, Michael took one last look at the awakening city. The meetings had prepared him, but they had also transformed him. He was no longer just a participant in the struggle; he was a leader, a protector, a beacon of hope for those who looked to him for guidance. The personal cost was high, but the cause was worth every sacrifice.

With a heart full of resolve and a mind sharpened by the debates, Michael stepped inside, ready to face whatever the future held. The commitment to the cause, strengthened by each meeting, each discussion, and each personal struggle, would guide him through the complexities of their fight for freedom.

Chapter 3: A Patriotic Flame Amidst The Fog Of War

N the shadowed corners of Belfast, under a blanket of uneasy darkness, Michael and his team huddled in a cramped, dimly lit room. The single bulb hanging from the ceiling flickered intermittently, casting erratic shadows on the peeling wallpaper. The air was thick with the scent of sweat and stale smoke, a tangible manifestation of the tension that gripped them all. Each creak of the floorboards, each distant sound from the street outside, seemed amplified in the oppressive silence, serving as a stark reminder of the peril that surrounded them.

Michael's heart pounded in his chest, a relentless rhythm that matched the urgency of their situation. His eyes, sharp and focused, scanned the faces of his comrades, each etched with a mixture of determination and fear. Beside him, Sean fidgeted nervously, his fingers tapping a restless beat on the wooden table. The usually stoic Liam, his jaw set in a grim line, stared at the map spread out before them, tracing potential escape routes with a calloused finger. Brendan adjusted the strap of his rifle, his gaze steely and unyielding, reflecting the fierce resolve that had become his trademark.

The room, once a modest living space, now served as their impromptu command center. The faded floral curtains did little to muffle the distant sounds of Belfast's troubled night – the sporadic bursts of gunfire, the wail of sirens, and the occasional roar of an armored vehicle passing by. These sounds, once alien, had become a grim symphony to their nightly activities.

They had just received urgent news: one of the IRA's safe houses, a covert repository of their arms, had been raided. The message had come through a breathless courier, a young lad who barely escaped the tightening net of British patrols. Now, they faced a critical mission – to relocate the remaining weapons cache before it fell into the hands of the British forces. The stakes were higher than ever; the loss of these arms could cripple their operations, and worse, lead to the capture of more of their comrades.

Michael broke the silence, his voice low and steady, yet brimming with a quiet intensity. "We don't have much time. We need to move fast and stay invisible. The British are combing the area, and they'll be on us in no time if we make a wrong move."

Sean nodded, his usual bravado tempered by the gravity of the situation. "I've scouted a couple of routes. They're risky, but it's our best shot."

Liam, still studying the map, added, "We'll need to split up to cover more ground and avoid detection. and I Brendan will take the east route. Michael, you and Sean cover the west. We'll regroup at the old distillery by dawn."

Brendan's eyes met Michael's, a silent exchange of trust and mutual resolve. "We've done this before, and we'll do it again," she said, her voice firm.

Michael took a deep breath, feeling the weight of responsibility settle on his shoulders. "Alright, let's get moving. Stay sharp, stay safe."

As they gathered their gear, the room buzzed with a renewed sense of purpose. The familiar clink of weapons being loaded, the rustle of maps being folded, and the murmured words of strategy blended into a ritual that, despite the danger, brought a sense of solidarity.

They were not just a team; they were a family, bound together by their shared struggle and unyielding spirit.

Outside, the night was thick with fog, the damp air chilling their bones as they stepped into the alley. Michael led the way, his senses heightened, every shadow and sound a potential threat. The city, shrouded in darkness, seemed to hold its breath, waiting for the next move in this deadly game of cat and mouse. As they navigated the labyrinthine streets, the weight of their mission pressed heavily on them, but so too did their determination to succeed.

Each step they took was a defiance, a testament to their resilience and their unwavering commitment to the cause. In the heart of Belfast's troubled night, amidst the shadows and the fear, Michael and his team moved with a singular purpose – to protect their people, to fight for their freedom, and to ensure that their struggle would not be in vain.

The room, usually a place for quiet planning and resolute decisions, was now a hub of hurried activity. The once orderly space was now chaotic, with maps spread out across the worn wooden table, edges curling from constant use. The dim light from the flickering bulb overhead cast long shadows, adding to the sense of urgency that pervaded the room.

Michael leaned over one of the maps, his brow furrowed in concentration as he traced possible routes with a finger. The others gathered around him, their faces illuminated by the pale light, reflecting a mixture of determination and anxiety. The air was thick with the scent of sweat and the faint, lingering smell of gun oil.

"We need to move these weapons tonight," Michael said, his voice barely above a whisper, yet carrying the weight of the situation.

"If the British forces get their hands on them, it could cripple our operations."

Brendan, standing next to him, nodded, her eyes scanning the map for potential pitfalls. "We've got two main routes, but both are risky," she said, her voice steady despite the tension. "The main road is faster, but it's likely to be patrolled. The back alleys are safer, but they'll take longer."

Sean, tapping his fingers on the table, added, "We could split the load, send some through each route. It's a gamble, but it might increase our chances."

Liam, always the pragmatist, shook his head. "Too many variables. If one group gets caught, we lose half the cache. We need to stick together, move quickly and quietly."

The room buzzed with the sound of rustling paper and the murmur of strategic discussions. The gravity of their task hung heavily in the air, an unspoken understanding that failure was not an option. The loss of the weapons would be a significant blow to their operations, a risk they couldn't afford.

Michael straightened up, his mind made up. "Alright, we go through the alleys. It's slower, but safer. We stick together, keep communication tight. If anything goes wrong, we regroup at the old distillery."

As they prepared to move, the tension in the room escalated. Each member of the team checked their gear, ensuring everything was in place. The familiar sounds of weapons being loaded, the click of safety catches being released, and the rustle of jackets filled the room, blending into a soundtrack of readiness.

Michael glanced around at his team, catching each of their eyes. "We've done this before. We know what's at stake. Let's get it done."

The room fell silent for a moment, a collective breath held as they steeled themselves for the task ahead. Then, with a final nod, Michael led the way, the team falling into step behind him.

Outside, the night was dense with fog, the air cool and damp. The city, usually bustling with activity, was eerily quiet, as if holding its breath in anticipation. The streets, illuminated only by the occasional flicker of a streetlamp, seemed to stretch endlessly into the darkness.

As they moved through the back alleys, every sound was amplified – the distant barking of a dog, the soft hum of an approaching car, the faint murmur of voices. The shadows seemed to close in around them, each step a careful, calculated move to avoid detection.

The importance of their task was clear in every glance, every whispered word of caution. The loss of the weapons would be a significant blow to their operations, a risk they couldn't afford. But as they navigated the labyrinthine streets of Belfast, their resolve hardened. They were not just fighting for their cause; they were fighting for each other, for the hope of a future free from oppression.

With each step, they moved closer to their goal, driven by a shared sense of purpose and the unyielding spirit that bound them together. In the shadowed corners of Belfast, under a blanket of uneasy darkness, Michael and his team pressed on, determined to succeed against all odds.

Ashling, with a calm demeanor that belied the racing of her heart, quickly assigned roles and divided the cache. The room, now a hive of activity, buzzed with a tense energy. The weight of their mission hung heavily over them, yet Ashling's steady voice provided a much-needed anchor. Her sharp eyes moved from one team member to the next, assessing and directing with practiced precision.

"Sean, you'll take the eastern route," she instructed, her tone firm. "Liam, you cover the north. Brendan, you and Michael will handle the west. We need to split the cache evenly."

Each member nodded, their faces set with determination. They moved with purpose, methodically concealing weapons beneath their coats and stowing smaller arms in unassuming bags. The clinking of metal was muted by layers of fabric, but the weight of the arsenal was a constant reminder of the perilous task at hand.

Ashling handed Michael a bag, her fingers brushing against his briefly, a silent exchange of trust and resolve. "Stay low and stay alert," she said, her voice barely above a whisper. "The streets are crawling with patrols."

Michael gave a curt nod, feeling the reassuring weight of the concealed weapon against his side. "We'll be careful," he promised, his voice steady despite the tension coiling in his chest.

The air outside was thick with the damp chill of an Irish night, and the fog that clung to the cobblestones seemed to swallow sound. Every step they took was measured, their breaths controlled, as they moved through the maze-like alleys of Belfast. The usual hum of the city was replaced by an eerie quiet, broken only by the occasional distant rumble of an armored vehicle or the sharp bark of orders from a patrol.

The group dispersed, each heading in their assigned direction. Ashling took a moment to steady herself, her back pressed against the cold stone of a building. The weight of responsibility pressed heavily on her shoulders, but she pushed it aside, focusing instead on the task at hand.

The streets were more dangerous than ever, with increased patrols and the watchful eyes of the British army at every turn. Ashling moved with a deceptive ease, her steps light and sure. She kept to the shadows, blending into the night, her senses heightened to every sound and movement around her.

She could hear the distant echo of boots on pavement, the low murmur of soldiers' voices as they passed by, oblivious to her presence. Each sound sent a spike of adrenaline through her, but she kept her breathing steady, her mind focused. The memory of the raided safe house was fresh in her mind, a stark reminder of the consequences of failure.

Ashling spotted a pair of soldiers at the end of the street, their silhouettes barely visible in the fog. She paused, pressing herself into a doorway, her heartbeat thundering in her ears. The soldiers exchanged a few words before continuing their patrol, their figures disappearing into the mist. She waited a few moments longer, ensuring they were gone, before slipping back into the shadows.

The weight of the concealed weapons was a constant reminder of their mission's urgency. Each step brought them closer to their goal, but also deeper into danger. The streets of Belfast, with their hidden corners and narrow passages, had become a treacherous landscape of potential traps and ambushes.

Michael and Brendan moved silently, their footsteps muffled by the thick fog. They communicated with brief, silent gestures, their movements synchronized by years of shared struggle. The familiarity of the alleys provided little comfort, as each turn held the possibility of an encounter with the enemy.

As they approached a known checkpoint, Michael signaled for them to stop. They crouched behind a low wall, peering through the gloom. The checkpoint was manned by three soldiers, their rifles slung casually over their shoulders. The light from their torches cut through the fog, creating shifting patterns of light and shadow.

"We need to find another way," Michael whispered, his breath visible in the cold night air. Brendan nodded, her eyes scanning their surroundings for an alternate route.

They backtracked, moving swiftly and silently through the narrow lanes. The tension was palpable, but so was their determination. Each of them carried not just weapons, but the hopes and future of their cause.

The night stretched on, a relentless test of their resolve and endurance. Ashling, Michael, Brendan, and the rest of the team navigated the dangerous streets with a blend of caution and courage, their every movement a testament to their unyielding spirit. In the heart of Belfast's uneasy darkness, they pressed on, driven by the necessity of their mission and the unwavering belief in their fight for freedom.

The team moved with efficiency, their actions driven by the pressing need for speed and stealth. The room, once a sanctuary of quiet planning and resolute decisions, was now a hub of hurried activity. Maps were spread out, routes discussed in hushed, urgent tones. The importance of their task was clear: the loss of the weapons would be a significant blow to their operations, a risk they couldn't afford.

As they readied themselves to step into the cool night air, there was a final exchange of determined glances. Ashling, with a calm demeanor that belied the racing of her heart, quickly assigned roles and divided the cache. Each member was to transport a part of the arsenal, concealing it beneath coats and in unassuming bags. Their movements had to be discreet, for the streets of Belfast were more dangerous than ever, with increased patrols and the watchful eyes of the British army at every turn.

The dim light from the single bulb overhead flickered, casting long, shifting shadows on the peeling wallpaper. The air was thick with the scent of sweat and stale smoke, the palpable tension a living, breathing entity among them. Ashling's voice, calm yet commanding, cut through the silence. "Sean, you'll take the eastern route. Liam, you cover the north. Brendan, you and Michael will handle the west."

Michael nodded, feeling the reassuring weight of the concealed weapon against his side. Brendan adjusted his coat, ensuring the hidden arsenal was secure. Sean and Liam shared a brief look of mutual understanding before turning back to their tasks. The gravity of the situation was unspoken but deeply felt by all.

As they stepped into the night, the chill of the air was a stark contrast to the stifling tension inside. The fog hung low, wrapping the streets in a blanket of anonymity. The distant sounds of Belfast's troubled night – the occasional bark of a dog, the muffled hum of a car engine – were absorbed into the dense, quiet night. Each footfall was deliberate and muted, their breaths controlled and shallow.

Ashling moved with a deceptive ease, her steps light and assured. The weight of the concealed weapons was a constant reminder of their mission's urgency. She led the way through the narrow alleys, her eyes constantly scanning the shadows for any sign of danger.

The team followed, their movements synchronized and silent, each step a testament to their discipline and resolve.

Every corner turned, every shadow passed, held the potential for danger. The watchful eyes of the British army were everywhere, and the increased patrols meant that even the smallest mistake could be catastrophic. As they navigated the maze-like streets, the familiar pathways provided little comfort; each turn was a calculated risk.

Approaching a known checkpoint, Ashling signaled for a halt. The team crouched low, their breaths barely audible in the still night. The faint glow of a torch and the low murmur of soldiers' voices indicated a patrol ahead. Michael and Brendan exchanged a quick look, their shared history and trust evident in their synchronized movements.

Ashling motioned for them to follow her lead. With the grace of a dancer and the precision of a soldier, she maneuvered around the checkpoint, using the shadows to her advantage. The team followed, their movements fluid and silent, blending seamlessly into the night.

Once past the checkpoint, they continued through the fog-shrouded streets, their destination drawing nearer with each step. The old distillery loomed ahead, a familiar silhouette emerging from the mist, promising refuge and the completion of their perilous task.

Before entering, there was a final exchange of determined glances. This was more than a mission; it was a testament to their commitment, a dangerous dance with fate they were all too willing to engage in for their cause. United by their shared purpose and the unyielding spirit that bound them, they pressed on into the night, ready to face whatever dangers lay ahead.

With the weight of the weapons pressing against them, both physically and metaphorically, they stepped out into the night. The city, a maze of shadows and uncertainty, lay before them, its once familiar streets now a treacherous path to navigate. The mission had begun, a race against time and enemy, fraught with peril at every turn.

The chill of the night air was a stark contrast to the oppressive heat inside, the fog wrapping around them like a shroud. Every sound was amplified – the soft scuff of boots on cobblestones, the distant murmur of a patrol, the occasional creak of a door – each one a potential threat.

Ashling led the way, her steps quick and silent, her eyes scanning the dimly lit streets for any sign of danger. Michael followed close behind, his senses heightened, every nerve on edge. The concealed weapons weighed heavily, a constant reminder of the high stakes.

The narrow alleys provided cover but also heightened the risk of ambush. The familiar routes now seemed alien, transformed by the oppressive presence of the British patrols. Each corner turned was a calculated risk, every shadow a potential hiding place for the enemy.

Brendan and Liam brought up the rear, their movements synchronized with the rest of the team. The fog thickened as they moved deeper into the heart of the city, muffling their footsteps but also obscuring their vision. The distant glow of streetlights created a surreal, shifting landscape, adding to the sense of disorientation.

As they approached the first checkpoint, Ashling raised her hand, signaling a halt. The team crouched low, their breaths shallow and controlled. The faint glow of a torch and the low murmur of soldiers' voices drifted through the fog. They exchanged quick, determined glances, the unspoken understanding clear: failure was not an option.

With a final nod from Ashling, they moved forward, slipping through the shadows with practiced ease. The checkpoint loomed ahead, a formidable obstacle in their path. The soldiers' voices grew louder, the torchlight cutting through the fog in erratic beams. The team pressed on, their movements a blend of stealth and urgency.

Navigating the checkpoint required precision and nerve. They moved in unison, their bodies tense with anticipation. Each step was deliberate, each movement calculated to avoid detection. The weight of the weapons pressed against them, a physical and metaphorical burden they bore with grim determination.

Once past the checkpoint, they continued through the labyrinthine streets, the old distillery drawing nearer with each step. The familiar silhouette of the building emerged from the mist, a beacon in the treacherous night. The team paused, taking a moment to gather their thoughts and reaffirm their resolve.

This mission was more than a task; it was a testament to their commitment, a dangerous dance with fate they were all too willing to engage in for their cause. United by their shared purpose and the unyielding spirit that bound them, they pressed on, ready to face whatever dangers lay ahead.

The streets of Belfast, usually familiar and navigable, now presented a labyrinth of risks. Sean led the team through less frequented alleys and side streets, his knowledge of the city's nooks and crannies more crucial than ever. Every shadow, every unexpected sound made them tense, ready to react.

The fog clung to the ground, weaving through the cobblestones and curling around their legs like a ghostly serpent. The cold air bit at their faces, but they pressed on, the urgency of their mission driving them forward. Sean moved with a cautious confidence, his eyes darting from side to side, ears tuned to the slightest noise. He knew these back alleys well – every twist, every turn – but tonight, they felt different, menacing.

Ashling, just behind him, kept her hand close to her concealed weapon, her breath steady but shallow. The weight of the arsenal was a constant reminder of the stakes. Michael, Brendan, and Liam followed, their movements synchronized, each step taken with deliberate care to avoid making a sound.

A distant clang of metal caused them to freeze, hearts pounding in unison. Sean raised a hand, signaling for silence. They listened, straining to hear through the thick silence of the night. The sound didn't repeat, but the tension remained, a coiled spring ready to snap.

The alleys, usually bustling with life during the day, were eerily silent, the usual noises of the city muffled by the dense fog. Their path was lit only by the occasional flicker of a streetlamp, casting long, distorted shadows that seemed to dance and shift as they moved. The fog played tricks on their eyes, making every shape and movement suspect.

Sean led them through a narrow passageway, the walls pressing in close. The air was thick with the smell of damp stone and decay. He paused at the entrance to a wider street, peering around the corner to check for patrols. The distant murmur of voices sent a chill down his spine, but the street ahead was clear.

"All clear," he whispered, his voice barely audible. The team moved swiftly but cautiously, their senses heightened. Every creak of a floorboard, every rustle of leaves was scrutinized, their nerves stretched thin by the ever-present threat of discovery.

As they continued, a dog barked somewhere in the distance, followed by a sharp command. The sound was too close for comfort. Sean signaled for them to duck into a nearby doorway, pressing themselves against the cold, rough brick. They waited, breaths held, as a patrol passed by, their boots clomping heavily on the cobblestones.

The team exchanged tense glances, the gravity of their situation mirrored in each other's eyes. The patrol moved on, the noise fading into the night. Sean gave a nod, and they slipped back into the alley, moving with renewed urgency.

The route Sean chose was winding and complex, taking them through seldom-used paths. The familiarity of the cityscape offered little comfort; each turn felt like a potential ambush. The fog thickened, and the air grew colder, but they pressed on, driven by their mission and the weight of their cause.

Every shadow, every unexpected sound made them tense, ready to react. They were a well-oiled machine, each member playing their part with precision. The labyrinthine streets of Belfast challenged them, but their resolve was unyielding.

As they neared their destination, the sense of peril grew, but so did their determination. The old distillery was just ahead, its silhouette barely visible through the fog. They paused one last time, exchanging determined glances. The mission had begun, a race against time and enemy, fraught with peril at every turn, but they were ready.

The presence of British military patrols, more frequent and vigilant in the wake of recent IRA activities, was a constant threat. The patrols, often abrupt and invasive in their searches, had become an ominous part of the city's nightly routine. Michael's team had to be vigilant, timing their movements with precision and care to avoid detection.

The fog-draped streets of Belfast were now a chessboard of potential danger, each move calculated to avoid the probing eyes of the patrols. The cold air was thick with tension, every breath taken with the awareness that discovery could be around any corner. The distant rumble of armored vehicles and the sharp clack of boots on cobblestones were intermittent reminders of the relentless surveillance.

Sean led the way, his knowledge of the city's back alleys and hidden routes more crucial than ever. Each step was deliberate, their movements synchronized like a well-rehearsed dance. The weight of the weapons hidden beneath their coats added a tangible sense of urgency, pressing against them with each cautious step.

Suddenly, the team halted. The murmur of voices and the harsh beam of a searchlight cut through the fog, signaling the approach of a patrol. They pressed themselves into the shadows, hearts pounding, as the light swept past their hiding place. The patrol moved slowly, their conversations a blend of clipped orders and terse remarks, the metallic jangle of their equipment sending shivers down the team's spines.

Michael glanced at Ashling, her face illuminated briefly by the passing light. Her calm exterior belied the intensity of her focus. He knew she was listening intently, counting the footsteps, gauging the distance. The torchlight flickered away, and they remained still, muscles taut, until the sounds faded into the distance.

"Go," Ashling whispered, her voice barely audible. The team moved swiftly, their senses sharpened by the close call. The streets ahead were shrouded in mist, each turn taken with caution, each alley navigated with care.

The city, usually a familiar and navigable landscape, had transformed into a series of traps and potential confrontations. The patrols were a looming presence, their routes unpredictable, their searches invasive. Michael's team had to be one step ahead, timing their movements with the precision of a finely tuned clock.

As they approached another intersection, Sean signaled for a stop. The glow of a streetlamp revealed the silhouette of a patrol vehicle parked at the corner, soldiers conducting a search on a group of young men. The soldiers' voices were harsh, their manner aggressive. The team watched, tense and silent, waiting for the right moment to move.

The search seemed to stretch on forever, the shouts and protests of the young men echoing off the buildings. Finally, the soldiers moved on, their captives released, looking shaken but unharmed. Sean motioned for the team to proceed, leading them down a narrow, twisting alley that bypassed the patrol.

Their journey was punctuated by these moments of high tension, each one a reminder of the stakes. The weight of the hidden weapons was a constant burden, both physically and mentally. The fog thickened as they moved deeper into the city, the once-familiar routes now alien and fraught with danger.

Every shadow, every unexpected sound was scrutinized with heightened vigilance. The distant crackle of a radio, the soft hum of a vehicle's engine – all became potential threats. The team's movements were fluid and coordinated, their survival dependent on their ability to anticipate and adapt.

Michael felt the pressure of each decision, the responsibility of leading his team through the labyrinthine streets without falling into the hands of the British forces. The patrols, an ever-present menace, required them to blend into the darkness, becoming ghosts in their own city.

As they neared their destination, the outline of the old distillery loomed through the fog. They paused one last time, checking their surroundings and ensuring they were not followed. The final leg of their journey was the most critical, requiring every ounce of their skill and composure.

The presence of the British military patrols, more frequent and vigilant than ever, was a constant shadow over their mission. But Michael's team, driven by their shared resolve and the necessity of their task, pressed on. Timing their movements with precision and care, they navigated the treacherous path through Belfast's darkened streets, determined to succeed against the odds.

As they moved, the team communicated with subtle signals, a silent language developed over months of working together. A raised hand, a quick nod, a flick of the wrist – each gesture conveyed a precise message, understood instantly by every member. The fog-draped streets of Belfast became their stage, the team moving in a choreographed dance of stealth and precision.

At one point, the distant sound of a patrol vehicle approached, its low rumble growing louder in the stillness of the night. Without a word, the team seamlessly dispersed, each finding a shadow to blend into, a doorway to obscure their presence. They were like phantoms in the night, their movements calculated and ghost-like.

Michael pressed himself against the cold, rough stone of a building, the weight of the concealed weapons pressing into his ribs. He could hear his own heartbeat, loud in his ears, as the patrol vehicle drew nearer. The beam of its headlights cut through the fog, sweeping the street in front of him. He held his breath, muscles tensed, ready to spring into action if necessary.

Ashling slipped into the narrow space between two buildings, her silhouette merging with the darkness. She glanced briefly at Sean, who had taken cover behind a stack of crates, his eyes scanning the street with the vigilance of a hawk. Brendan crouched low behind a parked car, his breathing steady, his hand resting on the handle of a concealed weapon. Liam flattened himself against a doorway, his profile invisible in the deep shadows.

The patrol vehicle passed slowly, the engine's growl reverberating off the buildings. The soldiers inside were alert, their eyes searching the fog for any sign of movement. The team remained perfectly still, each member a master of silence and invisibility. The vehicle's lights swept past, illuminating the street for a brief, blinding moment before moving on.

Once the danger had passed, Ashling emerged from her hiding place, signaling the all-clear with a series of quick hand gestures. The team regrouped, their movements fluid and practiced. The brief encounter had heightened their awareness, but their resolve remained unshaken.

As they continued through the labyrinthine streets, the fog seemed to thicken, muffling their footsteps and cloaking their movements. The city, usually familiar and navigable, now felt like a maze of shadows and unseen threats. Each step was taken with care, their senses attuned to every sound and shift in the darkness.

The team's silent communication was a testament to their bond, forged through countless nights of shared danger and unwavering trust. They moved as one, each member acutely aware of their role and the collective mission. The distant sounds of the city – a dog barking, a door creaking open – were carefully analyzed and swiftly dismissed as non-threats.

At another point, the team froze as the sound of voices echoed down a narrow alley. A group of soldiers, their laughter harsh and grating, were approaching from the opposite direction. With practiced ease, the team dispersed once more, each finding a place to hide. Michael slipped into the recess of a doorway, his heart hammering in his chest as the soldiers passed mere feet away.

The soldiers' boots clattered on the cobblestones, their voices a dissonant chorus of bravado and boredom. One of them stopped to light a cigarette, the brief flare of the match illuminating his face. Michael held his breath, willing himself to become one with the shadows. After what felt like an eternity, the soldiers moved on, their voices fading into the distance.

The team reassembled, their faces set with grim determination. The night's dangers were far from over, but their shared purpose propelled them forward. They moved with renewed urgency, each step a testament to their dedication and skill.

As they neared their destination, the old distillery loomed through the fog, its familiar outline a welcome sight. They paused one last time, checking their surroundings and ensuring they were not followed. The final leg of their journey was the most critical, requiring every ounce of their skill and composure.

Their movements were like a well-rehearsed ballet, each step, each gesture, perfectly timed. The presence of British patrols was a constant threat, but the team, united by their silent communication and unwavering resolve, navigated the treacherous streets of Belfast with ghost-like precision.

Despite the tension, there was a sense of camaraderie among the team, a shared understanding of the importance of their task. They were not just moving weapons; they were upholding their commitment to their cause, a cause that had become intertwined with their very identities.

The team moved with a quiet efficiency, their actions driven by both urgency and a deep-seated bond forged through countless missions. Michael could feel the unity in their steps, the silent coordination that came from knowing each other's movements and thoughts. They were more than comrades; they were a family bound by a shared purpose.

As they navigated the fog-laden streets of Belfast, Michael glanced at his teammates. Ashling, her calm exterior masking the fierce resolve within, led with a steady hand. Sean, his keen eyes always alert, scanned their surroundings with the vigilance of a hawk. Brendan, the quiet strength of the group, moved with a fluid grace, her every action precise and deliberate. Liam, bringing up the rear, exuded a quiet confidence, his presence a reassuring constant.

The distant rumble of a patrol vehicle approaching once again caused them to freeze. Instantly, they dispersed, each finding a shadow to blend into, a doorway to obscure their presence. Michael pressed himself against a cold, damp wall, the weight of the weapons concealed beneath his coat a constant reminder of their mission.

The patrol passed slowly, the harsh light of their searchlights cutting through the fog. The soldiers' faces were stern and watchful, their eyes scanning for any sign of movement. The team remained perfectly still, their breath held, each member becoming one with the darkness. The vehicle moved on, its noise gradually fading into the night, and the team reassembled, their movements synchronized and silent.

As they continued, a subtle gesture from Ashling directed them down a narrow side street. The camaraderie among the team was palpable, a shared understanding of the stakes and the significance of their mission. They communicated in a silent language developed over months of working together, each gesture conveying a wealth of meaning.

The fog thickened, muffling the sounds of the city and adding an eerie quality to their journey. The distant sounds of Belfast's troubled night – a dog barking, a door creaking open – were carefully noted and swiftly dismissed as non-threats. The team's senses were heightened, every nerve on edge, yet there was an unspoken trust that bound them together.

At another point, the sound of voices echoed through a narrow alley. Soldiers, their laughter harsh and jarring, approached from the opposite direction. The team dispersed seamlessly, each finding a hiding spot. Michael slipped into a doorway, his heart pounding as the soldiers passed mere feet away. The glow of a cigarette briefly illuminated a soldier's face, but they moved on, oblivious to the hidden presence of the team.

Once the soldiers were gone, the team regrouped, their resolve unshaken. There was a brief exchange of glances, a silent reaffirmation of their shared commitment. They moved on, the old distillery now visible through the fog, its silhouette a beacon of hope and refuge.

Despite the tension, there was a sense of camaraderie among the team, a shared understanding of the importance of their task. They were not just moving weapons; they were upholding their commitment to their cause, a cause that had become intertwined with their very identities. The weight of the weapons pressed against them was both a burden and a symbol of their dedication.

As they neared their destination, the sense of peril intensified, but so did their determination. The final leg of their journey required every ounce of their skill and composure. They moved with ghost-like precision, each step taken with care, each shadow navigated with expertise.

The presence of the British patrols was a constant threat, but the team, united by their silent communication and unwavering resolve, pressed on. The fog-shrouded streets of Belfast became a testament to their courage and commitment. They were more than a team; they were the embodiment of a cause that demanded everything of them, and they were ready to give it.

Navigating the streets of Belfast on this night was like traversing a different world. A world where the familiar had become dangerous, and the ordinary had turned extraordinary. Michael and his team, in their silent march, were acutely aware that the streets they walked were the same ones they hoped to free.

The fog enveloped the city, shrouding it in an eerie stillness. The once familiar landmarks, now obscured by mist, seemed ghostly and surreal. Every corner turned held the potential for danger, every shadow a possible threat. The team moved with heightened caution, their senses sharpened by the gravity of their mission.

Michael led the way, his footsteps barely making a sound on the damp cobblestones. The weight of the weapons concealed beneath his coat was a constant reminder of their task. Behind him, Ashling, Sean, Brendan, and Liam moved in sync, their silent communication a testament to their months of training and camaraderie.

The air was thick with tension, every distant sound amplified by the fog. The rumble of an approaching patrol vehicle sent a jolt through the team. Without a word, they dispersed, each finding cover in the shadows. Michael pressed himself against the cold, rough surface of a brick wall, his breath held as the vehicle passed by. The beam of the searchlight swept the street, highlighting the swirling fog before moving on.

The patrol moved slowly, the soldiers' eyes scanning for any sign of movement. The team remained perfectly still, their presence masked by the darkness and the fog. The vehicle's noise gradually faded, and Michael signaled for the team to regroup. They emerged from their hiding places, resuming their journey with renewed caution.

The streets of Belfast, usually bustling with life, were now silent and foreboding. The distant sounds of the city – the occasional bark of a dog, the faint hum of a passing car – were reminders of the ordinary life they were fighting to protect. The team navigated the labyrinthine alleys, their movements fluid and purposeful.

As they approached another intersection, the faint glow of a streetlamp revealed the silhouette of a patrol vehicle parked at the corner. Soldiers were conducting a search, their voices harsh in the quiet night. The team watched, hidden in the shadows, as the soldiers interrogated a group of young men. The sight was a stark reminder of the stakes of their mission.

When the soldiers moved on, Sean signaled the all-clear, and the team slipped past the checkpoint, moving with practiced ease. The fog seemed to thicken as they moved deeper into the city, the once-familiar streets now a maze of potential dangers. The weight of their concealed weapons was a constant burden, both physical and psychological.

Despite the tension, there was a palpable sense of camaraderie among the team. They were not just moving weapons; they were upholding their commitment to a cause that had become intertwined with their very identities. Each step they took was a testament to their shared purpose and unyielding resolve.

The final leg of their journey brought them to the old distillery, its outline barely visible through the fog. The sight of the building, a symbol of refuge and resistance, brought a sense of relief and renewed determination. They paused one last time, checking their surroundings before proceeding.

Navigating the streets of Belfast on this night was like traversing a different world. A world where the familiar had become dangerous, and the ordinary had turned extraordinary. Michael and his team, in their silent march, were acutely aware that the streets they walked were the same ones they hoped to free. Each step was a declaration of their commitment, a silent promise to reclaim their city from the shadow of oppression.

The tension among Michael and his team escalated as they entered one of Belfast's most tightly monitored areas. The streets here were suffused with an air of expectancy, every corner potentially hiding a new danger. It was in this nerve-wracking environment that they suddenly found themselves face-to-face with a British army patrol.

The fog seemed denser in this part of the city, the cold air carrying a sense of foreboding. The usual sounds of the night were replaced by an oppressive silence, broken only by the occasional distant rumble of an armored vehicle or the faint clink of metal from a soldier's gear. The team moved with heightened caution, their senses tuned to every possible threat.

As they turned a corner, the sharp beam of a searchlight suddenly pierced the fog, blinding them momentarily. Michael froze, his heart pounding in his chest. The harsh voices of the soldiers cut through the silence, their figures emerging from the mist like specters.

"Hold it right there!" barked one of the soldiers, his rifle raised. The patrol, a group of four heavily armed men, stood blocking their path. The team instinctively fanned out, each finding cover behind whatever meager protection the street offered – a lamppost, a parked car, a doorway.

Michael's mind raced, calculating their next move. The weight of the concealed weapons pressed against him, a reminder of both their mission and the immediate danger. He caught Ashling's eye; her calm demeanor was a stark contrast to the tension that gripped them all.

The lead soldier stepped forward, his eyes scanning each member of the team. "What are you doing out here at this hour?" he demanded, his tone suspicious and aggressive.

Ashling, ever the quick thinker, stepped slightly forward from her cover. "Just heading home, sir," she said, her voice steady despite the fear that gnawed at her insides. "Got caught up with some friends and lost track of time."

The soldier's eyes narrowed, his suspicion palpable. He looked back at his comrades, then returned his gaze to Ashling. "You and your friends, step into the light."

Michael knew they had to act fast. The risk of being searched and the weapons discovered was too great. He signaled subtly to the team, a series of quick hand gestures conveying the plan. As the soldiers advanced, the team tensed, ready to spring into action if needed.

"Come on, move it!" the soldier barked, his patience wearing thin. He raised his rifle, motioning them forward.

In that split second, Sean moved, diverting the soldiers' attention with a sudden shout from the opposite direction. "Over here!" he yelled, before disappearing into the fog. The soldiers turned, momentarily distracted by the noise.

Michael seized the opportunity, signaling the team to scatter. They moved as one, melting into the shadows, their movements swift and silent. The soldiers, confused by the sudden commotion, hesitated, giving the team the precious seconds they needed to escape.

Heart pounding, Michael ducked into a narrow alley, the sounds of the patrol fading behind him. He glanced back to ensure the others were following. Ashling, Sean, Brendan, and Liam regrouped with him, their breaths heavy but relieved.

"That was too close," Liam muttered, wiping sweat from his brow.

Ashling nodded, her face set with determination. "We need to keep moving. They'll be looking for us now."

The team pressed on, the encounter with the patrol a stark reminder of the dangers they faced. The streets of Belfast, once familiar and navigable, had become a perilous maze, each turn fraught with the potential for discovery. Yet their resolve remained unshaken. They moved with renewed urgency, each step a testament to their courage and commitment to their cause.

Navigating the tightly monitored area, the team knew they had to be more vigilant than ever. The tension was palpable, but so was their unyielding determination. They were not just moving weapons; they were carrying the hope of their cause, a cause that defined their very existence. And they would see it through, no matter the risks.

The patrol, a group of soldiers armed and alert, was methodically moving down the street. The air was thick with tension, the weight of recent unrest palpable. The soldiers stopped civilians at random, their interrogations thorough and intimidating. The soldiers' eyes were sharp, missing nothing, as they conducted their searches with a rigor born of the turmoil that had gripped Belfast.

Michael and his team could see the patrol's systematic approach from their vantage point in the shadows. The soldiers moved in a tight formation, their rifles at the ready, eyes scanning every nook and cranny. Each interaction with the civilians was a calculated display of authority, the soldiers' voices carrying a tone of undisguised suspicion and control.

One soldier, a tall man with a stern face and a prominent scar across his cheek, seemed particularly vigilant. His eyes darted around constantly, assessing every movement, every flicker of shadow. He barked questions at a nervous young man, his posture rigid, exuding an air of unquestionable dominance. The young man stammered out answers, his eyes wide with fear as the soldier patted him down, searching for anything that could be deemed suspicious.

Another soldier, shorter but equally intimidating, stopped a middle-aged woman carrying a basket of groceries. Her hands trembled as she handed over her identification, the soldier scrutinizing it under the harsh beam of his flashlight. The woman's anxiety was palpable, her eyes darting nervously as the soldier questioned her with a relentless barrage of questions.

The team watched, muscles tense, as the patrol moved closer to their position. Michael's heart pounded in his chest, the weight of their concealed weapons pressing heavily against his body. He signaled for the team to remain still, their only chance lying in the soldiers overlooking their hiding spots.

Ashling, crouched behind a low wall, kept her breathing slow and even, her eyes never leaving the patrol. The soldiers' boots clattered on the cobblestones, the sound echoing ominously in the silent night. Each step brought them closer, the beam of their searchlight sweeping perilously close to the team's hiding places.

Suddenly, the scarred soldier stopped, his head snapping in the direction of a faint noise down the alley. His hand went up, signaling the patrol to halt. The silence was deafening as the soldiers listened intently, their bodies tense, ready to spring into action.

Michael felt a bead of sweat trickle down his temple, his mind racing through their options. Any sudden move could betray their position, but staying hidden meant trusting the soldiers would overlook them. The tension was almost unbearable, the air thick with the promise of imminent danger.

The soldier with the scar slowly advanced towards the alley, his flashlight cutting through the fog. He moved with the precision of a predator, every step deliberate, every sense on high alert. The team held their breath, their bodies pressed tightly against the cold, rough surfaces that concealed them.

The flashlight's beam swept over the alley, illuminating the damp walls and slick cobblestones. Michael's pulse quickened as the light drew closer, the seconds stretching into an eternity. Just as the light was about to reveal their position, a loud crash echoed from the opposite direction. A stray cat had knocked over a garbage can, sending the metal lid clattering across the street.

The soldier turned sharply, his attention diverted by the sudden noise. He gestured to his comrades, and they moved off in the direction of the disturbance, their disciplined formation never breaking. The team exhaled collectively, the immediate danger averted but the tension still high.

As the patrol continued their methodical sweep, Michael and his team remained hidden, their resolve unshaken. They knew the risks were far from over. The soldiers' thoroughness was a stark reminder of the stakes, their sharp eyes missing nothing in their quest to maintain control over the unrest-ridden city.

Navigating the streets of Belfast was a perilous endeavor, but the team's commitment to their cause was unwavering. Each soldier they evaded, each shadow they utilized, was a testament to their dedication and the high stakes of their mission. They were not just moving weapons; they were carrying the hopes and dreams of a free Belfast, a cause worth every risk they faced.

In this moment, Michael's training kicked in. He knew they had to remain calm, to blend in as just another group of locals out for a nightly stroll. Any sign of panic could draw the soldiers' attention. So, they slowed their pace, adopting an air of casualness that belied their inner turmoil.

The team's synchronized movements shifted seamlessly, their previously urgent pace now a leisurely amble. Michael led the way, his posture relaxed, his eyes scanning the surroundings with a casual air. The tension in his muscles was tightly controlled, his mind working furiously to maintain the facade.

Ashling walked beside him, her steps light and unhurried. She adjusted her coat casually, the concealed weapons beneath remaining hidden. Her eyes flicked toward the patrol without seeming to, gauging their distance and readiness. Sean, Brendan, and Liam followed suit, their body language mirroring that of ordinary civilians on a quiet evening walk.

The streetlights cast a soft, yellow glow, creating long shadows that danced with their every movement. The fog swirled around their feet, adding an ethereal quality to the scene. The distant sounds of the city were muted, the occasional bark of a dog or the low hum of a car engine blending into the background.

As they neared the patrol, the soldiers' sharp eyes scanned them briefly. Michael made a show of pointing out a non-existent detail on a nearby building to Ashling, his voice low and conversational. "Did you hear about the new shop opening up down the road?" he asked, his tone deliberately mundane.

Ashling nodded, playing along effortlessly. "Yes, I heard it's supposed to be quite nice. We should check it out sometime," she replied, her voice steady and unconcerned.

Sean stretched his arms casually, stifling a yawn as if tired from a long day. Brendan adjusted the strap of his bag, his movements unhurried and natural. Liam kicked at a small pebble on the ground, his expression one of mild disinterest.

The patrol slowed as they passed the group, the soldiers' eyes lingering for a moment longer. Michael's heart pounded, but he kept his demeanor calm, offering a polite nod to the nearest soldier. The soldier, seemingly satisfied, returned the nod and continued his sweep of the area.

The team moved on, their pace remaining steady until they were well out of sight. Only then did they quicken their steps, the casual air dropping away as the urgency of their mission returned. Michael could feel the adrenaline coursing through his veins, the near encounter heightening his senses.

"That was close," Sean murmured, his voice low.

"Too close," Brendan agreed, his eyes scanning their surroundings.

"We need to keep moving," Ashling said, her tone firm. "We're not out of danger yet."

The team pressed on, their movements now a blend of stealth and speed. The fog thickened, providing them with some cover but also obscuring their vision. They navigated the narrow alleys with practiced ease, every step a testament to their training and cohesion.

Michael's mind raced with the implications of their near encounter. The patrols were more vigilant than ever, their searches thorough and intimidating. Any mistake, any lapse in their facade, could spell disaster. Yet, despite the danger, their resolve remained unbroken.

They reached a quieter part of the city, the oppressive presence of the patrols lessening but not disappearing entirely. The team's pace slowed once more, adopting the careful balance between urgency and caution. Every shadow was scrutinized, every sound analyzed.

In this moment, Michael's training kicked in. He knew they had to remain calm, to blend in as just another group of locals out for a nightly stroll. The team's casual facade had saved them from immediate danger, but the night was far from over. They moved with the silent understanding that their mission was a dangerous dance, one that required both skill and composure.

As they continued through the fog-shrouded streets, the sense of camaraderie and shared purpose kept them focused. They were not just moving weapons; they were fighting for their cause, for their city, and for each other. And they would not falter.

As the soldiers approached, the tension was almost tangible. Michael could feel the weight of the concealed weapons pressing against him, a constant reminder of the danger they were in. They were mere steps away from the patrol now, each second stretching out like an eternity.

The night air was thick with anticipation, the fog swirling around their feet as if trying to pull them into the shadows. The sound of the soldiers' boots clattering on the cobblestones echoed ominously, a stark contrast to the eerie silence that enveloped the team. Michael's breath was shallow, his heart pounding in his chest like a drumbeat of dread.

Ashling walked beside him, her face a mask of calm that belied the turmoil inside. Her eyes flicked to Michael, a silent reassurance passing between them. Sean, Brendan, and Liam moved with practiced ease, their casual demeanor a thin veil over the coiled tension that lay beneath.

The soldiers were now close enough that Michael could see the glint of their weapons in the dim light, their eyes sharp and watchful. The lead soldier, a tall man with a hardened expression, scanned the group with a suspicion born from countless nights of unrest. His gaze lingered on Michael for a moment, then moved on to Ashling.

Michael forced himself to breathe evenly, to project an air of casual indifference. He pointed to a nearby building, making small talk with Ashling. "That old pub over there used to be quite popular," he said, his voice steady despite the fear gnawing at his insides.

Ashling nodded, playing along seamlessly. "I remember. We should stop by sometime," she replied, her tone light.

The soldiers' footsteps grew louder, the gap between them closing rapidly. Michael could feel the tension in the air, the unspoken understanding that any misstep could lead to disaster. His grip tightened slightly on the strap of his bag, the concealed weapons a heavy burden both physically and mentally.

The lead soldier's eyes narrowed as he continued to scrutinize the group. "Evening," he said, his voice carrying an edge of authority. "What are you all doing out at this hour?"

Michael met his gaze, forcing a polite smile. "Just heading home after a late night with friends," he replied, keeping his tone casual. "Lost track of time, I suppose."

The soldier's eyes bored into him for a moment longer, and then he glanced at Ashling. "And you?" he asked, his tone no less probing.

"Same here," Ashling said smoothly. "It's been a long day."

The soldier seemed to consider this, his eyes moving to the rest of the team. Sean stretched his arms and yawned, Liam kicked at a loose stone on the ground, and Brendan adjusted the strap of her bag. They all mirrored the same air of casual indifference, masking the undercurrent of tension that thrummed between them.

Finally, the soldier seemed satisfied, giving a curt nod. "Alright then," he said. "Move along, and stay out of trouble."

Michael nodded in return, a wave of relief washing over him. "Will do. Have a good night," he said, and with that, he led the team forward, maintaining their leisurely pace until they were well past the patrol.

Only then did they allow themselves to breathe a collective sigh of relief. The danger had passed, but the tension remained, a constant companion on their perilous journey. The weight of the concealed weapons pressed against them, a reminder of the high stakes and the need for constant vigilance.

They continued down the fog-shrouded streets, their steps quickening once they were out of sight. Michael's mind raced with the implications of their near encounter, but their resolve remained unshaken. They were not just moving weapons; they were carrying the hope and determination of their cause, a cause worth every risk they faced.

The night stretched on, each step bringing them closer to their destination and the fulfillment of their mission. The tension among Michael and his team was almost palpable, but so was their unwavering commitment to their shared purpose. As they navigated the treacherous streets of Belfast, they knew that every moment, every breath, was a testament to their courage and their cause.

In this moment, Belfast's streets transformed from a familiar cityscape into a stage for a high-stakes game of deception and survival. As the British patrol drew closer, the imminent threat of discovery loomed large over Michael and his team. They could feel the gaze of the soldiers inching closer, threatening to unravel their mission in mere moments. In this tense atmosphere, quick and decisive action was imperative.

The fog clung to the ground, creating an almost surreal atmosphere that distorted the usual landmarks of the city. The streetlights cast long, eerie shadows, making every corner and alley a potential hiding spot or a trap. The once familiar sounds of the city were now sinister, every distant footstep and murmur amplified by the stillness of the night.

Michael's heart pounded in his chest, each beat a reminder of the concealed weapons pressing against his body. He signaled subtly to his team, a series of quick hand gestures that conveyed the urgency of the situation. Ashling, Sean, Brendan, and Liam moved into position, their casual demeanor masking the intense focus that gripped them all.

The soldiers advanced methodically, their boots hitting the cobblestones with a rhythmic precision that seemed to echo in the tense silence. The lead soldier, a tall man with a stern face and an air of authority, scanned the area with sharp, unyielding eyes. His flashlight cut through the fog, illuminating patches of the street in harsh, white light.

Michael knew they had to remain calm, to blend in as just another group of locals out for a nightly stroll. Any sign of panic could draw the soldiers' attention. He slowed his pace, adopting an air of casualness that belied the turmoil churning inside him. He pointed to a nearby building, engaging Ashling in light conversation. "That old pub there," he said, his voice steady, "used to be quite the spot."

Ashling nodded, playing along effortlessly. "Yes, I've heard stories. We should visit sometime," she replied, her tone light and unconcerned.

The soldiers' eyes narrowed as they drew nearer, their suspicion palpable. The leader's voice rang out, commanding and direct. "What are you doing out at this hour?" he demanded, his tone leaving no room for evasion.

Michael forced a smile, keeping his demeanor relaxed. "Just heading home after catching up with some friends," he replied. "Lost track of time, I'm afraid."

The soldier scrutinized each member of the team, his gaze lingering a fraction longer on Michael. Sean yawned theatrically, stretching his arms, while Brendan adjusted her bag with a casual air. Liam kicked a small stone, his expression one of mild disinterest.

The soldier seemed to consider their story, his eyes flicking back and forth between them. Finally, he nodded, a curt acknowledgment of their explanation. "Move along, and stay out of trouble," he said, his tone grudgingly accepting.

Michael nodded, leading the team forward, their pace slow and measured until they were well past the patrol. Each step away from the soldiers felt like a small victory, but the tension didn't fully dissipate until they were out of sight. Only then did they quicken their pace, the urgency of their mission returning in full force.

The encounter with the patrol had been a stark reminder of the stakes. The weight of the concealed weapons pressed against Michael, a constant reminder of the danger they were in. The tension was almost unbearable, each second stretched out like an eternity as the soldiers' gaze threatened to unravel their mission.

As they continued through the fog-shrouded streets, the transformation of Belfast's streets from a familiar cityscape into a stage for a high-stakes game of deception and survival became all the more apparent. Every step was a calculated risk, every shadow a potential threat. The team moved with a renewed sense of purpose, knowing that quick and decisive action was imperative.

They were not just moving weapons; they were fighting for their cause, for their city, and for each other. The imminent threat of discovery loomed large, but their resolve remained unshaken. Together, they pressed on, navigating the treacherous streets with a silent determination, each step a testament to their courage and commitment.

It was Brendan, the oldest among them, who stepped forward with a plan. His expression was resolute, a stark determination in his eyes. "I'll create a diversion," he whispered, his voice barely audible yet carrying the weight of a profound sacrifice. Brendan was armed, and he understood the risks of what he was about to do. A confrontation with the patrol could lead to his capture or worse, but it was a risk he was willing to take for the sake of the mission.

Michael hesitated, the protective instinct for his comrade clashing with the understanding that Brendan's plan was their best chance. After a tense moment, he gave a subtle nod. The unspoken bond between them, forged in the fires of shared struggles, spoke volumes. They all knew what this decision meant, and the gravity of Brendan's sacrifice was not lost on any of them.

Brendan casually broke away from the group, his movements calculated to avoid drawing immediate suspicion. The rest of the team continued forward, their pace steady but their hearts racing, each step taking them further away from their comrade and deeper into the uncertainty of the night.

The fog thickened, cloaking the streets of Belfast in a heavy, almost oppressive silence. The once-familiar landmarks now appeared ghostly and distorted, each shadow a potential threat. The team moved with a practiced fluidity, their footsteps barely audible on the damp cobblestones.

In the background, the sound of Brendan's distraction began to unfold, a carefully orchestrated chaos designed to divert the patrol's attention. A sudden loud crash echoed through the streets, followed by Brendan's shouted taunts aimed at the soldiers. The patrol's attention snapped towards the noise, their disciplined formation breaking as they rushed to investigate.

Michael and his team seized the moment, slipping away into the shadows. The distant shouts and the clatter of pursuit filled the night air, but they pushed on, their resolve unwavering. The weight of the concealed weapons pressed against them, a constant reminder of the stakes.

The streets seemed to twist and turn in a maze-like fashion, each corner turned with a mixture of caution and urgency. The familiar sights of the city were transformed into a treacherous landscape, the danger of discovery ever-present. The team moved as one, their silent communication and shared purpose guiding them through the labyrinth.

Every now and then, a distant shout or a burst of noise from Brendan's diversion would reach their ears, spurring them forward. They knew the risks Brendan faced, and the thought of his sacrifice fueled their determination. They navigated the narrow alleys and backstreets, their senses heightened, every nerve on edge.

As they approached their destination, the silhouette of the old distillery loomed through the fog, a beacon of hope amidst the uncertainty. They quickened their pace, the urgency of their mission propelling them forward. The final stretch felt like an eternity, but their focus never wavered.

In the quiet moments between Brendan's orchestrated chaos and their own careful steps, the reality of their situation settled in. They were not just moving weapons; they were carrying the hopes and dreams of their cause, a cause that demanded everything from them.

Reaching the relative safety of the distillery, Michael allowed himself a brief moment to reflect on Brendan's bravery. The sound of the diversion gradually faded into the background, replaced by the oppressive silence of the night. The team exchanged solemn glances, the weight of their comrade's sacrifice heavy in the air.

Brendan's plan had worked, buying them the precious time they needed to complete their mission. The streets of Belfast, a stage for their high-stakes game of deception and survival, had once again witnessed the profound depths of their commitment.

Michael led the team, weaving through the chaos with a singular focus. Every step was a gamble, every movement a dance with danger. The air was thick with tension and the acrid smell of gunfire. They ducked between alleys and behind cars, using the urban landscape to their advantage.

As they navigated the bedlam, the reality of the situation was stark. Civilians, innocent bystanders, were thrust into the heart of the conflict, their evening routines turned into a nightmare. The team moved past them, acutely aware of the innocent lives disrupted by their struggle.

The sounds of Brendan's diversion grew distant as they put space between themselves and the clash. The realization of what Brendan had sacrificed for their escape weighed heavily on Michael's heart. His act of defiance, while crucial for their mission's success, had escalated the situation beyond their worst fears.

This tense sequence of distraction and escape was not just a testament to their mission's dangers but also a grim reminder of the conflict's cost. For Michael, it underscored the complex interplay of their fight for freedom and the unintended consequences that often shadowed their path.

As Michael and his team disappeared into the shadows of Belfast, the focus shifted back to Brendan, now alone in his standoff against the British patrol. The air was thick with tension and the acrid smell of gunfire as the firefight raged on.

Brendan, positioned behind a derelict car, exchanged fire with the soldiers. His movements were swift and calculated, betraying his training and determination. Despite being outnumbered, he fought with a ferocity that spoke of his deep commitment to the cause. Each shot he fired was deliberate, aimed at keeping the soldiers at bay and drawing their attention away from the fleeing team.

The firefight intensified, the night air filled with the deafening sounds of gunfire. Brendan's sharp eyes tracked every movement, his mind focused on the task at hand. He aimed with precision, each pull of the trigger a testament to his resolve. The soldiers, though numerous and well-armed, found themselves momentarily held back by Brendan's relentless defense.

Bullets ricocheted off the car and nearby buildings, the metallic clangs adding to the chaos. Brendan's cover was meager, but he used it expertly, shifting positions to avoid being pinned down. His breath came in controlled bursts, each inhalation a reminder of the life-or-death stakes.

The soldiers advanced cautiously, their formation tightening as they responded to Brendan's fire. He could see their determined faces, the discipline in their movements, but he remained undeterred. Every second he held them off was a second gained for Michael and the team to escape.

With each shot, Brendan's thoughts were on his comrades. He knew the risks he faced, but his commitment to the mission and his friends fueled his bravery. The exchange of fire was relentless, the night around him alive with the flash of gunfire and the acrid smell of smoke.

As the soldiers began to close in, Brendan's resolve never wavered. He fought with the fierce intensity of someone who knew that his actions, even in isolation, were part of a larger struggle. His sacrifice was not just a diversion; it was a statement of defiance, a testament to the unbreakable spirit that drove him and his comrades forward.

The soldiers, recovering from the initial surprise of the ambush, coordinated their response. They moved tactically, trying to flank Brendan and cut off his escape routes. Their commands were sharp, a series of orders barked amidst the chaos. They advanced with caution, aware of the potential danger posed by this lone but determined IRA member.

Brendan could see the shift in their strategy, their movements becoming more calculated and precise. He adjusted his position behind the derelict car, his eyes scanning for any opportunity to counter their advance. The tension was palpable, the air thick with the smell of gunpowder and the echoes of gunfire.

The soldiers moved in a coordinated dance, their training evident in every step. They communicated with hand signals and terse shouts, their focus unwavering. Brendan fired strategically, aiming to disrupt their formation and buy more time. Each shot was a deliberate act of defiance, a testament to his unwavering commitment to the cause.

As the soldiers attempted to flank him, Brendan shifted his position, using the car as a shield. The sound of bullets striking metal and the crumbling facade of nearby buildings added to the cacophony. He knew he was outnumbered and outgunned, but his determination did not falter.

The lead soldier, recognizing Brendan's skill and resolve, directed his men with increased urgency. They advanced in a pincer movement, closing in from both sides. Brendan's sharp eyes caught their approach, and he fired rapidly, aiming to slow their progress. The exchange of fire was intense, the night lit by the muzzle flashes of their weapons.

Brendan's heart pounded in his chest, his breath coming in quick, controlled bursts. The weight of the situation pressed heavily on him, but he remained resolute. He had to keep the soldiers focused on him, to ensure that Michael and the team had the chance to escape. His sacrifice was necessary, and he embraced it with a fierce pride.

The soldiers' tactics began to take effect, their flanking maneuver cutting off Brendan's potential escape routes. He was pinned down, but not defeated. His movements were swift and precise, each action calculated to maximize his impact. The soldiers pressed closer, their determination matching his own.

In the midst of the chaos, Brendan's thoughts remained clear. He was a part of something larger, a cause that demanded everything from him. The soldiers might have the upper hand, but Brendan's spirit was unbreakable. He would fight to the last, a beacon of defiance amidst the storm of battle.

The street, once a quiet residential area, had transformed into a miniature warzone. The sound of gunfire echoed off the buildings, shattering the night's peace. Windows in nearby houses were hastily shuttered as residents sought cover from the crossfire.

The once serene neighborhood was now filled with the acrid smell of gunpowder and the deafening roar of firearms. Brendan, still positioned behind the derelict car, exchanged fire with the soldiers. His every movement was deliberate and calculated, a testament to his training and determination.

The soldiers, now fully recovered from the initial surprise, coordinated their response with precision. Their commands were sharp, a series of orders barked amidst the chaos. They moved tactically, attempting to flank Brendan and cut off his escape routes. The lead soldier directed the advance, his voice cutting through the cacophony.

Nearby, the sounds of civilians scrambling for safety added to the chaos. Families huddled behind closed doors, their fear palpable. Brendan could hear the muffled cries of children and the frantic whispers of parents trying to reassure them. Each gunshot echoed through the narrow streets, amplifying the sense of dread that hung in the air.

Brendan fired strategically, aiming to keep the soldiers at bay. His shots were precise, each one designed to disrupt their formation and buy more time. The soldiers advanced cautiously, aware of the danger posed by this lone but determined IRA member.

As the firefight raged on, the street bore the scars of the conflict. Bullet holes riddled the walls of houses, and shattered glass littered the pavement. The once familiar surroundings were now a testament to the violence that had erupted.

Despite being outnumbered, Brendan fought with a ferocity that spoke of his deep commitment to the cause. Each shot he fired was deliberate, aimed at keeping the soldiers at bay and drawing their attention away from the fleeing team. His resolve was unshaken, his focus unwavering.

The soldiers, intent on ending the standoff, pressed their advantage. They moved in a coordinated dance, their tactics honed by countless operations. Brendan adjusted his position, his eyes constantly scanning for threats. He could feel the weight of the situation, but he refused to yield.

The firefight had transformed the quiet residential street into a battleground, the sounds of conflict reverberating through the night. Brendan's determination was matched by the soldiers' resolve, each side committed to their cause. In the midst of the chaos, the once peaceful neighborhood stood as a stark reminder of the cost of their struggle.

Brendan, aware that his time was limited, fought with a sense of desperation. He knew he couldn't hold them off indefinitely but was determined to give his comrades the best chance of escape. His actions were those of a man who had accepted his fate, sacrificing himself for the larger mission.

The sound of gunfire continued to echo through the street, the once-quiet residential area now a battleground. Brendan's movements were swift and precise, his training evident in every calculated shot. He aimed to disrupt the soldiers' advance, each pull of the trigger a testament to his resolve.

The soldiers, recognizing his determination, pressed forward with increased caution. Their coordinated efforts to flank Brendan were met with fierce resistance, each attempt countered by his well-aimed shots. Brendan's heart pounded in his chest, but he maintained his focus, the desperation fueling his determination.

He glanced around, taking in the transformed landscape. The shattered windows, the bullet-riddled walls, and the hastily shuttered homes painted a stark picture of the night's chaos. The air was thick with the acrid smell of gunpowder, and the once-familiar street now felt foreign and hostile.

Brendan knew that every second he held the soldiers back was a second gained for Michael and the team. The thought of his comrades slipping away into the night, their mission continuing because of his actions, brought him a sense of grim satisfaction. He accepted his fate with a clear mind, his purpose giving him strength.

As the soldiers advanced, their formation tightening, Brendan fought with the desperation of a man who knew his time was running out. He moved quickly, using the derelict car for cover, his eyes scanning for any opportunity to slow their progress. The realization that he couldn't hold them off indefinitely was ever-present, but it did not deter him.

His thoughts briefly flickered to his comrades, now moving further away from the danger. Brendan's sacrifice was their chance, and he embraced it fully. The firefight intensified, each shot a reminder of the stakes, each breath a testament to his unyielding spirit.

The soldiers, driven by their own determination, continued to close in. Brendan's actions were those of a man resigned to his fate but committed to making every moment count. His desperation translated into a fierce resolve, every movement purposeful and defiant.

The once-quiet residential street bore witness to his stand, the sounds of conflict a stark contrast to the peace that had once prevailed. Brendan's sacrifice was not just for his comrades but for the larger mission, a cause that demanded everything from him.

As the soldiers finally began to overwhelm his position, Brendan's thoughts remained on the mission and the comrades he had given everything for. His final moments were a blend of desperation and fierce resolve, his actions a testament to the unbreakable spirit that defined their struggle.

Brendan, aware that his time was limited, fought with a sense of desperation. He knew he couldn't hold them off indefinitely but was determined to give his comrades the best chance of escape. His actions were those of a man who had accepted his fate, sacrificing himself for the larger mission.

The intensity of the firefight reflected the stark reality of the conflict in Northern Ireland – moments of intense violence breaking the veneer of normalcy that tried to persist in the city. The sound of gunfire continued to echo through the street, the once-quiet residential area now a battleground. Brendan's movements were swift and precise, his training evident in every calculated shot. He aimed to disrupt the soldiers' advance, each pull of the trigger a testament to his resolve.

The soldiers, recognizing his determination, pressed forward with increased caution. Their coordinated efforts to flank Brendan were met with fierce resistance, each attempt countered by his well-aimed shots. Brendan's heart pounded in his chest, but he maintained his focus, the desperation fueling his determination.

He glanced around, taking in the transformed landscape. The shattered windows, the bullet-riddled walls, and the hastily shuttered homes painted a stark picture of the night's chaos. The air was thick with the acrid smell of gunpowder, and the once-familiar street now felt foreign and hostile.

Brendan knew that every second he held the soldiers back was a second gained for Michael and the team. The thought of his comrades slipping away into the night, their mission continuing because of his actions, brought him a sense of grim satisfaction. He accepted his fate with a clear mind, his purpose giving him strength.

As the soldiers advanced, their formation tightening, Brendan fought with the desperation of a man who knew his time was running out. He moved quickly, using the derelict car for cover, his eyes scanning for any opportunity to slow their progress. The realization that he couldn't hold them off indefinitely was ever-present, but it did not deter him.

His thoughts briefly flickered to his comrades, now moving further away from the danger. Brendan's sacrifice was their chance, and he embraced it fully. The firefight intensified, each shot a reminder of the stakes, each breath a testament to his unyielding spirit.

For Brendan, this stand was a manifestation of his dedication to the IRA's cause, a willingness to face overwhelming odds for what he believed in. The soldiers, driven by their own determination, continued to close in. Brendan's actions were those of a man resigned to his fate but committed to making every moment count. His desperation translated into a fierce resolve, every movement purposeful and defiant.

The once-quiet residential street bore witness to his stand, the sounds of conflict a stark contrast to the peace that had once prevailed. Brendan's sacrifice was not just for his comrades but for the larger mission, a cause that demanded everything from him.

As the soldiers finally began to overwhelm his position, Brendan's thoughts remained on the mission and the comrades he had given everything for. His final moments were a blend of desperation and fierce resolve, his actions a testament to the unbreakable spirit that defined their struggle.

The firefight between Brendan and the British soldiers intensified, the street resonating with the sound of continuous gunfire. Brendan, using the derelict car as cover, managed to keep the soldiers at bay. His shots were precise, each one aimed with a purpose. Amid the chaos, he was grazed by a bullet, a sharp pain searing through his arm, but he pushed through the pain, his focus unwavering.

The soldiers, realizing the seriousness of the situation, radioed for backup. Their voices were tense as they requested assistance from the local police, acknowledging that the situation had escalated beyond a routine patrol encounter. They continued their advance, cautiously moving closer to Brendan's position, their training evident in their coordinated movements.

In an act of sheer determination and skill, Brendan managed to take down three of the advancing soldiers. Each shot was a calculated risk, exposing him to return fire, but he seized the opportunities with a combination of bravery and desperation. The street echoed with the sound of his successful hits, adding to the chaos of the night.

Despite his injury and the growing odds against him, Brendan continued to hold his ground. His actions were not just about delaying the soldiers but also about sending a message of resistance. He knew that every minute he fought was another minute gained for his comrades to escape.

The firefight intensified, the night air filled with the acrid smell of gunpowder and the deafening roar of gunfire. Brendan's determination shone through his every movement, his resolve unbroken despite the searing pain in his arm. His training and experience guided him, each shot a testament to his skill and unwavering commitment.

The soldiers pressed on, their formation tightening as they moved closer. Brendan could see their faces, the tension and determination mirrored in their eyes. He adjusted his position, using the derelict car to his advantage, every shot a precise effort to keep the soldiers at bay.

The radio chatter from the soldiers became more frantic as they realized the gravity of the situation. Brendan's resistance was fiercer than they had anticipated, and their calls for backup grew more urgent. The tension in their voices underscored the escalating danger of the encounter.

As Brendan fired, he felt the sharp sting of a bullet grazing his arm, but he gritted his teeth and pushed through the pain. His focus remained on the task at hand, each movement deliberate and purposeful. He knew the stakes, and his resolve only hardened with each passing second.

In a moment of sheer determination, Brendan took down three soldiers, their bodies hitting the ground with finality. The sound of his successful hits echoed through the street, adding to the chaotic symphony of the night. His actions were a blend of bravery and desperation, each shot a calculated effort to delay the soldiers and protect his comrades.

The odds were against him, but Brendan's spirit remained unbroken. His stand was more than just a tactical maneuver; it was a symbol of resistance, a message that their fight was far from over. Every minute he held his ground was a victory, a testament to his unyielding commitment to the cause.

As the soldiers continued their advance, Brendan's thoughts remained on his comrades. He knew that his actions were buying them precious time, each moment a chance for them to escape and continue their mission. His sacrifice was a powerful statement, a reminder of the unwavering spirit that fueled their struggle.

The street, once a quiet residential area, had transformed into a warzone, the sounds of gunfire and the cries of civilians caught in the crossfire creating a stark contrast to the peace that had once prevailed. Brendan's stand was a powerful testament to the intensity and complexity of their fight, a struggle marked by moments of profound sacrifice and unwavering determination.

The arrival of local police units added to the tension, their sirens piercing the night as they approached the scene. The once quiet residential street had now become the epicenter of a significant conflict, a testment to the ongoing struggle that gripped Belfast and the lengths to which both sides were willing to go. Brendan, isolated but resolute, prepared to continue his stand, embodying the fierce spirit of resistance that defined the IRA's fight.

As the firefight raged on, the balance seemed to tip in favor of the British Army. Brendan, though wounded and outnumbered, continued his valiant stand against the overwhelming force. The relentless advance of the soldiers, coupled with their strategic maneuvers, appeared to be closing in on him. The night air was filled with the sound of gunfire, shouts, and the approaching sirens of the RUC (Royal Ulster Constabulary), signaling that reinforcements were just moments away.

Brendan, positioned behind his meager cover, knew the odds were stacking against him. The British Army, a symbol of the might and reach of the state, seemed on the verge of overpowering him. The realization that he was one man against the formidable machinery of the British war effort dawned on him, yet his resolve did not waver.

The sirens grew louder, their wails mingling with the cacophony of gunfire and shouted commands. The flashing lights of the RUC vehicles cast an eerie glow on the chaotic scene, illuminating the determined faces of the advancing soldiers. Brendan's heart pounded, but his hands remained steady, his aim precise as he continued to fire.

The soldiers, emboldened by the impending arrival of reinforcements, pressed their advantage. Their movements were coordinated and disciplined, a testament to their training and experience. Brendan, despite his wounds, matched their intensity with sheer determination, each shot a defiant stand against the overwhelming odds.

The street, once a place of quiet normalcy, was now a warzone, the air thick with smoke and the acrid smell of gunpowder. Windows that had once framed peaceful domestic scenes were now shattered, the buildings scarred by bullet holes. The cries of frightened civilians added to the sense of urgency and chaos.

Brendan could feel the pressure mounting, the soldiers' strategic maneuvers slowly but surely closing in on his position. He shifted behind the derelict car, the pain in his arm a constant reminder of his vulnerability. Yet, he fought on, driven by a fierce dedication to his cause and a resolve that refused to break.

The realization that he was one man against the formidable machinery of the British war effort settled in his mind, yet it only steeled his resolve. Brendan knew that his stand, no matter how brief, was a powerful statement of resistance. Each minute he delayed the soldiers was a minute gained for his comrades, a testament to his unyielding spirit.

The gunfire intensified as the soldiers closed the distance, their shouts growing louder. Brendan's cover was being steadily eroded, the relentless advance of the soldiers a stark contrast to his solitary stand. He fired with precision, each shot an act of defiance against the overwhelming force arrayed against him.

As the RUC vehicles screeched to a halt and officers began to deploy, Brendan knew the end was near. The combined might of the British Army and the local police was an insurmountable force, yet he faced it with unwavering determination. The approaching sirens, the flashing lights, the advancing soldiers – all were symbols of the formidable opposition, but also of the courage it took to stand against it.

Brendan's thoughts were with his comrades, now far from the danger. His sacrifice was their opportunity, and he embraced it fully. The night air was filled with the sounds of battle, the echoes of his resistance a lasting testament to his bravery.

In these critical moments, as the RUC neared the scene, the tension reached its peak. The street, illuminated by the flashing lights of approaching police vehicles, took on an eerie glow. Brendan could hear the crackling of radio communication, the voices of the RUC coordinating their approach. He understood that his time was running out, yet he stood firm, determined to fight until the very end.

His thoughts flashed back to his comrades, hoping his actions had bought them enough time to escape. He knew the significance of what his stand represented – not just a physical confrontation, but a symbol of defiance against a conflict that had long gripped his homeland.

As the RUC vehicles pulled into the street, the soldiers intensified their efforts, eager to end the standoff. Brendan, amidst the noise and chaos, prepared for the final confrontation, his spirit undeterred. He stood, a lone figure of resistance, against the backdrop of a conflict that was larger than any individual, a poignant symbol of the struggle that defined Northern Ireland.

The flashing lights cast long, shifting shadows, creating a surreal battlefield. The tension in the air was palpable, every second feeling like an eternity. Brendan's grip tightened on his weapon, his eyes sharp and focused. He could feel the weight of his responsibility, the need to hold the line just a little longer.

The crackling of the RUC radios mixed with the shouts of the soldiers, their coordinated movements becoming more aggressive. The intensity of their approach was a clear sign that they intended to bring the standoff to a swift and decisive end. Brendan took a deep breath, steeling himself for what was to come.

His mind was a whirlwind of thoughts – memories of his comrades, the cause they all fought for, and the hope that his sacrifice would not be in vain. He knew that every second he could keep the soldiers and the RUC at bay was a victory, a testament to his unwavering dedication.

The soldiers, spurred on by the arrival of the RUC, moved with renewed vigor. Their voices grew louder, commands barked with urgency as they closed in on Brendan's position. He could see their determined faces, the resolve in their eyes mirroring his own.

Brendan's heart pounded in his chest, but his spirit remained unbroken. He was not just fighting for his life, but for the ideals that had brought him to this moment. The street, now a cacophony of sirens, gunfire, and shouted orders, became the stage for his final act of defiance.

As the RUC vehicles screeched to a halt and officers began to deploy, the tension reached its zenith. The combined might of the British Army and the local police bore down on him, but Brendan faced them with unwavering determination. His actions were not just a stand against his immediate enemies, but a broader statement against the oppression that had long plagued his people.

The soldiers, now mere meters away, intensified their efforts. Brendan fired back with precision, each shot a deliberate attempt to hold his ground. The pain in his arm was a distant memory, overshadowed by the adrenaline and resolve that coursed through him.

In these final moments, Brendan's thoughts were with his comrades, now hopefully far from danger. His stand, though destined to be overwhelmed, was a beacon of resistance. The street, bathed in the eerie glow of flashing lights, bore witness to his bravery and sacrifice.

As the soldiers and RUC officers finally closed in, Brendan's actions remained a powerful symbol of defiance. He stood firm, a lone figure against a formidable force, embodying the struggle that had defined Northern Ireland for so long.

Just as the situation seemed dire for Brendan, a twist of fate occurred that would change the dynamics of the night. From the shadows of a doorway behind the British soldiers' position, a figure emerged, almost like a specter from the past. It was Old Danny O'Toole, a man in his late seventies, with a lifetime of conflict etched into the lines of his face. In his hands, he clutched an old but well-maintained rifle, his eyes burning with a fire that belied his age.

The soldiers, focused on Brendan and unaware of this new development, were caught off guard. Danny, a veteran of past conflicts and a legend in his own right within the community, had been watching the firefight unfold. Despite his age, he moved with a purpose and determination that spoke of his experience and the depth of his convictions.

As he stepped into the open, Danny took aim. His presence was a game-changer, providing Brendan with the distraction he desperately needed. The soldiers, now realizing the threat behind them, scrambled to reposition. The street, already a scene of chaos, descended further into confusion.

Danny's shot rang out, echoing sharply through the night. The bullet struck true, hitting one of the soldiers who had been closing in on Brendan. The unexpected attack threw the soldiers into disarray, their formation breaking as they sought cover and tried to identify the new threat.

Brendan seized the moment, firing with renewed vigor. The sudden appearance of an ally gave him the boost he needed. Each shot was precise, a deliberate effort to keep the soldiers at bay and exploit their confusion.

The street, already chaotic, erupted into further turmoil. The soldiers, now facing attacks from two fronts, struggled to maintain their advance. Danny, moving with surprising agility for his age, shifted positions to keep the soldiers guessing. His presence was a living testament to the community's enduring spirit of resistance.

Brendan's heart surged with hope and determination. The arrival of Old Danny O'Toole was more than just a tactical advantage; it was a symbolic reinforcement of their shared struggle. He fought with renewed intensity, each shot fired with the knowledge that he was not alone in this fight.

The soldiers, now caught between Brendan and Danny, found themselves at a disadvantage. Their initial confidence wavered as they faced the combined resistance of two determined fighters. The air was thick with tension and the acrid smell of gunpowder, the street illuminated by the sporadic flashes of gunfire.

Danny's shots were measured and precise, each one a reminder of his storied past. His presence added a layer of unpredictability to the firefight, forcing the soldiers to constantly adjust their tactics. The voices on the RUC radios grew more frantic, the situation spiraling out of their control.

For Brendan, the sight of Danny in action was a powerful motivator. He pushed through the pain of his injuries, his focus sharp and unwavering. Together, they created a formidable defense, turning the tide of the confrontation.

The soldiers, recognizing the escalating threat, called for immediate reinforcements. The RUC officers, already on the scene, scrambled to respond, their sirens adding to the night's chaotic soundtrack. The once quiet residential street was now a battlefield, each moment filled with uncertainty and danger.

Old Danny O'Toole, with his unyielding spirit and sharp aim, embodied the resilience of the community. His intervention was a reminder that the fight for freedom and justice spanned generations, each one contributing to the cause in their own way.

As the firefight raged on, the balance of power shifted. Brendan and Danny, though outnumbered, fought with a fierce determination that kept the soldiers at bay. Their combined efforts were a testament to the enduring spirit of resistance, a powerful statement against the forces that sought to oppress them.

In the midst of the chaos, the significance of their stand was clear. This was more than just a tactical skirmish; it was a symbol of defiance, a reminder that the struggle for their homeland's future was far from over. Brendan and Danny, standing shoulder to shoulder, represented the unbreakable will of a community that refused to be subdued.

Brendan, seizing the opportunity provided by Danny's unexpected intervention, adjusted his tactics. He knew that this might be his only chance to escape. The old man's actions, brave and reckless, had tilted the scales, however briefly.

The sound of Danny's rifle joined the symphony of gunfire, adding to the intensity of the battle. The RUC, now arriving at the scene, faced a situation more complex than they had anticipated. The standoff was no longer a clear-cut engagement but had transformed into a multi-front confrontation.

In these moments, the street of Belfast became a testament to the enduring spirit of resistance that had characterized the city's history. Danny O'Toole, standing his ground against the might of the British forces, symbolized a defiance that transcended generations, his actions a reminder of the long and tumultuous struggle for Irish independence.

Brendan, recognizing the narrow window of opportunity, moved with renewed purpose. The distraction created by Danny allowed him to shift his position, taking advantage of the chaos to find better cover. His shots were now more strategic, aiming to create further confusion among the soldiers.

The combined gunfire from Brendan and Danny echoed through the night, creating an overwhelming cacophony that disoriented the advancing soldiers. The RUC officers, arriving on the scene, quickly realized that the situation had escalated beyond their expectations. Their sirens added to the chaos, flashing lights casting eerie shadows on the war-torn street.

Danny's rifle cracked again, another soldier falling as the old man's aim proved unerring. His presence was not just a tactical advantage; it was a powerful symbol of resistance. His figure, silhouetted against the backdrop of flashing lights and gunfire, stood as a living testament to the city's unyielding spirit.

Brendan felt a surge of hope and determination. The sight of Danny fighting with such vigor was inspiring, a reminder of why they fought and what was at stake. He pushed through his pain, every shot fired with renewed energy. The soldiers, now caught between two fronts, struggled to maintain their coordinated advance.

The RUC, attempting to establish control, found themselves in a complex and volatile situation. Their radio communications crackled with frantic updates, the officers trying to assess and respond to the dual threats. The street, once a quiet residential area, had become a battlefield, a vivid tableau of the ongoing conflict.

Brendan's movements were swift and calculated, each step taking him closer to a potential escape. He knew that Danny's brave stand had bought him precious time. The old man's defiance was a powerful motivator, driving Brendan to fight harder and smarter.

The street of Belfast, under siege, was alive with the sounds of resistance. Danny's actions were a stark reminder of the city's storied past, each shot he fired echoing the defiance that had long characterized their struggle. His presence was a beacon, illuminating the path for those who continued the fight for freedom.

As Brendan and Danny continued to hold their ground, the balance of power in the confrontation remained uncertain. The soldiers, now fully aware of the unexpected threat, tried to adapt their tactics. But the spirit of resistance embodied by Brendan and Danny was a formidable force, one that could not be easily subdued.

In the heart of the chaos, the significance of their stand was clear. This was more than just a tactical skirmish; it was a symbol of defiance, a reminder that the struggle for their homeland's future was far from over. Brendan, seizing the moment provided by Danny's intervention, continued to fight with a fierce determination, his actions echoing the resilient spirit of Belfast.

The firefight, now raging with renewed intensity, had taken an unexpected turn with the arrival of this unlikely ally, proving that even in the face of overwhelming odds, the spirit of resistance in Belfast was far from extinguished. In the midst of the firefight, the momentum began to shift unexpectedly. The remaining British soldiers, disoriented by Old Danny O'Toole's sudden appearance and the ensuing chaos, found themselves under siege from two fronts. One by one, they were being picked off, their systematic approach unraveling in the face of this unforeseen resistance.

The arrival of the RUC only added to the confusion. Caught in the midst of the chaos, they struggled to coordinate their response. The officers, still within their armored vehicles, were hesitant to disembark into the unpredictable and dangerous fray that the street had become. Their presence, rather than being a reinforcement, seemed momentarily paralyzed by the complexity of the situation.

Amid this turmoil, Brendan, recognizing the unexpected advantage they had gained, quickly reassessed his position. With the soldiers now distracted and the RUC's response stalled, he saw an opportunity to make his escape. Moving with a combination of stealth and urgency, he repositioned himself, taking advantage of the cover provided by the urban landscape.

The gunfire intensified, each shot echoing through the narrow streets. The flashes from the muzzle blasts illuminated the scene in brief, harsh bursts, highlighting the confusion and desperation of the soldiers. Danny's steady, calculated shots continued to disrupt their formation, each bullet a reminder of the indomitable spirit of resistance.

Brendan moved swiftly, his heart pounding in his chest. The sound of gunfire and the shouts of disoriented soldiers created a cacophony that masked his movements. He used the shadows and the cover of parked cars and alleyways to his advantage, each step bringing him closer to safety.

The RUC officers, still struggling to make sense of the chaos, communicated frantically over their radios. The complexity of the situation had caught them off guard, their initial confidence giving way to hesitation. The flashing lights of their vehicles added an eerie glow to the chaotic scene, casting long, distorted shadows.

Danny's presence was a beacon of hope. His unwavering stance and expert marksmanship were pivotal in shifting the momentum. He moved with the agility of a man half his age, his experience and determination evident in every action. Each shot he fired was precise, a testament to his lifelong dedication to the cause.

Brendan glanced back briefly, his eyes meeting Danny's. In that moment, a silent understanding passed between them. Brendan knew that Danny's intervention had not only saved his life but had also reignited a spark of resistance that could not be easily extinguished. With renewed determination, Brendan pressed on.

The British soldiers, realizing their precarious position, attempted to regroup. Their systematic approach had been shattered, and now they faced a formidable resistance from two determined fighters. The street, once a scene of quiet residential life, had become a battlefield, the air thick with smoke and the acrid smell of gunpowder.

Brendan moved with purpose, each step calculated to maximize his cover and minimize exposure. The urban landscape, with its labyrinthine alleys and concealed corners, provided the perfect terrain for his escape. He slipped through the shadows, his movements fluid and precise.

The RUC, finally beginning to disembark from their vehicles, faced an uphill battle. The chaotic scene before them was a testament to the resilience of the resistance fighters. Their hesitance had cost them precious time, and now they had to contend with a situation spiraling out of their control.

As Brendan neared the edge of the conflict zone, he felt a surge of relief mixed with determination. The unexpected advantage provided by Danny's arrival had turned the tide, allowing him to escape from what seemed like a certain demise. The firefight, still raging behind him, was a powerful reminder of the enduring struggle for freedom.

With one last glance at the scene, Brendan disappeared into the night, his heart filled with gratitude and resolve. The spirit of resistance in Belfast was far from extinguished, and as long as there were fighters like Danny O'Toole, their cause would live on.

He moved swiftly, darting between the shadows, his steps measured but quick. Every movement was calculated to keep him out of the line of sight of both the soldiers and the RUC. His mind was racing, planning his route, looking for the best path to safety.

Brendan's escape was not just a flight from immediate danger, but a strategic withdrawal, ensuring he could continue to fight another day. His actions were driven by a keen survival instinct honed through his involvement in the IRA's operations.

The narrow alleyways and the maze of backstreets became his allies. Brendan moved with the agility of a seasoned fighter, his footsteps light on the cobblestones. The dim light from the streetlamps cast long shadows, providing him with the cover he needed to evade detection. He hugged the walls, using every available obstruction to shield himself from view.

His heart pounded in his chest, the adrenaline coursing through his veins sharpening his senses. Every sound, every flicker of movement was analyzed in an instant. The chaos behind him, with the soldiers and the RUC struggling to regain control, provided the perfect backdrop for his escape.

Brendan's mind worked rapidly, mapping out his route. He knew these streets well, their twists and turns ingrained in his memory from years of clandestine operations. He anticipated potential obstacles, adjusting his path with each step to avoid potential traps and dead ends.

The muffled sounds of gunfire and shouting faded as he put more distance between himself and the epicenter of the conflict. He remained vigilant, aware that any misstep could lead to his capture. His eyes scanned the path ahead, his body ready to react at a moment's notice.

The urgency of his movements was tempered by his need for stealth. Brendan understood that a hasty, reckless dash could draw attention just as easily as standing still. He moved with purpose, each stride calculated to maintain his low profile while covering as much ground as possible.

As he navigated the labyrinthine streets, Brendan's thoughts were a mixture of relief and determination. The night's events had taken an unexpected turn, and he was grateful for the intervention that had provided him with this opportunity. But his focus remained on the mission – on surviving this night so he could continue the fight for his cause.

He turned a corner, slipping into an even narrower alley, the darkness enveloping him like a protective cloak. The distant sounds of the conflict were now a mere echo, but he knew better than to let his guard down. He maintained his pace, every muscle poised for action.

Brendan's path led him through a series of interconnected backstreets, each turn bringing him closer to safety. His survival instincts, honed by countless missions, guided him unerringly. The familiar terrain of Belfast's underbelly was both his refuge and his battlefield.

With each step, Brendan reinforced his resolve. His escape was not just a retreat; it was a tactical maneuver, a means to preserve his strength for the battles yet to come. He moved with the knowledge that every minute he remained free was a victory in itself.

Finally, as he reached a more secluded part of the city, Brendan slowed his pace. He found a concealed spot, allowing himself a moment to catch his breath and assess his surroundings. The immediate danger had passed, but the night's events were far from over in his mind.

Brendan's escape was a testament to his resilience and the enduring spirit of the resistance. As he prepared to move again, he knew that his fight was far from finished. The streets of Belfast had witnessed another chapter in their long history of struggle, and Brendan was determined to see it through to the end.

The scene on the street was one of intense conflict, a microcosm of the larger struggle that had been playing out in Northern Ireland. Old Danny O'Toole, standing firm with his rifle, represented a bridge between the past and present – a symbol of the enduring nature of the conflict. Meanwhile, Brendan's calculated escape epitomized the younger generation's involvement in the ongoing struggle, a blend of daring and tactical prudence.

The firefight raged on, the crack of gunfire echoing through the narrow streets of Belfast. The air was thick with smoke and the acrid smell of gunpowder. Danny, with his weathered face and steely gaze, stood resolute, his rifle steady in his hands. Every shot he fired was precise, a testament to his lifetime of experience and unwavering dedication to the cause.

The soldiers, disoriented by the unexpected resistance from both fronts, struggled to maintain their formation. The arrival of the RUC had only added to the chaos, their sirens and flashing lights creating a surreal backdrop to the conflict. The officers, still hesitant to disembark from their armored vehicles, were caught in a moment of indecision, their response paralyzed by the complexity of the situation.

Amid this turmoil, Brendan moved with calculated precision. His steps were swift but measured, each movement designed to keep him out of sight. He darted between shadows, using the urban landscape to his advantage. His heart raced, but his mind remained sharp, planning his route and anticipating potential obstacles.

Brendan's escape was not just a retreat from immediate danger but a strategic withdrawal to ensure he could continue the fight another day. His involvement in the IRA's operations had honed his survival instincts, blending daring with tactical prudence. He knew the importance of living to fight another day, and his actions were driven by this keen sense of purpose.

As he navigated the labyrinthine backstreets, Brendan's thoughts flickered back to Danny. The old man's brave stand was more than just a tactical maneuver; it was a powerful symbol of resistance that spanned generations. Danny's presence on the battlefield was a reminder of the long and tumultuous struggle for Irish independence, a struggle that had shaped the lives of so many.

The street, illuminated by the sporadic flashes of gunfire, was a testament to the enduring spirit of resistance in Belfast. The conflict, embodied by figures like Danny and Brendan, was a vivid portrayal of the ongoing struggle that had gripped Northern Ireland for decades. Danny's firm stance with his rifle, a bridge between the past and present, and Brendan's calculated escape, a blend of youthful daring and strategic thinking, epitomized the resilience and determination of their cause.

As Brendan put more distance between himself and the conflict, the sounds of battle began to fade, replaced by the steady rhythm of his footsteps on the cobblestones. He moved with purpose, his mind focused on the next steps, the next fight. The night's events had reinforced his resolve, each moment a reminder of what they were fighting for.

The scene on the street was a powerful microcosm of the larger struggle, a snapshot of the enduring conflict in Northern Ireland. Danny's presence, a symbol of the historical roots of the resistance, and Brendan's escape, a testament to the ongoing fight and the involvement of the younger generation, painted a poignant picture of their shared struggle.

As Brendan disappeared into the shadows, his mind remained sharp, planning his next move. The conflict on the street, a moment of intense violence and defiance, was just one chapter in the ongoing story of resistance. Both Danny and Brendan, through their actions, had shown that the spirit of resistance in Belfast was far from extinguished.

As Brendan made his escape, the situation on the street reached a tragic climax. Old Danny O'Toole, the unexpected ally who had so dramatically altered the course of the night's events, continued to stand his ground. His rifle, steady in his aged hands, kept firing at the British soldiers and RUC, who were now converging on his position with a determined ferocity.

The RUC, recovering from their initial hesitation, coordinated with the remaining soldiers to launch a concentrated assault on Danny's position. The air was filled with the deafening sound of gunfire, and the street lit up with the flashes of muzzle fire. Danny, undeterred, continued to fight with a resolve that seemed to transcend his physical limitations.

However, the odds were heavily stacked against him. The combined firepower of the RUC and the soldiers was overwhelming, and despite his valiant efforts, Danny could not withstand the onslaught. In a final act of defiance, he continued to fire his rifle until the very end, refusing to yield even as the bullets closed in on him.

The moment Danny fell was one of poignant tragedy. His death was not just the loss of a life, but a symbol of the sacrifices made in the name of the struggle. He had fought with the spirit of generations of Irish resistance, a spirit that would outlive him.

His sacrifice, however, was not in vain. The diversion he created, even at the cost of his own life, provided Brendan with the critical chance to escape. As the RUC and soldiers focused on Danny, Brendan slipped away into the darkened streets of Belfast, his heart heavy with the weight of what had transpired.

Danny's last stand, a testament to his unwavering commitment to the cause, would be remembered in the annals of the community's history. As Brendan disappeared into the night, he carried with him not just the responsibility of continuing the fight but also the memory of Danny O'Toole – a man who had given everything for the cause he believed in.

The intensity of the firefight had reached its zenith. The crackle of gunfire and the shouts of the soldiers and RUC filled the air, creating a cacophony of chaos. The street, once a quiet residential area, was now an arena of conflict, each shot a stark reminder of the violence that gripped Belfast.

Danny, with his unwavering resolve, continued to fire, his movements deliberate and precise despite the overwhelming odds. The determination in his eyes shone through, a beacon of defiance against the forces closing in on him. His actions were driven by a lifetime of struggle, a commitment that refused to waver even in the face of certain death.

The RUC and soldiers, now fully coordinated, advanced with relentless force. Their combined firepower was devastating, and Danny, though valiant, was pushed to his limits. He took down several more soldiers, each shot a testament to his skill and resolve. But the tide was against him.

As the bullets tore through the air, Danny's body finally succumbed to the relentless assault. He fell, his rifle slipping from his hands, the light in his eyes dimming but not extinguished. The silence that followed his fall was deafening, a somber testament to his sacrifice.

For Brendan, Danny's final stand was a poignant and powerful moment. He knew that the old man's actions had bought him the time he needed to escape. The weight of Danny's sacrifice pressed heavily on him, but it also fueled his determination to continue the fight.

As Brendan navigated the darkened streets, each step took him further from the immediate danger but closer to the enduring conflict. The memory of Danny O'Toole, standing firm in the face of insurmountable odds, would stay with him. It was a reminder of the spirit of resistance that burned within the community, a spirit that could not be easily extinguished.

Danny's death, while tragic, was not the end. It was a continuation of a struggle that had been fought for generations, a struggle that Brendan was now a part of. His escape, made possible by Danny's ultimate sacrifice, was a victory in itself, a testament to the unbreakable will of those who fought for their homeland.

In the quiet moments that followed, as the RUC and soldiers secured the area, the impact of Danny's actions began to sink in. He had fought with a courage that would be remembered, his name etched into the history of their resistance. Brendan, now a part of that legacy, moved forward with a renewed sense of purpose.

The streets of Belfast, scarred by the night's violence, stood as silent witnesses to the bravery and sacrifice of Old Danny O'Toole. His spirit lived on in the hearts of those who continued the fight, a beacon of hope and defiance in the face of oppression.

Before the chaos erupted on the street, Danny O'Toole was in his modest home, a small, unassuming house nestled in the heart of Belfast. The night had been like any other, quiet and uneventful, until the distant sound of gunfire pierced the stillness. Danny, a man in his late seventies with a lifetime of memories marked by the struggle for Irish independence, was no stranger to such sounds. Yet, each echo of gunfire stirred something deep within him.

Sitting in his worn armchair, Danny's ears tuned to the growing commotion outside. He could hear the distinct sounds of a firefight – the rapid bursts of gunfire, the shouts of men, the urgency that tinged the air. His old, yet keen mind began piecing together the scenario unfolding just beyond his doorstep. The realization that the IRA and British forces were engaged in a confrontation nearby quickly dawned on him.

In the quiet of his living room, surrounded by mementos of the past, Danny felt a familiar fire ignite within him. His years had been marked by resistance, by a deep-seated belief in the cause of Irish freedom. The walls of his home were adorned with photographs and relics of a life spent in the shadows of the Troubles, each item a testament to his unwavering commitment.

As the sounds of battle intensified, Danny's resolve strengthened. He knew that young men like Brendan, whom he had seen grow up in the neighborhood, were out there, risking their lives for the same ideals he had once fought for. The thought of these young lives in peril, caught in the crossfire of a seemingly endless conflict, stirred a deep sense of duty within him.

Rising from his chair with a determination that belied his age, Danny moved to a corner of the room where an old, but well-maintained rifle was hidden. It was a relic from his past, a weapon that had seen many battles and had been a silent witness to the turbulent history of Belfast. Danny's hands, though aged, were steady as he retrieved the rifle and checked its readiness.

With a last glance around his home, Danny took in the memories of a lifetime – the faces of friends and comrades who had fought and fallen, the symbols of a cause that had defined his existence. Each photograph, each artifact, seemed to impart a silent blessing, a call to arms that resonated deeply within him.

He stepped out into the cool night air, the sounds of the firefight growing louder with each step. The streets of Belfast, once familiar and quiet, were now a battleground, and Danny's heart pounded with a mix of fear and fierce determination. His eyes, still sharp, scanned the darkness as he made his way towards the source of the commotion.

As he approached the scene, the sight of the British soldiers and RUC officers converging on the IRA fighters filled him with a sense of urgency. The younger generation was embroiled in a fight that had consumed his own youth, and Danny knew that he could not stand idly by.

Positioning himself in the shadows of a doorway, Danny raised his rifle and took aim. The years seemed to fall away as he focused on his target, the weight of the weapon familiar and reassuring in his hands. He fired, the sharp crack of the rifle cutting through the night, and a soldier fell, caught off guard by the unexpected assault.

The soldiers, disoriented by this new threat, scrambled to reposition themselves. Danny, moving with a purpose and determination that spoke of his experience, continued to fire, each shot a deliberate act of defiance. His presence was a game-changer, providing Brendan and the other IRA fighters with the distraction they desperately needed.

As the firefight intensified, Danny stood his ground. The RUC, now arriving at the scene, faced a situation more complex than they had anticipated. The street, already a scene of chaos, descended further into confusion. The combined forces of the RUC and the soldiers launched a concentrated assault on Danny's position, the air filled with the deafening sound of gunfire and the street lit up with the flashes of muzzle fire.

Despite the overwhelming odds, Danny fought with a resolve that seemed to transcend his physical limitations. The odds were heavily stacked against him, but his spirit remained unbroken. In a final act of defiance, he continued to fire his rifle until the very end, refusing to yield even as the bullets closed in on him.

The moment Danny fell was one of poignant tragedy. His death was not just the loss of a life, but a symbol of the sacrifices made in the name of the struggle. He had fought with the spirit of generations of Irish resistance, a spirit that would outlive him.

His sacrifice, however, was not in vain. The diversion he created, even at the cost of his own life, provided Brendan with the critical chance to escape. As the RUC and soldiers focused on Danny, Brendan slipped away into the darkened streets of Belfast, his heart heavy with the weight of what had transpired.

Danny's last stand, a testament to his unwavering commitment to the cause, would be remembered in the annals of the community's history. As Brendan disappeared into the night, he carried with him not just the responsibility of continuing the fight but also the memory of Danny O'Toole – a man who had given everything for the cause he believed in.

With a final glance at his home, a bastion of memories and dreams, Danny O'Toole stepped out into the night. The door closed behind him, marking the threshold between his past and the decisive action he was about to take – an action that would resonate through the streets of Belfast and in the hearts of those fighting for their cause.

The night air was cool and filled with the distant echoes of conflict. Danny's heart pounded with a mixture of resolve and anticipation. Each step he took away from his home was a step into a familiar yet daunting battlefield. The quiet streets he had known for decades were now shrouded in tension and uncertainty.

Danny moved with purpose, his aged yet steady hands gripping the old rifle. The weapon, a relic from his days of active resistance, felt reassuringly solid. Every corner he turned brought him closer to the sounds of gunfire and shouts, the chaotic symphony of a firefight in progress.

The streets, normally quiet and peaceful, had transformed into a theater of war. The flashes of gunfire illuminated the buildings, casting fleeting shadows that danced with the chaos of the night. Danny's keen eyes scanned the scene ahead, assessing the positions of the British soldiers and the RUC.

As he approached the scene, he could see the young men, including Brendan, engaged in a desperate struggle against the better-equipped forces. The sight fueled his determination. These were the same streets he had fought on years ago, and now it was time for him to stand once more.

Positioning himself in the shadows of a doorway, Danny took a deep breath and steadied his aim. His first shot rang out, a sharp crack that sliced through the night and found its mark. A British soldier fell, the element of surprise firmly in Danny's favor.

The soldiers, momentarily thrown into disarray, began to scramble. Danny fired again, each shot deliberate and calculated. The years seemed to melt away as he moved with the precision and focus of his younger self. His presence on the battlefield was a beacon, a symbol of the enduring spirit of resistance that defined his life.

The RUC, arriving at the scene, found themselves caught in an unexpectedly complex situation. Their sirens and flashing lights added to the chaos, but their response was hampered by the ferocity of Danny's attack. The officers hesitated, their initial confidence shaken by the fierce resistance they encountered.

In the midst of the chaos, Brendan seized the opportunity provided by Danny's intervention. Moving with a blend of stealth and urgency, he navigated the urban landscape, each step taking him closer to safety. The sounds of the firefight provided the cover he needed to slip away.

Danny, aware of the growing danger, continued to hold his ground. The combined firepower of the RUC and the soldiers was overwhelming, but his resolve remained unbroken. He fought with the spirit of a man who had dedicated his life to a cause greater than himself.

As the soldiers and RUC officers converged on his position, the air was thick with gunfire. The street lit up with the flashes of muzzle fire, the intensity of the battle reaching its peak. Danny's shots, though fewer, were still precise, each one a final act of defiance.

In his last moments, Danny's thoughts were with Brendan and the younger fighters. His sacrifice was for them, for the future they represented. The bullets that finally brought him down did not extinguish his spirit but rather solidified his legacy as a symbol of unwavering resistance.

Danny's fall was a moment of poignant tragedy. His death, while a significant loss, was also a testament to the enduring fight for Irish independence. His actions had provided Brendan with the critical chance to escape, ensuring that the struggle would continue.

As Brendan disappeared into the night, his heart was heavy with the weight of Danny's sacrifice. The old man's final stand would be remembered, not just as a tactical maneuver, but as a powerful symbol of the sacrifices made in the name of freedom. Danny O'Toole, through his brave actions, had bridged the past and present, leaving a legacy that would inspire generations to come.

Brendan, having narrowly escaped the intense firefight, found himself plunging deeper into the labyrinthine streets of Belfast. His heart pounded against his chest, not just from the exertion but from the weight of what had just transpired. Behind him, the sound of gunfire had ceased, marking the tragic end of Danny O'Toole's last stand. The night, however, was far from over.

The narrow alleys and winding streets of Belfast became both his refuge and his obstacle. Each corner he turned was a step further into the city's shadowy depths, away from the conflict but not the memories. The air was thick with the lingering tension of the firefight, the acrid smell of gunpowder still heavy in the air.

Brendan's mind raced as he navigated the darkened streets. The sacrifice of Danny O'Toole weighed heavily on him, a poignant reminder of the cost of their struggle. Danny's final stand was not just an act of defiance but a gift of time – precious moments that Brendan was determined not to waste.

His movements were swift but calculated, each step taken with care to avoid drawing attention. The city's familiar streets offered some comfort, their twists and turns etched into his memory from years of clandestine activities. He knew where to hide, where to move quickly, and where to blend into the night.

The silence that followed the cessation of gunfire was deafening. It was as if the city itself was holding its breath, mourning the loss of one of its own. Brendan's thoughts flickered back to Danny's resolute figure, standing firm in the face of overwhelming odds. That image fueled his resolve to keep moving, to survive.

As he moved through the backstreets, Brendan encountered the occasional civilian peeking cautiously from behind closed doors and shuttered windows. Their eyes, wide with fear and curiosity, watched him pass. He offered no explanation, only a silent nod of acknowledgment. They understood the silent language of a city in conflict.

Brendan's route took him through a series of interconnected alleys, each darker and narrower than the last. The distant wail of sirens and the occasional shout of soldiers searching for him punctuated the otherwise eerie quiet. He knew he had to keep moving, to stay ahead of any potential pursuit.

His goal was to reach a safe house, a hidden sanctuary known only to a select few within the IRA. It was a place where he could regroup, gather his thoughts, and plan the next steps. Every decision he made was guided by the need to honor Danny's sacrifice by continuing the fight with renewed vigor.

As he approached a particularly narrow alley, Brendan paused, listening intently for any signs of pursuit. Hearing nothing but the distant hum of the city, he pressed on. His footsteps echoed softly against the cobblestones, a steady rhythm that kept him grounded amidst the chaos.

The night was far from over, and Brendan knew that his journey was just beginning. The memory of Danny O'Toole, standing defiantly in the face of overwhelming force, was a beacon guiding him through the darkness. The old man's spirit seemed to infuse him with strength, each step a testament to their shared cause.

Finally, Brendan reached a nondescript door hidden in the shadows of a dilapidated building. He knocked in a specific pattern, a coded signal that identified him as a friend. The door creaked open, revealing a safe haven where he could catch his breath and plan his next move.

Inside, the atmosphere was tense but supportive. Fellow fighters greeted him with solemn nods, understanding the gravity of what had just transpired. Brendan, though weary, felt a renewed sense of purpose. Danny's last stand had not been in vain, and he was determined to honor that sacrifice.

As he sat down to rest, Brendan's thoughts remained on the night's events. The streets of Belfast, scarred by the conflict, were a stark reminder of the ongoing struggle for freedom. Danny's sacrifice had given him a chance to continue that fight, and he would not let it go to waste.

The night was far from over, but Brendan was ready for whatever came next. The spirit of resistance that Danny embodied lived on in him, driving him forward. With each breath, he prepared for the battles yet to come, knowing that the fight for their homeland's future was far from over.

As word of Danny's death spread like wildfire, a palpable wave of anger and grief swept through the community. Danny was not just an old man; he was a symbol, a beacon of the long-standing struggle, a living testament to their enduring fight for freedom. His death at the hands of the British forces and the RUC sparked a fury that had been simmering under the surface.

The streets of Belfast, which had only moments ago been a battleground, now became the stage for a different kind of conflict. Residents, galvanized by the news of Danny's sacrifice, poured out of their homes. What started as a gathering of mourners quickly escalated into a full-blown riot. The community, united in their grief and rage, began to rally against the symbols of the authority they viewed as oppressors.

Brendan, still evading capture, witnessed the transformation of the neighborhood. The sounds of sorrow had turned into chants of defiance, the mourning into mobilization. People young and old, fueled by a mix of respect for Danny and anger at the ongoing conflict, took to the streets. They built barricades, lit fires, and confronted the incoming waves of RUC and military reinforcements.

The riots unfolded with a ferocity that shook the city. The air was filled with the acrid smell of burning tires, the clamor of improvised weapons, and the shouts of the rioters. The confrontation was not just physical; it was a profound expression of a community pushed to its breaking point, a cry for justice and autonomy.

The streets, now ablaze with flames and fury, bore witness to the community's unyielding spirit. Makeshift barricades rose quickly, constructed from whatever materials could be found – old furniture, debris, and overturned vehicles. The fires cast an orange glow, illuminating the determined faces of the residents who had taken up the fight.

Brendan, navigating the chaos, felt a deep connection to the people around him. Danny's death had ignited something powerful, a unified resistance that transcended individual grief. He moved through the throng with a mix of urgency and awe, his heart heavy with the weight of loss but buoyed by the collective resolve he witnessed.

The RUC and military reinforcements, taken aback by the sudden uprising, struggled to regain control. Their presence, once a symbol of order, now faced a wall of defiance. The air crackled with tension as the two sides clashed, the sounds of batons against shields mingling with the roar of the crowd.

In the midst of the turmoil, Brendan saw familiar faces – neighbors, friends, and even strangers united by a common cause. The chants of defiance grew louder, a rhythmic declaration of their determination to fight back. The community, long accustomed to the weight of oppression, now stood together, refusing to be silenced.

As the night wore on, the intensity of the riots only increased. The flames from burning tires and barricades sent plumes of smoke into the sky, creating an almost apocalyptic scene. The shouts of the rioters, filled with anger and sorrow, echoed through the streets, a testament to their collective grief and unwavering resolve.

Brendan, finding temporary refuge in a hidden alley, took a moment to catch his breath. The events of the night had taken a toll on him, both physically and emotionally. But as he listened to the sounds of the uprising, he felt a renewed sense of purpose. Danny's sacrifice had not been in vain – it had sparked a fire that would not easily be extinguished.

The RUC and military forces, despite their training and equipment, found themselves overwhelmed by the sheer determination of the community. Every attempt to push forward was met with fierce resistance. The streets, once symbols of division, now became the battlegrounds of unity and defiance.

Brendan knew that the night was far from over. The struggle for freedom and justice continued, fueled by the memory of Danny O'Toole and the countless others who had given their lives for the cause. As he prepared to move again, he carried with him the spirit of resistance that had been reignited in the hearts of Belfast's residents.

The riots, though chaotic and destructive, were a powerful reminder of the community's strength and resilience. Danny's death had transformed grief into action, mourning into mobilization. As the flames continued to burn and the chants of defiance echoed through the night, the fight for freedom and autonomy pressed on, undeterred by the forces that sought to suppress it.

In this tumultuous upheaval, Brendan found himself swept along. The pulse of the crowd matched his own, their collective heart beating with the rhythm of resistance that drove the community. As he navigated the chaotic streets, images of Danny's sacrifice flashed through his mind, mingling with the unyielding spirit of the people who refused to be silenced.

Belfast's night air crackled with tension and resolve. The streets, once familiar, now felt like a battleground transformed by the raw energy of defiance. Shouts of protest echoed off the buildings, intermingling with the acrid scent of burning tires. The community, galvanized by grief and anger, surged forward in waves.

Brendan moved through the throng, feeling the vibration of their footsteps resonating through the ground. Each step taken by the crowd was a statement, a refusal to back down. Faces around him were set in grim determination, eyes ablaze with the fire of resistance. The scene was alive with the sound of makeshift barricades being erected and the rhythmic chants that grew louder with each passing moment.

Danny's name was on everyone's lips, whispered in reverence and shouted in fury. Candles flickered at makeshift memorials, their flames dancing in the night breeze, casting a soft glow on the flowers and handwritten notes left by mourners. The scent of fresh blooms mixed with the heavy air, creating an almost sacred atmosphere around these impromptu altars.

Families emerged from their homes, clutching photographs and mementos, tears mingling with expressions of fierce pride. Children, eyes wide with a mixture of fear and awe, clung to their parents, absorbing the gravity of the moment. Brendan saw elderly neighbors, faces etched with years of struggle, standing tall amidst the chaos, their presence a silent testament to resilience.

The community's response was immediate and profound. Makeshift banners appeared, scrawled with messages of defiance and unity. Impromptu marches snaked through the streets, their participants' footsteps a steady drumbeat of solidarity. Voices rose in unison, a powerful chorus that demanded to be heard. The chants, raw and unfiltered, spoke of a collective pain and an unyielding desire for justice.

Brendan felt the weight of the night's events pressing down on him, yet also lifting him. The sight of neighbors, once mere acquaintances, now standing shoulder to shoulder, sharing stories of Danny and their own brushes with the conflict, filled him with a sense of kinship. This was a community transformed, united by a shared history and a newfound determination.

As the night wore on, the initial outpouring of grief evolved into something more formidable. The streets, lit by the soft glow of candlelight and the harsh glare of burning barricades, became a canvas for the community's collective expression. Acts of resistance took shape, each one a tribute to Danny's legacy and a defiant stand against oppression.

Brendan paused at one of the memorials, his eyes tracing the flickering light of the candles. He saw messages written with trembling hands, words of love, loss, and an unwavering pledge to continue the fight. The air was thick with emotion, the raw, unfiltered energy of a people united in their grief and anger.

He joined the marchers, his steps falling in line with theirs. The rhythm of their movement was hypnotic, a physical manifestation of their collective resolve. The city that had borne witness to so much pain and struggle now resonated with a powerful declaration: they would not be broken.

As dawn approached, the fervor of the night began to settle, but the resolve remained unshaken. The streets of Belfast, marked by the night's events, stood as a testament to the community's unyielding spirit. Brendan knew that Danny's sacrifice had not only sparked a night of profound resistance but had also etched a powerful chapter in their ongoing struggle for freedom and recognition.

As the night turned into dawn, the streets of Belfast bore the marks of the night's events. Burned-out fires, charred barricades, and the quiet but resolute presence of the community spoke of a night where grief had turned into action, and mourning had transformed into a collective assertion of identity and solidarity.

The first light of morning revealed the scars of the night's fierce resistance. Smoke still curled from smoldering tires, and the acrid scent lingered in the cool air. Streets that had been battlegrounds were now littered with the debris of makeshift defenses—splintered wood, twisted metal, and fragments of shattered glass.

Residents, their faces etched with exhaustion but eyes still burning with resolve, began to emerge from the shadows. They surveyed the aftermath of their spontaneous uprising, their expressions a mix of sorrow for the loss of Danny O'Toole and pride in their unyielding defiance. The night's chaos had given way to a quiet but powerful determination that hung in the air like the morning mist.

Among the remnants of barricades, impromptu memorials stood as silent witnesses to the night's events. Candles, now melted to stubs, flickered weakly in the early light. Flowers and handwritten notes, damp with dew, lay scattered at the site of Danny's last stand, their presence a poignant reminder of the community's grief and unity.

Brendan, weary but driven, moved through the streets with a sense of purpose. The echoes of chants and shouts still reverberated in his mind, a soundtrack to the night's tumult. He passed groups of neighbors who had once been strangers but now shared a bond forged in the fires of resistance. They exchanged nods, silent acknowledgments of their shared struggle and newfound solidarity.

The community's spontaneous uprising was more than a reaction; it was a testament to their resilience in the face of ongoing strife. Each person, each act of defiance, was a clear message: while individuals like Danny might fall, the spirit of the community and their quest for justice and freedom would endure.

Children, clinging to their parents, walked the streets with wide eyes, taking in the transformed landscape. Their parents pointed out the remnants of the night's battles, their voices filled with a mixture of sorrow and pride. Stories of bravery and sacrifice were whispered, ensuring that the legacy of Danny and the spirit of resistance would be passed to the next generation.

As Brendan continued his journey, he encountered more signs of the community's resolve. Graffiti had appeared overnight on walls and buildings, messages of defiance and hope scrawled in bold letters. "Freedom," "Justice," and "Remember Danny" were emblazoned across surfaces, visible to all who passed by.

The early morning light cast long shadows across the streets, but the people of Belfast stood tall, unbowed. The night had tested them, but it had also united them in a way that few other events could. Their collective grief had been transformed into a powerful force, a beacon that would guide their continued fight for recognition and autonomy.

Brendan knew that the coming days would be challenging. The authorities would undoubtedly respond to the night's uprising, but the community had shown that they were not easily subdued. They had demonstrated their willingness to stand together, to fight for their beliefs, and to honor the memory of those who had sacrificed everything.

As he walked, Brendan felt a renewed sense of purpose. The events of the night had reinforced his commitment to the cause, his resolve strengthened by the sight of his neighbors' unwavering spirit. The memory of Danny O'Toole, and the uprising sparked by his death, would serve as a rallying cry for the days ahead.

Dawn in Belfast revealed not just the aftermath of a night of resistance but the enduring spirit of a community determined to fight for their future. The scars of the night's events would remain, but so too would the indomitable will of the people. Their message was clear: the struggle for justice and freedom would continue, undimmed and unbroken.

A mile away from the tumultuous events of the night, in a secluded backstreet shrouded in darkness, Michael and the remaining members of his team reconvened. The quiet of the alley stood in stark contrast to the chaos they had left behind. As they gathered, the palpable sense of relief at seeing each other safe was tempered by the gravity of what had transpired.

Shadows cloaked the alley, the dim light from a distant streetlamp casting long, eerie silhouettes. The team members, emerging from different directions, exchanged quick, hushed updates. Their faces, illuminated sporadically by the faint light, bore expressions of fatigue, concern, and lingering adrenaline from the night's events.

Michael scanned the faces of his comrades, noting the absence of Brendan. The silence hung heavy, each of them acutely aware of the sacrifice that had enabled their escape. The weight of Brendan's absence pressed down on them, a silent testament to the cost of their mission.

Taking a deep breath, Michael stepped forward. "We made it," he said, his voice low but steady, echoing softly in the narrow alley. "But Brendan..." His words trailed off, the unspoken acknowledgment of their comrade's fate hanging in the air. The team bowed their heads briefly, a silent tribute to Brendan's sacrifice.

The news of the community's response had reached them – the riots, the loss of Danny O'Toole. Each detail painted a vivid picture of the night's full impact. The alley, though quiet, seemed to reverberate with the distant echoes of the community's uproar, a stark reminder of the ongoing struggle.

In the dim light, the team pieced together the timeline of the night. Michael listened intently as each member recounted their escape, their voices filled with a mix of urgency and sorrow.

"The raid on the safe house," one began, eyes darting to each team member, "it happened so fast. We barely had time to react."

"We had to move the weapons," another added, gripping their coat as if still feeling the weight of the cache hidden within. "There was no choice."

"The patrol," a third interjected, voice trembling slightly, "they came out of nowhere. Brendan's diversion... it gave us the chance we needed."

Michael nodded, absorbing their words. The night had been a whirlwind of strategic decisions and unforeseen encounters, each moment a precarious balance between survival and sacrifice.

"Brendan's bravery," Michael said, his voice firm, "won't be in vain. He gave us a chance, and we need to honor that by continuing our mission."

Their expressions, though weary, hardened with resolve. The night's events had forged an even stronger bond among them, each member silently vowing to carry on in Brendan's memory. The news of Danny O'Toole's death and the subsequent riots only fueled their determination.

As the first light of dawn began to creep into the alley, Michael looked at his team with a mixture of pride and sorrow. "We need to move forward," he said quietly. "For Brendan, for Danny, for everyone counting on us."

The team nodded in unison, the quiet resolve in their eyes reflecting the shared understanding of their mission's importance. They knew the path ahead would be fraught with danger, but they also knew that their fight was just one part of a larger struggle.

With a final, silent acknowledgment of their fallen comrades, Michael led the team out of the alley. The streets of Belfast, still bearing the scars of the night's upheaval, awaited their continued defiance. Their steps were firm, each one a tribute to the sacrifices made and a commitment to the cause that bound them together.

The conversation then turned to the community's uprising. The fervent response from the residents of Belfast had ignited a fire within the team. As they spoke in hushed tones, the gravity of the night's events became apparent. Danny's stand and subsequent death had transformed grief and anger into a powerful display of unity.

In the dim alley, surrounded by the quiet aftermath of chaos, the team reflected on the significance of the night. What had begun as a mission to safeguard their resources had evolved into a pivotal moment in their struggle. The community's reaction, the loss of Danny, and the impact on the neighborhood were all testaments to the complexity and depth of the conflict they were engaged in.

Michael, stepping into his role as leader, addressed the team with a tone of cautious optimism. "This night has shown us the strength of our community," he said, his voice steady but filled with the weight of responsibility. "We must be more strategic, more careful. The path ahead is fraught with challenges, and we must navigate it wisely."

The team nodded, the flickering light of the distant streetlamp casting determined shadows on their faces. They understood the necessity of calculated actions, each move carrying the potential to either strengthen their cause or endanger their community.

As the first light of dawn began to creep into the sky, casting a pale glow over the alley, the team members prepared to disperse. Their footsteps echoed softly on the cobblestones as they disappeared into the waking city, each carrying the weight of the night's events. The night's story was etched in their minds – a tale of resilience, sacrifice, and the unyielding spirit of a community ensnared in a long-standing conflict.

Just as the last of the team members turned to leave, a shadowy figure emerged from the dim light of the early morning. The silhouette, moving slowly and with evident fatigue, became clearer as it approached. It was Brendan, against all odds, making his way back to the rendezvous point. His appearance was disheveled, his face etched with exhaustion and the residue of the night's harrowing events, but he was alive.

Michael's eyes widened in surprise and relief as he rushed forward to meet Brendan. "Brendan!" he called out, his voice a mix of disbelief and joy. The team quickly gathered around, their expressions reflecting a mixture of astonishment and gratitude.

Brendan, breathing heavily, managed a weary smile. "I made it," he said, his voice hoarse from the night's exertion. He looked at the familiar faces around him, finding solace in their presence.

The team, momentarily forgetting their fatigue, surrounded Brendan with relief and support. The alley, which had been a place of quiet reflection, now buzzed with a renewed sense of hope. Brendan's return was more than just a reunion; it was a symbol of resilience, a testament to the indomitable spirit that defined their cause.

As the dawn light grew stronger, casting long shadows on the cobblestones, Michael addressed the team once more. "Brendan's return is a reminder of why we fight," he said, his voice filled with conviction. "We do this for each other, for our community, and for the future we believe in."

With Brendan's safe return, the team felt a renewed sense of purpose. They knew that the road ahead would be difficult, but their unity and determination had been strengthened by the night's events. As they quietly dispersed into the city, each member carried with them the memory of Danny's sacrifice and the powerful uprising of their community.

The story of the night, now etched into their hearts, would guide them in the days to come. It was a story of defiance, of standing together against overwhelming odds, and of the unbreakable bond that held them together. As the first rays of the sun illuminated the streets of Belfast, the team moved forward, ready to face whatever challenges lay ahead, their spirits undimmed by the trials of the night.

The team, stunned and relieved, quickly gathered around Brendan. Whispered questions and expressions of disbelief filled the air as they tried to process his return. Brendan, with a weary but resilient smile, recounted his miraculous escape from the chaos. After creating the diversion, he had managed to evade capture in the confusion and turmoil, using his knowledge of the city's back alleys and hidden passages to escape.

Brendan's voice, though tired, carried the weight of his harrowing journey. He painted vivid pictures of chaotic scenes, close calls, and moments when he thought he wouldn't make it. He spoke of darting through shadowy alleys, heart pounding as he narrowly avoided patrols, and slipping through narrow gaps in fences. Each detail he shared pulled the team deeper into his experience, making them feel the tension and desperation of his escape.

"The streets were a maze," Brendan said, his eyes distant as he recalled the night. "I could hear the soldiers shouting, the crack of gunfire echoing off the buildings. At one point, I had to hide in a rubbish bin to avoid a patrol."

The team listened intently, their faces a mix of awe and concern. Brendan described how the escalating violence and Danny O'Toole's stand had ignited a fierce response from the residents. He painted a picture of the community's rage boiling over, leading to widespread riots and confrontations with the authorities.

"The people... they just poured out of their homes," he continued, his voice gaining strength. "Danny's death... it was like a spark in dry tinder. The whole neighborhood erupted. Barricades went up, fires lit the sky, and the chants... you could feel the anger, the grief."

Each team member absorbed the details of Brendan's ordeal, feeling the weight of the night's events. His return was not only a relief but also a catalyst for renewed purpose. Brendan's escape was a testament to his skills and determination, qualities that were invaluable to their cause.

Michael, watching his team, saw the impact Brendan's words had on them. He stepped forward, his voice steady and clear. "Brendan's return reminds us of why we fight," he said, his gaze moving from one team member to the next. "Our unity and commitment are our greatest strengths. The events of tonight have shown us the risks we face, but also the power of our actions."

The first rays of sunlight began to break through the horizon, casting a soft glow over the city. The team, standing together in the dim alley, shared a moment of quiet solidarity. They had faced one of their most challenging nights, but they had emerged intact, their resolve strengthened by the trials they had endured.

The light of dawn bathed the alley in a gentle, golden hue, symbolizing a new beginning. The team's faces, though weary, reflected a renewed determination. They understood the significance of their actions, the ripple effect that one night could have on their struggle and on the community they sought to protect.

Brendan, looking around at his comrades, felt a deep sense of belonging. His ordeal had tested him, but it had also reinforced the bond he shared with these people. "We carry on," he said softly, echoing Michael's sentiment. "For Danny, for our community, for each other."

With the dawn breaking, the team knew their path was fraught with danger, but they were united in their mission. The memory of Danny's sacrifice and the community's uprising would fuel their fight. As they dispersed into the waking city, each member carried the night's lessons with them, ready to face the challenges ahead with an unyielding spirit.

Brendan's return marked not just the end of a perilous night but also the beginning of a new chapter in their struggle. With renewed determination, the team melted away into the waking city, each member carrying with them the experiences of the night and a deepened commitment to their cause. The story of their fight was far from over, but they faced the future with a united front, bolstered by the resilience and spirit they had all shown.

In the relative safety of a secluded alleyway, away from the prying eyes of patrols and the chaos of the streets, Michael's team finally found a moment to regroup. The darkness of the alley provided a brief respite, a sanctuary where they could let down their guard for a moment and process the events of the night.

Huddled together, the team was visibly shaken. The adrenaline that had fueled their escape was now giving way to the realization of just how close they had come to capture or worse. The gravity of their situation hung heavily in the air, a tangible reminder of the risks inherent in their cause.

Michael, leaning against the cold, damp wall of the alley, took a deep breath. His eyes scanned the faces of his comrades, each one etched with exhaustion and lingering fear. "We made it through the night," he began, his voice steady but filled with the weight of their ordeal. "But we need to talk about what happened."

One by one, the team members shared their experiences, their voices low but urgent. Sean recounted darting through narrow passageways, his heart pounding as he barely evaded a patrol. Brendan described the harrowing moment when he hid in a cellar, the footsteps of soldiers echoing above her. Each story was a vivid tapestry of fear, quick thinking, and sheer luck.

"I thought they'd found me for sure," Liam admitted, his hands trembling slightly as he relived the moment. "But then there was this loud crash, and they all ran off. I still don't know what caused it, but it gave me the chance to slip away."

The intensity of their shared experiences was evident in their voices and expressions – a mixture of relief at having evaded capture and a sobering understanding of the dangers they had just faced. Michael listened intently, absorbing each detail, his mind already working on strategies to improve their chances in future missions.

Brendan, still catching his breath from his own ordeal, spoke last. His voice was rough, each word carrying the weight of his narrow escape. "Danny's stand... it was something else. It wasn't just a fight. It was a message. And the people... they responded."

The team fell silent, the mention of Danny bringing a fresh wave of emotion. His sacrifice had not been in vain; it had sparked a fierce response from the community, a testament to the unbreakable spirit of their fight. The impact of his actions was still reverberating through the city, and through their hearts.

Michael, sensing the need to refocus their energies, addressed his team with renewed resolve. "Danny showed us what's at stake. We need to be smarter, more strategic. The path ahead won't be easy, but we have each other. And we have the community behind us."

As the first light of dawn began to filter into the alley, casting a soft glow on their weary faces, the team felt a renewed sense of purpose. They had faced one of their most challenging nights and emerged intact, their resolve strengthened by the trials they had endured.

Michael's words hung in the air, a rallying cry for the days ahead. "Let's move out, stay safe, and keep fighting. For Danny, for Brendan, for all of us."

With that, the team dispersed quietly into the city, each member carrying the night's lessons with them. The dawn brought a new beginning, but the struggle was far from over. As they disappeared into the waking streets of Belfast, their steps were firm, their spirits undimmed by the night's trials.

The alleyway, now empty, stood as a silent witness to their resilience. The story of their fight would continue, each chapter written with the blood, sweat, and unyielding spirit of a community determined to reclaim their freedom.

Michael's reflection went beyond the physical risks they faced; it delved into the emotional and moral complexities of their struggle. Each decision, each action, rippled outward, affecting not just themselves but the entire community they were fighting for. The night's events had illuminated this intricate web of responsibility and consequence.

As he watched the city slowly come to life, the first light of dawn casting a gentle glow over the rooftops, Michael felt a renewed sense of purpose. The close call had reinforced his commitment to the cause, a cause that was bigger than any individual. It was a struggle for freedom, for justice, and for the right to determine their own future.

The camaraderie and sacrifice he had witnessed reaffirmed his belief in the IRA and its members. They were more than just fighters; they were brothers and sisters in arms, bound together by a shared vision and a common goal. The faces of his comrades, etched with fatigue yet shining with resolve, mirrored his own unwavering determination.

The rising sun cast long shadows across the rooftops, painting the city in hues of gold and gray. Michael stood up, the weight of the night's events settling into a determined resolve. It was time to blend back into the city, to become once again a part of the community he was fighting for. The events of the night would stay with him, a constant reminder of the risks, the commitment, and the deep bonds that defined their struggle.

He turned to his team, their eyes meeting in silent understanding. The close calls and near misses of the night had forged an even stronger bond between them. Each face bore the marks of exhaustion, but also a steely determination that spoke of their shared resolve.

"We've got work to do," Michael said quietly, his voice carrying the weight of their mission. "Let's get back out there and make sure Danny's sacrifice wasn't in vain."

The team nodded, their expressions reflecting a unity that went beyond words. They dispersed into the waking city, each step taken with a renewed sense of purpose. The story of their fight was far from over, but they were ready to face whatever the future held, united and resolute in their mission.

As Michael walked through the alleys and side streets, he couldn't help but notice the small signs of resilience and defiance scattered throughout the city. The graffiti on the walls, the whispered conversations of neighbors, the determined faces of those who had taken to the streets—all of it reminded him why they fought.

The morning air was crisp, carrying with it the promise of a new day. Michael felt a deep connection to the city and its people, a sense of belonging that fueled his determination. The night had tested them, but it had also shown them the strength of their collective spirit.

The memories of the night's events would stay with him, a constant reminder of the sacrifices made and the challenges yet to come. But as the sun rose higher in the sky, casting its light on the city below, Michael felt a renewed sense of hope. They were not alone in their struggle; they were part of a community united by a shared vision of freedom and justice.

With each step, Michael blended back into the fabric of the city, ready to continue the fight. The path ahead was uncertain, but their resolve was unwavering. Together, they would face whatever came their way, united by the bonds of camaraderie and the spirit of resistance.

The story of their fight was one of resilience, sacrifice, and an unyielding commitment to their cause. And as Michael and his team moved forward, they carried with them the lessons of the night, ready to write the next chapter in their struggle for freedom.

In the quiet aftermath of the night's tumultuous events, Michael found himself wandering through the awakening streets of Belfast. The city was slowly coming to life, seemingly oblivious to the undercurrents of the conflict that had shaped its recent history. This moment of solitude gave Michael an opportunity to reflect on the broader context of the Troubles, to consider the complex tapestry of political and social nuances that defined the conflict.

As he walked, the sights and sounds of the city sparked a series of reflections. The soft hum of morning traffic, the distant clatter of market stalls being set up, and the chirping of birds in the early light all contrasted starkly with the echoes of gunfire and shouts that had filled the night. Each familiar scene was a reminder of the city's resilience and the ever-present tension beneath its surface.

Passing by a mural depicting scenes of resistance, Michael's mind wandered back to the historical roots of the Troubles. He saw in his mind's eye the colonial history, the centuries-old religious divisions, and the long-standing fight for national identity that had brought them to this point. The mural, vibrant with colors and defiance, encapsulated the struggle that was both deeply personal and profoundly historical.

He continued his walk, the path taking him past a solemn memorial. The names etched into the stone spoke of lives lost, each one a story of its own. Michael pondered the aspirations and fears of both sides, realizing that beneath the veneer of violence lay a myriad of human stories, hopes, and tragedies. The Troubles were more than a conflict; they were a tapestry woven with the threads of countless lives, each strand representing a different perspective, a different pain.

The political intricacies of the conflict weighed heavily on his mind. As he walked, Michael thought about the roles of various entities – the IRA, the British government, the loyalist paramilitaries, and the international community. Each player brought their agendas and perspectives, contributing to a complex and often volatile situation. He recalled the peace talks and ceasefires, the fragile efforts to find a resolution amidst seemingly insurmountable differences. The distant memory of political speeches and negotiations echoed in his thoughts, a reminder of the tenuous balance they all sought to maintain.

Walking past a row of houses, their walls adorned with slogans and graffiti, symbols of resistance and defiance, Michael reflected on the social impact of the Troubles. He saw the faces of families torn apart by violence, the hollow eyes of children growing up in a world divided by fear and hatred. The conflict had seeped into every aspect of life in Northern Ireland, shaping identities and worldviews, creating a landscape where hope and despair coexisted uneasily.

A group of schoolchildren crossed his path, their laughter momentarily lifting the heavy veil of his thoughts. Michael watched them, thinking about the younger generation, about the world they were inheriting. These children, growing up amidst the remnants of conflict, were the ones who would carry forward the legacy of their parents' struggles. He hoped they would find a way to transcend the divisions, to build a future where the echoes of the past were not chains but lessons.

The sun climbed higher, casting long shadows that stretched across the city. Michael's steps led him to a quiet park, a place of temporary reprieve from the turmoil. He sat on a bench, the events of the night still vivid in his mind. The park, with its green expanse and blooming flowers, felt like an oasis of normalcy amidst the chaos. It was a stark contrast to the scenes of violence and resistance that had played out in the dark hours before dawn.

As he rested, Michael's thoughts returned to his team, to Brendan's miraculous return, and to the memory of Danny O'Toole's sacrifice. The close call had reinforced his commitment to the cause, but it had also deepened his understanding of the complexities they navigated every day. Their fight was not just about survival; it was about justice, about the right to determine their own future.

Michael stood up, feeling the weight of his reflections settling into a renewed resolve. The story of their fight was far from over, and the path ahead was uncertain. But as he walked back into the city, blending once again into the fabric of Belfast, he carried with him the lessons of the past and the hope for a future defined by unity and peace.

The rising sun cast a golden light over the rooftops, illuminating the murals, the memorials, and the faces of those starting their day. Each step Michael took was a testament to their resilience, to the unyielding spirit of a community that had endured so much yet remained unbroken. The fight for freedom, for justice, continued, and with each new day, they moved closer to the world they envisioned, one where the shadows of the past no longer dictated the possibilities of the future.

In the quiet aftermath of the night's tumultuous events, Michael found himself wandering through the awakening streets of Belfast. The city was slowly coming to life, seemingly oblivious to the undercurrents of the conflict that had shaped its recent history. This moment of solitude gave Michael an opportunity to reflect on the broader context of the Troubles, to consider the complex tapestry of political and social nuances that defined the conflict.

As he walked, the sights and sounds of the city sparked a series of reflections. The soft hum of morning traffic, the distant clatter of market stalls being set up, and the chirping of birds in the early light all contrasted starkly with the echoes of gunfire and shouts that had filled the night. Each familiar scene was a reminder of the city's resilience and the ever-present tension beneath its surface.

Passing by a mural depicting scenes of resistance, Michael's mind wandered back to the historical roots of the Troubles. He saw in his mind's eye the colonial history, the centuries-old religious divisions, and the long-standing fight for national identity that had brought them to this point. The mural, vibrant with colors and defiance, encapsulated the struggle that was both deeply personal and profoundly historical.

He continued his walk, the path taking him past a solemn memorial. The names etched into the stone spoke of lives lost, each one a story of its own. Michael pondered the aspirations and fears of both sides, realizing that beneath the veneer of violence lay a myriad of human stories, hopes, and tragedies. The Troubles were more than a conflict; they were a tapestry woven with the threads of countless lives, each strand representing a different perspective, a different pain.

The political intricacies of the conflict weighed heavily on his mind. As he walked, Michael thought about the roles of various entities – the IRA, the British government, the loyalist paramilitaries, and the international community. Each player brought their agendas and perspectives, contributing to a complex and often volatile situation. He recalled the peace talks and ceasefires, the fragile efforts to find a resolution amidst seemingly insurmountable differences. The distant memory of political speeches and negotiations echoed in his thoughts, a reminder of the tenuous balance they all sought to maintain.

Walking past a row of houses, their walls adorned with slogans and graffiti, symbols of resistance and defiance, Michael reflected on the social impact of the Troubles. He saw the faces of families torn apart by violence, the hollow eyes of children growing up in a world divided by fear and hatred. The conflict had seeped into every aspect of life in Northern Ireland, shaping identities and worldviews, creating a landscape where hope and despair coexisted uneasily.

A group of schoolchildren crossed his path, their laughter momentarily lifting the heavy veil of his thoughts. Michael watched them, thinking about the younger generation, about the world they were inheriting. These children, growing up amidst the remnants of conflict, were the ones who would carry forward the legacy of their parents' struggles. He hoped they would find a way to transcend the divisions, to build a future where the echoes of the past were not chains but lessons.

The sun climbed higher, casting long shadows that stretched across the city. Michael's steps led him to a quiet park, a place of temporary reprieve from the turmoil. He sat on a bench, the events of the night still vivid in his mind. The park, with its green expanse and blooming flowers, felt like an oasis of normalcy amidst the chaos. It was a stark contrast to the scenes of violence and resistance that had played out in the dark hours before dawn.

As he rested, Michael's thoughts returned to his team, to Brendan's miraculous return, and to the memory of Danny O'Toole's sacrifice. The close call had reinforced his commitment to the cause, but it had also deepened his understanding of the complexities they navigated every day. Their fight was not just about survival; it was about justice, about the right to determine their own future.

Michael stood up, feeling the weight of his reflections settling into a renewed resolve. The story of their fight was far from over, and the path ahead was uncertain. But as he walked back into the city, blending once again into the fabric of Belfast, he carried with him the lessons of the past and the hope for a future defined by unity and peace.

The rising sun cast a golden light over the rooftops, illuminating the murals, the memorials, and the faces of those starting their day. Each step Michael took was a testament to their resilience, to the unyielding spirit of a community that had endured so much yet remained unbroken. The fight for freedom, for justice, continued, and with each new day, they moved closer to the world they envisioned, one where the shadows of the past no longer dictated the possibilities of the future.

Michael also considered the internal dynamics within the IRA. He thought about the debates and discussions they had, the differing opinions on strategy and tactics, and the challenges of balancing the fight for freedom with the moral implications of their actions. He realized that the struggle was not just against an external adversary but also about defining their path, one that aligned with their vision of a free and united Ireland.

These reflections brought a deeper understanding of the conflict's complexity. Michael recognized that the Troubles were not just a black-and-white narrative but a multi-faceted issue, steeped in history and human experience. This understanding reaffirmed his commitment but also highlighted the need for a thoughtful approach, one that considered the broader implications of their actions.

As Michael continued his walk, the city fully awoke around him. Shops began to open, the smell of freshly baked bread wafted through the air, and the chatter of early risers filled the streets. The normalcy of these scenes stood in stark contrast to the turmoil of the night, a reminder of what they were fighting for: a peaceful, ordinary life free from the shadow of conflict.

Michael meandered through the waking streets, each step a meditation on the night's events and the road ahead. The challenges they had faced, the loss they had endured, and the outpouring of communal emotion had not weakened his determination; rather, they had served to strengthen it.

He passed by a group of children on their way to school, their laughter and chatter a poignant symbol of innocence amidst the conflict. Michael's thoughts turned to the future they were fighting to secure – a future where these children could grow up in a united, peaceful Ireland. The weight of this responsibility settled on his shoulders, but it also fueled his resolve.

Michael's mind wandered back to the internal debates within the IRA. He recalled heated discussions about the best path forward, the tension between aggressive tactics and the moral high ground. He remembered voices calling for more militant actions and others urging caution and diplomacy. These debates were a microcosm of the larger conflict, reflecting the struggle to balance immediate needs with long-term goals.

His reflections deepened his understanding of the complexity of their cause. The Troubles were not a simple battle between good and evil, but a tangled web of history, politics, and human experiences. Every action had consequences that rippled through the community, affecting lives in ways that were often hard to predict.

Michael felt a renewed sense of purpose taking shape within him. The night's harrowing experiences had crystallized his understanding of the importance of their struggle. It was not just about the immediate fight or the tactical victories; it was about the larger quest for Irish independence, a cause steeped in a history of resistance and the pursuit of self-determination.

As he walked, the sights and sounds of Belfast in the early morning filled him with a sense of calm determination. The city, with its scars and resilience, was a testament to the enduring spirit of its people. Michael knew the road to peace and unity in Northern Ireland was long and fraught with challenges, but it was a road he was willing to travel.

He thought of Danny O'Toole and Brendan, of the sacrifices made and the bonds forged in the crucible of conflict. Their stories were part of a larger narrative, one that spanned generations and encompassed countless acts of bravery and resistance. Michael felt a deep connection to this narrative, a sense of belonging that transcended the immediate struggles.

As the sun climbed higher, casting a golden light over the city, Michael felt his resolve solidify. The events of the night had tested them, but they had also brought them closer together. They had shown that their fight was not just about resisting oppression, but about building a future rooted in justice and equality.

With each step, Michael felt his commitment to the IRA and its cause deepen. The night's experiences had crystallized his understanding of the importance of their struggle. It was about more than just the immediate fight; it was about the larger quest for Irish independence, a cause steeped in a history of resistance and the pursuit of self-determination.

The city's morning bustle continued to grow, a symphony of everyday life that underscored the significance of their mission. Michael knew that the path ahead would be difficult, but he was ready to face it with a renewed sense of purpose and an unshakable belief in their cause. As he walked back into the heart of Belfast, he carried with him the lessons of the past and the hope for a future defined by unity and peace.

As the chapter drew to a close, Michael stood atop a small hill overlooking Belfast. The city lay spread out before him, a tapestry of history and conflict, of resilience and struggle. In these quiet moments, Michael's thoughts turned to the future, to the challenges and decisions that lay ahead in his journey with the IRA.

The first light of dawn bathed Belfast in a soft, golden glow. From his vantage point, Michael could see the intricate network of streets, the familiar landmarks, and the pockets of the city that had witnessed so much turmoil. The distant hum of morning activity was just beginning, a stark contrast to the chaos of the night before.

He knew that the events of the past night were just the beginning. The successful transport of the weapons, the tragic loss of Danny O'Toole, and the ensuing riots had marked a significant turn in the conflict. They had not only shown the IRA's capability and resolve but had also highlighted the deep-rooted tensions within Belfast. Michael understood that these events would have repercussions, setting off ripples that would touch every corner of the community.

The increasing militarization of the city, the heightened surveillance, and the British government's response to the IRA's activities were all factors that Michael knew would shape their future operations. He anticipated more aggressive tactics from the British forces, and with it, the need for the IRA to adapt and evolve. The path ahead would require careful planning, strategic thinking, and, above all, a unity of purpose among the IRA members.

As he scanned the cityscape, his mind raced with thoughts of strategy and survival. He could almost see the British patrols tightening their grip, the watchful eyes of surveillance cameras, and the ever-present tension that had become part of daily life in Belfast. He imagined the streets he had walked earlier, now potentially hotspots for future conflicts, each alley and corner a potential battlefield.

Michael also foresaw difficult decisions in his future. The moral complexities of their fight for independence, the impact of their actions on the civilian population, and the ever-present risk to himself and his comrades were all considerations that would weigh heavily on him. He knew that each decision would carry with it a weight of responsibility, not just for the immediate outcome, but for the broader implications on the cause they were fighting for.

His thoughts drifted to the faces of the people affected by the conflict: the grieving families, the children growing up amidst violence, and the community members whose lives were entwined with the struggle. Each face represented a story, a reason to continue fighting, but also a reminder of the human cost of their actions.

As he looked out over the city, Michael felt a renewed sense of purpose. The struggle for Irish independence was a long and arduous journey, one that required sacrifice, resilience, and an unwavering commitment to the cause. The weight of responsibility settled on his shoulders, but with it came a steely resolve.

The sky began to lighten, the sun's rays piercing through the morning mist and illuminating the city below. Michael took a deep breath, feeling the crisp air fill his lungs. The road ahead was fraught with challenges, but he was ready to face them. The memory of Danny O'Toole's sacrifice and the community's fierce response fueled his determination.

Michael turned away from the panoramic view, his mind set on the tasks ahead. The city below, with all its scars and hopes, awaited his return. Each step he took down the hill was imbued with a sense of purpose, each footfall a promise to continue the fight for a free and united Ireland.

As he descended, the sounds of Belfast waking up grew louder. The city, resilient and unbroken, was a testament to the enduring spirit of its people. Michael knew that the story of their struggle was far from over. There were battles yet to be fought, decisions to be made, and a future to be shaped.

With a final glance back at the city, Michael reaffirmed his commitment. The challenges were daunting, but they were not insurmountable. United in their cause, he and his comrades would continue their journey, each step forward driven by the unwavering belief in the justice of their fight.

The sun fully emerged, casting a warm light over Belfast. Michael's heart swelled with determination as he rejoined the waking city, ready to face the future with a renewed sense of purpose. The struggle for independence, for justice, was not just a fight; it was a testament to the resilience and spirit of the people of Northern Ireland. And Michael was ready to play his part in the next phase of the IRA's fight.

Chapter 4: Chess With The Empire

The basement, hidden in the labyrinthine streets of Belfast, was shrouded in shadows, with only a few flickering bulbs casting an eerie glow. This dimly lit refuge had become a sanctuary, a clandestine haven where plans were meticulously crafted, and destinies were irrevocably altered. The air was thick with the mingled scents of damp earth and musty wood, a constant reminder of their underground existence.

Michael and his IRA team clustered around an old, rugged table scarred by years of use and conflict. Each creak of the wooden chairs, each rustle of clothing seemed amplified in the tense silence. The men exchanged glances, their eyes reflecting a blend of determination and unease, the weight of their mission pressing heavily on their shoulders.

On the table, a detailed map of a rural area in the Republic of Ireland lay spread out, its edges curling slightly from age. The map was their blueprint, the pathway to their ambitious target – a secluded police station. The marked location stood out sharply, a bold red circle that seemed to pulse with the gravity of what it represented. The men leaned in, the soft rustling of paper and the muted murmur of their voices the only sounds in the room, as they plotted the intricate steps of their perilous journey.

SEAN, A SEASONED STRATEGIST with a rugged demeanor shaped by countless battles, stood authoritatively at the head of the table. The dim light cast sharp shadows across his face, highlighting the deep lines etched by years of conflict and strategy. He surveyed the room, his intense gaze lingering on each member, silently conveying the gravity of their task.

As he began outlining the mission, his voice cut through the tension, a blend of seriousness and unspoken urgency that commanded attention. "This isn't just about acquiring more arms," he declared, his tone steady and resolute. His words seemed to hang in the air, heavy with meaning. "It's about making a statement, asserting that our reach extends beyond Northern Ireland."

The room fell silent, the weight of his words sinking in. Sean's eyes blazed with conviction as he continued, "This raid is going to send a bold message, not just to our supporters but to our adversaries as well." The murmurs of agreement and the firm nods from his team reflected their shared understanding of the mission's significance. This wasn't just an operation; it was a declaration, a testament to their determination and resolve.

Michael's eyes were glued to the map, his mind meticulously visualizing every detail Sean described. The police station, nestled in a serene, rural part of the Republic of Ireland, seemed almost innocuous at first glance. Its isolation, surrounded by rolling green fields and distant farmhouses, and relatively lax security made it an enticing target.

As Sean's words painted the scenario, Michael could almost hear the rustling of leaves and the distant chirping of birds that would surround their approach. Yet, beneath the surface of this tranquil scene, he sensed the gravity of their mission. The secluded location, while advantageous for a swift raid, underscored the audacity of their plan.

Michael was acutely aware of the broader implications. Raiding a target in the Republic of Ireland marked a significant escalation in their operations. It was a bold, risky maneuver that could shift the dynamics of their struggle, drawing a sharp line in the sand. The potential to alter the course of their fight loomed large, and with it, the likelihood of attracting international scrutiny. The stakes were higher than ever, and Michael could feel the weight of responsibility pressing down on him as he prepared to turn their plans into reality.

The team leaned in closer, their collective focus sharpening as they absorbed the specifics of the plan. The room buzzed with a quiet intensity, each member hanging on Sean's every word. Discussions ensued, their voices low but urgent, as they dissected the layout of the police station. Diagrams were sketched, routes traced with pointed fingers, and escape paths debated with fervor.

"The timing is crucial," Sean emphasized, his finger tapping on the map. "We strike at dawn, just as the shift changes, to catch them off guard and minimize conflict." The men nodded, their faces a mix of determination and wariness.

Each member was acutely aware of the risks involved. They talked through potential scenarios, from the moment they breached the station to the swift, silent retreat they hoped to execute. Every angle was considered, every possible outcome weighed.

Such an operation was more than a tactical maneuver; it was a leap into uncharted territory. The gravity of the mission hung heavy in the air, the understanding that this raid could dramatically alter the landscape of their conflict. It would blur the lines in a struggle that had long been confined to Northern Ireland, thrusting them onto a broader, more perilous stage. The room was filled with the silent acknowledgment of the gamble they were about to take, the recognition that success would bring not just victory, but a seismic shift in their battle for freedom.

Brendan, now recovered from the ordeal of the previous night, leaned forward, his eyes sharp with renewed energy. His voice, steady and confident, cut through the low murmurs of the group. "We'll need a fast getaway. A quiet approach, swift action, and then out before they even realize what's hit them," he suggested, his tone leaving no room for doubt.

He traced potential escape routes on the map with his finger, the lines he drew almost coming to life under his touch. "Here," he said, pointing to a narrow path winding through the fields, "this route will give us cover and a quick exit. It's secluded enough to avoid immediate detection." The team watched intently, nodding in agreement.

Brendan's insights, born from hard-earned experience, added a layer of precision to their plan. His calm demeanor belied the intensity of his focus, each word he spoke imbued with the clarity of someone who had faced peril before and emerged wiser. The details he provided—timing, speed, stealth—painted a vivid picture of their escape, solidifying their strategy and boosting the team's confidence in their mission's success.

Her hands moved deftly over the map, outlining critical points with practiced ease. "Coordination and communication will make or break this operation," she continued, her tone leaving no room for ambiguity. "Every move must be synchronized. We need clear signals and backup plans for every possible scenario."

The room grew quiet, the weight of her words sinking in. Aisling's meticulous nature, usually a source of gentle teasing among the team, now commanded their respect and attention. Her unwavering focus and thoroughness brought a sense of order and clarity to the chaotic energy of the room.

"We'll establish checkpoints," she said, marking them on the map with precise taps. "And designate roles to ensure everyone knows their part. This isn't just about speed; it's about flawless execution." Her voice softened slightly, but her resolve remained firm. "We can do this, but we have to be perfect."

The team nodded in unison, their determination solidifying under Aisling's methodical guidance. Her emphasis on precision and communication resonated deeply, reinforcing the critical nature of their mission and the need for absolute cohesion.

The room buzzed with a dynamic exchange of ideas, plans, and possible contingencies, the air thick with the intensity of their discussion. Voices overlapped as each member contributed their expertise, sketching out scenarios and debating the best course of action. The table, now cluttered with maps, notes, and diagrams, became the epicenter of their collective effort.

This raid represented more than just a tactical operation; it was a strategic move in the grander scheme of their struggle. The implications of their plan stretched far beyond the immediate goal, carrying the potential to reshape their fight in profound ways. Each detail they hammered out, every contingency they planned for, underscored the gravity of their mission.

The atmosphere crackled with a blend of anticipation and resolve. They were not merely preparing for a raid; they were orchestrating a pivotal moment in their battle, a decision that could shift the balance of power and draw attention from all corners. The magnitude of their endeavor was not lost on them. They were poised on the edge of a significant turning point, aware that the success of this mission could alter the trajectory of their struggle and etch their actions into the annals of history.

As ideas flowed and plans solidified, the team felt the weight of their responsibility, yet also a surge of unity and purpose. They were ready to step into the unknown, driven by the hope that this bold move would carve a path toward their ultimate goal.

s the meeting continued, a renewed sense of determination settled over Michael like a warm, steady flame. This mission marked a significant step in their journey, a bold and daring venture that could redefine the very nature of their fight. Each word exchanged, every strategy debated, added layers to his resolve.

Michael's mind churned with the enormity of their undertaking. He understood the gravity of what they were about to embark upon, the weight of their decision pressing heavily upon him. The details of the plan crystallized in his thoughts—the quiet approach, the swift execution, the precise escape. It wasn't just the logistical challenges that occupied his mind but the broader implications of their actions.

The room's atmosphere grew denser with the collective focus of the team, yet Michael felt a clarity cutting through the tension. This mission was more than a tactical operation; it was a statement, a leap into a new phase of their struggle. The potential to alter their trajectory, to draw international attention and shift perceptions, hung in the balance.

Michael's gaze drifted over his comrades, seeing in their faces a reflection of his own determination. Their shared resolve, their commitment to the cause, bolstered his spirit. He felt the weight of responsibility, but also a surge of unity and purpose that strengthened his resolve. This was their moment, a daring step into the unknown, driven by the hope that this mission would carve a decisive path toward their ultimate goal.

The exchange concluded with the team finalizing their plans, each member fully aware of the mission's immense significance. They were not just participants in an operation; they were key players in a pivotal new chapter of their struggle. Each person felt the weight of their role, acutely aware of the critical moment they were about to step into.

After setting the mission's goals, Michael and his team delved into the intricate strategic planning for the raid on the rural police station in the Republic of Ireland. The basement, once a mere meeting place, had now transformed into a war room, its atmosphere charged with a sense of urgency and purpose. Maps, diagrams, and documents sprawled across the old table, each item a piece of the complex puzzle they were assembling.

Every detail of the operation was meticulously scrutinized. Timelines were established, routes plotted, and contingencies discussed with painstaking precision. The team moved with synchronized efficiency, their minds honed on the task ahead. Sean's authoritative voice provided guidance, while Aisling's meticulous nature ensured that no detail was overlooked. Brendan's insights into escape routes and timing added a layer of practicality that was indispensable.

The basement walls seemed to close in, not with confinement, but with the intensity of their focus. The faint smell of dampness mingled with the sharper scent of ink and paper, creating an environment that was both oppressive and electrifying. The team's whispered discussions and the soft rustle of maps were the only sounds, amplifying the gravity of their mission.

Each member of the team felt the transformation. They were no longer just planning a raid; they were orchestrating a decisive maneuver that could reshape their fight. The basement had become a crucible, forging their resolve and sharpening their strategy. As they reviewed their plans one final time, a shared sense of determination solidified among them. They were ready to step into the breach, united by their cause and the knowledge that this mission could be the turning point in their struggle for freedom.

In the days leading up to the planned raid, Michael and a small subgroup of his team embarked on a covert mission to scout the rural police station in the Republic of Ireland. Their goal was clear: gather as much intelligence as possible to ensure the success and safety of their operation.

Blending seamlessly into the local scene, they arrived in the small town under the guise of travelers, their demeanor relaxed and unremarkable, careful to avoid any behavior that might arouse suspicion. The police station stood on the outskirts of the town, a seemingly quiet building that belied its significance in their upcoming mission.

Michael, with his keen eye for detail, surveyed the station's layout with the precision of a seasoned strategist. He noted the main entrance, the position of the windows, and any secondary access points that could be used for entry or escape. The team discreetly took photographs where possible, capturing angles and details that would be crucial in planning their entry and exit. The click of the camera was almost inaudible, each shot carefully framed to avoid detection.

The number of personnel at the station was a key factor in their planning. They meticulously counted the officers coming in and out, timing their observations to coincide with shift changes. It was during these transitions that they noticed a slight relaxation in the station's security—an opportunity they could potentially exploit. The officers' routines, their casual interactions, and even the occasional cigarette break outside the back entrance were all noted with precision.

The station itself seemed innocuous under the midday sun, its brick walls warmed by the light. Yet, Michael could almost feel the tension in the air as he imagined the chaos they would unleash. He watched the officers move about with a deceptive sense of normalcy, their uniforms blending into the rural backdrop, oblivious to the scrutiny they were under.

The team's conversations were hushed, their movements synchronized as they navigated the town. Aisling, with her meticulous nature, jotted down notes in a small, inconspicuous notebook, recording times, faces, and patterns. Brendan, ever the strategist, suggested potential scenarios for their entry, escape routes, and fallback plans. Their combined efforts painted a comprehensive picture of the station's vulnerabilities and strengths.

As dusk approached, casting long shadows across the landscape, Michael and his team made their way back to their temporary lodgings. The day's reconnaissance had been fruitful, providing them with the critical insights needed to refine their strategy. The quiet of the evening contrasted sharply with the intensity of their planning session, the team's whispered discussions filled with a renewed sense of purpose.

Each member knew that the success of the mission hinged on the intelligence they had gathered. The small town, with its picturesque charm and unassuming police station, would soon be the stage for a daring raid that could alter the course of their struggle. The covert mission had brought them one step closer to that decisive moment, their preparations now grounded in the detailed knowledge of their target.

Security systems were the next focus. The team meticulously observed the presence of CCTV cameras and any visible alarms. From a distance, they made mental notes of camera positions and the areas they covered, identifying blind spots that could provide crucial cover during the raid. The slow, mechanical sweep of the cameras was memorized, each arc of motion committed to memory.

Michael and his team extended their observations to the area surrounding the station as well. They identified potential hiding spots—dense foliage that could obscure their movements, narrow back alleys that offered quick escape routes, and even an abandoned barn that could serve as temporary cover if things went awry. The barn, with its weathered wood and overgrown surroundings, seemed like a relic of another time, now repurposed in their strategic calculations.

Local traffic patterns were carefully noted, determining the least busy times and the natural flow of vehicles that could provide incidental cover for their movements. Michael watched the rhythm of the town, the ebb and flow of cars, the sporadic hum of activity that peaked during the day and lulled into quiet in the early hours of the morning. They timed the intervals between passing cars, understanding the moments of opportunity when they could move undetected.

The streets around the station were mapped in their minds, every twist and turn, every potential obstruction. They observed the habits of the local residents, the routines that could either pose a risk or offer unwitting assistance. Brendan pointed out a narrow lane that led to the rear of the station, often deserted and perfect for a covert approach. Aisling highlighted a thick cluster of trees that bordered one side of the property, providing a natural screen from prying eyes.

With each piece of intelligence gathered, their plan grew more detailed and precise. The station, once just a dot on a map, now loomed large in their minds as a complex puzzle to be solved. The team's discussions became more focused, their strategies more refined, as they wove together their observations into a coherent plan.

As night fell, cloaking the town in darkness, Michael felt a surge of determination. They had identified the weaknesses in the station's defenses, pinpointed their entry and exit points, and mapped out their hiding spots and escape routes. The success of their mission now hinged on their ability to execute these plans with precision and stealth.

The team's covert scouting had provided them with the knowledge they needed. They returned to their base with a sense of readiness, their minds sharp and their resolve unshaken. The rural police station, with its quiet exterior and hidden vulnerabilities, was now a well-charted target in their audacious campaign. The days of preparation had steeled them, transforming their intent into a finely tuned strategy, poised for action.

Back in their secret hideout, Michael and his team huddled around the table, their faces illuminated by the dim glow of a single overhead lamp. They pored over the details gathered from the scouting mission, every note and photograph laid out before them. The focus now shifted to one of the most critical aspects of their plan—timing the raid. Every member understood that success hinged not just on what they did, but when they did it.

The room was thick with tension as they debated the best time to strike. Maps and notes were passed around, each observation scrutinized under the collective gaze of the team. The air was filled with a mix of determination and apprehension, the weight of their impending action pressing down on them.

After much deliberation, the team agreed on a late-night raid. The cover of darkness would provide an added layer of stealth, enveloping their movements in shadows. The late hour was likely to coincide with a period of reduced activity at the station, a time when the town slept and vigilance waned. They hypothesized that the guards' attentiveness might lapse in the early hours of the morning, creating a window of opportunity they intended to exploit.

Michael glanced around the table, his eyes meeting those of his comrades. He saw in their expressions a reflection of his own resolve, the shared understanding of the risks and the stakes. Brendan, always the tactician, outlined the timeline, his finger tracing the path they would take under the cloak of night. Aisling added her insights on synchronizing their movements, ensuring that each step was taken with precision.

"The guard change happens at 3 AM," Brendan noted, pointing to the spot on the map where the shift transitions. "We'll move in just after, when they're least alert and their defenses are down."

Aisling nodded, adding, "We'll need to synchronize our watches. Every second counts. Any deviation could jeopardize the entire operation."

The team nodded in agreement, the gravity of their mission evident in their focused expressions. They discussed the specifics—how they would approach the station, the signals they would use, the exact timing of each move. Every contingency was considered, every potential obstacle planned for.

As the final details were hammered out, a sense of unity and purpose solidified among them. The room, filled with the quiet hum of strategizing minds, felt charged with the energy of their resolve. They were not just planning a raid; they were preparing to take a decisive step in their struggle, a bold move that could tip the scales in their favor.

With the plan set and the timing agreed upon, the team dispersed to make their final preparations. Michael lingered for a moment, looking at the maps and notes one last time. The late-night raid was a calculated risk, a gamble that could redefine their fight. He felt the weight of leadership, the responsibility of guiding his team through the darkness that lay ahead.

As he extinguished the light and left the room, Michael carried with him the silent determination of his comrades, each one ready to move under the cover of night, their collective fate resting on the precision and courage of their actions. The stage was set, and the countdown to their daring mission had begun.

Sean, always meticulous about details, leaned forward, his eyes sharp with intensity. "Timing is everything," he said, his voice underscored with the gravity of their undertaking. "We synchronize our watches, and we move in unison. A minute's delay or rush could unravel everything."

The team gathered around, the room hushed with the weight of the moment. This synchronization was more than a mere adjustment of timepieces; it was a ritual that marked the seriousness of their mission. Each member extended their arm, the dim light casting long shadows over their faces, as they adjusted their watches to match Sean's precisely. The quiet ticking of each watch seemed amplified, a countdown to their decisive action.

They set a specific time for the raid, ensuring that each member knew the schedule down to the second. The chosen hour was critical, a carefully calculated moment when the station's defenses would be at their weakest. The synchronicity was crucial—it meant that every action, from the initial breach to the escape, was perfectly timed to minimize exposure and maximize efficiency.

Sean's voice, calm but firm, guided them through the final adjustments. "We move at 3:05 AM sharp. Not a second before, not a second after. Each step we take, each move we make, must be in perfect harmony."

The team nodded in understanding, the gravity of their shared commitment clear in their expressions. Michael glanced at his watch, the second hand ticking steadily forward, each movement bringing them closer to the moment of truth. He felt the collective resolve around him, the unity of purpose that bound them together.

As they synchronized their watches, an unspoken bond of trust and reliance formed, each member keenly aware of their role and the precise timing required. The tension in the room was almost tangible, the air thick with anticipation and determination. This was their pact, a promise to move as one, to execute their plan with the precision of a well-oiled machine.

The team dispersed to make their final preparations, the synchronized watches a constant reminder of the ticking clock and the impending raid. The late-night hour loomed ahead, shrouded in darkness and the promise of action. As they moved through the shadows, each step timed to perfection, they carried with them the silent understanding that their success depended on unwavering precision and unyielding unity.

In those quiet moments before the storm, the synchronized watches became symbols of their collective fate, each tick echoing the seriousness of their mission and the resolve that would carry them through the night.

Michael took a moment to stress the importance of this timing to the group. He stood, his posture commanding attention, and looked each team member in the eye. "Once we're in motion, every second counts," he said, his voice firm and unwavering. "We stick to the plan, and we stick to the timing. We're a single unit, and our movements need to be like clockwork." His tone left no room for doubt about the stakes at hand.

The gravity of his words settled over the group, each member absorbing the weight of their mission. They acknowledged the importance of this precision with a series of resolute nods. The room, filled with the quiet hum of synchronized determination, felt like a ticking timepiece itself, every second bringing them closer to the raid.

Michael continued, "Time is both our ally and our enemy. Mastering it is crucial to our success." He paused, letting the silence amplify the significance of his statement. The faint sounds of the outside world seemed distant and irrelevant, their focus honed sharply on the task ahead.

The team's expressions were set with steely determination, their minds aligning with Michael's instructions. They knew that in operations like these, even the slightest deviation could mean the difference between success and disaster. The synchronization of their watches was not just a formality but a lifeline, a tether that connected each of them to the plan and to each other.

As Michael finished speaking, the room seemed to breathe as one, a collective inhalation of purpose and resolve. The importance of timing, the necessity of flawless execution, and the understanding of the stakes at hand forged an unspoken bond among them. They were ready to act, every tick of the clock echoing the precision and unity required for their mission.

In that moment, they were more than just a team; they were a single, cohesive unit, bound by a shared commitment to their cause and to each other. The countdown had begun, and with it, the relentless march towards their moment of action.

As the meeting carried on, each team member internalized the plan, mentally rehearsing their movements against the backdrop of the ticking clock. The late-night raid was not just a tactical decision; it was a dance with time itself, a carefully choreographed sequence where every tick of the clock was a step closer to either triumph or disaster.

In the strategic hush of their clandestine meeting room, the IRA team, led by Michael, gathered to commence the next critical phase of their daring raid's planning. The atmosphere was charged with a sense of urgency and purpose, the air almost crackling with anticipation. Michael, known for his seasoned leadership and tactical acumen, stood at the head of the table, his presence commanding and reassuring.

"Alright, let's assign roles," Michael began, his voice steady and authoritative. He understood that the success of their operation depended on leveraging the unique strengths of each individual and executing every part of the plan flawlessly.

He turned to Brendan first, his trusted strategist. "Brendan, you'll lead the entry team. Your knowledge of the station's layout and escape routes is vital. Ensure everyone knows their positions and stick to the timing."

Brendan nodded, his eyes sharp with focus. "Got it. We'll move in and out swiftly."

Next, Michael looked at Aisling, whose meticulous nature made her the perfect fit for coordinating communications. "Aisling, you'll handle our comms. Keep everyone updated on the guards' positions and any changes. We need real-time information."

Aisling gave a firm nod, already mentally mapping out her tasks. "I'll make sure we're all in sync."

Michael then addressed Sean, the veteran with a knack for managing security systems. "Sean, you're on the tech. Disable the cameras and any alarms we might trigger. We need as much time as possible before they realize what's happening."

Sean's face was set in determination. "I'll take care of it. They won't know what hit them."

Turning to the rest of the team, Michael assigned specific roles—lookouts, backup, and the driver for their getaway vehicle. Each role was critical, each member a cog in the finely tuned machine they had become.

"The success of this raid hinges on each of us performing our roles to perfection," Michael emphasized, his gaze sweeping across the room. "Remember, we're not just a team; we're a single unit. Our movements must be synchronized, our actions precise."

The room was filled with a shared sense of resolve, the importance of their mission reflected in each face. They were ready to move, each step meticulously planned, each second accounted for.

As they dispersed to make their final preparations, the weight of their upcoming task settled over them. This was more than a mission; it was a pivotal moment in their struggle, a chance to make a statement and alter the course of their fight. The clock continued its relentless march forward, each tick a reminder of the delicate balance between success and failure.

In the silence of the meeting room, now empty but for the lingering tension, Michael felt a surge of determination. They had planned for every eventuality, prepared for every possible outcome. Now, all that remained was to execute their plan with the precision and unity that defined their team.

The countdown to their daring raid had begun, and with it, the hope that this meticulously choreographed dance with time would lead them to triumph.

Michael's first focus was on forming the infiltration team—a group tasked with the crucial job of breaching the police station. He carefully selected members known for their agility and stealth, ensuring that each individual could move silently and efficiently under pressure. Brendan, with his recent experiences and proven ability to navigate high-risk environments, was an ideal candidate. His sharp instincts and quick reflexes made him invaluable to the team.

Michael himself, with his calm demeanor and quick decision-making skills, was a natural choice to lead this team. He had a clear head in the most stressful situations, a trait that inspired confidence and trust in his comrades. His responsibility was to ensure that each stage of the infiltration—from entry to execution—was carried out with military precision.

"We move swiftly and silently," Michael instructed, his voice low but firm. "Every step, every action, needs to be executed flawlessly. There's no room for error."

Brendan nodded, his expression determined. "We'll get in and out before they know what's happened."

Turning his attention to the perimeter security team, Michael selected members with exceptional observational skills and situational awareness. This team's role was vital for maintaining a secure boundary and providing early alerts to any external threats. Their vigilance was crucial to the operation's success, acting as the operation's eyes and ears.

Sean, with his keen eyesight and ability to remain undetected, was appointed to lead this team. His experience in scouting and surveillance made him perfect for the role. He would coordinate their positions around the station, ensuring maximum coverage and quick communication of any signs of trouble.

"We need you to be our first line of defense," Michael told Sean and his team. "If anything or anyone approaches, we need to know immediately. Your alertness could mean the difference between success and failure."

Sean gave a curt nod, his eyes already scanning the map for the best vantage points. "We'll cover every angle. Nothing will get past us."

The teams were now set, each member aware of their role and the importance of their contribution. Michael's careful selection and strategic planning had created a well-balanced operation force, ready to move with the precision and coordination of a finely tuned machine.

As the final preparations were made, the atmosphere in the room was charged with anticipation. The infiltration team reviewed their entry points and escape routes, their minds focused on the tasks ahead. The perimeter security team planned their positions and communication signals, ensuring they were prepared for any eventuality.

Michael took a moment to address both teams together. "Remember, we are a single unit. Our success depends on our ability to work together seamlessly. Stay sharp, stay focused, and we will accomplish our mission."

The room filled with a quiet determination as the team members absorbed his words. They knew the risks, but they also understood the significance of their mission. With everything in place, they were ready to embark on their daring raid, each second bringing them closer to their moment of action.

The countdown had begun, and with it, the unwavering resolve of a team poised to make history.

The final group, which included Aisling with her meticulous attention to detail, was tasked with the critical job of retrieving the arms. This team required individuals who were not only physically capable but also able to maintain composure under the intense pressure of the raid. Quick, efficient, and careful handling of the weapons was paramount to avoid any accidental discharges or damage.

Aisling's precision and calm demeanor made her an ideal leader for this group. Her ability to stay focused and maintain control in high-stress situations was essential for the task at hand. She meticulously reviewed the inventory lists and ensured that each member of her team was familiar with the types of arms they were to retrieve and handle.

Once the roles were delineated, Michael took the time to meet with each subgroup, discussing their specific responsibilities in detail. He emphasized the need for seamless coordination and clear communication throughout the operation, constantly reminding them that their collective effort was the key to their success.

"Remember, we're only as strong as our weakest link," Michael stated emphatically, ensuring his message resonated with each team member. "We need to operate as a single unit, trusting each other implicitly. Every move, every decision must be in perfect sync."

He first met with the infiltration team, reiterating the importance of stealth and precision. "Our entry has to be silent and swift. Brendan, ensure everyone knows their positions and timings down to the second."

Next, he convened with the perimeter security team. "Your vigilance is our first line of defense," Michael reminded them. "Sean, your eyes and ears on the surroundings are crucial. Any sign of trouble, and we need to know immediately."

Finally, Michael turned to Aisling and her team. "Your task is critical," he said, his tone serious. "Handling the arms requires utmost care. Ensure everything is secure and accounted for. A single mistake could cost us dearly."

Aisling nodded, her face set with determination. "We'll handle it with precision, Michael. You can count on us."

The room buzzed with a shared sense of purpose as each team member internalized their role. Michael's thorough briefings left no room for ambiguity, his strategic mind anticipating every possible scenario. The meticulous planning and clear delineation of tasks created a unified force, each subgroup aware of how their actions intertwined with the others.

As the final preparations were made, Michael gathered everyone for a last briefing. "This is it," he said, his voice filled with resolve. "We've planned for this moment, and now we execute. Trust in each other and in the plan. We move as one."

The team responded with a collective nod, their faces reflecting a mixture of determination and focus. They were ready, their minds and bodies aligned with the mission's demands. The countdown to the raid had reached its final moments, and with it, the culmination of their meticulous planning and unwavering resolve.

With everything in place, they moved out, each step taken with silent precision. The night air was thick with anticipation as they approached their target, their synchronized movements a testament to their training and unity. The raid was about to begin, and with it, the hope of a significant victory in their ongoing struggle.

As the team members absorbed their roles, a sense of unity and shared purpose filled the room. They were not merely individuals assigned tasks; they were integral parts of a larger, well-oiled machine, each playing a critical role in the operation.

As the meeting concluded, the team members dispersed to prepare for their respective roles, internalizing every aspect of the mission ahead. Michael watched them depart with a mixture of pride and responsibility. He knew that the night ahead would test their skills, courage, and commitment to their cause. Yet, he also knew they were ready, each member trained and prepared for the task at hand, united in their collective aim to strike a decisive blow for their cause.

In the final stages of their meticulous planning for the raid, Michael and his team shifted their focus to one of the most critical aspects of any covert operation: escape routes and contingency plans. In the confines of their dimly lit meeting room, they pored over maps of the area surrounding the police station, marking out multiple exit strategies to cater to a range of possible scenarios.

Michael stood at the head of the table, pointing to various routes on the map. "We need to be prepared for anything. If Plan A goes south, we switch to Plan B without hesitation," he explained, his voice steady and authoritative. "Sean, you'll lead the first escape route. Brendan, you'll be responsible for coordinating any fallback to the secondary routes."

Sean nodded, tracing his finger along a path through the nearby woods. "This route offers the most cover. If we need to retreat, we'll use the dense foliage to our advantage."

Brendan added, "I've identified several choke points where we can slow down any pursuers. We'll plant diversions here and here," he said, marking specific spots on the map.

Aisling, always attentive to detail, raised a concern. "What about communication if things go awry? We need a reliable way to stay in touch without compromising our positions."

Michael responded, "We'll use short-range radios with encrypted channels. Each team leader will have one. If we get separated, we stick to the predetermined signals and rendezvous points."

The team meticulously reviewed each escape route, discussing potential obstacles and how to overcome them. They planned for every eventuality, from unexpected patrols to blocked exits, ensuring that no detail was overlooked. The maps, now covered in notes and markers, reflected their thorough preparation.

"We need to be adaptable," Michael emphasized. "Our success depends not just on our initial plan but on our ability to react quickly and effectively to any changes. Trust in each other and stay focused."

As the night of the raid approached, the team's preparations reached a fever pitch. Each member double-checked their equipment, mentally rehearsing their roles and the contingency plans. The tension in the air was palpable, but so was their determination.

Michael took one last look at the maps, committing every detail to memory. He then gathered the team for a final briefing. "Tonight, we make our move. Remember, we've prepared for this. Trust your training, trust each other, and we will succeed."

The team responded with silent nods, their resolve clear in their eyes. They were ready to face whatever challenges lay ahead, united in their mission and driven by a shared purpose.

As they moved out under the cover of darkness, the quiet confidence of their preparations filled the night. The police station loomed in the distance, a silent testament to their upcoming challenge. Each step taken was a step towards their goal, each breath a reminder of the gravity of their mission.

In those final moments before the raid, Michael felt a surge of pride for his team and a deep sense of responsibility for the outcome. They were more than a team; they were a brotherhood, bound by their commitment to each other and to their cause. The countdown to their daring raid had reached its end, and with it, the hope that their meticulous planning and unwavering resolve would lead them to victory.

Each escape route was carefully analyzed and chosen based on its ease of access, level of cover it provided, and proximity to safe houses. Brendan, with his recent experience in evading capture, played a crucial role in this process. He suggested routes that were less likely to be monitored or patrolled, emphasizing the importance of blending into the environment to avoid detection.

"These paths here and here," Brendan pointed out on the map, "are shielded by dense foliage and natural barriers. They're less likely to be patrolled and offer excellent cover."

Aisling, ever the detail-oriented planner, had already compiled a list of safe houses in the area. These locations were vetted for security and accessibility, offering immediate refuge for the team if the situation escalated beyond their control. She briefed the team on the specifics of each safe house, ensuring everyone was familiar with the locations and their various entry and exit points.

"The safe house on Mill Road has a concealed entrance at the back," Aisling explained, her finger tracing the path on the map. "It's crucial that you remember this, as it provides a quick and hidden entry."

The team also spent considerable time discussing and establishing contingency plans for a range of unexpected situations. Michael led this discussion, stressing the importance of being prepared for any eventuality. "If we're spotted during the operation, we need to disperse according to the pre-planned routes and regroup at the designated safe house," he instructed, his voice carrying the weight of their mission.

They also considered the possibility of encountering more guards than anticipated. In such a case, the plan was to abort the operation if it risked turning into a direct confrontation. Michael was adamant about avoiding unnecessary risks to the team and civilians.

"If we face unexpected resistance," Michael stated firmly, "we abort. Our goal is the mission's success, not unnecessary heroics."

The triggering of an alarm was another scenario they planned for. The team agreed on a rapid extraction protocol, where speed and immediate withdrawal would be prioritized to minimize the time of exposure and risk of engagement.

Sean elaborated on this point, "If the alarm goes off, we follow Route B immediately. No hesitation. Speed is our ally in those moments."

As the meeting concluded, each team member had a clear understanding of the escape routes and contingency plans. They had rehearsed each scenario, committing the details to memory. The atmosphere in the room was one of solemn determination; they knew that despite their best planning, unpredictability was an inherent part of such operations.

The room fell into a contemplative silence as they absorbed the final instructions. Each member was deep in thought, visualizing their roles and the routes they would take. The weight of their mission settled heavily upon them, but so did a shared sense of resolve.

Michael looked around at his team, pride and concern etched on his face. "Remember," he said quietly but firmly, "we move together, we leave no one behind, and we adapt to whatever comes our way."

The team members dispersed, each retreating into their own preparations. The silence of the night was punctuated by the distant sounds of the city, a reminder of the world outside their clandestine planning. As they readied themselves for the mission, they carried with them the knowledge of their meticulous planning, the strength of their unity, and the hope that their efforts would strike a significant blow for their cause.

In the quiet moments before action, Michael felt the weight of leadership more acutely than ever. He knew that the success of this mission rested not only on their planning but on their ability to adapt, to trust each other, and to move as one. The night ahead would test them all, but they were ready, bound together by a shared purpose and an unwavering determination.

Michael watched as his team prepared to leave, each moving with a sense of purpose. He felt a quiet confidence in their readiness and their ability to adapt to any situation. The chapter closed with the team dispersing into the shadows of Belfast, the night ahead holding both danger and the hope of a successful mission.

As the planning meeting for the raid drew to a close, Michael initiated the final, crucial phase: a comprehensive review and refinement of the plan. The team gathered around, their faces illuminated by the soft glow of a single lamp in the otherwise dim room, symbolizing the gravity and focus of their mission.

Michael methodically went through the entire plan, starting from the initial approach to the police station to the final escape and regrouping. He carefully reiterated each team member's role, the timing of each action, and the specific details of their tasks. As he spoke, he maintained eye contact with each member, ensuring their engagement and understanding.

As the review progressed, team members were encouraged to provide feedback and raise any concerns. Brendan, with his recent field experience, suggested a slight tweak in the escape route, considering a potential construction site that might obstruct their original path. Aisling, keen on ensuring seamless communication, recommended a backup signal in case their primary non-verbal cues were compromised.

Michael listened attentively to each suggestion, acknowledging the value of collective input. He understood that the success of their operation depended not only on his leadership but on the collective experience and wisdom of his team. Each piece of feedback was discussed and considered, and adjustments were made to the plan where necessary.

This collaborative approach fostered a sense of unity and mutual trust among the team. They were not just following orders; they were active participants in shaping their mission, their insights and perspectives contributing to a more robust and foolproof plan.

The final review served not only as a means to refine their strategy but also as a reinforcement of each member's commitment to the mission. It was an opportunity for the team to mentally walk through the entire operation, visualizing their actions and anticipating potential challenges.

As the meeting concluded, there was a collective sense of readiness and resolve. The team members had not only internalized their roles but had also contributed to a plan that was comprehensive and adaptable. The chapter closed with the team dispersing, each member carrying with them the weight of the task ahead. They left the meeting with a heightened sense of purpose, ready to face the challenges of the night, united in their mission to strike a decisive blow for their cause.

With their meticulously crafted plan securely in place, the next pivotal step for Michael and his IRA team was the acquisition of essential resources and the mobilization of allies for the raid on the secluded police station. This phase, demanding as much stealth and precision as the planning itself, was critical to the operation's success.

Michael and his team knew they couldn't carry out the raid alone. They needed the support and cooperation of local sympathizers who could provide the necessary resources and cover. Over the next few days, Michael discreetly reached out to trusted contacts within the community, individuals who shared their commitment to the cause and had the means to assist.

One evening, Michael met with Connor, a reliable ally known for his resourcefulness and connections. In the back room of a quiet pub, they discussed the specifics of the operation. Connor agreed to supply vehicles, weapons, and safe houses, ensuring that everything was in place for the night of the raid.

"We'll need everything ready by the end of the week," Michael said, his voice low but firm. "The timing has to be perfect. We can't afford any delays."

Connor nodded, understanding the urgency. "I'll have it all arranged. You can count on me."

Meanwhile, Brendan and Aisling focused on securing additional equipment and supplies. They visited various locations, picking up radio sets, medical kits, and other essential gear. Each item was carefully chosen to ensure it met their specific needs, balancing the need for functionality with the necessity of discretion.

The team also conducted final drills, rehearsing their movements and refining their timing. These practice sessions, held in secluded areas away from prying eyes, were crucial for ensuring that everyone was prepared for the high-stakes operation.

As the day of the raid approached, the tension within the team was palpable, but so was their determination. They had planned meticulously, secured the necessary resources, and mobilized their allies. Now, all that remained was to execute their plan with the precision and unity they had cultivated through their extensive preparation.

On the eve of the raid, Michael gathered the team one last time. "We've done everything we can to prepare," he said, his voice steady and resolute. "Now it's time to act. Trust in your training, trust in each other, and we will succeed."

The team responded with a unified nod, their resolve unwavering. As they dispersed to their positions, the weight of the night ahead settled over them. They moved with purpose, their minds focused on the task at hand, ready to face whatever challenges lay ahead.

The night was dark and still, the silence broken only by the distant sounds of the city. As they approached the police station, their shadows blended with the darkness, a testament to their stealth and readiness. The stage was set for their daring raid, and with it, the hope of a significant victory in their ongoing struggle.

Brendan, known for his resourcefulness, led a select subgroup to a concealed arms cache in a derelict barn on the outskirts of Belfast. The cache, a well-kept secret, was a treasure trove of arms suited for their mission. In the dim light of the barn, they carefully selected an array of lightweight, easy-to-handle, and reliable weapons. Each firearm was meticulously inspected and tested, ensuring flawless functionality. Ammunition, critical to their operation, was carefully counted and packed into nondescript bags. This cautious approach was designed to avoid drawing any attention during their transportation to the raid site.

Transportation was a key consideration in their operation. Aisling, with her network of contacts, coordinated with a trusted ally who provided an unremarkable van. The vehicle, bland and easily overlooked, was ideal for discreetly transporting both the team and their arsenal. Its ordinariness was its greatest asset, allowing it to blend seamlessly into everyday traffic, a crucial advantage for the covert nature of their operation.

Equally important were the disguises for the raid. Operating outside their familiar terrain meant they needed to assimilate unnoticed into the local environment. The team opted for simple, everyday attire that mirrored the local population's dress. Michael stressed the importance of these disguises, knowing well that their ability to blend in could mean the difference between a successful operation and a compromised one.

The final, and perhaps most vital, element of their preparation was securing the support of local sympathizers in the Republic of Ireland. Michael had previously cultivated relationships with individuals sympathetic to their cause. These contacts now proved invaluable, providing critical on-the-ground intelligence about the current situation, including any recent changes in police routines or signs of increased military presence. These allies also agreed to serve as lookouts, adding an extra layer of security for the team during the operation.

As each team member returned to their base with the resources in hand, a tangible sense of anticipation and readiness permeated the air. The weapons, transportation, and disguises were more than just tools; they symbolized the team's readiness to execute their meticulously laid plans.

The tasks concluded with the team in a state of heightened preparation, double-checking each element of their strategy and reviewing their roles. The atmosphere was charged with focused determination, each member acutely aware of the operation's stakes. They were not merely gearing up for a raid; they were steeling themselves for a significant escalation in their ongoing struggle, a bold move that could redefine their standing in the conflict.

The team's final gathering was marked by a solemn sense of camaraderie and resolve. Michael, reviewing the checklist of resources and plans, felt a profound sense of responsibility. He knew that the night ahead would not only test their skills and courage but also their commitment to their cause. Yet, as he looked around at his team, he saw a group united by a shared goal, each member embodying the strength and determination that had become the hallmark of their struggle.

"Remember," Michael said, his voice steady and low, "this mission is about more than just the raid. It's about showing our resolve and our ability to strike where it's least expected. Trust in each other, trust in our plan, and we'll succeed."

As the day ended, the team dispersed, disappearing into the shadows of the evening, each carrying with them the weight of the task ahead. They left with a quiet confidence, ready to face the challenges of the night, united in their aim to strike a decisive blow for their cause. The stage was set for a raid that would not only challenge the status quo but also demonstrate the IRA's resolve and resourcefulness in their continued fight for independence.

The night descended on Belfast, cloaking the city in a blanket of darkness, as Michael and his team moved towards their objective. The quiet hum of the van blended into the ambient noise of the night, each member focused and prepared. As they approached the secluded police station, the magnitude of their mission became palpably real, their collective breaths held in anticipation of the challenge ahead.

In the stillness of the night, the final preparations were made. Weapons were distributed, final checks completed, and the team members exchanged silent nods of reassurance. They were ready, each one a crucial cog in the well-oiled machine they had become. As the first moments of their meticulously planned raid began to unfold, they moved with precision and purpose, their actions a testament to their shared determination and unyielding resolve. The night held both danger and the hope of a successful mission, and as they advanced, they did so united, ready to make their mark in the ongoing struggle for their cause.

HERE'S THE ENHANCED version with added drama, more scenes, and communication between the characters to show the plot:

UNDER THE CLOAK OF night, the team convened at a secluded, predetermined location on the outskirts of Belfast. The air was thick with a blend of anticipation and tension as they prepared for the raid. One by one, they arrived, each blending into the shadows, their faces obscured by the disguises that would allow them to meld into the rural landscape.

In the dim light, they methodically donned their disguises and checked their equipment for the last time. Weapons were loaded and secured, communication devices tested, and disguises adjusted.

Every movement was precise, every action deliberate, reflecting the gravity of the task ahead.

Michael stood amongst his team, his expression calm yet resolute. He surveyed the group, ensuring that each member was adequately prepared. Then, drawing everyone's attention, he delivered a final brief. His voice, steady and clear, cut through the night air.

"This operation hinges on our ability to move undetected and execute our plan flawlessly," Michael began, locking eyes with each team member. "Remember, timing and stealth are our greatest allies tonight. We must be like shadows – seen by none, felt by none."

He reiterated key aspects of the plan – the approach, the entry, the retrieval of arms, and the escape. He emphasized the importance of non-verbal communication and the need to stay vigilant at all times.

"Stick to the plan, trust in your training, and trust in each other," Michael concluded, instilling a final dose of confidence and camaraderie among the team. "We've prepared for this, and we're ready. Let's do what we came to do."

As the briefing ended, a sense of unity and purpose enveloped the group. They were more than a team; they were a single entity moving towards a common goal. With a final nod from Michael, they moved to their vehicles, ready to embark on their mission. The night of the raid had begun, and each team member was acutely aware of the role they had to play in the unfolding events.

The team, huddled in the nondescript van, made their way through the winding roads leading to the outskirts of the police station. The van, carefully chosen for its inconspicuous appearance, blended seamlessly into the late-night traffic. Inside, the atmosphere was tense yet focused, with each member mentally rehearsing their role in the operation.

Michael, sitting in the front with a steady hand on the steering wheel, led the convoy. His eyes were fixed on the road, but his mind was acutely attuned to the mission ahead. Beside him, Aisling kept a vigilant eye on a discreet GPS device, ensuring they stayed on course while avoiding any well-lit areas or busy intersections.

As they neared their destination, Michael signaled for radio silence. The only sound in the van was the low hum of the engine and the occasional gravel crunching under the tires. Every team member knew the importance of maintaining silence to avoid any potential interception of their communications.

They parked the van in a secluded area, shrouded by trees and far enough from the station to avoid drawing attention. With a final check of their gear, the team disembarked quietly. The darkness of the night enveloped them, providing a cloak of invisibility as they began their stealthy approach to the station.

Moving in a tight formation, they communicated through pre-arranged non-verbal signals. A tap on the shoulder, a hand gesture, a subtle nod – each signal was a language they all understood, a silent conversation that guided their movements.

The team traversed the terrain with practiced ease, their steps light and calculated. Brendan, with his keen sense of direction, led the way, using the knowledge gained from their reconnaissance to avoid open areas and navigate through the safest paths.

Every member was on high alert, their senses heightened to detect any sign of movement or sound that could indicate a threat. The stillness of the night was their ally, masking their movements as they edged closer to their target.

As they approached the perimeter of the police station, the outline of the building emerged from the darkness, a shadowy figure against the night sky. The moment of action was drawing near, and the team tightened their formation, ready to execute the plan they had so meticulously prepared for.

Having approached the police station under the veil of darkness, Michael and his team were now at the crux of their mission – the breach and entry. The station loomed before them, a silent edifice in the dead of night. Every team member knew that the next few moments would be critical.

The team split into their designated roles with practiced precision. One subgroup, including Brendan, adept in lock-picking, approached the back entrance of the station. Brendan knelt by the door, his tools in hand, working meticulously to unlock it without a sound. Beside him, another team member held a device designed to jam any electronic alarm systems, ensuring their entry would go undetected.

Meanwhile, Michael and the rest of the infiltration team positioned themselves near the front entrance. They relied on their technical gadgets to silently disable any external alarms. Aisling, who was part of this group, kept a watchful eye on the surroundings, ready to signal at the first sign of trouble.

The tension was palpable as Brendan successfully unlocked the door. A soft click was the only sound, lost in the stillness of the night. The team exchanged quick, confirming glances before proceeding. They entered the station with a fluid, ghost-like movement, each step calculated and silent.

Inside, the team split up again, each subgroup heading towards their predetermined objectives within the station. Michael led his group down a dimly lit corridor, moving towards the central control room. Their movements were swift but controlled, their training evident in their disciplined approach.

The station, seemingly deserted in these late hours, was easier to navigate than they had anticipated. However, the team remained on high alert, aware that even the slightest noise could betray their presence and jeopardize the entire operation.

As they progressed deeper into the building, the reality of their situation set in. They were now in the heart of enemy territory, every moment increasing the risk of discovery. Yet, with each step, they moved closer to achieving the primary objective of their mission – securing the arms and equipment crucial for their ongoing struggle.

With the successful breach of the police station, Michael's team swiftly transitioned to the next critical phase of their mission: seizing the arms. Inside the dimly lit station, the team split into their pre-assigned groups with practiced efficiency. One group, led by Brendan, made a beeline for the armory, while another, under Michael's command, moved to secure the exits.

The armory group moved with precision and speed; their footsteps barely audible on the cold floor. Brendan, with his intimate knowledge of weapons and armaments, identified the key storage areas. The doors to the armory were secured with heavy locks, but the team was prepared. Using the lock-picking tools and gadgets they had brought, they gained access with minimal noise.

Inside the armory, they found racks of firearms and shelves lined with ammunition boxes. The sight of such an arsenal was a stark reminder of the stakes of their operation. Brendan and his team worked quickly and silently, carefully selecting the most valuable and useful weapons. Each firearm was inspected briefly to ensure functionality before being packed.

The weapons were carefully wrapped in cloth to prevent any clanking sounds during transport. Ammunition was distributed evenly among the team members to avoid overburdening any single person. Despite the urgency, the team's movements were methodical and calm, a testament to their training and preparation.

Meanwhile, Michael's group had taken positions at strategic points near the exits. They kept a vigilant watch for any signs of movement or incoming personnel. Their role was crucial to provide early warning and to ensure a clear path for the quick evacuation of the armory group.

The operation inside the station was a delicate balance of speed and silence. Every second inside the building increased their risk, but the team's efficiency and coordination made the process seem almost effortless.

As the last of the arms were securely packed, Brendan gave a subtle signal, and the team prepared to exit. The armory, now significantly lighter of its contents, stood as a testament to the team's effectiveness. The chapter closed with the team retracing their steps, arms in tow, ready to execute their escape plan. Their mission inside the station had been accomplished with precision, but they were not out of danger yet. The true test would be making it back to safety with their newly acquired arsenal.

With the unexpected challenge skillfully navigated, Michael's team swiftly transitioned to the next critical phase of their operation: a rapid escape. The arms, now secured in their grasp, were not just a symbol of their potential strength but also a beacon of the immediate danger they carried.

The team, each member acutely aware of their individual escape routes, moved with a renewed sense of urgency. The quiet of the night was punctuated only by the muffled sounds of their careful footsteps as they navigated through the labyrinthine paths leading away from the police station. The weight of the arms added a physical strain to their stealthy movements, but their resolve did not waver.

Michael, leading the charge, kept a vigilant eye on their surroundings, ensuring that they remained unseen. Brendan, with his keen situational awareness, acted as the rear guard, ensuring that no one was left behind and that they left no trace of their passage.

The team's escape was a blend of precision and speed, a testament to their rigorous training and preparation. They avoided well-lit areas and main roads, instead opting for the shadowed back alleys and overgrown fields that provided cover.

Upon reaching the van, parked discreetly at a safe distance from the station, the team acted swiftly to transfer the seized arms. Each weapon and box of ammunition was moved with precision and haste, a well-orchestrated dance dictated by the urgency

of their situation.

The van's doors closed with a soft thud, sealing away the evidence of their daring raid. As Michael gave the signal, the van pulled away, melting into the night as if it had never been there. The escape, though rapid, was marked by a collective breath held and then slowly released; they had managed to avoid direct confrontation, a key objective in their operation.

With the van disappearing into the darkness, the team inside allowed themselves a moment of silent celebration. They had executed their escape plan flawlessly, but the night's operation was not yet complete. The journey back to their base, with the newly acquired arsenal, was the final stretch of their mission, a path fraught with its own dangers and challenges.

With the stolen arms safely stowed and the van in motion, Michael's team transitioned into the next critical phase of their operation: evading any potential pursuit. The success of their raid had so far hinged on stealth and precision, but now, as they made their way back to the safety of their base, the risk of being trailed by police or other security forces loomed large.

Inside the van, the atmosphere was tense but focused. Every team member was acutely aware of the potential dangers that lay in the journey ahead. Michael, who took the driver's seat, navigated the vehicle with a calm efficiency, his eyes constantly scanning the rearview mirrors for any signs of pursuit.

Beside him, Aisling monitored a portable scanner, listening intently for any police chatter that might indicate they were being followed. Her fingers moved deftly over the device, adjusting frequencies and keeping an ear out for any mention of their raid. The scanner crackled intermittently, a constant reminder of the perilous situation they were in.

In the back of the van, Brendan and other members of the perimeter team peered out through small, discreet openings. Their role was to provide cover and to alert the driver of any potential threats. They were the team's last line of defense, a critical element in ensuring a safe escape.

The route back was carefully chosen to avoid major roads and populated areas. They took back roads and lesser-known paths, areas where a large police presence was less likely. The van moved at a steady pace, fast enough to make good time but careful not to attract unwanted attention.

As they wound their way through the dark, quiet streets, the team maintained a silent vigilance. Every passing car was a potential threat, every distant siren a cause for concern. But as the miles passed and they moved further away from the scene of the raid, the initial tension began to ease slightly.

The van successfully navigated its way out of the area. The perimeter team's watchful eyes and Michael's skilled driving, combined with Aisling's diligent monitoring, had allowed them to leave undetected. The risk of pursuit was ever-present, but for now, they had managed to evade any immediate detection, bringing them one step closer to completing their mission successfully.

After a tense journey marked by vigilance and caution, Michael's team reached a remote location, deemed safe for a brief but crucial debrief. The van, still holding the night's spoils, rolled to a stop in an abandoned warehouse far from the city's prying eyes. The team, though weary, remained alert as they filed out of the vehicle, each member carrying the weight of the night's events.

In the dimly lit expanse of the warehouse, Michael quickly accounted for each member, a silent headcount confirming that everyone had made it back safely. The sense of relief at this realization was palpable yet tempered by the seriousness of their situation.

Michael initiated the debrief with a concise efficiency. "Let's make this quick. We need to know what went right, what went wrong, and how we can improve," he stated. The team members, in turn, provided brief reports on their respective roles during the raid. They discussed the challenges encountered, particularly the unexpected change in the guard routine, and how their contingency plans had effectively countered this potential threat.

Aisling confirmed that the arms and ammunition were all accounted for, and Brendan reported no signs of pursuit or compromise during their escape. The success of their mission was clear, but Michael reminded them that analysis and improvement were ongoing processes.

With the debrief concluded, the next step was dispersal. It was crucial to their safety and the continued secrecy of their operations. The team members changed out of their disguises, donning their regular clothes. They meticulously wiped down the van and their equipment, eradicating any fingerprints or traces of their presence.

One by one, they left the warehouse in different directions, each heading to a pre-arranged location. Some went alone, while others left in pairs, blending back into the night as seamlessly as they had emerged from it. The van, with its contents, was taken to a secure location for unloading and storage.

The events closed with the empty warehouse echoing the silence of their efficient dispersal. The successful raid and their subsequent escape were a testament to their planning, skills, and unity as a team. But more than that, their ability to vanish into the fabric of their surroundings underscored the clandestine nature of their struggle, a struggle that continued even as they disappeared into the night.

In the solitude of the early dawn, after the adrenaline of the night had ebbed away, Michael found himself in a rare moment of quiet reflection. The successful execution of the raid was not just a tactical victory but a profound statement in their ongoing struggle. As he sat alone, the events of the night replayed in his mind, each decision, each move, a testament to the capability and determination of his team.

The significance of their achievement extended far beyond the physical arms they had seized. For Michael, it was a demonstration of their resilience, their ability to strike effectively despite the odds. It sent a powerful message to their allies, bolstering morale and showcasing their strength and commitment to the cause. It was a beacon of hope and a tangible display of their resolve.

But the raid had another audience – their adversaries. Michael knew that their bold action would not go unnoticed. It was a direct challenge to the authorities, a clear indication that their fight for independence was far from over. He anticipated the heightened scrutiny and potential backlash that would come from this, but there was a part of him that welcomed it. It meant that they were being taken seriously, that their actions were having an impact.

As the first light of dawn began to creep over the horizon, Michael steeled himself for the days to come. The raid was a success, but it was also a reminder of the continuous effort and vigilance required in their struggle. He stood up, the weight of leadership settling back onto his shoulders, and prepared to face whatever came next, knowing that his team was ready to meet the challenges ahead with the same determination and unity they had shown tonight.

Here's the enhanced version with deeper emotional insights and character interactions:

MICHAEL ALSO CONTEMPLATED the broader implications of the raid. It was a strategic move that would undoubtedly shift the dynamics of their struggle. He pondered how this would change their operations, the increased need for caution, and the inevitable escalation of conflict. Yet, despite these considerations, there was an undeniable sense of accomplishment.

As the first light of day crept through the window, Michael's thoughts turned toward the future. The raid was a milestone, but the journey was far from over. There were challenges ahead, undoubtedly more difficult than what they had just faced. But in this moment of reflection, Michael felt a renewed sense of purpose and clarity. The path ahead was fraught with danger, but it was a path they were willing to tread for the sake of their cause. The chapter closed with Michael standing up, his resolve hardened, ready to face whatever the future held.

As Michael stood up, his resolve hardened by the events of the night and the contemplation of their implications, his thoughts seamlessly transitioned to the impact of the raid on their greater struggle for independence. In the quiet of the dawn, with the first light filtering through the window, he could feel the weight of history on his shoulders and the stirrings of change in the air.

The raid, he knew, marked a significant turning point in their fight. It was more than just a successful operation; it was a statement, a demonstration of their strength and a testament to their commitment to the cause of independence. Michael could almost sense the ripple effect it would have, not just within his own group but across the wider movement. The success of their operation would undoubtedly inspire others, kindling a flame of resistance and determination that could spread far and wide.

He considered the potential increase in support from sympathizers. The news of their bold and successful raid would resonate with those who had, until now, been hesitant to lend their support. Michael envisioned the influx of new recruits, bolstered resources, and a strengthened network of allies and informants. The raid was not just a victory in terms of the arms they had acquired but a victory in the hearts and minds of those who shared their dream of independence.

Yet, with these hopeful prospects, Michael was also acutely aware of the challenges that lay ahead. He expected a significant escalation in response from the authorities. The raid would not go unanswered, and he anticipated a robust and possibly severe crackdown. Increased security measures, heightened patrols, and intensified surveillance were all likely outcomes of their actions. The authorities would be eager to demonstrate their control and deter any similar future actions.

As Michael pondered these future challenges, he recognized the need for a strategic shift in their operations. The increased scrutiny from the authorities meant that they would have to be more cautious, more cunning in their future endeavors. The landscape of their struggle had changed, and they would need to adapt to continue their fight effectively.

The chapter concluded with Michael looking out at the dawning day, his mind a whirlwind of thoughts and plans. The raid had indeed marked a new chapter in their struggle for independence, bringing with it both hope and the promise of harder days to come. Michael knew that the path ahead would be fraught with challenges, but he also knew that they were ready to face them. The resolve that had carried them through the night would carry them into the future, no matter what it held.

In the seclusion of an abandoned farmhouse, well away from prying eyes, Michael's team reconvened for a crucial meeting. The air was thick with a sense of purpose as they gathered around an old wooden table, each member keenly aware of the gravity of their recent actions and the need to strategize for the future.

Michael initiated the discussion, his voice low but firm. "We've made our mark," he began, "but this is just the beginning. We need to be smart about our next steps."

The team nodded in agreement; their faces etched with the seriousness of the situation. Brendan, leaning against a weathered wall, spoke up first. "The raid was a success, but we've surely stirred the hornet's nest. We should expect increased patrols and possibly military involvement in the coming days."

Aisling, sitting across from Michael, added, "We need to heighten our surveillance and gather intel more diligently. Knowing their next move before they make it will be crucial."

The team discussed the need for increased caution in their daily activities. They agreed that maintaining a low profile was essential to avoid drawing attention. "We can't afford any slip-ups. Even our usual meeting spots might need to change," Michael emphasized.

The conversation then shifted to potential retaliatory actions by the police or military. The team brainstormed various scenarios, from increased raids and checkpoints to more aggressive tactics aimed at flushing them out. "We need contingency plans for each possibility," Michael stated, "and everyone must be prepared to act on a moment's notice."

The discussion was not just tactical but also philosophical. They talked about the importance of keeping their cause at the forefront of their actions, ensuring that their response to any retaliation was measured and aligned with their principles. "We're not just fighting for our independence," Michael reminded them, "but for the hearts and minds of the people. Our actions must reflect that."

In the rustic setting of the abandoned farmhouse, Michael's team delved deeper into their discussion, focusing now on the repercussions they anticipated in the wake of their bold raid. The wooden table around which they sat became a war room of sorts, with maps, reports, and notes scattered across its surface.

Michael leaned forward, his eyes scanning the faces of his team. "We've struck a significant blow, but we must be ready for the fallout," he stated, setting the tone for the next phase of their discussion. The team leaned in; their attention sharpened.

Brendan, with his tactical acumen, was the first to address the potential consequences. "Heightened security measures are a given. We should expect more checkpoints, raids, and general scrutiny in our areas of operation," he said. His comment was met with nods of agreement, each member mentally bracing for the increased pressure.

Aisling chimed in; her voice laced with strategic insight. "We need to be smarter in how we move and communicate. Changing our patterns, varying our routes, and maybe even using decoys could help us stay under the radar."

The conversation shifted to the likelihood of intensified surveillance. The team agreed on the need to enhance their counter-surveillance measures. "We'll need to sweep for bugs regularly and be cautious with our communication channels," suggested one of the team members, a note of resolve in his voice.

Michael then steered the discussion towards strategies for handling the heightened attention. "We can't let increased scrutiny paralyze us. Our operations must continue, but with greater discretion and intelligence," he asserted. The team brainstormed ways to carry out their activities without drawing unnecessary attention, discussing everything from coded messages to the use of trusted intermediaries for communication.

The philosophical aspect of their struggle was not lost in the tactical discussion. Michael reminded the team of the need to maintain the moral high ground. "Our actions should always reflect the righteousness of our cause. We're fighting a just battle, and our methods must align with our principles," he said, his words resonating with a sense of ethical commitment.

As the morning light began to filter through the cracks of the old farmhouse, Michael and his team turned their focus to adapting their strategies in response to the anticipated increase in security measures. They knew that their recent actions would not only heighten the authorities' vigilance but also bring about more sophisticated surveillance tactics.

Gathered around the worn-out table, laden with maps and various communication devices, the team delved into a detailed discussion on how to counter this increased security presence. Michael, always two steps ahead in his thinking, initiated the conversation. "We've shown our hand, and now they'll be watching us more closely. We need to be smarter, more elusive."

Brendan, with a tactical map spread in front of him, pointed out potential hotspots for increased patrols and surveillance. "We'll need to avoid these areas as much as possible. Alternate routes and safe houses should be identified and used unpredictably," he suggested.

Aisling, the communications expert, proposed enhancements to their communication protocols. "We'll need to use more secure channels, maybe even consider old-school methods like dead drops and coded messages. Anything that can't be easily intercepted or traced back to us."

The team agreed on the importance of improving their intelligence-gathering capabilities. "We need eyes and ears everywhere," Michael emphasized. "More informants, more reconnaissance, and constant monitoring of police and military frequencies."

They discussed the need for training sessions to enhance their skills in counter-surveillance and evasion techniques. "It's not just about being discreet. It's about being invisible," Michael added, the seriousness of his tone underscoring the importance of these new measures.

One of the team members, an expert in digital surveillance, brought up the possibility of using technology to their advantage. "If we can hack into their systems, we could stay one step ahead. It's risky, but the rewards could be substantial."

As the clandestine meeting in the old farmhouse came to a close, the team found themselves enveloped in a state of heightened awareness, tempered with a palpable sense of motivation stemming from their recent success. The early morning sun, now casting long shadows across the room, served as a reminder of the new day and the new challenges that awaited them.

Michael stood at the head of the table, his gaze passing over each team member. There was a shared understanding that their bold action had irreversibly changed the landscape of their struggle. They had stepped into uncharted territory, one that promised greater risks but also the potential for significant gains in their fight for independence.

He addressed the team with a firm resolve, "What we've done last night is more than a successful raid. We've sent a message. We've shown that we are a force to be reckoned with. But this is just

the beginning. We need to be ready for what comes next."

The team members nodded in agreement, their faces a mix of determination and contemplation. The success of the raid had bolstered their confidence, but they were acutely aware of the need for increased vigilance and strategic planning. The road ahead was going to be more challenging, requiring them to muster even greater resilience and determination.

Michael continued, "We've set the stage for the next phase of our operations. We must stay focused, adaptable, and above all, united. Our cause demands it, and we owe it to those who believe in our fight."

As the team dispersed, there was a sense of quiet solidarity among them. They left the farmhouse with their commitment renewed and their spirits fortified by the knowledge that their actions were part of a larger narrative in their quest for independence.

The chapter concluded with Michael alone in the room, looking out at the rising sun. He allowed himself a moment to reflect on the path they had chosen. It was fraught with peril, but it was a path paved with the hopes and dreams of their cause. The raid had indeed set the stage for future operations, and Michael knew that their journey ahead would require all the courage, wisdom, and strength they could muster. As he stepped out of the farmhouse, he did so with an unwavering commitment to lead his team through whatever lay ahead, ready to face the future with unflinching resolve.

Chapter 5 Fox and the hound

In the seclusion of a nondescript safe house nestled in the outskirts of the city, Michael and his team gathered for what was intended to be a routine strategy meeting. The atmosphere inside was casual yet focused, a testament to the many similar gatherings they had held in the past. Sunlight filtered through the curtains, casting a warm glow over the room, while a pot of tea sat in the middle of the table, steam gently rising from its spout.

Around the old wooden table, team members were sprawled out with maps and documents, engaged in earnest discussions about their future operations. The mood was relaxed; there were occasional jokes and laughter as they debated tactics and shared ideas. Michael, sitting at the head of the table, listened intently, interjecting with guidance and making notes in his well-worn notebook.

Brendan, leaning back in his chair with a mug in hand, was mid-sentence, discussing potential routes for their next supply run. Aisling, her eyes scanning over a map, chimed in with suggestions on safe drop-off points. The team operated like a well-oiled machine, each member contributing their expertise and experience to the collective goal.

Outside, the world was oblivious to the gathering of this covert group, dedicated to their cause and hidden away from prying eyes. The safe house had always been their haven, a place where they could plan and strategize without fear of interruption or discovery.

However, this sense of security was about to be shattered in the most violent way possible. Without any warning, the tranquility of the meeting was abruptly ruptured by a barrage of gunfire. Bullets pierced through the windows, shattering the glass and sending shards flying across the room. The walls reverberated with the sound of the assault, and the air was filled with the acrid smell of gunpowder.

In an instant, the room transformed from a place of strategic planning to a chaotic battleground. Papers fluttered to the floor, and cups of tea spilled over as the team members instinctively ducked for cover. The suddenness of the attack sent a shockwave of confusion and panic through the room.

Michael, his instincts as a leader kicking in amidst the chaos, shouted orders over the din of gunfire, trying to coordinate a defense. "Take cover! Return fire!" he yelled, as the team scrambled to respond to the unexpected onslaught.

The calm of the safe house was shattered in an instant. Without any warning, a hailstorm of bullets tore through the tranquility of the morning, bombarding the safe house with merciless ferocity. The windows, once casting a serene light, shattered into a thousand pieces, sending shards flying like lethal rain. Bullets thudded into the walls, boring through the plaster and wood with ruthless precision.

The team, caught completely unawares, was thrown into disarray. One moment they were engaged in strategic discussions, and the next, they were diving for cover under a barrage of gunfire. The room, which had been filled with the hum of conversation, was now echoing with the sounds of destruction and chaos.

In those first few seconds, confusion reigned supreme. No one had expected an attack, especially not in their sanctuary, which had always been a bastion of safety. The suddenness and intensity of the onslaught left them momentarily stunned. Chairs were knocked over, and documents scattered in a mad scramble as each member sought cover wherever they could find it.

Michael, despite the shock, tried to rally his team. "Down! Everyone down!" he shouted, his voice barely audible over the cacophony of gunfire and breaking glass. His mind raced, trying to make sense of the situation, to figure out a response to this unexpected threat.

The team members, trained for combat but not prepared for an attack in their own base, reacted instinctively. Some returned fire towards the shattered windows, while others tried to shield their more vulnerable comrades. The room was filled with the sounds of gunfire, both incoming and outgoing, creating a terrifying symphony of survival.

As the initial shock wore off, the team began to move with more purpose, driven by survival instincts honed through years of conflict. The realization that they were in the midst of a well-planned ambush set in, and the need for a coordinated defense became urgently clear.

As the initial shock of the ambush began to dissipate, a surge of adrenaline kicked in, and Michael's team transitioned from defense to offense. Amidst the debris of their shattered sanctuary, they rallied to return fire, driven by a fierce determination to survive and fight back.

Michael, crouched behind an overturned table that now served as a makeshift barricade, quickly assessed their defensive position. "Return fire!" he commanded, his voice steady despite the chaos. "Aim for the flashes from their muzzles!"

Sean, a veteran in combat tactics, peered through a narrow gap in the shattered window frame. With controlled breaths, he squeezed the trigger of his rifle, sending precise shots towards the unseen assailants outside. Each shot was a calculated response, aimed at suppressing the enemy's fire and buying them crucial time.

Aisling, alongside Michael, coordinated their counterattack, shouting updates on enemy movements based on the fleeting glimpses and sounds of the assailants. Her eyes were sharp, her instructions clear, enabling her team members to focus their fire more effectively.

The team, despite being caught off guard, exhibited remarkable resilience and tactical acumen. They moved fluidly within the confined space of the safe house, finding vantage points amidst the chaos. The sound of their returning gunfire melded with that of the attackers, creating a fierce and desperate symphony.

In those intense moments, the team's training and instinct took over. They operated as a cohesive unit, each member covering the others, their movements synchronized amidst the disarray. The air was thick with the smell of gunpowder, and the sound of bullets striking wood and plaster was relentless.

As the retaliatory strike continued, the team managed to push back the initial wave of the ambush. Their return fire became more confident, more controlled, as they worked to gain the upper hand in the firefight. Michael's leadership and the team's collective experience in combat were evident in their measured yet aggressive response.

The intensity of the ambush was nothing short of harrowing. As the Ulster Freedom Fighters (UFF) launched their surprise attack on Michael's team, the safe house, once a haven of planning and camaraderie, was transformed into a frenzied battleground.

The air was immediately filled with the cacophony of gunfire, a relentless and deafening barrage that echoed through the rooms. Bullets zipped through the space, embedding into walls, shattering what little remained of the windows, and piercing the furniture that the team desperately used for cover. The sound was accompanied by the splintering of wood and the clatter of falling objects, adding to the chaos.

Michael's team, caught completely off guard, found themselves at a grave disadvantage. They were in a defensive position they had never anticipated needing at their safe house. The surprise attack left them scrambling for weapons and returning fire in a disoriented state. They had trained for combat, but the suddenness of the assault in a place they considered safe left them momentarily stunned.

Despite their shock, the team's survival instincts kicked in. They ducked behind whatever cover they could find – overturned tables, couches, even the thick walls offered some protection. Bullets whizzed by, creating a perilous environment where every move could mean the difference between life and death.

Shouts filled the air – calls for ammunition, warnings of enemy movements, and the groans of the injured. Michael, trying to maintain some semblance of order, shouted commands, directing his team's fire, and organizing a semblance of a counterattack. But the UFF's overwhelming firepower and strategic positioning outside the house made it clear that this was not a battle on equal footing.

The UFF, having planned the ambush meticulously, seemed to anticipate and counter every move Michael's team made. Their gunfire was concentrated and relentless, pinning down the team and limiting their ability to fight back effectively. The team, usually so controlled and strategic in their operations, was forced into a reactive stance, fighting not just for their cause but for their very survival.

In the thick of the battle, Michael's team fought with a desperation borne of survival. Every member, despite the shock and disorientation, rallied to fend off the UFF's relentless assault. The once strategic and composed group was now driven by a raw, primal instinct to protect one another and survive.

The din of the firefight was overwhelming. The air inside the safe house was thick with gunpowder smoke, making it hard to see and breathe. The confined space became an echo chamber for the sounds of war – the continuous rattle of gunfire, the shattering of what was left of the windows, and the dull thuds of bullets embedding into the walls.

Michael, positioned behind a makeshift barricade, provided cover fire, trying to create an opportunity for his team to regroup. He knew they were outgunned and at a tactical disadvantage, but surrender was not an option. Every shot he fired was aimed at giving his team a fighting chance.

Brendan, despite the chaos, managed to maintain a level of tactical thinking. He directed some team members to flank the attackers, creating a crossfire that could potentially turn the tide in their favor. This maneuver was risky, but in the face of overwhelming odds, bold actions were necessary.

Aisling, meanwhile, was attending to the injured while also keeping an eye on the safe house's exits. The situation was dire, and she knew they needed an escape plan. "We need to find a way out," she shouted over the noise, her mind racing through potential exit strategies.

The team's response to the ambush, although reactive, displayed their resilience and training. They moved with purpose, each covering the other's

back, fighting a battle they hadn't prepared for but were determined to survive.

Outside, the UFF continued their onslaught, capitalizing on the team's momentary lapse. Bullets continued to fly, walls continued to be punctured, and the air was thick with the smell of gunpowder and blood.

In the turmoil of the ambush, with Sean critically wounded and the safe house under siege, Michael faced the monumental task of rallying his team amidst chaos. They were outnumbered, outflanked, and fighting in a location that was never meant to be a battleground. Yet, in these dire moments, Michael's leadership was more crucial than ever.

With a mix of determination and urgency, Michael began to formulate a rapid response plan. "Brendan, Aisling, cover the east side! The rest of you, with me on the west! We need to hold them off!" he commanded, trying to carve out a defensive strategy amidst the disarray. His voice was a beacon of focus in the pandemonium, providing much-needed direction to his team.

Brendan, who had momentarily taken charge in Michael's stead, nodded in understanding and moved to execute the orders. He and Aisling quickly positioned themselves, laying down suppressive fire to keep the UFF attackers at bay. Their movements were swift and coordinated, a testament to their training and experience, but the uncertainty of the situation weighed heavily on them.

Meanwhile, Michael led the rest of the team in fortifying their position on the west side of the house. They hastily stacked whatever furniture was left to create a makeshift barrier, all the while exchanging fire with the UFF operatives who were relentlessly closing in.

The team's struggle to maintain cohesion was palpable. They were a unit that thrived on strategy and planning, but the ambush had forced them into a reactive stance. Every decision, every action was made under extreme pressure, with the knowledge that one misstep could mean disaster.

Despite these challenges, there was a sense of unity among them, a resolve to stand together against overwhelming odds. They moved with a grim determination, covering each other's backs, communicating non-verbally amidst the noise, and adapting to the rapidly evolving situation.

The intensity of the firefight reached its peak as the UFF continued to press their advantage. The sounds of bullets, shouts, and breaking wood filled the air, creating a chaotic symphony that underscored the ferocity of the attack.

As the relentless barrage of gunfire and the chaos of the ambush reached a fever pitch, there came an abrupt, almost disorienting lull in the fighting. The hail of bullets from the UFF attackers began to subside, giving way to a tense and uncertain quiet. The sudden shift from intense combat to an eerie stillness left Michael and his team in a state of shock, their ears still ringing from the cacophony of the assault.

In the aftermath of the initial onslaught, the safe house was a scene of devastation. The air was thick with dust and gunpowder, and the smell of spent ammunition and fear hung heavily in the space. The team members, visibly shaken, slowly emerged from their cover, their weapons still at the ready, not yet convinced that the danger had passed.

The most pressing concern was Sean's critical condition. Lying motionless on the floor, with Aisling desperately trying to staunch the bleeding, he was a stark reminder of the brutal reality of their situation. The team gathered around him, their expressions a mix of concern, anger, and helplessness. Sean, once a pillar of strength and guidance, now lay vulnerable and fighting for his life, a visual representation of the cost of their struggle.

Michael, while deeply concerned for Sean, maintained a semblance of composure. He knew they were not out of danger yet. "Stay alert," he instructed, his voice low but firm. "They could still be out there. We need to be ready for anything." His leadership, even in the face of such adversity, was a grounding force for the team.

As the team members processed the end of the assault, they were acutely aware that this ambush marked a turning point in their conflict with the UFF. The intensity and coordination of the attack were unlike anything they had faced before. It was a clear indication that the UFF viewed them as a significant threat and that the nature of their struggle had escalated to a new, more dangerous level.

In the wake of the initial assault, the team, surrounded by the wreckage of what was once their sanctuary, scrambled to regroup. The chaos of the ambush had left its mark, both physically and mentally, on each team member. Amidst the broken furniture, shattered glass, and bullet-riddled walls, they tried to make sense of the situation and plan their next move.

The distant sound of sirens pierced the heavy air, adding a new layer of urgency to their predicament. The Royal Ulster Constabulary (RUC), the local police force, was on its way. For Michael and his team, the approach of the RUC was a critical development; getting caught would mean the end for all of them. Arrests, interrogations, and possibly even worse fates awaited them if they fell into the hands of the authorities.

Michael, acutely aware of the gravity of the situation, quickly assessed the room. His gaze moved from one team member to another, each showing signs of shock, fatigue, and the strain of the ambush. Despite their training and experience, the intensity of the attack had shaken them to their core.

"We need to move, now!" Michael's voice cut through the lingering tension. "Gather what you can. We can't be here when the RUC arrives." His directive was met with nods of understanding, though the team's movements were slower, weighed down by the events of the day.

The sound of the approaching sirens grew louder, a constant reminder that time was running out. Aisling, still tending to Sean, looked up with a mix of fear and determination. "We can't leave him," she said firmly, her hands still pressing down on Sean's wound in a futile attempt to stop the bleeding.

Brendan, quickly taking stock of their arsenal and supplies, replied, "We take him with us. We leave no one behind." The team rallied around this decision, a testament to their bond and unwavering loyalty to one another.

As Michael's team prepared to flee the battered safe house, they were confronted with a harrowing moral dilemma. Sean, critically wounded and barely clinging to life, lay before them – a brother-in-arms whose life was rapidly slipping away. The team faced an agonizing choice: attempt to carry Sean with them, jeopardizing their slim chances of escape, or leave him behind to ensure the survival and continued fight for their cause.

The air was thick with tension as the team weighed their options. The sound of approaching sirens served as a grim reminder of the impending danger. To linger any longer could mean capture or death for them all, but the thought of abandoning Sean was unbearable. He had been more than a comrade; he was a mentor and friend whose guidance had steered them through many perils.

Michael, torn between his duty to the team and his loyalty to Sean, faced an excruciating decision. The ideals they fought for – freedom, brotherhood, the cause – all seemed to converge in this singular, pivotal moment. "We can't leave him," he finally said, his voice strained with emotion. "But we can't all stay and risk capture. We have to keep the fight alive."

Aisling, still at Sean's side, looked up with tears in her eyes, understanding the gravity of Michael's words. She knew the importance of their mission, the sacrifices they had all agreed to make, but the reality of leaving one of their own was a stark reminder of the cost of their struggle.

The team was faced with an impossible choice, one that tested the very principles they fought for. To leave Sean was to abandon a part of themselves, but to stay meant the potential end of everything they had worked for. The decision was heart-wrenching, but in the end, the survival of the group and the continuation of their cause took precedence.

Under the dimming light of the safe house, a heavy air of sorrow enveloped Michael and his team. There, lying grievously wounded, was Sean, a stalwart of their cause, now reduced to a painful emblem of the sacrifices demanded in their quest for Ireland's freedom. The team stood at a crossroads, grappling with a decision that pitted their loyalty to a fallen comrade against the overarching mission for national liberation.

Michael's face, a canvas of internal conflict and grief, conveyed the gravity of their situation. Breaking the heavy silence, he uttered the excruciating verdict, "We must continue the fight for Ireland's freedom. It's bigger than any one of us." His voice, though firm, barely masked the turmoil churning within him.

This stark reality resonated deeply with the team. They understood the enormity of their cause, the relentless pursuit of independence that had always demanded immense personal sacrifices. To linger or attempt a perilous rescue could spell disaster for them all, potentially derailing the very movement Sean had dedicated his life to.

With heavy hearts, the team made the gut-wrenching decision to leave Sean behind. Brendan, his eyes lingering on his fallen comrade, expressed a silent promise, "We'll make sure your sacrifice wasn't in vain." The resolve in his voice was tinged with pain, reflecting a bond forged in the crucible of their shared struggle.

The task of obliterating any traces of their presence fell upon them with a grim finality. They methodically doused the safe house in fuel, the pungent smell of gasoline permeating the already tense atmosphere. Each pour was a farewell, each match struck a tribute to their comrade's bravery.

As the team stepped out of the safe house for

the last time, they cast one final, lingering glance at Sean. The ensuing flames engulfed the building, symbolically consuming their collective anguish and the physical remnants of their ordeal. The fire raged with a ferocity that mirrored their inner turmoil, a beacon of their painful sacrifice.

As the engulfing flames illuminated the night sky, the piercing wail of sirens announced the arrival of the Royal Ulster Constabulary (RUC). Their vehicles, bathed in flashing blue lights, skidded to a halt near the fiery chaos of the safe house. The officers, dressed in standard uniforms, stepped out briskly, their expressions a blend of professional resolve and wariness.

The scene before the RUC was one of destruction and enigma. The safe house, now partially consumed by the inferno, seemed to offer little in the way of immediate answers. The officers, maintaining a safe distance from the intense heat, surveyed the area cautiously. Their trained eyes scanned for any indicators of the occupants or clues to the events that led to this fiery end.

Amidst the group of officers, a distinct figure emerged. Dressed not in uniform but in plain clothes, this man's presence marked him as different. He was an MI5 agent, a 'spook' integrated within the RUC team. His involvement was a clear sign of the incident's significance in the complex tapestry of Northern Ireland's ongoing conflict.

The agent's gaze swept across the scene with a critical, analytical sharpness. He took in every detail: the flames' reach, the spread of the debris, the distinct marks of an intense firefight. His assessment went beyond the immediate visual cues, probing for deeper insights into the incident's perpetrators and their potential motives.

As the RUC officers commenced securing the perimeter and awaited the fire brigade's intervention, the MI5 agent remained observant but detached, his thoughts veiled behind a stoic facade. He understood that the fire's aftermath was more than a mere consequence of violence; it was a deliberate message, a calculated move in the complex chess game of Northern Irish politics.

Suddenly, the routine operation took an unexpected turn. As the flames were brought under control and the RUC officers prepared to investigate, they made a startling discovery. Amidst the charred remnants and smoky haze, they found Sean – injured and barely alive, but a critical piece in the puzzle of the night's events.

As the RUC team worked amidst the aftermath of the fire, the discovery of Sean, barely clinging to life, shifted the dynamics of the scene dramatically. The officers, trained for such emergencies, immediately sprang into action, radioing for an ambulance with the urgency the situation demanded. They carefully extracted Sean from the ruins, providing him with critical first aid as they awaited the medical team's arrival.

The MI5 agent, observing from a slight distance, could barely conceal his astonishment at this unexpected turn of events. In his mind, the survival of a member of Michael's team was an unforeseen boon. Sean's presence offered a rare opportunity to glean firsthand information about the inner workings and future plans of a key republican faction. The agent's thoughts were already racing ahead to the interrogation possibilities and the intelligence that could be extracted from Sean.

Meanwhile, Michael and his team, having made the harrowing decision to leave Sean behind, were in the midst of their escape. The night enveloped them as they moved swiftly, the burning safe house casting a haunting glow behind them. The team was shrouded in a mix of emotions – relief at their escape, guilt over leaving Sean, and a renewed sense of urgency for their cause.

Unbeknownst to them, the fate of their comrade Sean was taking a dramatic turn in the hands of the RUC and the MI5. As they disappeared into the cover of the city, their thoughts were with Sean, unaware that he had survived and was now in the custody of the authorities.

The contrast between the two scenes was stark. While Michael and his team melted into the shadows, seeking refuge and planning their next move, the RUC, with the MI5 agent in tow, were preparing to transport Sean to a secure location. The agent knew that time was of the essence; Sean's condition was critical, and every moment they delayed could mean a loss of valuable information.

In the relative safety of a new hideout, Michael's team took a moment to pause and assess the aftermath of the harrowing attack they had just endured. The atmosphere was heavy, laden with a mix of relief, grief, and simmering anger. The safe house, their once secure haven, was now just a memory engulfed in flames, and the cost of their escape weighed heavily on their minds.

As they gathered in the dimly lit room, each member was visibly shaken. The sounds of the ambush still echoed in their ears, a stark reminder of their narrow escape from death. The loss of Sean, left behind in their desperate flee, cast a long shadow over the group. His absence was a palpable presence in the room, a silent testament to the sacrifice they had all been forced to accept.

Michael, still reeling from the decisions he had made, looked around at his team. His eyes met theirs, each exchange a wordless conversation of shared sorrow and resilience. He cleared his throat, breaking the silence. "We need to take stock of our situation," he began, his voice steady despite the turmoil he felt. "We've lost a lot, but we're still here, and our fight is far from over."

The team proceeded to inventory their remaining resources. Ammunition, weapons, medical supplies – each item was carefully cataloged, a necessary step to plan their next move. Yet, the practicalities of their situation did little to alleviate the emotional toll the ambush had taken. The reality of their vulnerability had been laid bare, and the threat of further attacks loomed large in their thoughts.

The emotional impact of the ambush was profound. Feelings of guilt for leaving Sean, anger at the UFF and the authorities, and a deep-seated resolve to continue their struggle were all intermingled. Each member dealt with these emotions in their own way, some in silent contemplation, others in soft murmurs of conversation.

The ambush's aftermath had a profound and altering impact on the team's dynamics and morale. In the wake of losing Sean and enduring such an unexpected and violent attack, each member of the group found themselves grappling with a complex mix of emotions and the daunting task of recalibrating their approach to the struggle they were deeply embedded in.

For Michael, the leader whose decisions had always been guided by a blend of strategic acumen and a deep sense of responsibility for his team, the loss of Sean was both a personal and a professional blow. It was a loss that went beyond the physical absence of a key team member; it was a stark reminder of the perils they all faced and the harsh realities of the conflict they were engaged in. Michael felt the weight of leadership more heavily than ever, his mind constantly revisiting the events of the ambush, analyzing what could have been done differently.

The team members, too, were visibly affected. There was an air of somber reflection as they each dealt with their grief and anger. Sean had been more than just a comrade; he was a mentor, a friend, and a symbol of their shared cause. His absence left a void that was hard to fill, both in their operations and in their hearts.

This emotional turmoil was coupled with the need to reassess their strategy. The attack had exposed vulnerabilities they hadn't fully appreciated, and there was a collective understanding that their approach needed to adapt to this new level of threat. Discussions were held, with each member contributing their thoughts on how they could improve their security, enhance their operational tactics, and ensure better preparedness for such unforeseen incidents in the future.

However, amid this strategic re-evaluation, there was an undeniable sense of resilience. The ambush, though a harsh blow, had not dampened their resolve. If anything, it had reinforced their commitment to their cause. The discussions often circled back to how they could honor Sean's memory and sacrifice – by continuing their fight with even greater determination.

Several days after the ambush, Michael's team, immersed in their heightened security measures and strategic planning, was interrupted by an unexpected and unsettling update. Word had reached them through a convoluted network of contacts, finally arriving from Sean's wife. The news she relayed was both shocking and laden with grave implications: Sean had survived the ambush and was now in the hands of the authorities.

The team received this news with a complex mix of emotions. Relief that Sean was alive was intertwined with a deep sense of foreboding about what his capture could mean for their safety and the future of their operations. Sean, with his extensive knowledge of their activities and plans, was a valuable asset to the authorities. The risk of him divulging critical information, whether through coercion or otherwise, was a serious threat they couldn't ignore.

Gathered in a makeshift meeting room, the team listened intently as Michael relayed the message. "Sean is alive, but he's been captured," he announced, his voice heavy with the weight of this revelation. The room fell into a tense silence as the team processed the news, each member grappling with their thoughts and fears.

The conversation gradually turned towards the implications of Sean's capture. "We need to assume the worst," Michael said, a note of urgency in his voice. "We have to operate under the assumption that our security has been compromised. It's time to implement contingency plans and tighten our operations even further."

The team discussed various measures to enhance their security – changing communication codes, relocating to new safe houses, and possibly even breaking contact with some of their associates to prevent any potential leaks. The reality that one of their own was now in enemy hands forced them to re-evaluate their every move and strategy.

Despite the shock of the news, there was also a palpable sense of determination in the room. The team knew that they couldn't afford

to be paralyzed by fear or uncertainty. "We carry on," Michael stated resolutely. "For Sean, for us, and for the cause we believe in. We owe it to him to keep fighting."

In response to the shocking news of Sean's capture, Michael's team embarked on an immediate and comprehensive reorganization of their local network. Understanding the heightened risks and the possibility of Sean divulging critical information, they knew they had to act swiftly to secure their operations and protect their members.

The process was exhaustive and meticulous. Every aspect of their network – from safe house locations to communication methods – was scrutinized and altered. Trusted contacts were informed of the changes through secure channels, and some connections were temporarily severed to avoid potential leaks. The team understood that even the smallest oversight could lead to disastrous consequences.

This reorganization also meant going into deeper hiding. The team members, once active in various covert operations, now found themselves confined to the shadows, their movements limited and always shrouded in caution. The constant threat of being discovered by the RUC loomed over them, adding a persistent edge of tension to their daily lives.

Michael, ever the strategic leader, coordinated these changes with a calm but firm hand. He knew that the morale and mental well-being of his team were just as crucial as their physical safety. "We need to stay sharp and focused," he reminded them regularly. "But we also need to support each other. Now, more than ever, we're all we've got."

Each night, the team members went to bed with the unsettling uncertainty of what the next day might bring. The fear of waking up in the arms of the RUC was a constant companion, a silent shadow that followed them into their dreams. Despite the precautions they had taken, the risk of capture or worse was an ever-present reality.

Amidst this backdrop of intensified conflict, the civilian population of Northern Ireland found themselves caught in the crossfire. The daily lives of ordinary people were marked by checkpoints, curfews, and a pervasive sense of uncertainty. The fear of being in the wrong place at the wrong time was a constant concern, as was the anguish of living in a deeply divided society.

In this tense and uncertain environment, Michael's team found themselves navigating not only their immediate challenges but also considering their role in the broader context of the Northern Irish conflict. Their story was a microcosm of the larger struggle – a struggle that was as much about ideas and identity as it was about territory and power.

Several weeks had elapsed since the ambush and the subsequent upheaval in the operations of Michael's team and the broader conflict in Northern Ireland. During this time, little information had filtered through about Sean's fate. The uncertainty surrounding his condition and whereabouts weighed heavily on the team, a constant source of concern amidst their ongoing struggles.

Finally, a fragment of news broke through the silence. It was revealed that Sean had been interned, a term that in the context of Northern Ireland's troubled history, carried ominous connotations. He was reportedly being held in a secure medical wing within the infamous Maze Prison, a facility known for housing paramilitary prisoners from both sides of the conflict.

The Maze, with its high-security measures and notorious reputation, was a place that many in the republican movement knew all too well – either through personal experience or through the stories that permeated their communities. The fact that Sean was placed in the medical wing provided a sliver of hope about his survival but did little to alleviate the concerns about his well-being and the potential pressures he might be facing.

Internment, particularly in a place like the Maze, was more than just imprisonment. It was a symbol of the broader conflict, a reflection of the harsh measures employed by the authorities, and a stark reminder of the personal costs of the struggle. For those interned, it often meant prolonged detention without trial, and for their comrades and families, it meant grappling with the uncertainty of their loved ones' fates.

For Michael and his team, this news about Sean stirred a complex mix of emotions. There was relief that he was alive, but this was tempered by worries about his treatment and the potential for him to be coerced into providing information. The fact that he was in the medical wing suggested he was still dealing with the severe injuries sustained during the ambush, adding another layer of concern.

The news of Sean's internment at the Maze served to reinforce the team's resolve. It was a harsh reminder of the stakes of their involvement in the struggle and the need to continue their fight with even greater caution and determination. As they processed this information, their thoughts were with Sean, hoping for his strength and resilience in the face of adversity. The chapter closed on a note of solidarity among the team members, their bond strengthened in the face of shared challenges and the ever-present reminder of the sacrifices they had all made.

Chapter 6: Betrayal

The chapter begins in the aftermath of the ambush, set in the same safe house now littered with broken glass and spent bullets. The air is thick with the acrid smell of gunpowder and the faint metallic tang of blood. The room, once a sanctuary for Michael and his comrades, now feels like a tomb, haunted by the echoes of gunfire and the specter of betrayal.

Michael stood in the center of the room, his eyes scanning the wreckage around him. Chairs were overturned, papers scattered, and the walls were pocked with bullet holes. The dim light from a single, flickering bulb cast long shadows, accentuating the chaos. His heart pounded in his chest, not just from the physical exertion of the fight but from the gnawing suspicion that one of their own had betrayed them.

His comrades moved around him in a daze, tending to minor injuries, checking weapons, and trying to restore some semblance of order. The silence was heavy, only broken by the occasional groan of pain or whispered curse. Each man wore the same haunted look, eyes darting nervously, reflecting their shared fear and mistrust.

Michael's thoughts raced, replaying the events leading up to the ambush. He had gone over the plans meticulously, ensuring every detail was accounted for, every precaution taken. Yet, the British forces had known exactly when and where to strike. Someone had tipped them off. His mind wandered to each member of the team, evaluating their potential for betrayal.

He moved towards a corner of the room where Brendan sat, nursing a graze on his arm. Brendan's usually bright eyes were now clouded with pain and confusion. Michael knelt beside him, placing a comforting hand on his shoulder.

"How are you holding up?" Michael asked, his voice low and strained.

"I'll live," Brendan replied, wincing as he shifted his arm. "But what about Sean? They took him, didn't they?"

Michael nodded, the weight of Brendan's words pressing heavily on his shoulders. Sean, one of their most trusted members, had been captured. The implications were dire, not just for Sean, but for the entire group. If Sean talked, if he revealed their plans and hideouts, their fight could be over before it had truly begun.

"We'll get him back," Michael said, trying to inject confidence into his voice. But even as he spoke, doubt gnawed at him. The Maze Prison was notorious, a fortress from which few ever escaped. The reality of Sean's situation was grim.

As Michael stood, his eyes met those of Aisling, who stood across the room. She was watching him intently, her expression a mix of determination and concern. She stepped forward, her voice cutting through the oppressive silence.

"We need to find out who did this," she said, her tone leaving no room for argument. "Someone betrayed us, and we need to root them out before they can do any more damage."

Michael nodded, his resolve hardening. He looked around the room at his comrades, each one a potential suspect, and felt a chill run down his spine. The hunt for the informant had begun, and Michael knew that this betrayal could tear their group apart from within.

"Gather everyone," he instructed, his voice firm. "We need to talk. Now."

As the remaining members of the group assembled, Michael took a deep breath, preparing himself for the difficult task ahead. Trust had been shattered, and the path to uncovering the traitor would be fraught with tension and danger. But it was a path they had to walk if they were to survive and continue their fight for freedom.

The safe house, once their stronghold, now felt eerily quiet despite the presence of the entire team. The flickering bulb overhead cast an intermittent light that played tricks on their weary eyes, making every shadow seem like a lurking threat. Michael could feel the tension rising, a palpable force pressing down on everyone in the room.

He moved methodically, his boots crunching over broken glass as he checked on each member of the team. Aisling had already started gathering the scattered papers, her movements brisk and efficient, trying to bring some semblance of order to the chaos. She glanced up at Michael as he approached, her eyes conveying a silent message of solidarity and urgency.

"We need to secure this place first," Michael said, his voice steady despite the turmoil inside him. "Make sure there are no more surprises waiting for us."

Aisling nodded and began directing the others to fortify the entrances and check for any remaining threats. Michael turned his attention to the rest of the room, taking in the damage and the faces of his comrades. They were a mix of anger, fear, and suspicion, each one grappling with the same horrifying realization: someone among them had betrayed their trust.

As the team worked, Michael's mind kept drifting back to Sean. The Maze Prison was infamous for its brutal conditions and the relentless pressure placed on inmates to turn informant. He knew Sean was strong, but everyone had their breaking point. The thought of Sean enduring that kind of torment fueled Michael's determination to find the traitor quickly.

Finally, with the room as secure as it could be under the circumstances, Michael called everyone together. They formed a loose circle, their faces illuminated by the unsteady light. The air was thick with anticipation, each person waiting for Michael to speak.

"We were betrayed," Michael began, his voice cutting through the silence like a knife. "The British knew exactly where to find us and when. Someone here tipped them off."

A murmur of shock and anger rippled through the group. Michael held up a hand to quiet them.

"We need to figure out who it was," he continued. "We can't move forward until we know we can trust each other again. This isn't just about Sean – it's about all of us. Our lives depend on rooting out this traitor."

He looked around the circle, meeting each pair of eyes in turn. Some held defiance, others fear, and a few flickered with guilt. Michael knew this was going to be the hardest part of their journey so far, but it was necessary.

"We're going to do this systematically," Aisling said, stepping forward to stand beside Michael. "We'll start by going over the events of the past few days. Every interaction, every conversation. We'll find the leak."

The team nodded, some more reluctantly than others. Michael took a deep breath, feeling the weight of the moment. The hunt for the informant had begun, and it would test their resolve and unity like never before.

As they began the painstaking process of retracing their steps and scrutinizing each other's actions, Michael couldn't shake the feeling that this betrayal was just the beginning. The real challenge would be in rebuilding the trust that had been shattered and finding a way to move forward together despite the scars of treachery.

The team gathered in a rough circle, the remnants of the safe house's furniture creating an uncomfortable but necessary arrangement. Michael stood at the center, his gaze firm and unwavering as he addressed his comrades.

"We need to start asking hard questions," he said, his voice steady despite the underlying tension. "We'll go through each person's movements and interactions over the past few days. No detail is too small. We need to find out who betrayed us."

The room fell silent, the weight of the situation pressing heavily on everyone present. Aisling stepped forward, a notebook in hand, ready to document every statement and piece of evidence.

"We'll go one by one," she said. "Start with what you were doing the day before the ambush, and who you were with."

First to speak was Liam, a wiry man with a perpetually nervous demeanor. He shifted uncomfortably under the scrutiny, his eyes darting around the room.

"I was on lookout duty," Liam began, his voice shaky. "Didn't see anything unusual. After that, I went to the pub to gather intel.

Talked to a few regulars, then headed back here. Didn't talk to anyone else."

The group listened intently, but Michael noticed a few skeptical glances exchanged among the members. Brendan, his arm now bandaged, leaned forward.

"Anyone can vouch for you?" Brendan asked, his tone sharp.

Liam hesitated, then shook his head. "No one from our group. Just locals, but they wouldn't know anything."

Next was Connor, a burly man with a calm demeanor that belied the intensity of his loyalty. He recounted his activities, mostly involving logistics and planning sessions. His account was detailed, yet Michael noticed a few gaps in his timeline.

"What about the hour before the ambush?" Michael pressed. "Where were you?"

Connor frowned, clearly trying to recall. "I was with Aisling, discussing the next mission. You can ask her."

Aisling nodded in confirmation, but the room's tension didn't ease. The process continued, each member recounting their actions, defending their loyalty under the harsh glare of suspicion.

As the interrogations proceeded, minor details began to surface, each one a potential clue in unraveling the betrayal. Aisling noted everything down meticulously, her sharp mind piecing together the fragments of information.

Michael listened carefully; his instincts finely tuned to detect any inconsistencies. It was during Connor's second recounting of his activities that something caught Michael's attention.

"You said you were with Aisling before the ambush," Michael repeated. "But earlier, you mentioned running an errand alone. Which was it?"

Connor's eyes narrowed, a flicker of uncertainty crossing his face. "I—I might have mixed up the times. It's been a chaotic few days."

Another clue surfaced when Liam recounted his visit to the pub. One of the regulars he mentioned, a known informant, had been seen speaking with British soldiers recently. The room grew colder as the implications sank in.

"That informant,"

Brendan interjected, "did he see you leave? Could he have followed you back here?"

Liam's face paled, realization dawning. "I—I don't know. I didn't think he'd... he's been around forever. Didn't seem a threat."

The tension in the room was palpable as each revelation added to the growing unease. The group's unity was fraying, suspicion and paranoia gnawing at the bonds that had held them together.

Tempers flared as the interrogation intensified. Voices rose, accusations flying across the room. Connor accused Liam of negligence, while Liam fired back, questioning Connor's sudden need for solo errands. Even Aisling wasn't spared, her interactions with external contacts brought into question.

"Enough!" Michael's voice cut through the chaos, restoring a semblance of order. "This isn't helping. We need to stay focused and methodical. We're all on edge but turning on each other won't solve anything."

The room fell silent again, the tension still thick but now laced with a grudging acceptance of Michael's authority. He turned to Aisling, who nodded, signaling it was time to take a different approach.

"We need to narrow this down," Michael said, taking a deep breath. "Let's focus on the solid leads we have – the informant at the pub and the inconsistencies in timelines. We'll cross-check everyone's statements and find the truth."

As the interrogation continued, Michael felt the weight of responsibility pressing heavily on his shoulders. The betrayal had cut deep, but he knew that finding the traitor was essential not just for their survival, but for the integrity of their cause. With each question and answer, they moved one step closer to uncovering the truth, even as the path grew darker and more perilous.

The air grew heavier with each passing minute as they meticulously went through everyone's statements again. Michael's mind was a whirlpool of thoughts, sifting through every minor inconsistency, every hint of doubt.

Connor's alibi seemed solid when cross-referenced with Aisling's account, yet his errand remained a point of contention. Michael decided to probe further.

"What was the nature of your errand, Connor?" Michael asked, his tone neutral but probing.

Connor shifted uncomfortably. "I went to pick up some supplies from a contact in the outskirts. We needed more medical supplies and ammunition."

"Who was this contact?" Aisling asked, her pen poised over the notebook.

"Tommy, the usual guy we get our supplies from," Connor replied. "He's trustworthy."

"We need to verify that," Michael said, turning to Brendan. "Can you reach out to Tommy discreetly?"

Brendan nodded and moved to a corner to make the call. The room waited in tense silence, every eye on Brendan as he spoke in hushed tones.

After a few minutes, Brendan returned, his expression grim. "Tommy confirmed the meeting, but he mentioned something strange. He said Connor seemed agitated, more than usual."

Michael turned to Connor, his eyes narrowing. "Why were you agitated, Connor? What aren't you telling us?"

Connor's face flushed with frustration. "I was on edge because we're all on edge! This isn't just a walk in the park. We're fighting for our lives here."

Before Michael could respond, Liam spoke up, his voice trembling. "There's something else. I saw Connor talking to someone in an alley before he came back. I didn't think much of it at the time, but now..."

Connor's eyes widened in shock. "What are you implying, Liam? That I'm the traitor?"

Michael raised a hand to calm the escalating tension. "We're not making accusations without proof. But we need to investigate every lead."

"We'll verify every detail, cross-check every alibi," Michael said. "No stone unturned. Aisling, continue documenting. Brendan, stay on Tommy's contact. Liam, describe the person Connor was talking to."

Liam hesitated, then spoke. "It was dark, but the guy was tall, wearing a long coat. Couldn't see his face clearly."

Michael nodded, turning to the group. "We'll follow these leads. No assumptions, just facts. We'll find the truth."

The room's tension eased slightly as they settled into a methodical investigation. Michael felt the weight of leadership more than ever, knowing that every decision could mean the difference between survival and annihilation.

With each step, they moved closer to the truth, even as the shadows of betrayal loomed large. The path was fraught with danger, but Michael knew that uncovering the traitor was their only hope for redemption and unity.

Hours turned into an agonizing wait as the team pursued every lead and verified every alibi. The tension in the room was suffocating, each person grappling with their own doubts and fears. Michael felt the pressure mounting, knowing that a wrong move could shatter what remained of their fragile unity.

Finally, Brendan returned with a crucial piece of information. "I found someone who saw Liam talking to a British agent. It was a brief encounter, but it matches the description of the man in the alley."

The room fell silent, all eyes on Liam. Michael felt his heart sink as he turned to Liam. "Is this true?"

Liam's face was ashen, his voice a whisper. "I... I didn't know who he was. He approached me, said he could help with my debts. I didn't tell him anything important, I swear."

Michael's eyes hardened. "But you did talk to him. You put us all at risk."

Liam's shoulders slumped, the weight of his actions finally crashing down on him. "I'm sorry. I was desperate. I didn't mean for any of this to happen."

Michael felt a mixture of anger and pity. "You betrayed our trust, Liam. You endangered us all. We have to decide what to do with you."

The room's atmosphere grew even tenser as the group faced the harsh reality of their situation. The shadows of betrayal had been illuminated, but the path to redemption was still uncertain.

The group gathered once more, their faces a mix of anger, sadness, and determination. Michael stood at the center, his resolve firm despite the emotional toll.

"Liam's actions have put us all in danger," Michael said. "But we must remember that we are fighting for a cause greater than ourselves. We cannot afford to let this betrayal tear us apart."

He looked around the room, meeting each pair of eyes in turn. "We will decide Liam's fate together. But let this be a lesson to us all – trust is fragile, and we must protect it with everything we have."

The group nodded, their unity restored, albeit with scars. They knew that the road ahead would be difficult, but they were resolved to face it together. The shadows of betrayal had been confronted, and now they could begin the process of healing and moving forward.

As they prepared to continue their fight, Michael felt a renewed sense of purpose. The path to victory was long and arduous, but with trust and unity, they could overcome any obstacle. The battle was far from over, but they were ready to face whatever came next, together.

Liam had always been a bit of an enigma within the group. While his loyalty to the cause was never outright questioned, his personal life and habits often made him the subject of silent scrutiny. Now, under the intense pressure of betrayal, those past indiscretions came back to haunt him, painting a more detailed picture for both his comrades and the readers.

Liam's background was a mix of tragedy and resilience. He had grown up in a tough part of Belfast, his family struggling to make ends meet amidst the chaos of the Troubles. His father had been a staunch supporter of the IRA, and Liam grew up idolizing him. However, his father's arrest and subsequent imprisonment had left a void in their family, thrusting young Liam into the role of provider.

As he matured, Liam's responsibilities weighed heavily on him. The streets of Belfast offered few opportunities, and the allure of quick money from gambling was too tempting to resist. His habit started small—friendly bets with neighbors—but it quickly spiraled into something more insidious.

Liam's gambling problem became a dark secret he carried, a constant source of stress and shame. He owed money to dangerous people, and the pressure to repay those debts grew with each passing day. This desperation drove him to make risky decisions, often clouding his judgment and leading him down a path of self-destruction.

The group knew about Liam's gambling issues, but they never realized the extent of his debt or the danger it posed to their operations. Liam had always managed to keep it under wraps, presenting a facade of control. However, the recent ambush and subsequent investigation had stripped away those layers, revealing the fragility beneath.

Liam's vulnerabilities made him an easy target for manipulation. British agents and informants were skilled at identifying and exploiting such weaknesses. When a well-dressed man approached Liam in a dark alley, promising help with his debts in exchange for information, Liam's desperation overpowered his loyalty. He believed he could handle it, that he wouldn't betray anything significant. But in his panic, he didn't realize the full implications of his actions.

As the group delved deeper into the investigation, these facets of Liam's life came to light. They saw a man torn between his commitment to the cause and the personal demons that plagued him. His erratic behavior, the shifty glances, the nervous energy—all pointed to a man on the edge, struggling to maintain his composure under immense pressure.

The confrontation with Michael and the group brought Liam's internal conflict to the forefront. He was forced to confront his actions, the lies he told himself, and the reality of the consequences he now faced.

"Liam," Michael's voice

was softer now, tinged with a mix of disappointment and understanding. "We all have our battles, but this... this has put us all at risk. You need to be honest with us, and with yourself."

Liam's shoulders shook as he spoke, his voice cracking. "I didn't mean for it to go this far. I thought I could control it, that I could fix things without anyone getting hurt. I was wrong."

The room was silent, the weight of Liam's words sinking in. His comrades saw not just a traitor, but a man broken by his own choices, caught in a web of circumstances he couldn't escape.

As they prepared to decide Liam's fate, the group was torn between empathy and the harsh reality of their situation. They understood his struggles, but they also knew the importance of maintaining trust and security within their ranks.

"Liam, we have to protect ourselves and our mission," Aisling said, her voice firm but compassionate. "We need to know that we can trust each other implicitly. Your actions have endangered that trust."

Michael felt a mixture of anger and pity. "You betrayed our trust, Liam. You endangered us all. We have to decide what to do with you."

Given the gravity of the situation, the group knew there could be only one outcome. Historically, the IRA dealt with informers, known as "touts," through brutal interrogation followed by execution. The fear of informants was a significant threat, and they were dealt with ruthlessly to maintain discipline and security within the ranks.

The room grew colder as Michael delivered the final verdict. "Liam, your actions have left us no choice. You will be taken to a secure location for interrogation. If you are found guilty of betraying us, the punishment will be severe."

Liam's face paled as the reality of his situation sank in. He knew what was coming. His fate was sealed, and there would be no second chances.

After restraining Liam, Michael and Aisling composed a message detailing the findings of their internal investigation. The message was sent to the IRA's Army Council, outlining the evidence and requesting a decision on Liam's fate. This process was crucial, as the Army Council held the authority to sanction any severe actions, including executions.

As they waited for the council's response, the group made their peace with what was likely to come. The decision to execute an informant was never taken lightly, but it was a necessary evil to protect the integrity and safety of the organization.

Liam was taken to a secure location where he was interrogated by the group's internal security team. The interrogation was intense, designed to extract any additional information and confirm the extent of his betrayal. Liam, already broken by guilt and fear, confessed to everything.

Within hours of their message to the Army Council, the response came back swiftly. Liam was found guilty, and the order for his execution was given. The gravity of the situation sank in quickly. Michael gathered the group for a final meeting to ensure everyone understood their roles and the gravity of what lay ahead.

As they prepared to carry out the sentence, the group's unity was both tested and solidified. The decision to execute Liam, while brutal, was necessary to maintain the integrity of their cause. Each member of the group understood the harsh realities of their struggle, and this grim task brought them closer together, reinforcing their commitment to one another and their mission.

"We're all in this together," Michael said, his voice steady but heavy with emotion. "This isn't easy, but it has to be done. Liam's betrayal endangered us all, and we can't afford to let this happen again."

Aisling nodded, her eyes reflecting the weight of their decision. "We need to be vigilant. Trust is our most valuable asset, and we have to protect it at all costs."

Each member of the group shared their thoughts, the conversation filled with a mix of anger, sadness, and resolve. They spoke about their commitment to the cause, the sacrifices they had made, and the need to stay united in the face of adversity.

In the dim light of early morning, the group prepared for the execution. Liam was brought to a secluded location, his hands bound and his face pale with fear. Despite his betrayal, there was a sense of solemnity and respect for the life that was about to be taken.

Michael stood before Liam; the weight of leadership heavy on his shoulders. "Liam, you betrayed us, and for that, you must pay the price. We all understand the consequences of our actions, and today, you face yours."

Liam's eyes were filled with regret and sorrow. "I'm sorry," he whispered, his voice breaking. "I never meant for it to go this far."

The group formed a circle around Liam, their faces grim but resolute. Aisling stepped forward, reading the final judgment from the Army Council. "Liam, you have been found guilty of betraying the trust of your comrades and endangering the mission. The punishment is death."

Liam was given a moment to say a final prayer. The silence was heavy, each member of the group reflecting on the severity of their actions and the cost of their fight for freedom.

Michael raised his weapon, his hands steady despite the turmoil inside him. With a final look at Liam, he pulled the trigger. The sound of the gunshot echoed through the still morning air, marking the end of Liam's life and the group's painful resolution to the betrayal.

The group returned to the safe house in silence, the reality of their actions weighing heavily on them. They had done what was necessary, but the emotional toll was undeniable. Michael gathered them together once more, knowing that their unity was crucial in the days to come.

"We move forward from this," Michael said, his voice firm but gentle. "We honor Liam's memory by learning from this experience and ensuring it never happens again. Our fight continues, and we need each other now more than ever."

In the hours following Liam's execution, the group took time to reflect on their mission and the sacrifices they had made. The weight of their decision lingered, but it also served as a stark reminder of the seriousness of their struggle.

Michael and Aisling worked closely to strengthen their security measures and ensure that trust was maintained within the group. They held regular meetings, encouraging open communication and addressing any concerns that arose.

Brendan, who had been particularly close to Liam, found solace in the solidarity of his comrades. They supported him through his grief, reinforcing the bonds that held them together.

With the shadows of betrayal behind them, the group refocused on their mission with renewed determination. They knew the road ahead was fraught with danger, but their unity and resolve were stronger than ever. The execution of Liam had reinforced the importance of loyalty and trust, and they were prepared to face any challenges that lay ahead.

As they continued their fight for freedom and justice, Michael felt a renewed sense of purpose. The path to victory was long and arduous, but with trust and unity, they could overcome any obstacle. The battle was far from over, but they were ready to face whatever came next, together, with a deeper understanding of the sacrifices required and the strength found in their shared commitment.

In the quiet that followed the grim events, Michael found a secluded corner of the safe house. He pulled out his battered journal, the pages already filled with the trials and tribulations of their struggle. The ink flowed smoothly, almost cathartically, as he began to write.

"Today, we lost more than a comrade. We lost a part of our trust, our unity. The betrayal of Liam has left scars that will take time to heal. It was a necessary evil, a decision no leader wants to make, yet one that could not be avoided. The path we walk is fraught with peril, and each step demands sacrifice."

Michael paused, the weight of their cause pressing heavily on his shoulders. He reflected on the brutal actions they had taken, the life they had extinguished. His thoughts wandered to Sean, still trapped in the Maze Prison, and the countless others who had fallen for their cause. The faces of lost comrades haunted him, each one a stark reminder of the high stakes they faced daily.

"I must stay strong for them, for all of us. This fight is far from over, and we must steel ourselves for the battles yet to come. Our enemies are relentless, and the British forces grow bolder. The risk of future betrayals is ever-present, a shadow lurking in the corners of our minds."

He set the pen down, the ink drying quickly on the page, and closed the journal. The future of their cause seemed more uncertain than ever, but Michael knew that his resolve needed to be unbreakable. He looked around at his comrades, each one bearing the weight of their own grief and determination. Aisling was organizing their scattered plans, her face a mask of focused intensity. Brendan, normally a pillar of strength, looked weary and withdrawn, the strain of their recent losses etched deeply into his features.

Hints of increased pressure from British forces began to infiltrate their discussions, whispers of new strategies and tighter security measures. They spoke of surveillance sweeps, stricter curfews, and the ominous presence of more informants embedded within their ranks. The fear of another informant gnawed at their trust, a silent enemy that threatened to unravel them from within.

Michael steeled himself, knowing that the difficult path ahead would test their limits. The internal conflict was far from resolved, and every decision carried the weight of their shared fate. He recalled the coded messages intercepted in recent weeks, hinting at escalated operations and tighter grips on their movements. The need for vigilance was paramount, and Michael understood that his leadership would be critical in navigating the treacherous waters ahead.

As the group gathered for a final meeting of the day, Michael addressed them with a renewed sense of purpose. "We must remain united," he said, his voice steady. "Trust

is our greatest weapon and our most fragile asset. We need to be vigilant, but we also need to support each other. The road ahead is daunting, but together, we can face whatever comes our way."

The room settled into a somber silence; each member lost in their thoughts. The future was a daunting expanse, but together, they would face it, one step at a time, their unity forged anew in the fires of their recent trials. The bonds between them, tested by betrayal, were now tempered by their shared resolve to continue the fight for their cause. Michael's gaze lingered on each of his comrades, his heart heavy but his spirit unbroken.

With the echoes of their past still resonating around them, they prepared to forge ahead, their determination steeled against the challenges that lay in wait.

Chapter 7: The Maze

Sean sat in the back of the blacked-out van, feeling every jolt and bump as it sped along the uneven road. The darkness was almost complete, save for the occasional beam of light seeping through the cracks, flashing across his face for just a moment before plunging him back into blackness. His mind was a tumult of fear and determination, memories of the ambush replaying in vivid detail.

The sudden attack had come without warning. One moment, Michael and his team had been gathered around the table in the safe house, discussing future operations, and the next, chaos had erupted. Bullets shattered the windows, and the air was filled with the acrid smell of gunpowder. Michael's shouts of "Take cover! Return fire!" were barely audible over the cacophony. Sean had dived for cover, his heart pounding as he fired back at the unseen assailants. The room, once a place of strategic planning, had transformed into a battleground.

Sean remembered the sting of the bullet that had hit him, the sharp, searing pain that had dropped him to the ground. He had watched as his comrades tried to defend their position; their faces set in grim determination. The UFF's attack was relentless, their firepower overwhelming. Sean had struggled to stay conscious, but the pain and blood loss had been too much.

Now, he was being taken to one of the most notorious prisons in Northern Ireland, the Maze. He had heard the stories—of the brutal conditions, the psychological torment, the unyielding struggle for dignity and recognition. He tried to steel himself, repeating silently, "Stay strong. Don't break."

The van came to an abrupt halt, and Sean was roughly pulled from the vehicle, the blinding daylight assaulting his eyes after the prolonged darkness. As his vision adjusted, the imposing structure of the Maze loomed before him. Tall fences topped with barbed wire stretched out as far as he could see, and high concrete walls surrounded the facility, giving it the appearance of a fortress. Watchtowers dotted the perimeter, manned by armed guards whose eyes tracked his every movement. The heavy gates clanked open with a foreboding finality, and Sean was led through them, the sound of his footsteps echoing off the cold, gray walls.

Inside, the silence was broken only by the occasional clanking of cell doors and the distant, muffled voices of other prisoners. The interior was a labyrinth of corridors and cells, designed to disorient and intimidate. The medical wing, where Sean was taken due to his injuries, was no exception. It was stark and clinical, the antiseptic smell doing little to mask the underlying scent of fear and despair.

As Sean was processed—stripped, searched, and given a prison uniform—the weight of the Maze's notorious reputation pressed down on him. The guards' indifferent, almost mechanical treatment of him added to his sense of dread. He knew this place was not just about confinement; it was about breaking the spirit. The stories of the blanket protests and the dirty protests, of men smeared in their own filth in a desperate bid for recognition and basic human rights, were all too real now.

Each clank of a cell door, each barked order from a guard, was a reminder of the psychological warfare he was about to endure. He could feel the oppressive atmosphere trying to seep into his mind, but he clung to the thought of his comrades, of the cause they were fighting for. He couldn't afford to break. Not here, not now.

As he was led deeper into the prison, the reality of his situation began to set in. The Maze was not just a physical place; it was a battleground of wills. Sean knew he would need every ounce of strength and determination to survive this place, to resist the efforts to break him down. The walls around him seemed to close in, but he forced himself to stand tall, to face the challenges ahead with the same resolve that had kept him fighting all these years.

Sean's thoughts wandered back to the safe house, where the ambush had changed everything in a matter of seconds. The room had been filled with the smell of freshly brewed tea and the warmth of sunlight filtering through the curtains. Maps and documents sprawled across the table as the team discussed potential routes for their next supply run. Brendan had been mid-sentence, his voice steady and confident, when the first bullet shattered the tranquility. The safe house, once a haven of strategy and camaraderie, became a war zone.

The memory of the attack was vivid. The sound of glass shattering, the sharp cracks of gunfire, and the shouts of his comrades all blended into a chaotic symphony. Sean had fired back, his training taking over even as fear gripped him. The sting of the bullet that struck him was a fiery pain, and he had crumpled to the ground, clutching his wound as his vision blurred. The last thing he remembered was Michael's voice, strong and commanding, trying to organize their defense.

As Sean was led through the Maze, the physical pain from his injuries was overshadowed by the mental strain. The stories he had heard about the Maze—of men driven to the brink of madness, of the constant struggle for basic human dignity—played on a loop in his mind. The blanket protests and dirty protests were legendary acts of defiance, but they came at a tremendous cost. Sean knew he would have to draw on every ounce of his strength and resilience to withstand what was to come.

The guards' treatment was cold and impersonal, designed to strip away any sense of individuality. Sean was just another prisoner, another body to be controlled and broken. As he was led to his cell in the medical wing, he could feel the weight of the prison bearing down on him. The antiseptic smell of the medical wing did little to comfort him; it was just another reminder of the clinical efficiency with which the prison operated.

Inside his cell, the walls seemed to close in, the silence almost suffocating. Sean lay on the hard cot, staring at the ceiling, his thoughts racing. He knew he would need to stay strong, not just for himself but for his comrades still fighting outside these walls. The Maze was designed to break men, but Sean vowed to resist, to hold on to his spirit and determination. He repeated his mantra silently: "Stay strong. Don't break."

The clanking of cell doors and the distant sounds of other prisoners added to the oppressive atmosphere. Sean forced himself to think of his comrades, of the cause they were fighting for. The memory of the ambush, the image of his friends battling against overwhelming odds, gave him strength. He would survive this, he would endure. The Maze would not break him.

Sean was led to his cell in the medical wing, still weak and disoriented from the severe injuries he had sustained during the ambush. The stark, clinical environment provided little comfort. The fluorescent lights overhead cast a harsh glow, amplifying the sterile and unwelcoming atmosphere. The cot he was placed on was hard and unyielding, a far cry from the semblance of safety he had known in the safe house. Every movement was a reminder of his physical pain, but it was the psychological weight of his new reality that pressed down on him most heavily.

The medical wing was eerily quiet, the only sounds being the occasional distant clank of metal and the soft murmur of voices. Sean lay on the cot, staring at the ceiling, trying to process the whirlwind of events that had led him here. The attack had been swift and brutal, a stark reminder of the dangers they faced. Now, confined within the walls of the Maze, he felt the enormity of his predicament fully settle in. The pain from his wounds was constant, a sharp reminder of the chaos that had brought him to this point.

The medical staff were professional but distant. They treated Sean's wounds with practiced efficiency, their faces void of any warmth or compassion. Each interaction was brief and impersonal, as if they were tending to an object rather than a person. The guards, ever-present, added to the oppressive atmosphere, their eyes cold and watchful. Sean's attempts to engage with the staff were met with curt responses, their demeanor making it clear that any form of rapport was unwelcome.

Sean also met a few inmates in the medical wing. Some offered silent nods of solidarity, acknowledging the shared plight without words. Others were too engrossed in their own pain and despair to engage, their eyes glazed over with a sense of hopelessness. One older inmate, with a face etched in lines of suffering and resilience, whispered a few words of encouragement to Sean, telling him to stay strong and not let the prison break his spirit.

"Hang in there, lad," the older man muttered. "Don't let them get to you. We've all been through hell, but we keep fighting."

Sean nodded, absorbing the wisdom in those words. The small acts of solidarity, the shared understanding of their struggle, provided a glimmer of hope in an otherwise bleak situation. This camaraderie, even in silence, was a lifeline in the cold, indifferent world of the Maze.

Sean quickly learned the rigid routines of the Maze. The day started with early wakeups, the harsh clang of metal on metal echoing through the corridors as guards banged on cell doors. Head counts were conducted with military precision, the guards barking orders and making sure every prisoner was accounted for. Meals were meager and barely enough to sustain, served in small portions that left most prisoners perpetually hungry.

The hours in between were long and monotonous, filled with the hum of fluorescent lights and the distant murmurs of other prisoners. Sean spent much of his time lying on the cot, trying to conserve his strength and deal with the pain from his injuries. The only break in the monotony came when he overheard conversations about the blanket and dirty protests, legendary acts of resistance that had taken place within these very walls. These stories of defiance, of men refusing to be broken despite the brutal conditions, gave Sean a glimmer of hope and a sense of connection to a larger struggle.

Through these overheard conversations, Sean began to understand the deep-seated resistance among the prisoners. The blanket protest had started when inmates refused to wear prison uniforms, instead wrapping themselves in blankets. This act of defiance escalated into the dirty protest, where prisoners smeared their cells with their own excrement to protest the inhumane treatment. These stories were a testament to the unyielding spirit of the prisoners, their refusal to be dehumanized despite the prison's efforts to break them.

Sean knew he would need to draw on this same spirit to survive. Each day in the Maze was a battle, not just against the physical confines but against the psychological pressure designed to crush their resolve. The harsh realities of prison life were unrelenting, but Sean was determined to stay strong, to hold on to the hope that one day he would be free again, and to continue the fight for his cause.

He often thought back to the ambush, using the memory as fuel to keep his resolve strong. The image of his comrades fighting valiantly, refusing to give in, became a mantra of sorts. He would repeat silently to himself, "Stay strong. Don't break." The clanking of cell doors and the distant sounds of other prisoners added to the oppressive atmosphere. Sean forced himself to think of his comrades, of the cause they were fighting for. The memory of the ambush, the image of his friends battling against overwhelming odds, gave him strength. He would survive this, he would endure. The Maze would not break him.

The medical wing, while devoid of the overt violence of other areas of the prison, was no less a place of torment. The antiseptic smell, the impersonal treatment, the ever-watchful guards—all served to remind Sean of his precarious position. Yet, amidst this, he found small acts of resistance. A nod from a fellow prisoner, a shared glance of defiance, the whispered stories of protests past—these were the threads that wove together to form a tapestry of resilience and hope. Sean clung to these, knowing that as long as the spirit of resistance lived within him, the Maze could never truly imprison him.

One evening, as Sean lay on his cot in the Maze Prison, the oppressive silence of the cell block was broken by a whispered conversation from two nearby inmates.

The voices were low and urgent, barely above a murmur. Sean, ever vigilant and desperate for any news from the outside world, strained to listen, catching snippets of their exchange.

"Did you hear about the ambush?" one inmate whispered, his voice tinged with a mix of excitement and fear.

"Yeah, the safe house got hit hard. They say someone on the inside tipped off the Brits," the other replied, his tone grim.

Sean's heart skipped a beat. The ambush. Betrayal. Someone had betrayed them. His mind raced as he pieced together the fragments of the conversation. The memory of that chaotic day flashed through his mind: the sudden attack, the bullets shattering windows, the smell of gunpowder, and the pain of being hit.

"Michael's trying to find out who did it," the first inmate continued. "But it's a mess. Trust is shattered."

Sean's thoughts turned to his comrades. Michael, Brendan, Aisling—all of them were now grappling with the fallout of the betrayal. He felt a surge of anger and frustration, mixed with a deep sense of helplessness. Trapped within the Maze, he could do nothing to help them, nothing to uncover the traitor who had endangered them all.

The whispered conversation continued, filling in more details. The group's safe house had been compromised; their plans disrupted. Michael and the others were conducting a thorough investigation, scrutinizing every detail, every interaction, in a desperate bid to root out the informant.

"They're going through everyone's movements," the second inmate added. "Questioning every little thing. It's tearing them apart."

Sean clenched his fists, his knuckles white against the rough fabric of his prison-issue blanket. The betrayal had struck at the heart of their cause, threatening to unravel everything they had fought for. He knew the stakes were higher than ever, and the need for vigilance and unity was paramount. He could only imagine the atmosphere of suspicion and fear that must be pervading their ranks, each comrade eyeing the other with doubt and mistrust.

As he lay back on the cot, Sean felt a renewed sense of determination. He might be trapped in the Maze, but his spirit remained unbroken. He would endure the hardships of prison life, hold on to the hope of freedom, and continue to fight for their cause in any way he could. The betrayal might have shaken them, but it would not defeat them. They would emerge stronger, more resolute, and ready to face whatever challenges lay ahead.

Sean's thoughts turned to practical matters. He began to mentally prepare for the possibility of interrogation by the prison guards, knowing they would try to break him for information. He rehearsed his responses, steeling himself against the psychological and physical torment that he knew lay ahead.

Every day in the Maze was a battle of wills. The guards aimed to strip the prisoners of their humanity, to reduce them to numbers and broken spirits. But Sean clung to his identity, his purpose. He thought of Michael's determination, Aisling's unwavering resolve, Brendan's loyalty. These thoughts fortified him, became his armor against the daily assaults on his mind and body.

That night, as the prison lay in silence, Sean made a vow to himself and to his comrades. He would survive this ordeal, and when the time came, he would return to them. They would find the traitor, and they would continue their fight for freedom, undeterred by the obstacles thrown in their path.

as Sean lay on his cot in the Maze Prison, the oppressive silence of the cell block was broken by a whispered conversation from two nearby inmates. The voices were low and urgent, barely above a murmur. Sean, ever vigilant and desperate for any news from the outside world, strained to listen, catching snippets of their exchange.

"Did you hear about the ambush?" one inmate whispered, his voice tinged with a mix of excitement and fear.

"Yeah, the safe house got hit hard. They say someone on the inside tipped off the Brits," the other replied, his tone grim.

Sean's heart skipped a beat. The ambush. Betrayal. Someone had betrayed them. His mind raced as he pieced together the fragments of the conversation. The memory of that chaotic day flashed through his mind: the sudden attack, the bullets shattering windows, the smell of gunpowder, and the pain of being hit.

"Michael's trying to find out who did it," the first inmate continued. "But it's a mess. Trust is shattered."

Sean's thoughts turned to his comrades. Michael, Brendan, Aisling—all of them were now grappling with the fallout of the betrayal. He felt a surge of anger and frustration, mixed with a deep sense of helplessness. Trapped within the Maze, he could do nothing to help them, nothing to uncover the traitor who had endangered them all.

The whispered conversation continued, filling in more details. The group's safe house had been compromised; their plans disrupted. Michael and the others were conducting a thorough investigation, scrutinizing every detail, every interaction, in a desperate bid to root out the informant.

"They're going through everyone's movements," the second inmate added. "Questioning every little thing. It's tearing them apart."

Sean clenched his fists, his knuckles white against the rough fabric of his prison-issue blanket. The betrayal had struck at the heart of their cause, threatening to unravel everything they had fought for. He knew the stakes were higher than ever, and the need for vigilance and unity was paramount. He could only imagine the atmosphere of suspicion and fear that must be pervading their ranks, each comrade eyeing the other with doubt and mistrust.

As he lay back on the cot, Sean felt a renewed sense of determination. He might be trapped in the Maze, but his spirit remained unbroken. He would endure the hardships of prison life, hold on to the hope of freedom, and continue to fight for their cause in any way he could. The betrayal might have shaken them, but it would not defeat them. They would emerge stronger, more resolute, and ready to face whatever challenges lay ahead.

Sean's thoughts turned to practical matters. He began to mentally prepare for the possibility of interrogation by the prison guards, knowing they would try to break him for information. He rehearsed his responses, steeling himself against the psychological and physical torment that he knew lay ahead.

Every day in the Maze was a battle of wills. The guards aimed to strip the prisoners of their humanity, to reduce them to numbers and broken spirits. But Sean clung to his identity, his purpose. He thought of Michael's determination, Aisling's unwavering resolve, Brendan's loyalty. These thoughts fortified him, became his armor against the daily assaults on his mind and body.

As days turned into a few agonizing days, Sean maintained a routine of mental and physical exercises. He exchanged coded messages with fellow prisoners when possible, fostering a network of resistance within the Maze. The knowledge of the betrayal fueled his resolve, turning his anger into a cold, focused determination.

One night, as the prison lay in silence, Sean made a vow to himself and to his comrades. He would survive this ordeal, and when the time came, he would return to them. They would find the traitor, and they would continue their fight for freedom, undeterred by the obstacles thrown in their path.

The betrayal might have cast a long shadow over their cause, but it also cast a light on their resilience. The Maze could confine his body, but it could not imprison his spirit. With each passing day, Sean's determination grew stronger, a beacon of hope in the darkness of his captivity.

As the days turned into a few agonizing days, the tension within the Maze Prison grew palpable. Sean continued to gather information from the other inmates, piecing together the details of the outside world. One evening, a new piece of information reached his ears, sending a shockwave through his system.

"I heard they found out who the traitor was," one inmate whispered, his voice barely audibles in the dark.

"Yeah, it was Liam," the other inmate responded, his tone heavy with disbelief. "He sold them out to the Brits."

Sean felt a chill run down his spine. Liam. The same Liam who had fought by their side, shared their hardships, and vowed loyalty to their cause. The revelation hit him like a physical blow, and he struggled to process the betrayal.

"Liam?" Sean muttered under his breath, disbelief and anger mingling in his voice. "How could he?"

The first inmate continued, oblivious to Sean's inner turmoil. "Apparently, he had some serious gambling debts. The Brits offered him a way out, and he took it. That's how they knew about the safe house."

Sean's mind raced as he absorbed this new information. Liam's betrayal had not only led to the ambush but also to his own capture. The sense of betrayal was overwhelming, and he could feel his anger bubbling to the surface. He clenched his fists, his knuckles white with the intensity of his emotions.

"Michael found out," the second inmate added. "They confronted Liam and... well, let's just say Liam won't be betraying anyone else."

Sean's thoughts turned to Michael and the rest of the team. He could only imagine the pain and betrayal they must have felt upon discovering that one of their own had sold them out. The sense of helplessness he had felt before was now replaced with a burning resolve. He would survive this. He would return to them. And they would continue their fight for freedom, undeterred by Liam's betrayal.

That night, as Sean lay on his cot, he felt a renewed sense of purpose. The Maze could confine his body, but it could not imprison his spirit. With each passing day, his determination grew stronger, fueled by the knowledge of Liam's betrayal and the unwavering resolve of his comrades. They would emerge from this stronger, more united, and ready to face whatever challenges lay ahead.

The betrayal might have cast a long shadow over their cause, but it also cast a light on their resilience. Sean knew that their fight was far from over. They would find a way to overcome this, and when the time came, he would be there to stand with them once more.

Sean lay on his cot, the cold, unyielding surface pressing against his back. The darkness of the cell seemed to close in on him, mirroring the turmoil in his mind. The whispered conversation he had just overheard reverberated through his thoughts, each word a dagger plunging deeper into his heart.

Liam. A name that had once been synonymous with camaraderie and loyalty now tasted bitter on his tongue. The man who had shared their victories and defeats, who had stood by their side in the heat of battle, had been the one to betray them. Sean's mind struggled to reconcile the image of the friend he had known with the traitor who had sold them out.

A surge of anger coursed through him, tightening his chest and clenching his fists. How could Liam have done this? Sean remembered the nights they had spent planning their operations, the risks they had taken together, the blood they had shed. And for what? For a few pieces of silver to settle gambling debts? The betrayal cut deeper than any wound, leaving a scar that would never fully heal.

As he lay there, Sean's thoughts drifted back to the day of the ambush. The room had been filled with the smell of freshly brewed tea and the warmth of sunlight filtering through the curtains. Maps and documents had sprawled across the table as the team discussed potential routes for their next supply run. Brendan had been mid-sentence, his voice steady and confident, when the first bullet shattered the tranquility. The safe house, once a haven of strategy and camaraderie, had become a war zone in an instant.

The memory of the attack was vivid. The sound of glass shattering, the sharp cracks of gunfire, and the shouts of his comrades all blended into a chaotic symphony. Sean had fired back, his training taking over even as fear gripped him. The sting of the bullet that struck him was a fiery pain, and he had crumpled to the ground, clutching his wound as his vision blurred. The last thing he remembered was Michael's voice, strong and commanding, trying to organize their defense.

Now, he understood the root of that chaos. Liam's betrayal had set the events in motion, had led to the shattering of their sanctuary and the scattering of their hopes. Sean felt a deep sense of helplessness, trapped within the Maze, unable to do anything to help his comrades or bring the traitor to justice. The walls of his cell seemed to close in tighter, suffocating him with the weight of his rage and frustration.

But amidst the anger and despair, a spark of determination flared within him. Sean knew he couldn't let this betrayal break him. He had to stay strong, not just for himself, but for Michael, Brendan, Aisling, and the rest of the team. They were counting on him, even if they didn't know it. The Maze could confine his body, but it could not imprison his spirit.

He thought of Michael's resolve, Aisling's unwavering commitment, and Brendan's fierce loyalty. They had always been stronger together, and Sean believed that even in the face of this betrayal, they would find a way to overcome it. They had to.

Liam's actions had sown seeds of doubt and mistrust, but Sean was determined that those seeds would not take root. He would survive this ordeal, return to his comrades, and they would continue their fight for freedom, undeterred by Liam's treachery. The betrayal might have cast a long shadow over their cause, but it also cast a light on their resilience.

With each passing day, Sean's determination grew stronger. He would endure the hardships of prison life, hold on to the hope of freedom, and continue to fight for their cause in any way he could. He repeated his silent mantra: "Stay strong. Don't break."

The Maze could confine his body, but it could not imprison his spirit. He would emerge from this stronger, more resolute, and ready to face whatever challenges lay ahead. The betrayal might have shaken them, but it would not defeat them. They would emerge from this stronger, more united, and ready to continue their fight for freedom.

Sean lay on his cot, the cold, unyielding surface pressing against his back. The darkness of the cell seemed to close in on him, mirroring the turmoil in his mind. The whispered conversation he had just overheard reverberated through his thoughts, each word a dagger plunging deeper into his heart.

Liam. A name that had once been synonymous with camaraderie and loyalty now tasted bitter on his tongue. The man who had shared their victories and defeats, who had stood by their side in the heat of battle, had been the one to betray them. Sean's mind struggled to reconcile the image of the friend he had known with the traitor who had sold them out.

A surge of anger coursed through him, tightening his chest and clenching his fists. How could Liam have done this? Sean remembered the nights they had spent planning their operations, the risks they had taken together, the blood they had shed. And for what? For a few pieces of silver to settle gambling debts? The betrayal cut deeper than any wound, leaving a scar that would never fully heal.

As he lay there, Sean's thoughts drifted back to Liam's background. Liam had always been a bit of an enigma within the group. He had grown up in a tough part of Belfast, his family struggling to make ends meet amidst the chaos of the Troubles. His father had been a staunch supporter of the IRA, and Liam grew up idolizing him. However, his father's arrest and subsequent imprisonment had left a void in their family, thrusting young Liam into the role of provider.

As he matured, Liam's responsibilities weighed heavily on him. The streets of Belfast offered few opportunities, and the allure of quick money from gambling was too tempting to resist. His habit started small—friendly bets with neighbors—but it quickly spiraled into something more insidious. Liam's gambling problem became a dark secret he carried, a constant source of stress and shame. He owed money to dangerous people, and the pressure to repay those debts grew with each passing day.

Sean remembered how Liam had always managed to keep it under wraps, presenting a facade of control. The group knew about his gambling issues, but they never realized the extent of his debt or the danger it posed to their operations. Now, under the intense pressure of betrayal, those past indiscretions came back to haunt him, painting a more detailed picture for both his comrades and Sean himself.

Sean tried to imagine the desperation that must have driven Liam to betray them. British agents and informants were skilled at identifying and exploiting such weaknesses. When a well-dressed man approached Liam in a dark alley, promising help with his debts in exchange for information, Liam's desperation must have overpowered his loyalty. He probably believed he could handle it, that he wouldn't betray anything significant. But in his panic, he didn't realize the full implications of his actions.

A wave of sadness washed over Sean, mingling with his anger. He thought about the internal conflict Liam must have faced, torn between his commitment to the cause and the personal demons that plagued him. Sean could almost hear Liam's voice, cracking with guilt and fear, trying to explain himself. "I didn't mean for it to go this far. I thought I could control it, that I could fix things without anyone getting hurt. I was wrong."

Sean's mind wandered back to the safe house, where the ambush had changed everything in a matter of seconds. The room had been filled with the smell of freshly brewed tea and the warmth of sunlight filtering through the curtains. Maps and documents sprawled across the table as the team discussed potential routes for their next supply run. Brendan had been mid-sentence, his voice steady and confident, when the first bullet shattered the tranquility. The safe house, once a haven of strategy and camaraderie, became a war zone.

The memory of the attack was vivid. The sound of glass shattering, the sharp cracks of gunfire, and the shouts of his comrades all blended into a chaotic symphony. Sean had fired back, his training taking over even as fear gripped him. The sting of the bullet that struck him was a fiery pain, and he had crumpled to the ground, clutching his wound as his vision blurred. The last thing he remembered was Michael's voice, strong and commanding, trying to organize their defense.

Now, he understood the root of that chaos. Liam's betrayal had set the events in motion, had led to the shattering of their sanctuary and the scattering of their hopes. Sean felt a deep sense of helplessness, trapped within the Maze, unable to do anything to help his comrades or bring the traitor to justice. The walls of his cell seemed to close in tighter, suffocating him with the weight of his rage and frustration.

But amidst the anger and despair, a spark of determination flared within him. Sean knew he couldn't let this betrayal break him. He had to stay strong, not just for himself, but for Michael, Brendan, Aisling, and the rest of the team. They were counting on him, even if they didn't know it. The Maze could confine his body, but it could not imprison his spirit.

He thought of Michael's resolve, Aisling's unwavering commitment, and Brendan's fierce loyalty. They had always been stronger together, and Sean believed that even in the face of this betrayal, they would find a way to overcome it. They had to.

Liam's actions had sown seeds of doubt and mistrust, but Sean was determined that those seeds would not take root. He would survive this ordeal, return to his comrades, and they would continue their fight for freedom, undeterred by Liam's treachery. The betrayal might have cast a long shadow over their cause, but it also cast a light on their resilience.

With each passing day, Sean's determination grew stronger. He would endure the hardships of prison life, hold on to the hope of freedom, and continue to fight for their cause in any way he could. He repeated his silent mantra: "Stay strong. Don't break."

The Maze could confine his body, but it could not imprison his spirit. He would emerge from this stronger, more resolute, and ready to face whatever challenges lay ahead. The betrayal might have shaken them, but it would not defeat them. They would emerge from this stronger, more united, and ready to continue their fight for freedom.

As Sean's condition stabilized, he began to interact more with the other inmates in the Maze. The medical wing, though stark and clinical, became a place where bonds were formed, and stories were shared. Among the prisoners, there were seasoned IRA members who had spent years in the Maze, their resilience and determination shining through the harsh conditions.

One evening, after a particularly grueling day, Sean found himself sitting with a group of these veterans. They were a mix of ages and backgrounds, each with a story to tell. Paddy, an older man with a grizzled beard and kind eyes, was the first to speak.

"Welcome to the Maze, Sean," Paddy said, his voice a rough whisper from years of shouting in protests and battles. "It's not the place any of us want to be, but we're here, and we make do."

Sean nodded, grateful for the warm reception. "Thanks, Paddy. It's been... overwhelming."

Paddy chuckled; a sound more akin to a rumble. "Aye, it is at first. But you'll get used to it. And you'll find we look out for our own here."

Another inmate, Fergus, who had a wiry build and a sharp wit, leaned in. "Tell us about the outside, Sean. How's the fight going?"

Sean hesitated; the memories of the ambush still raw. But he knew these men needed to hear it, and he needed to share it. He recounted the events leading up to his capture, the betrayal, and the ongoing efforts of his comrades. As he spoke, he saw the flicker of determination in their eyes, a shared resolve that transcended the prison walls.

"We're still fighting," Sean concluded, his voice firm. "And we'll keep fighting, no matter what."

Paddy placed a hand on Sean's shoulder, his grip firm. "That's the spirit, lad. Remember, we're all in this together. They can lock us up, but they can't break us."

Over the following days, Sean began to bond more deeply with his fellow inmates. During exercise periods, they would walk the yard together, discussing strategies for coping with the harsh conditions and sharing stories of their past battles. It was during these times that Sean learned the true meaning of solidarity.

Eamon, a tall and imposing figure with a gentle demeanor, shared his own story one afternoon. "I was in the Maze during the blanket protest," he said, his voice tinged with both pride and pain. "We refused to wear prison uniforms, wrapped ourselves in blankets instead. It was brutal, but it showed them we wouldn't be broken."

Sean listened, his respect for Eamon growing. "How did you manage to keep going?"

Eamon smiled, a distant look in his eyes. "We had each other. When one of us was weak, the others lifted him up. We sang, we prayed, we supported each other. That's what you have to do here, Sean. Find strength in your comrades."

During mealtimes, the sense of camaraderie was palpable. The prisoners shared their food, meager as it was, and talked about everything from the latest news to personal anecdotes. Fergus, with his sharp wit, often kept their spirits high with jokes and stories from his childhood.

One evening, as they sat in the dimly lit dining area, Fergus recounted a humorous tale of outsmarting a British soldier during a protest. The group erupted in laughter, the sound echoing off the cold, gray walls. For a moment, they could forget where they were and simply enjoy each other's company.

Sean found that these moments of solidarity were crucial. They provided a respite from the constant tension and reminded him that he was not alone in his struggle. The guidance and support from his fellow inmates became his lifeline, reinforcing his commitment to their cause.

He also noticed the subtle ways they supported each other. Paddy would always share his extra piece of bread with the younger inmates, while Eamon organized nightly prayers and songs to lift their spirits. Fergus, despite his own hardships, made it his mission to bring a smile to everyone's face at least once a day.

One night, as Sean lay on his cot, he reflected on the bonds he had formed. The Maze was designed to break them, to strip away their humanity and reduce them to mere numbers. But within these walls, he had found a family, a group of men who were as committed to the cause as he was. They had shown him that even in the darkest of times, solidarity and mutual support could light the way.

With each passing day, Sean's resolve grew stronger. He knew that as long as they stood together, they could endure anything the Maze threw at them. The bonds of camaraderie they forged in the face of adversity would not only sustain them but also strengthen their fight for freedom.

One particularly cold morning, Sean and his comrades huddled together in the exercise yard, their breaths visible in the frosty air. Paddy began to speak about the early days of the IRA, recounting stories of legendary figures and their sacrifices.

"Back then," Paddy said, his voice filled with reverence, "we didn't have the numbers or the resources we have now. But we had heart. We had each other. And that's what kept us going."

Eamon nodded in agreement. "And that's what will keep us going now. The Maze is meant to break us, but we've turned it into a fortress of our own. They can't break what they can't see."

As the days turned into weeks, Sean noticed how the camaraderie among the inmates deepened. They developed a system of mutual support, ensuring that no one felt isolated or abandoned. During the harshest moments, they leaned on each other, sharing their burdens and finding strength in their unity.

One evening, as they gathered for their nightly ritual of songs and prayers, Sean felt a profound sense of belonging. Eamon led them in a traditional Irish ballad, his voice carrying a sense of both sorrow and hope. The other inmates joined in, their voices rising together in a powerful chorus that echoed through the cold, stone walls.

Sean closed his eyes, letting the music wash over him. In that moment, he realized that their shared struggle had forged an unbreakable bond. The Maze might be a place of confinement, but within its walls, they had found a sense of freedom and solidarity that no prison could take away.

As he drifted off to sleep that night, Sean felt a renewed sense of peace. He was part of something greater than himself, a brotherhood bound by shared sacrifice and unwavering determination. And with the support of his comrades, he knew they would emerge from this ordeal stronger, more united, and ready to continue their fight for justice.

The Maze had not broken them. It had only made them stronger.

As Sean's condition improved, he was moved out of the medical wing and into the general population of the Maze. The transition marked the beginning of a new and grueling chapter in his imprisonment: the interrogations.

The authorities wasted no time. On his first day outside the medical wing, Sean was dragged into a dimly lit interrogation room. The walls were bare and cold, the only furniture a metal table and two chairs bolted to the floor. The atmosphere was oppressive, designed to intimidate and disorient.

Two men entered the room, their faces hardened by years of breaking prisoners. The first, a tall and imposing figure, introduced himself as Inspector Collins. The second, a shorter man with piercing blue eyes, was Sergeant Mitchell. They sat across from Sean, their gazes locked onto him like predators eyeing their prey.

"Let's cut to the chase," Collins began, his voice a low growl. "We know your part of the IRA. We know about the ambush, and we know you're protecting someone. Tell us what we want to know, and this can end quickly."

Sean remained silent; his eyes fixed on a spot on the table. He had prepared for this moment, mentally rehearsing his responses—or lack thereof. He knew that anything he said could endanger his comrades.

Mitchell leaned forward; his voice softer but no less menacing. "You don't have to go through this, Sean. Just give us the names, and you can avoid a lot of pain."

Sean continued to stare at the table, refusing to engage. The interrogators exchanged a glance, and then the real ordeal began.

Over the next hours, Sean was subjected to a barrage of physical and psychological tactics. Collins and Mitchell took turns, their methods varying from threats and intimidation to beatings and sleep deprivation. They played mind games, trying to confuse and break him down. They showed him photos of his comrades, suggesting that they had already betrayed him, that he was the only one holding out.

Despite the relentless pressure, Sean remained silent. He drew strength from the stories he had heard from his fellow inmates, particularly those of past hunger strikers who had endured unimaginable suffering for the cause. Men like Bobby Sands, who had starved himself to death in the name of freedom, became his source of inspiration.

During the rare moments of solitude, Sean practiced mental exercises to keep his mind sharp and focused. He recited poems, remembered the faces and voices of his comrades, and envisioned the Irish countryside he fought to liberate. These mental routines became his armor, shielding him from the psychological assaults of his captors.

One day, after a particularly brutal session, Sean was left alone in the interrogation room, his body aching and his mind reeling. As he lay on the cold floor, he thought of Paddy, Eamon, Fergus, and the others. Their strength and solidarity had become his lifeline. He could not let them down.

He remembered Eamon's words: "When one of us is weak, the others lift him up." Sean felt that support now, even in his isolation. The knowledge that his comrades were enduring similar hardships and standing strong gave him the resolve to continue.

The interrogations became a grim routine. Each session blurred into the next, days losing their distinction. But Sean held firm, his silence becoming his act of defiance. He knew that every moment he resisted was a victory, a testament to his commitment to the cause and his comrades.

The authorities tried to exploit his weaknesses, using hunger, thirst, and exhaustion as weapons. But Sean turned these hardships into sources of strength, reminding himself that his suffering was part of a larger struggle. He was not just enduring for himself but for everyone who believed in their fight for freedom.

One particularly grueling night, as the rain pounded against the small window of his cell, Sean felt a moment of doubt. The pain and exhaustion seemed insurmountable. But then he thought of the stories he had heard, the men who had come before him, who had endured and survived. He thought of Michael and Aisling, still fighting outside these walls, counting on him to stay strong.

With renewed determination, Sean picked himself up from the floor and sat back in the chair. He focused on his breathing, slow and steady, grounding himself in the present moment. The rain became a steady rhythm, a backdrop to his silent vow: he would not break.

As the days turned into weeks, Sean's resilience became a source of frustration for his captors. They intensified their efforts, but Sean's silence only hardened. He knew that his strength came not just from within but from the unbreakable bond with his comrades, the shared cause that united them.

In the darkest moments, Sean clung to the belief that his endurance would inspire others, that his refusal to break would become a beacon of hope for those still fighting. And with each interrogation, he reaffirmed his commitment to the cause, to his comrades, and to the dream of a free Ireland.

Sean's ordeal in the Maze was far from over, but he had found his strength. The interrogations, with all their brutality, could not break the spirit forged in solidarity and mutual support. And as he faced each new challenge, he knew that he was not alone. The bonds he had formed with his fellow inmates, the shared stories and sacrifices, would see him through.

The Maze could confine his body, but it could not imprison his spirit. And with that unbreakable resolve, Sean continued to endure, his silence a testament to the strength and resilience of a united cause.

As Sean endured the relentless interrogations, he found himself back in his cell, battered and bruised. The days blurred together in a haze of pain and exhaustion. It was during one of these bleak days that he first noticed her—the prison nurse with kind eyes and a gentle touch.

Her name was Moira, and she moved through the prison with a quiet efficiency that belied the harsh environment. She treated the wounds of the inmates with a professionalism that was rare in the Maze, where brutality and indifference were the norms. Moira's presence was a small comfort in the oppressive atmosphere.

One evening, after a particularly brutal interrogation, Sean was lying on his cot, struggling to find any semblance of comfort. The cell door clanged open, and Moira entered, her face calm and composed. She carried a small medical kit and a tray with a bit more food than usual.

"Let's take a look at those wounds," she said softly, her voice barely above a whisper.

Sean sat up slowly, wincing at the pain that shot through his body. Moira began to clean his wounds, her touch gentle but sure. As she worked, she spoke in low tones, careful not to be overheard by the guards.

"You're doing well, Sean," she murmured. "Keep holding on. There are those of us who believe in your cause."

Sean looked at her, surprised by her words. He had learned to be wary of any kindness in this place, often a precursor to further manipulation. But Moira's eyes held a sincerity that was hard to fake.

"Why are you helping me?" he asked, his voice hoarse from days of silence and screaming.

Moira paused for a moment, considering her response. "I've seen too much suffering here. Too much cruelty. Not everyone within these walls agrees with what's happening. Some of us want to help, even in small ways."

Sean nodded, understanding the risks she was taking. "Thank you," he whispered, grateful for the kindness.

Over the following weeks, Moira's visits became a regular occurrence. She continued to treat his injuries, but also brought small comforts—a piece of bread, a whispered word of encouragement, sometimes even a book smuggled in from outside. Her presence was a beacon of hope in the darkness of the Maze.

During one particularly difficult evening, Moira entered Sean's cell with a piece of paper hidden in her medical kit. As she tended to his wounds, she slipped the note into his hand.

"Read this when you're alone," she whispered.

Later, when the guards had finished their rounds and the prison had settled into an uneasy silence, Sean unfolded the note. It was a message of solidarity and hope, written in careful, neat handwriting.

"Sean,

There are those within these walls who support your cause. Stay strong. We are doing what we can to help you and your comrades. Keep faith and know that you are not alone.

A Friend"

The message brought a surge of strength to Sean's weary heart. The knowledge that there were allies even within the prison walls gave him renewed determination. He shared the note with Paddy, Eamon, and Fergus, who were equally buoyed by the revelation.

Moira's subtle acts of kindness continued. She provided extra food during her rounds and offered words of encouragement when the guards were not watching. She even managed to smuggle a small radio into the prison, which Sean and his comrades used to keep informed about the outside world and their ongoing struggle.

One day, during a particularly harsh winter, Moira brought Sean a woolen blanket, a luxury in the frigid confines of the Maze. As she draped it over his shoulders, she leaned in close and whispered, "There's a plan to get messages out. Be ready."

Sean's heart raced with anticipation. The hope of communicating with his comrades outside the prison walls was a lifeline. He shared the news with Paddy, Eamon, and Fergus, and together they devised a system to pass messages to Moira, who would smuggle them out.

The bond between Sean and Moira grew stronger with each act of defiance. She became more than just a nurse; she was an ally, a confidante, and a symbol of resistance within the prison walls. Her courage and compassion reminded Sean that the fight for freedom extended beyond the physical battles. It was also a fight for humanity, for kindness, and for the belief that even in the darkest places, there could be light.

One night, as Sean lay on his cot, he reflected on the unexpected ally he had found in Moira. Her whispered words and subtle acts of kindness had given him the strength to endure the brutality of the Maze. He knew that with her support, and the solidarity of his comrades, they could continue their fight for freedom, even from within the prison walls.

The Maze could confine their bodies, but it could not imprison their spirits. And with allies like Moira, their hope for liberation burned brighter than ever.

Absolutely! Let's delve into the theme of covert resistance, highlighting Sean's involvement in these activities and how they boost morale and solidarity among the prisoners:

As Sean settled into the grim routine of life in the Maze, he became increasingly involved in covert resistance activities. The knowledge that there were allies within the prison walls, like Moira, fueled his determination to resist from within. These small acts of defiance, though risky, became a vital part of maintaining the prisoners' morale and solidarity.

One evening, after another brutal interrogation session, Sean returned to his cell to find a small piece of paper hidden under his blanket. It was a message from Moira, detailing the time and place for a secret meeting among the inmates.

That night, under the cover of darkness, Sean slipped out of his cell and made his way to the designated spot—a secluded corner of the exercise yard, hidden from the guards' view. There, he found Paddy, Eamon, Fergus, and a few other trusted inmates already gathered.

Paddy, the de facto leader of the group, spoke in hushed tones. "We need to stay united and keep our spirits high. Small acts of resistance can make a big difference. We have to show them that we won't be broken."

Eamon nodded; his face set in determination. "I've been in touch with some of the other lads. We can start by smuggling messages to our contacts outside. Moira has agreed to help us."

Sean felt a surge of hope. "What can I do to help?"

Fergus, ever the strategist, outlined the plan. "We'll need to coordinate our efforts. Each of us will have specific tasks. Sean, you'll be in charge of passing messages to Moira. Paddy and I will work on creating distractions to keep the guards occupied."

Over the next few weeks, the covert resistance activities began to take shape. Sean and his comrades used every opportunity to disrupt the daily routines of the prison, creating small but significant disturbances that kept the guards on edge. They smuggled messages out through Moira, who risked her position to aid their cause.

One of their first successes came during a routine inspection. Sean and Fergus had managed to rig a simple contraption using a piece of string and a few discarded metal parts. When the guards entered the cell block, the contraption triggered, causing a loud clatter that sent the guards scrambling to investigate. In the chaos, Sean slipped a message to Moira, who was waiting nearby.

The message contained vital information about their comrades' activities and morale within the prison. It also included requests for supplies and news from the outside world. Moira, ever resourceful, managed to smuggle the message out, ensuring it reached the right hands.

The impact of these small acts of defiance was profound. Each successful disruption, each smuggled message, became a beacon of hope for the inmates. They saw that even within the oppressive confines of the Maze, they could still fight back. Their resistance, though covert, was a testament to their unbreakable spirit.

One particularly daring act of defiance involved the prison's mealtime. Eamon and Paddy had noticed a pattern in the guards' routines and devised a plan to exploit it. During a meal, as the guards were distracted by an argument staged by a few inmates, Sean and Fergus quickly distributed hidden notes to their comrades, instructing them to synchronize a loud, coordinated chant demanding better conditions.

The sudden eruption of voices took the guards by surprise. The chant echoed through the dining hall, a powerful reminder of the inmates' unity and resolve. Though the guards swiftly moved to quell the disturbance, the prisoners felt a surge of pride. They had made their voices heard, if only for a moment.

Moira continued to be an invaluable ally, providing not only medical care but also smuggling in small items that boosted morale—books, extra food, even a few letters from the outside. Each item was a precious link to the world beyond the prison walls, a reminder that their struggle was recognized and supported.

One evening, as Sean met with his comrades in their hidden corner of the exercise yard, he felt a deep sense of camaraderie. The small victories they achieved together strengthened their bonds and reinforced their commitment to the cause.

"Every act of resistance matters," Paddy said, his voice filled with conviction. "We might be locked up, but we're not defeated. As long as we stand together, they can't break us."

Sean looked around at the faces of his fellow inmates, seeing the same determination reflected in their eyes. The Maze had tried to strip away their humanity, to reduce them to mere numbers. But through their covert resistance, they reclaimed their identity and dignity.

As the months passed, the covert activities continued to evolve. The prisoners became more adept at communicating and coordinating their efforts. Sean, with his growing network of contacts and his unwavering resolve, became a key figure in the resistance movement within the Maze.

Each act of defiance, no matter how small, was a victory. Each smuggled message, a lifeline. And with each passing day, Sean's belief in their eventual liberation grew stronger.

The Maze could confine their bodies, but it could not imprison their spirit. Through their covert resistance, Sean and his comrades found a way to fight back, to hold on to their hope and their humanity. And in the darkest of places, they discovered that solidarity and mutual support were their greatest weapons against oppression.

As Sean settled into the grueling routine of the Maze, he was assigned a role as an orderly. This position, though physically demanding, provided him with a unique opportunity to access different parts of the prison. He quickly realized the potential advantages of his new role and began to gather intelligence, carefully listening to guards and noting schedules and vulnerabilities.

Each day, Sean moved through the various wings of the prison, delivering supplies, cleaning cells, and assisting in the medical wing. He paid close attention to the guards' routines, observing their behavior and listening in on their conversations. His keen eyes and ears picked up on details that others might overlook—changing guard shifts, security weaknesses, and the subtle dynamics between staff members.

One evening, as he was cleaning the guard's break room, Sean overheard a conversation that piqued his interest. Two guards were discussing an upcoming transfer of prisoners, including the time and route they would take. Sean made a mental note of the details, knowing this information could be invaluable for their resistance efforts.

During his nightly meetings with his trusted comrades, Sean shared the intelligence he had gathered. Paddy, Eamon, and Fergus listened intently; their expressions serious as they absorbed the information.

"This is good, Sean," Paddy said, his eyes reflecting a glimmer of hope. "If we can coordinate our efforts, we might be able to create enough distractions to disrupt their plans."

Eamon nodded; his face set in determination. "We'll need to be careful, but this could give us an advantage. Let's plan our next move carefully."

The group spent the next few nights strategizing. They decided to use the upcoming transfer as a diversion to smuggle out a detailed message about the prison's layout and guard schedules. Moira, their invaluable ally, agreed to help them once again.

On the day of the transfer, tension hung in the air. Sean and his comrades were on edge, knowing that their plan carried significant risks. As the guards prepared for the transfer, the prisoners initiated a carefully orchestrated series of distractions. Paddy and Fergus staged a fight in the yard, drawing the guards' attention, while Eamon and a few others created a disturbance in the dining hall.

Amidst the chaos, Sean slipped away, making his way to the medical wing where Moira was waiting. He handed her the message, wrapped in a piece of cloth, and gave her a brief nod.

"Be careful," Sean whispered.

Moira nodded; her eyes filled with resolve. "You too, Sean. We'll get this out."

As Sean returned to his duties, he couldn't help but feel a surge of adrenaline. The success of their plan depended on precise timing and coordination. He moved quickly but cautiously, avoiding any unnecessary attention.

Later that evening, the prison was abuzz with activity as the guards dealt with the aftermath of the prisoners' disruptions. Sean and his comrades regrouped, exchanging nervous glances.

"Did it work?" Fergus asked, his voice low.

Sean nodded. "Moira has the message. Now we wait."

Days passed, and the tension slowly began to ease. The guards remained on high alert, but they had no idea about the smuggled message. Sean continued his duties as an orderly, gathering more information and sharing it with his comrades.

One night, as they met in their secluded corner of the exercise yard, Moira approached them discreetly. She had a look of triumph in her eyes.

"The message got out," she said softly. "Our contacts received it and are already working on coordinating with us. Your information is making a difference."

The group exchanged relieved smiles. Their efforts were paying off, and their resistance was growing stronger. Sean felt a renewed sense of purpose, knowing that their actions were contributing to the larger struggle.

As weeks turned into months, Sean's role as an orderly became increasingly valuable. He learned to navigate the prison's complex layout, identifying hidden corners and unused rooms that could serve as meeting spots or hideaways for contraband. He listened carefully to the guards' conversations, piecing together their routines and identifying potential allies and threats among the staff.

Sean also discovered that some of the newer guards were less vigilant, their inexperience making them easier to deceive. He noted their schedules and used this information to plan further acts of resistance, coordinating with his comrades to ensure maximum impact.

One day, while cleaning an unused storage room, Sean found a stash of old uniforms and tools. He quickly realized the potential uses for these items and shared his findings with Paddy and Fergus.

"We could use these for disguises," Sean suggested. "It might help us move around more freely during our operations."

Paddy grinned; his eyes gleaming with excitement. "Good thinking, Sean. Let's keep these hidden for now and figure out how to use them best."

The group's morale continued to grow as their covert resistance efforts bore fruit. They managed to smuggle more messages out, disrupt the guards' routines, and maintain a network of communication within the prison. Each small victory strengthened their resolve and brought them closer together.

Moira remained a crucial part of their efforts, her bravery and resourcefulness earning her the inmates' deep respect and gratitude. She continued to provide extra food, medical supplies, and encouragement, her presence a constant reminder that they had allies even in the darkest places.

One day, as Sean was delivering supplies to the kitchen, he overheard a conversation between two guards about an upcoming inspection. The guards mentioned that several high-ranking officials would be present, which meant increased security but also potential distractions.

Sean shared this information with his comrades during their next meeting. "If we time it right, we can use the inspection to our advantage. The guards will be focused on the officials, giving us a chance to move more freely."

Eamon nodded thoughtfully. "We can stage another diversion, something that will draw their attention away from us. Maybe a small fire in one of the unused storage rooms?"

Paddy agreed. "It's risky, but it could work. We need to make sure everyone is in position and ready to move quickly."

As the day of the inspection approached, the group meticulously planned their actions. Sean used his role as an orderly to gather more information, noting the guards' shifts and the areas that would be less monitored during the inspection.

When the day finally arrived, the prison buzzed with tension. High-ranking officials moved through the halls, escorted by the prison's warden and senior guards. Sean and his comrades prepared for their operation, each aware of the risks but determined to make it a success.

At the agreed time, Eamon and Fergus ignited a small fire in an unused storage room, setting off the alarms. As the guards scrambled to contain the fire and ensure the safety of the officials, Sean and Paddy moved swiftly through the less guarded areas, passing messages and coordinating with other inmates.

The diversion worked perfectly. Moira, ever vigilant, used the chaos to smuggle out another message, detailing the latest intelligence and requesting further support from their contacts outside the prison.

Later that evening, as the prison returned to its uneasy routine, Sean and his comrades gathered to review their actions. Despite the dangers, their plan had succeeded, and the sense of accomplishment was palpable.

"We did it," Paddy said, a rare smile crossing his face. "This is just the beginning. We can keep this up, and we'll make a real difference."

Sean felt a surge of pride and determination. The Maze was designed to break them, to strip away their humanity and reduce them to mere numbers. But through their covert resistance, they had reclaimed their identity and dignity. They had shown that even within the confines of the prison, they could fight back and make a difference.

The bonds of camaraderie and mutual support had become their greatest strength. With each passing day, Sean's determination grew stronger. He knew that as long as they stood together, they could endure anything the Maze threw at them.

The Maze could confine their bodies, but it could not imprison their spirits. Through their intelligence-gathering and resistance activities, Sean and his comrades found a way to fight back, to hold on to their hope and their humanity. And in the darkest of places, they discovered that solidarity and mutual support were their greatest weapons against oppression.

In the quiet moments between the relentless routines of the Maze, Sean often found himself lost in thought, his mind drifting back to his life before imprisonment. These reflections and flashbacks provided him with a mental escape from the harsh reality of the prison and reminded him of what he was fighting for.

One evening, as he lay on his cot after a particularly grueling day, Sean's mind wandered back to his childhood in Belfast. He remembered the small, cluttered kitchen where his mother would prepare meals, her soft humming filling the room with warmth. His father, a staunch supporter of the IRA, would sit at the table, discussing politics and the struggle for freedom with a quiet intensity. These early memories instilled in Sean a deep sense of purpose and commitment to their cause.

He recalled a specific day when he was about ten years old. His father had taken him to a secret meeting in a dimly lit basement. The room was filled with men and women, their faces set with determination. Sean had felt a mix of fear and pride as he listened to the impassioned speeches about their fight against British rule. It was that day he had vowed to follow in his father's footsteps, to do whatever it took to free their homeland.

As Sean grew older, his involvement in the IRA deepened. He remembered the camaraderie of his comrades, the shared sense of mission that bound them together. One of his most vivid memories was of a mission they had undertaken a few years before his capture. They had planned an ambush on a British patrol, a risky operation that required precise coordination and nerves of steel.

The night before the ambush, Sean and his closest friend, Brendan, had sat by a fire, their faces illuminated by the flickering flames. Brendan had been like a brother to Sean, his loyalty unwavering.

"Do you ever wonder if it's all worth it?" Brendan had asked, his voice soft but earnest.

Sean had looked at him, seeing the same doubts reflected in his friend's eyes. "I do. But then I think about our families, our future generations. If we don't fight, who will?"

Brendan had nodded, a determined smile crossing his face. "You're right, Sean. We'll make them proud."

The ambush had been a success, but it came at a cost. Sean remembered the look of relief and triumph on Brendan's face as they retreated to their safe house, only to be shattered by the news that Brendan had been captured during the escape. That moment had seared itself into Sean's memory, fueling his resolve to continue the fight, even when it seemed impossible.

In the Maze, these memories were both a comfort and a source of pain. Sean often found himself reflecting on the last moments with his family before his capture. His mother had hugged him tightly, tears streaming down her face as she whispered, "Be safe, Sean. Come back to us."

His father's parting words had been more stoic but no less heartfelt. "Remember why we fight, son. Stay strong, no matter what."

These reflections strengthened Sean's resolve, reminding him of the people he loved and the sacrifices they had made. He knew that his suffering in the Maze was part of a larger struggle, one that transcended his own hardships. Each time he thought of his family, his comrades, and the cause they fought for, his determination to resist grew stronger.

One particularly quiet night, as the prison lay in an eerie silence, Sean's thoughts turned to Aisling, a woman who had been a crucial part of their group. She was fierce and intelligent, her tactical acumen saving them more than once. Sean remembered the long nights they had spent planning missions, her eyes alight with passion and resolve.

He recalled a moment when they had narrowly escaped a raid, finding refuge in a cramped attic. They had sat in the darkness, their breathing heavy and hearts racing.

"We can't let fear control us," Aisling had whispered, her hand gripping his. "We have to stay focused. For everyone counting on us."

Her words had become a mantra for Sean in the Maze. Whenever the interrogations became too brutal or the isolation too suffocating, he would remember Aisling's fierce determination and draw strength from it.

These reflections and flashbacks were not just memories; they were lifelines. They provided Sean with the strength to endure, the motivation to continue resisting, and the hope that one day, he would be reunited with his loved ones and comrades.

In the Maze, Sean had learned that the battle was not just physical but also psychological. The authorities tried to break him, but his memories and the bond he shared with his family and comrades were unbreakable. Each recollection of his past life fortified his resolve, making him more determined to survive and resist.

As he lay on his cot, Sean vowed once again to stay strong. The Maze could confine his body, but it could not imprison his spirit. He was fighting for something greater than himself, and no matter how dark the days became, he would hold on to the hope of freedom and the memories of those he loved.

With each passing day, Sean's determination grew, fueled by the reflections of his past and the unwavering belief that their cause was just. The Maze could not break him, and as long as he held on to his memories and the solidarity of his comrades, he knew they would eventually prevail. In the oppressive silence of the Maze, Sean often found solace in imagining the efforts of his friends and comrades on the outside. The thought of their relentless fight for freedom and their attempts to support him even while he was imprisoned gave him a sense of hope and connection that transcended the bleakness of his surroundings.

Lying on his cot, Sean would close his eyes and envision the familiar faces of Michael, Aisling, Brendan, and others, their expressions filled with determination and resolve. He knew that they would not abandon him, that their loyalty and commitment to the cause extended beyond the physical barriers of the prison walls.

Sean imagined Michael, his unwavering leader, meticulously planning operations to disrupt British control and gather intelligence. Michael was always the strategist, able to foresee and counter the enemy's moves with precision. Sean pictured him hunched over a map, surrounded by trusted comrades, plotting their next move with a fierce intensity. In his mind's eye, he saw Michael's brow furrowed in concentration, his finger tracing potential routes for their next operation.

"Stay strong, Sean," he could almost hear Michael say. "We're working to get you out of there. Hold on."

Aisling's fierce determination was another source of inspiration for Sean. He imagined her leading raids and gathering critical information, her tactical mind always a step ahead of the enemy. Aisling's ability to inspire and lead had always been a cornerstone of their group's success. Sean could see her rallying the others, her eyes blazing with passion. He pictured her in action, moving through the shadows with a quiet grace, orchestrating their efforts with precision and unyielding resolve.

"We'll find a way to communicate," he imagined her saying, her voice filled with resolve. "And we'll get you out, no matter what."

Brendan, his closest friend, often occupied Sean's thoughts. Despite Brendan's capture during an earlier mission, Sean held on to the hope that Brendan was still fighting in his own way, perhaps even within another prison. The memory of their shared moments, their plans and dreams for a free Ireland, fueled Sean's determination to stay strong. He remembered their late-night conversations, huddled around a small fire, discussing their hopes and fears.

"I'm with you, Sean," he could almost hear Brendan's voice, a comforting presence in the darkness. "We'll get through this together."

These imagined conversations and scenarios were more than just wishful thinking; they were a lifeline. They kept Sean connected to his purpose and his comrades, reminding him that he was not alone in his struggle. He knew that every day he resisted, he was honoring their efforts and sacrifices.

The small acts of resistance within the Maze, the messages smuggled out, and the disruptions they caused were all part of a larger effort. Sean imagined his friends on the outside receiving those messages, coordinating with Moira and others to support their covert activities. He pictured them spreading the word, rallying more support for their cause, and planning operations that would one day lead to their liberation.

In the darkest moments, when the interrogations were particularly brutal or the isolation seemed unbearable, these thoughts provided Sean with a beacon of hope. He imagined his friends deciphering coded messages, finding ways to communicate with him through Moira, and plotting daring plans to aid in his escape.

One evening, after a day of harsh interrogations, Sean lay on his cot, exhausted but not broken. He closed his eyes and let his mind wander to the outside world. He pictured Michael and Aisling meeting in a safe house, discussing strategies and rallying support. He imagined Brendan, perhaps working on the inside to gather information or orchestrate a distraction.

Sean's heart swelled with pride and determination. He could almost feel their presence, a comforting and motivating force that pushed him to endure. Their ongoing efforts, though unseen, were a powerful reminder that their fight was far from over.

"We're with you, Sean," he imagined them saying in unison. "Stay strong. We'll get you out of there."

These thoughts of his friends' efforts gave Sean a renewed sense of purpose. The Maze could confine his body, but it could not imprison his spirit. He was part of a larger struggle, a movement that spanned beyond the prison walls. Each act of defiance, each moment of resistance, was a tribute to the bond he shared with his comrades and the cause they fought for.

As he drifted off to sleep, Sean held on to the hope that their combined efforts would one day lead to his freedom. The thought of his friends working tirelessly on the outside filled him with a sense of connection and solidarity that no prison could take away.

The Maze might be designed to break them, but Sean knew that as long as they stood together, they could endure anything. With his friends' efforts fueling his resolve, he was determined to stay strong and continue the fight from within.

As the days turned into weeks and the weeks into months, these visions of his friends' relentless fight gave Sean the strength to endure the daily grind of the Maze. He imagined the coded messages being passed from hand to hand, the secret meetings held in dimly lit basements, and the whispered plans of future operations. Each thought was a thread that connected him to a larger tapestry of resistance and hope.

He could almost see Aisling, her face set with determination, rallying new recruits and coordinating with other cells across Belfast. He pictured Michael in intense discussions with other leaders, planning the next big move that would bring them closer to their goal of a free Ireland. And Brendan, his spirit unbroken, finding ways to resist from within his own confines, perhaps even planning a coordinated escape.

Sean's reflections were not just a means of escape; they were a strategy for survival. By holding on to the thought of his friends' efforts, he could maintain his sanity and his resolve. Each imagined scenario was a reminder of the larger cause, the shared dream that bound them all together. It was a dream worth fighting for, worth enduring the hardships and the pain.

One night, after a particularly brutal session with the interrogators, Sean lay on his cot, battered but unyielding. He closed his eyes and let the memories and imaginings wash over him. He saw his friends not as distant figures but as tangible presences, their voices and actions vivid in his mind.

"We won't let you down," he imagined them saying. "We'll keep fighting, and we'll get you out. Just hold on."

These visions provided a profound sense of solidarity, reinforcing his belief that he was not alone. The Maze might be designed to isolate and break him, but the connections he held in his mind and heart were stronger than any physical barrier. His friends' imagined efforts were a beacon in the darkness, guiding him through the most challenging moments.

The thought of their unwavering support and relentless struggle filled Sean with a fierce determination. He knew that every act of defiance, every small victory within the Maze, was a step towards their shared goal. The knowledge that his friends were fighting for him, just as he was fighting for them, was a powerful motivator.

As he drifted into an uneasy sleep, Sean clung to the hope that one day, their combined efforts would lead to freedom. The bonds of friendship and shared purpose were his lifeline, providing the strength to endure and resist. The Maze could confine his body, but it could not imprison his spirit. He was part of a larger struggle, and with his friends' efforts fueling his resolve, he was determined to stay strong and continue the fight from within.

The Maze might be designed to break them, but Sean knew that as long as they stood together, they could endure anything. With his friends' efforts fueling his resolve, he was determined to stay strong and continue the fight from within.

In the oppressive confines of the Maze, Sean's mental resilience was continuously tested. The brutal interrogations, the isolation, and the constant threat of violence were designed to break the spirit of even the most steadfast prisoners. But Sean was determined to endure, transforming the hardships into sources of strength. Over time, he developed a mental fortitude that became a symbol of unbreakable spirit, not just for himself but for his fellow inmates as well.

From the moment Sean was assigned as an orderly, he began to form bonds with seasoned inmates who had spent years in the Maze. These men had faced the worst the prison had to offer and had survived through sheer willpower and mental resilience. They shared their experiences and techniques with Sean, helping him build a mental toolkit to withstand the daily pressures.

One of the first techniques Sean learned was from Paddy, the older inmate with a grizzled beard and kind eyes. Paddy had been in the Maze for over a decade and had seen countless prisoners come and go. He knew that mental strength was the key to survival.

"Focus on your breathing," Paddy advised one evening as they sat in a quiet corner of the yard. "When the pain gets too much, when the walls close in, just breathe. Slow, deep breaths. It centers you, helps you take control."

Sean practiced this technique diligently, finding that it helped him endure the long hours of interrogation and the suffocating isolation of his cell. By focusing on his breath, he could calm his mind and keep the panic at bay.

Eamon, the tall and imposing figure with a gentle demeanor, taught Sean another valuable lesson. "Visualize your happy place," Eamon said during one of their nightly meetings. "For me, it's the green hills of Ireland, the sound of the wind rustling through the grass. Picture it in your mind, and it will help you escape, even if just for a moment."

Sean embraced this technique as well, often closing his eyes and imagining the lush landscapes of his homeland. He would see the rolling hills, hear the distant sound of a river, and feel the warmth of the sun on his face. These mental escapes provided a much-needed respite from the grim reality of the Maze.

Fergus, with his sharp wit and unyielding spirit, shared stories of past resistance that served as both inspiration and a reminder of their shared struggle. He recounted tales of legendary fighters who had endured unimaginable hardships for the cause of freedom.

"Remember Bobby Sands," Fergus would say, his eyes alight with admiration. "He starved himself to death for our cause, Sean. If he could endure that, we can endure this."

These stories of past resistance became a wellspring of strength for Sean. He often thought of Bobby Sands and the hunger strikers, their unbreakable resolve in the face of such suffering. He drew parallels between their sacrifices and his own struggles, finding a sense of solidarity that transcended time and place.

The Hunger Strikes

During Sean's time in the medical wing, he witnessed the start of the hunger strikes. Bobby Sands, a prominent figure in their struggle, was one of the first to volunteer. Sean admired Bobby's courage and commitment, feeling a profound sense of solidarity with him and the others who chose to fight in such a drastic manner.

While Sean was not picked to go on hunger strike due to his injuries, he felt deeply connected to the cause. The hunger strikes were more than just a protest; they were a powerful statement of resistance against the British government's refusal to recognize the political status of IRA prisoners.

Sean recalled the conversations he had with Bobby before the strikes began. Bobby's determination was palpable, his eyes burning with a fierce resolve.

"This isn't just about us, Sean," Bobby had said one evening, his voice steady despite the gravity of their situation. "It's about sending a message to the world that we will not be broken. Our fight is just, and we will endure, no matter the cost."

Sean had nodded, feeling a deep respect for Bobby's unwavering spirit. "I'll do what I can from here, Bobby. We all will."

The hunger strikes began, and Sean watched as his comrades endured unimaginable suffering. The medical wing became a place of both hope and despair, as the strikers' health deteriorated but their resolve remained unbroken. Sean felt a mixture of pride and sorrow, knowing that their sacrifice was a testament to their commitment to the cause.

Mental Fortitude and Solidarity

During the hunger strikes, Sean's mental resilience grew as he used techniques learned from fellow inmates to withstand daily pressures. He drew strength from memories and the stories of past resistance, becoming a symbol of unbreakable spirit. The knowledge that he was part of a larger struggle, one that transcended his own hardships, fortified his resolve.

Each day, Sean maintained a routine of mental and physical exercises. He practiced the breathing techniques taught by Paddy, visualized his happy place as suggested by Eamon, and reflected on the stories of resistance shared by Fergus. These rituals became his lifeline, helping him stay grounded and focused amidst the chaos.

The solidarity among the inmates was palpable. They supported each other through the darkest times, sharing food, stories, and words of encouragement. The bonds of camaraderie and mutual support became their greatest strength, reinforcing their commitment to the cause and each other.

Sean also developed his own rituals to strengthen his mental resilience. Each morning, he would silently recite a mantra he had crafted: "Stay strong. Stay focused. Endure." This mantra became his shield against the relentless pressure, a reminder of his purpose and the importance of his struggle.

In the evenings, Sean would reflect on his memories of life before the Maze. He thought of his family, their faces filled with love and hope. He remembered the nights spent with his comrades, planning missions and dreaming of a free Ireland. These memories were not just a source of comfort; they were a lifeline, grounding him in the reality that there was a world worth fighting for beyond the prison walls.

One particularly brutal night, after hours of interrogation, Sean lay on his cot, every muscle aching, his spirit weary. He closed his eyes and took slow, deep breaths, focusing on each inhale and exhale. He visualized the green hills of Ireland, the place that brought him peace. He thought of Bobby Sands and the hunger strikers, their sacrifices fueling his resolve.

"We won't let you down," he whispered to himself, imagining his friends and comrades saying those words. "We'll keep fighting. Stay strong."

As weeks turned into months, Sean's mental resilience grew. He became a symbol of unbreakable spirit within the Maze. Fellow inmates looked to him for strength, inspired by his ability to withstand the daily pressures with grace and determination. He shared the techniques he had learned, helping others to develop their own mental fortitude.

The guards, too, noticed the change in Sean. Despite their efforts to break him, he remained steadfast, his eyes filled with a quiet defiance that unnerved them. Sean's unyielding spirit became a thorn in their side, a reminder that their control was not absolute.

Sean's resilience was tested time and again, but each challenge only strengthened his resolve. He continued to pass messages, coordinate resistance efforts, and support his comrades. The thought of his friends' ongoing efforts on the outside, their unwavering commitment to the cause, gave him hope and a sense of connection that no prison could take away.

Through his mental fortitude, Sean discovered that the Maze could confine his body, but it could not imprison his spirit. He was part of a larger struggle, a movement that spanned beyond the prison walls. Each act of defiance, each moment of resistance, was a testament to the bond he shared with his comrades and the cause they fought for.

As he lay on his cot, reflecting on the progress they had made, Sean felt a renewed sense of purpose. The Maze was designed to break them, to strip away their humanity and reduce them to mere numbers. But through their mental resilience and solidarity, they had reclaimed their identity and dignity. They had shown that even within the confines of the prison, they could fight back and make a difference.

With each passing day, Sean's determination grew stronger. He knew that as long as they stood together, they could endure anything the Maze threw at them. The bonds of camaraderie and mutual support had become their greatest strength. And through his unbreakable spirit, Sean became a symbol of hope and resistance, inspiring his fellow inmates to stay strong and continue the fight for freedom.

Absolutely! Let's expand on Sean's relationship with the sympathetic nurse, emphasizing her role as a crucial ally, the support and vital information she provides, and the glimmer of hope she offers amidst the adversity.

IN THE HARSH, UNYIELDING environment of the Maze, allies were few and far between. However, for Sean, a sympathetic nurse named Moira became an unexpected and invaluable ally. Her presence provided not only physical relief but also a crucial source of support and information that would become pivotal in Sean's efforts to resist from within.

Moira was different from the other staff members. While most of the prison personnel carried out their duties with cold efficiency or overt cruelty, Moira moved through the corridors of the Maze with a quiet grace and a palpable sense of empathy. She treated the prisoners with a humanity that stood in stark contrast to the brutal conditions of their confinement.

Sean first met Moira during his stay in the medical wing, recovering from the injuries he had sustained during the ambush that led to his capture. Her gentle touch and kind eyes were a balm to his wounded body and spirit. It didn't take long for Sean to realize that Moira was not just a nurse; she was a potential ally.

One evening, as she was tending to his injuries, Moira leaned in close and whispered, "Stay strong, Sean. There are people who believe in your cause, even here."

Her words were like a lifeline, and Sean clung to them desperately. He nodded, his eyes meeting hers with a silent understanding. This was the beginning of a relationship that would offer him more than just medical care.

As days turned into weeks, Moira's subtle acts of kindness grew more pronounced. She would bring him extra food, small comforts like a book or a warm blanket, and always, words of encouragement. But it was the information she provided that proved most vital.

Moira had access to areas of the prison that were off-limits to the inmates. She overheard conversations between guards, learned about schedules and routines, and even picked up on the occasional snippet of strategic information. Realizing the importance of this intelligence, she began to share it with Sean in discreet ways.

One night, as she changed the bandages on his arm, she slipped a small piece of paper into his hand. "Read this when you're alone," she whispered, her eyes scanning the room to ensure they were not being watched.

Later, in the solitude of his cell, Sean unfolded the note. It contained details about an upcoming inspection, the guards' shifts, and a potential weak spot in the prison's security. This information was invaluable, and Sean knew it could make a significant difference in their covert resistance efforts.

During their interactions, Moira also hinted at a network of sympathizers within the prison. "You're not alone in here, Sean," she said quietly one evening. "There are others who want to help. We just have to be careful."

This revelation filled Sean with a renewed sense of hope. The idea that there were allies within the prison walls, people who believed in their cause and were willing to take risks to support them, was a powerful motivator.

Moira's support extended beyond physical aid and information. She became a confidante; someone Sean could trust in an environment where trust was a rare commodity. They would talk in hushed tones during her visits, sharing stories of the outside world, their hopes, and their fears.

One particularly cold night, as Moira brought him an extra blanket, she shared a piece of news that lifted Sean's spirits. "There are whispers of a coordinated effort on the outside to get more support for your cause. People are starting to take notice."

Sean's heart swelled with pride and determination. "Thank you, Moira," he said, his voice filled with genuine gratitude. "For everything."

She smiled, a rare and genuine expression in the Maze. "Just keep holding on, Sean. We're doing what we can."

Their relationship, though constrained by the dangers and limitations of the prison, grew stronger with each interaction. Moira's unwavering support and the vital information she provided became crucial components of Sean's resilience.

Sean shared the intelligence he received from Moira with his trusted comrades, Paddy, Eamon, and Fergus. Together, they used this information to plan their resistance activities more effectively. The knowledge of guard shifts, security weaknesses, and potential allies within the prison walls allowed them to coordinate their efforts with greater precision.

One day, Moira brought news that filled Sean with both anxiety and hope. "There's a plan in the works," she whispered. "A possible escape. It's risky, but there are people inside and outside working on it."

Sean's eyes widened. "An escape? How soon?"

Moira shook her head slightly. "I don't have all the details yet. But stay alert. Be ready."

The idea of escape was a dangerous hope, but it was hope, nonetheless. Sean knew the risks were enormous, but the thought of regaining his freedom and rejoining the fight for their cause was a powerful incentive.

As the days passed, Moira continued to be a vital link between Sean and the outside world. She provided not just physical sustenance, but the mental and emotional support that kept him going. Her whispered words, hidden notes, and acts of kindness were lifelines in the dark, oppressive environment of the Maze.

Through Moira, Sean learned that their struggle extended beyond the prison walls. The support from sympathizers within the Maze and the coordinated efforts from the outside gave him a sense of connection and solidarity that no prison could break. Her involvement hinted at the possibility of broader support and perhaps, one day, freedom.

In the Maze, allies were rare and precious. Moira's presence, her courage, and her commitment to their cause became a symbol of hope and resilience. She reminded Sean that even in the darkest places, there were glimmers of light, and that the fight for freedom and justice was far from over.

With each passing day, Sean's determination grew stronger, fueled by the support and information provided by Moira. The Maze could confine his body, but it could not imprison his spirit. He was part of a larger struggle, one that spanned beyond the prison walls, and with allies like Moira, he knew they would continue to resist, to fight, and to hope for a brighter future.

The Maze was notorious for its brutal interrogation methods, and Sean had endured countless grueling sessions. But this day felt different. As he was forcibly removed from his cell, an oppressive sense of dread settled over him. The guards moved with a sense of urgency; their grips unrelenting. They led him through the winding corridors of the prison, the only sound the echo of their footsteps against the cold, stone floors.

Sean's mind raced. Rumors had circulated about a new interrogator, someone brought in specifically to break him. His heart pounded, but he steeled himself. He had survived this long; he would continue to endure, no matter what they threw at him.

Upon reaching the interrogation room, Sean was roughly shoved into a metal chair. The room was dimly lit, the harsh fluorescent lights casting ominous shadows on the walls. He glanced around, his eyes adjusting to the dimness. Then, the door creaked open.

A man entered, his presence commanding and intimidating. Sean recognized him immediately. It was the spook who had dragged him from the burning safe house during the ambush—the MI5 agent who had orchestrated the attack. His entrance was theatrical, his eyes cold and calculating.

"Hello, Sean," the man said, his voice dripping with false camaraderie. "It's been a while. Your friends have been busy while you've been inside."

Sean's jaw tightened. The memories of the ambush surged back—the shattering glass, the hail of bullets, the flames consuming everything. He remembered being pulled from the fire, his body battered and broken. The memory fueled his anger, giving him the strength to face this new threat.

The spook leaned in closer, his eyes boring into Sean's. "I'm here for a chat," he said, mocking. "I have some questions, and I think you have the answers."

Sean remained silent; his gaze unwavering. He knew the game they were playing. The spook would try to break him, to extract information about his comrades and their plans. But Sean was prepared. He had rehearsed his responses, steeling himself against the psychological and physical torment.

The interrogation began in earnest. Questions came rapid-fire, each one designed to unsettle and provoke. The spook's methods were both cunning and cruel, alternating between threats and false promises of leniency. But Sean refused to be swayed. He drew strength from his memories, the faces of his friends and family flashing before his eyes.

"Your silence won't protect them," the spook hissed, his frustration growing. "We will find them, with or without your help."

Sean's lips remained sealed. He thought of Michael, Aisling, Brendan, and the others. He thought of their unwavering resolve, their shared commitment to the cause. He would not betray them.

The spook's tactics grew more brutal. Physical pain was excruciating, but Sean focused on his breathing, using the techniques Paddy had taught him. He visualized the green hills of Ireland, a place of peace and refuge. He thought of Bobby Sands and the hunger strikers, their sacrifices fueling his resolve.

Hours passed, the interrogation dragging on with relentless intensity. But Sean remained steadfast. His silence and unyielding spirit frustrated the spook. Every question met with defiance; every threat countered with inner strength.

Finally, the spook slammed his fist on the table, his composure cracking. "This isn't over, Sean," he spat. "We'll break you eventually."

Sean met his gaze, his eyes unwavering. "You'll never break me," he said, his voice steady. "I'm fighting for something bigger than myself. And I'll endure, no matter what."

The spook's face twisted with anger, but he knew he had been bested, at least for now. He motioned to the guards, and they dragged Sean back to his cell. As the door closed behind him, Sean allowed himself a moment of relief. He had faced the worst they could throw at him and emerged unbroken.

In the darkness of his cell, Sean reflected on the encounter. The spook's words had been meant to intimidate, but they only strengthened his resolve. He knew his friends were still fighting, working tirelessly to support him from the outside. Their efforts, their unwavering commitment, gave him hope.

Covert Communications and Resistance

Despite the constant surveillance, Sean and his comrades found ways to communicate and coordinate their resistance efforts. Moira, the prison nurse, continued to be an invaluable ally. Her subtle acts of kindness and bravery were lifelines in the oppressive environment.

One evening, Sean received a note from Moira, hidden in the bandages she used to treat his wounds. The message contained vital information about the prison's layout and guard schedules, gathered from the whispers and observations of other inmates.

During their nightly meetings in the secluded corner of the exercise yard, Sean shared the information with Paddy, Eamon, Fergus, and a few other trusted inmates. They devised a plan to use the upcoming inspection as a diversion to smuggle out a detailed message about their situation.

The plan required precise timing and coordination. On the day of the inspection, Eamon and Fergus staged a fight in the yard, drawing the guards' attention. Meanwhile, Sean slipped away to meet Moira, passing her the message wrapped in a piece of cloth.

Building Solidarity and Hope

The small victories achieved through their covert resistance efforts boosted morale among the inmates. Each successful disruption, each smuggled message, was a testament to their unbreakable spirit. The bonds of camaraderie grew stronger, and the knowledge that they were not alone in their struggle provided a sense of hope.

Moira continued to smuggle in small items that brought comfort and news from the outside world. Books, extra food, and letters became precious links to a reality beyond the prison walls. These acts of kindness reminded Sean and his comrades that their fight was recognized and supported.

One night, as Sean lay on his cot, he reflected on the strength and resilience of his fellow inmates. The Maze was designed to strip away their humanity, but through their solidarity and mutual support, they reclaimed their dignity. The stories of past protests and acts of defiance became their inspiration, fueling their determination to resist.

Sean often thought back to the ambush and the betrayal that had led to his capture. He remembered the chaos of the attack, the sting of the bullet, and the faces of his comrades fighting valiantly. These memories, though painful, reinforced his resolve.

He also drew strength from his reflections on his family and his life before imprisonment. The memories of his parents' teachings and the bond with his comrades provided a mental escape from the harsh reality of the Maze. Each recollection of his past life fortified his determination to survive and resist.

In his quiet moments, Sean imagined the efforts of his friends outside the prison. He pictured Michael, Aisling, and Brendan continuing their fight for freedom, rallying support and planning operations. These thoughts were not just wishful thinking; they were a strategy for survival, keeping him connected to his purpose and his comrades.

"We're with you, Sean," he imagined them saying. "Stay strong. We'll get you out."

These visions provided a profound sense of solidarity, reminding Sean that he was part of a larger struggle. The Maze could confine his body, but it could not imprison his spirit. The knowledge that his friends were fighting for him, just as he was fighting for them, was a powerful motivator.

The Maze might be designed to break them, but Sean knew that as long as they stood together, they could endure anything. With the imagined efforts of his friends and the solidarity of his fellow inmates, he was determined to stay strong and continue the fight from within.

The morning light barely penetrated the thick, oppressive walls of the Maze Prison when Sean was abruptly pulled from his cell. His mind, still groggy from a restless night, quickly sharpened as he was led down the cold, echoing corridors. The guards' rough hands and gruff commands reminded him of the ordeal awaiting him.

Sean was taken to a small, dimly lit room. The walls were bare, save for a single, flickering fluorescent light that cast long shadows. In the center of the room stood a metal table and two chairs. Seated in one of them was the spook, his cold eyes assessing Sean as he was roughly pushed into the other chair.

"Good morning, Sean," the spook began, his voice smooth yet menacing. "I trust you slept well?"

Sean remained silent; his eyes fixed on the table. He knew better than to engage in any pleasantries.

The spook leaned forward, his gaze piercing. "You know why you're here. We need information, Sean. Information about your comrades, their plans, their hideouts. You can make this easy on yourself, or you can make it very difficult."

For days, this routine continued. Each session was a relentless barrage of psychological and physical tactics designed to break Sean. The spook used a mix of threats, false promises, and brutal force. He showed Sean photos of his comrades, insinuating that they had already betrayed him. He described, in vivid detail, the supposed suffering of his friends, trying to instill doubt and fear.

Despite the spook's efforts, Sean remained resolute. He drew strength from his memories of Michael, Aisling, Brendan, and the cause they were all fighting for. Each time the spook tried to break him, Sean retreated into his mind, replaying moments of solidarity and resistance.

Day 1: The Initial Interrogation

Sean was led into the room, the guards' hands gripping his arms tightly. The spook sat behind the metal table, a slight smirk playing on his lips.

"Welcome back, Sean," he said, his voice dripping with false warmth. "Let's start with something simple. Where is Michael hiding?"

Sean stared at the table, his jaw set. The spook's smile faded.

"Very well," he said, standing up. "We can do this the hard way."

The session that followed was brutal. The spook's fists struck with precision; each blow calculated to inflict maximum pain. Sean gritted his teeth, refusing to give the spook the satisfaction of a response.

Day 4: The Psychological Assault

The spook changed tactics. He sat across from Sean, a folder of documents in front of him. He pulled out photos, spreading them across the table.

"These are your friends, Sean," he said, tapping each photo. "Michael, Aisling, Brendan. They've all talked. They've all betrayed you."

Sean's heart pounded, but he kept his expression neutral. The spook leaned closer, his voice a whisper.

"You're alone, Sean. They've left you behind. Just give us what we want, and this can all ends."

Sean closed his eyes, shutting out the spook's words. He focused on the memories of his comrades, their shared laughter and determination. He wouldn't let the spook's lies shake his resolve.

Day 7: The False Promises

The spook tried a different approach. He placed a piece of paper and a pen in front of Sean.

"Write down the locations of your safe houses, and I'll see to it that you're transferred to a better facility," he promised. "No more beatings, better food, maybe even a visit from your family."

Sean stared at the paper, his hand trembling. The spook's offer was tempting, but he knew better. He pushed the paper away, shaking his head.

The spook's face darkened. "You're a fool, Sean. You're throwing away a chance to end this."

Sean met his gaze, his voice steady. "I won't betray them."

Day 10: The Breaking Point

The sessions grew increasingly brutal. The spook's frustration was evident, his methods more desperate. Sean was left battered and bruised, but his spirit remained unbroken.

One evening, after a particularly brutal session, Sean was left alone in the room, his body aching and his mind reeling. He stared at the door, knowing the spook would return. As he lay on the cold floor, he whispered to himself, "Stay strong. Don't break."

The spook returned, his frustration palpable. He paced around Sean, his voice a low growl. "You think you're strong, Sean? You think your silence will protect them? You're only prolonging your own suffering."

Sean looked up; his eyes filled with determination. "I won't give you anything."

The spook smirked, leaning down to Sean's level. "We'll see about that."

As the days turned into weeks, the spook's methods grew increasingly desperate. He tried to exploit any perceived weakness, any crack in Sean's resolve. But Sean had built a fortress within his mind, drawing on the strength of his comrades and the shared belief in their cause.

One evening, after another grueling session, Sean was returned to his cell. As he lay on his cot, battered but unbroken, Moira entered with her usual tray of medical supplies. She tended to his wounds, her touch gentle and reassuring.

"He's not getting to you, is he?" Moira whispered; her eyes filled with concern.

Sean shook his head, his voice hoarse. "No. I'll never give him what he wants."

Moira nodded, a small smile on her lips. "Good. Just remember, you're not alone. We're all fighting with you."

Sean closed his eyes, taking a deep breath. The spook could try to break him, but he could never touch the core of his spirit, fortified by the unyielding bond with his comrades and the unwavering belief in their fight for freedom.

The Maze could confine his body, but it could not imprison his soul. And with each passing day, Sean's resolve grew stronger, his silence a testament to the strength and resilience of their cause. The spook's increasingly frantic efforts only served to deepen Sean's resolve. The interrogations became a battle of wills, each session a test of endurance and mental fortitude.

One particularly harrowing session involved sensory deprivation. Sean was left in complete darkness, deprived of any sound, sight, or sense of time. The spook's voice, a disembodied whisper, occasionally broke the silence, taunting and probing.

"How long do you think you can last, Sean?" the spook's voice echoed in the void. "Everyone has a breaking point."

Sean focused on his breathing, reciting poems and mantras in his mind to stay grounded. He pictured his comrades, their faces clear and vivid, and held onto the belief that they were fighting for him just as he was fighting for them.

The spook's frustration grew with each passing day. He resorted to more extreme measures, attempting to break Sean's spirit through starvation and sleep deprivation. Sean was left without food for days, his body weakening but his resolve unyielding.

During one such session, the spook entered the room with a sinister smile. "You're strong, I'll give you that. But strength can only take you so far."

Sean, barely able to stand, looked up at the spook. His eyes, though sunken and tired, still held a spark of defiance. "You can try to break me, but you'll never succeed."

The spook's smile faltered. He knew that Sean's strength was not just physical but deeply rooted in his unwavering belief in the cause and the solidarity of his comrades.

One evening, as Sean lay on his cot, battered but not broken, he reflected on the spook's words and tactics. He realized that the spook's desperation was a sign of his own victory. No matter what the spook tried, Sean's spirit remained unbroken.

Moira entered his cell, her presence a comforting balm to his battered body and soul. She brought not just medical supplies but also a small piece of bread, a rare and precious gift.

"Here, Sean," she whispered, pressing the bread into his hand. "Keep your strength up. We're all with you."

Sean took the bread, gratitude filling his heart. "Thank you, Moira. For everything."

She smiled; her eyes filled with determination. "You're not alone, Sean. Remember that.

As the days turned into weeks and weeks into months, Sean's resolve only grew stronger. The spook's increasingly desperate efforts were futile against the unbreakable spirit fortified by memories, solidarity, and the unwavering belief in their cause.

Sean's silence became a symbol of resistance, his unyielding spirit a beacon of hope for his comrades inside and outside the Maze. He knew that no matter how harsh the interrogations, how brutal the conditions, his resolve would not waver.

The Maze could confine his body, but it could never imprison his soul. With each passing day, Sean's silence spoke volumes, a testament to the strength and resilience of their shared cause. And in the darkest moments, he held onto the hope that one day, they would all be free.

The days dragged on, each one blending into the next in a relentless cycle of pain and resistance. Sean's body bore the marks of his ordeal, but his spirit remained unyielding. He had become a symbol of defiance, his silence a powerful act of rebellion against his captors.

One morning, as the dim light of dawn seeped through the tiny window of his cell, Sean was again pulled from his cot. The guards led him down the familiar, cold corridors to the interrogation room. This time, there was an air of finality in their rough handling, as if they too sensed that something had changed.

The door to the interrogation room creaked open, and Sean was shoved inside. The spook was already there, sitting behind the metal table. He looked more haggard than before, dark circles under his eyes betraying the toll these weeks of fruitless interrogations had taken on him.

"Sit," the spook ordered, his voice lacking its usual edge.

Sean complied, his body aching with every movement. He met the spook's gaze, his own eyes filled with a quiet determination.

The spook leaned back in his chair, exhaling slowly. "You've been a tough nut to crack, Sean. I'll give you that."

Sean remained silent; his expression impassive.

The spook's eyes narrowed. "This is your last chance. Give me something, anything, and I might be able to make things easier for you. Refuse, and..." He trailed off, the threat hanging in the air.

Sean took a deep breath, feeling a surge of strength. He knew this was a crucial moment. "You'll get nothing from me," he said, his voice steady. "My comrades, our cause, they're worth more than my own life. You can break my body, but you'll never break my spirit."

The spook's frustration boiled over. He slammed his fist on the table, causing the metal to rattle. "Damn it, Sean! Don't you see? You're only making this harder on yourself!"

Sean leaned forward; his eyes locked onto the spook's. "No, I'm making it harder for you. Because no matter what you do, you can't touch what's inside me. You can't touch my resolve, my hope, or my loyalty."

For a moment, the spook looked at Sean, a mix of anger and grudging respect in his eyes. He knew he had lost this battle of wills. The room fell into a tense silence, broken only by the distant sounds of the prison.

Finally, the spook stood up, his shoulders slumped. "Take him back to his cell," he ordered the guards, his voice devoid of the earlier menace.

Sean was pulled to his feet and led out of the room. As he walked down the corridor, he felt a sense of triumph. He had faced the spook's worst and emerged unbroken. His spirit, fortified by memories and solidarity, remained intact.

Back in his cell, Sean collapsed onto his cot, exhaustion washing over him. Moira soon arrived with her tray, her eyes reflecting both concern and pride.

"He's done, isn't he?" Sean asked, his voice a whisper.

Moira nodded, a small smile playing on her lips. "Yes, Sean. You've won. He's given up."

Sean closed his eyes, relief flooding through him. He had endured the worst and had not broken. The Maze had failed to crush his spirit.

As he lay on his cot, Sean allowed himself a moment of quiet reflection. He thought of his comrades, their shared struggles, and the cause they fought for. He knew that his resistance, his unyielding silence, would inspire others. It was a victory not just for him, but for everyone who believed in their fight for freedom.

The Maze could confine his body, but it could never imprison his soul. He was part of something greater, and that knowledge filled him with a renewed sense of purpose and hope.

With a deep sense of peace, Sean whispered to himself, "Stay strong. Don't break."

He knew that as long as he held onto his resolve, he would continue to be a beacon of hope for his comrades, both inside and outside the prison walls. And one day, they would all be free

As the days turned into weeks, the routine of relentless interrogations began to wear on the spook as much as it did on Sean. Each session became a bitter stalemate, a battle of wills with no clear winner. The spook's desperation grew palpable, his frustration evident in every harsh word and brutal tactic.

One particularly cold morning, Sean was dragged from his cell for what he sensed might be the final confrontation. The guards' grip was tighter than usual, their faces set in grim determination. Sean's body, though weakened by the constant abuse, moved with a resilience that defied his physical state.

The interrogation room felt different this time. The air was heavy with tension, and the spook's eyes were shadowed with exhaustion and something else defeat. He gestured for Sean to sit, his movements slow and weary.

"Sit down, Sean," the spook muttered, his voice devoid of its previous menace.

Sean sat, his eyes never leaving the spook's face. The silence stretched, a tangible thing in the cold room. Finally, the spook spoke, his voice a low, defeated murmur.

"You've held out longer than anyone I've ever met," he admitted, his tone a mix of anger and grudging respect. "But you need to understand, this isn't just about you. Your friends out there—they're still fighting, still getting hurt. You could save them a lot of pain."

Sean's eyes hardened. "And betray everything we stand for? Never."

The spook sighed, rubbing his temples. "You're a stubborn man, Sean. But even the strongest tree falls in a storm."

Sean leaned forward, his gaze unwavering. "I'm not just one tree. I'm part of a forest. You can cut down one, but you can't tell us all."

The spook stared at him, a long silence stretching between them. "You really believe that don't you?"

Sean nodded. "With all my heart."

For the first time, the spook looked genuinely defeated. He slumped back in his chair, the weight of his failure pressing down on him. "You win, Sean. I've done everything I can, and you haven't budged an inch."

Sean felt a surge of triumph. Despite the pain, the fear, and the relentless pressure, he had endured. He had protected his comrades, upheld their cause, and remained unbroken.

The spook stood up, signaling the guards. "Take him back to his cell."

As Sean was led away, the spook called after him. "I hope your comrades appreciate what you've done for them."

Sean turned back, his voice strong despite his exhaustion. "They do. And they always will."

Back in his cell, Sean collapsed onto his cot, exhaustion and relief washing over him. Moira soon arrived with her tray, her eyes reflecting both concern and pride.

"He's done, isn't he?" Sean asked, his voice a whisper.

Moira nodded, a small smile playing on her lips. "Yes, Sean. You've won. He's given up."

Sean closed his eyes, relief flooding through him. He had endured the worst and had not broken. The Maze had failed to crush his spirit.

As he lay on his cot, Sean allowed himself a moment of quiet reflection. He thought of his comrades, their shared struggles, and the cause they fought for. He knew that his resistance, his unyielding silence, would inspire others. It was a victory not just for him, but for everyone who believed in their fight for freedom.

He thought of Michael, Aisling, Brendan, and the countless others who fought alongside him, both inside and outside the Maze. Their faces, their voices, their unwavering resolve filled his mind, giving him strength. He knew that his victory over the spook was a testament to their collective will.

The Maze could confine his body, but it could never imprison his soul. He was part of something greater, and that knowledge filled him with a renewed sense of purpose and hope. With a deep sense of peace, Sean whispered to himself, "Stay strong. Don't break."

He knew that as long as he held onto his resolve, he would continue to be a beacon of hope for his comrades, both inside and outside the prison walls. And one day, they would all be free.

In the days following his final interrogation, Sean's life in the Maze returned to its harsh routine. However, something fundamental had changed. The guards seemed less harsh, their movements less aggressive, as if they, too, sensed the shift in the balance of power. The spook's defeat had rippled through the prison, a silent acknowledgment of Sean's unbreakable spirit.

Moira continued her visits, bringing not just medical supplies but also whispers of the outside world. "Your friends are still fighting," she would say, her eyes bright with hope. "They're stronger because of you."

Sean listened, his heart swelling with pride and determination. The thought of his comrades carrying on the fight filled him with a sense of purpose. He knew that his silence and resilience had not been in vain.

One evening, as Sean lay on his cot, he was roused by the sound of his cell door opening. Moira slipped inside, her movements quick and quiet. She handed him a small piece of paper, her eyes gleaming with excitement.

"Read this when you're alone," she whispered, squeezing his hand before leaving as silently as she had come.

Later, in the dim light of his cell, Sean unfolded the note. It was a message from Michael, smuggled in through their network of allies.

"Sean,

We hear you. Your silence speaks louder than words. We're fighting harder than ever, inspired by your strength. Hold on. We're with you, always.

Michael"

Tears filled Sean's eyes as he read the note. The message was a lifeline, a connection to the outside world and a reminder that he was not alone. His comrades were still with him, fighting for their shared cause. The note reaffirmed his belief in their struggle and gave him the strength to endure.

As the days turned into weeks, Sean's resolve only grew stronger. He continued to gather and share information with his fellow inmates, using every opportunity to resist their captors. The network they had built within the prison walls became a source of hope and solidarity, a testament to their unyielding spirit.

Sean knew that the fight for freedom was far from over. The Maze could confine his body, but it could never imprison his soul. He was part of a larger struggle, and with the support of his comrades, he was determined to continue the fight from within.

One night, as Sean lay on his cot, he reflected on the journey that had brought him to this point. The brutal interrogations, the relentless pressure, and the unyielding resistance had shaped him into a symbol of hope and defiance. His silence had become a powerful act of rebellion, a testament to the strength of the human spirit.

He thought of the spook, defeated and weary, and the small victories they had achieved within the prison walls. Each act of defiance, each smuggled message, was a step towards their ultimate goal. Sean knew that their struggle was not just about survival, but about preserving their dignity and humanity.

As he drifted off to sleep, Sean whispered his mantra once more, "Stay strong. Don't break." He knew that as long as he held onto his resolve, he would continue to inspire others, both inside and outside the Maze.

The Maze might be designed to break them, but Sean knew that as long as they stood together, they could endure anything. With his friends' efforts fuelling his resolve, he was determined to stay strong and continue the fight from within.

As the first light of dawn broke over the Maze, Sean awoke with a renewed sense of purpose. The fight for freedom was ongoing, and he was ready to face whatever challenges lay ahead. He was not alone in his struggle; he was part of a larger movement, a collective effort that transcended the walls of the prison.

Sean stood by the small window of his cell, looking out at the bleak landscape. The sight of the barbed wire and watchtowers no longer filled him with despair. Instead, he saw them as symbols of the strength and resilience that he and his comrades possessed.

He knew that the road to freedom would be long and difficult, but he was prepared to walk it. With the support of his friends and the unbreakable bond they shared, Sean was confident that they would one day achieve their goal.

The Maze could confine his body, but it could never imprison his spirit. And as long as he held onto his hope and determination, Sean knew that he would continue to be a beacon of resistance and resilience.

Years later, long after the Maze had become a distant memory, Sean stood on the steps of a newly liberated building, the sun shining brightly on his face. The struggle had been long and arduous, but they had finally achieved their goal. Ireland was free.

As he looked out over the crowd of supporters, Sean felt a deep sense of pride and accomplishment. The journey had been filled with hardship and sacrifice, but they had persevered. They had remained unbroken.

Michael, Aisling, and Brendan stood beside him, their faces filled with joy and relief. They had all played a part in this victory, their collective efforts culminating in this moment of triumph.

Sean stepped forward, raising his voice to address the crowd. "We have fought long and hard for this day. We have endured unimaginable hardships, but we never lost sight of our goal. Today, we stand here as free men and women, united in our shared belief in freedom and justice. Let us remember those who fought alongside us, those who sacrificed their lives for this cause. Their spirit lives on in us. And as we move forward, let us honour their memory by continuing to fight for a better future."

The crowd erupted in cheers, their voices echoing through the streets. Sean felt a tear slip down his cheek, a tear of joy and gratitude. They had done it. They were free.

As he stood there, surrounded by his comrades and supporters, Sean knew that their journey was not over. There were still challenges to face, still battles to be fought. But he was ready. He had faced the worst and emerged unbroken.

The Maze had tried to crush his spirit, but it had only made him stronger. And with his unbreakable resolve, Sean was determined to continue the fight for freedom, justice, and a better future for all.

In the months that followed the liberation, Sean, Michael, Aisling, and Brendan dedicated themselves to rebuilding their nation. The scars of conflict were everywhere, but so too was the spirit of resilience. Together with other leaders, they worked tirelessly to heal the divisions that had long plagued their homeland.

Sean found himself speaking at schools and community centres, sharing his story with the younger generation. He wanted them to understand the cost of freedom and the importance of unity. His words resonated with many, inspiring a new wave of hope and determination.

One afternoon, as Sean walked through the streets of Belfast, he was approached by a young man. "Mr. Sean," he said, his eyes wide with admiration, "thank you for everything you did. My father told me about your bravery in the Maze. You give us all hope."

Sean smiled, placing a hand on the young man's shoulder. "Remember, the real heroes are those who continue to fight for what's right, no matter the cost. Stay strong and never lose sight of the future we're building."

A significant part of their work involved honouring those who had sacrificed their lives. Sean and his comrades organized memorials and erected monuments to ensure that the stories of their fallen friends were never forgotten. One such ceremony took place at a new memorial site, where hundreds gathered to pay their respects.

Standing before the monument, which was inscribed with the names of the brave men and women who had given their lives, Sean felt a profound sense of responsibility. He stepped forward to address the crowd, his voice steady and filled with emotion.

"Today, we honor the heroes who are no longer with us," Sean began. "Their sacrifices have paved the way for our freedom. We must never forget the price they paid and must always strive to live up to the ideals they fought for. Their legacy lives on in us."

Despite his public role, Sean also embarked on a personal journey of reconciliation. He visited the families of his fallen comrades, sharing stories and offering his support. These visits were often emotional, but they were also healing.

One such visit took him to the home of Liam's family. Liam's betrayal had been a wound that had never fully healed, but Sean knew that forgiveness was a crucial part of moving forward.

"Liam made a terrible mistake," Sean told Liam's mother, his voice gentle but firm. "But he was also a brother to us. We honor his memory by acknowledging his humanity, by learning from his mistakes and striving to build a better future."

Liam's mother, tears in her eyes, reached out and took Sean's hand. "Thank you, Sean. Knowing that you've forgiven him means more than you can imagine."

As years passed, Ireland began to flourish. The wounds of the past were healing, and the nation was slowly but surely rebuilding itself. Sean, now an elder statesman, continued to advocate for peace and justice, his experiences shaping his every word and action.

One evening, as the sun set over the rolling hills of his beloved homeland, Sean sat on his porch, a sense of contentment settling over him. The journey had been long and fraught with challenges, but they had emerged victorious. His thoughts turned to his comrades, those who stood beside him and those who had fallen.

Michael, ever the strategist, had taken on a key role in the new government, ensuring that the principles they fought for were upheld. Aisling's fierce determination had translated into her work with community organizations, empowering the next generation of leaders. Brendan, his spirit unbroken, had become a renowned writer, chronicling their struggle and inspiring countless others.

Together, they had built a legacy that would endure. The Maze and its horrors were a distant memory, but the lessons learned within those walls had shaped a future filled with hope and promise.

Sean's thoughts returned to the present, to the young faces he saw every day, filled with hope and determination. He knew that the true measure of their success was not just in the liberation they had achieved, but in the future they were building.

As the first stars appeared in the twilight sky, Sean whispered a silent prayer for all those who had sacrificed so much. Their spirit, their courage, and their unbreakable resolve had made all of this possible.

"We did it," he murmured to the wind. "We stayed strong. We didn't break."

And as long as the memory of their struggle and the principles they stood for continued to inspire future generations, Sean knew that their victory was complete. Ireland was free, and its people, unbroken and united, were forging a new path forward.

Chapter 7 Along the silk of a spider's web

———

The heavy metal door of the interrogation room slammed shut with a deafening clang, the echo reverberating through the cold, sterile corridor of the Maze prison. The harsh fluorescent lights flickered momentarily, casting eerie shadows. Seán, shackled to the table, felt the reverberations through his bones. He exhaled a long, slow breath, the air escaping his lungs in a visible puff in the chilly room. He could almost taste the metallic tang of the air. Relief washed over him, as if a weight had been lifted from his shoulders. He believed he had outmaneuvered the spook in this round of their psychological duel, savoring the fleeting victory.

On the other side of the door, the spook strode down the corridor with a grin playing at his lips. The fluorescent lights flickered above him, casting long, intermittent shadows on the polished floor. A warder approached, his face eager for news.

"How did it go, sir? Did he talk?" the warder asked, his voice tinged with hope.

The spook paused, his eyes gleaming with calculated confidence. "My dear boy, this story has only just begun."

The spook then inquired if his escort was ready. They confirmed, "Ready and waiting." He stepped outside into the biting night air and got into a waiting car. As the vehicle drove through the darkened streets of Belfast towards a nondescript safe house on the outskirts, his mind was a whirl of calculations and strategies. He knew the next steps were crucial.

Inside the car, the spook's eyes flickered between the passing streetlights. The rhythmic hum of the engine served as a backdrop to his thoughts. He recalled the last debrief he had before the day's events, his superior's stern face etched in his memory.

As the car pulled into the driveway of the safe house, the spook took a deep breath, feeling the weight of his responsibilities settle more heavily upon his shoulders. These were the moments he thrived on. Stepping out, he walked briskly to the entrance, greeted by fellow operatives and junior officers who snapped to attention at his approach.

The spook entered a dimly lit room where a group of intelligence officers was gathered. The atmosphere was tense, filled with the hum of quiet conversations and the rustling of papers. The room was illuminated by dim, overhead lights, casting long shadows on the walls. A large map of Belfast dominated one wall, marked with pins and notes, a testament to their ongoing operations.

Suddenly, the phone rang, its sharp sound cutting through the room's murmurs. The spook picked up the receiver, and a stern female voice began to speak.

"Our friend Roger has informed me that you have some interesting developments happening, Mr. Spider. Why don't you explain to me why I'm risking the reputation of the British state on some silly girl fresh out of the academy parading around the Maze prison in a nurse's uniform?"

"Director, Moira is more than capable. Her position allows us unprecedented access to the prisoners' confidences. She's already proving invaluable in breaking down Seán's defenses. We're closer than ever to dismantling Michael's unit from the inside."

The director's patience was thin, her voice cutting through the spook's explanations. "This better not be a waste of resources, Spider. You know how thin our patience is running. If this operation falls apart, it's on your head."

"Understood. I assure you, Director, we are on the brink of a significant breakthrough."

As the call ended, the spook replaced the receiver and turned to face his team. The eyes of the junior officers were fixed on him, waiting for direction.

"Alright, everyone. Here's where we stand. Michael O'Connor has just completed a mission that significantly boosts the IRA's operational capabilities. This success has placed him in our sights more prominently than ever."

The spook pointed to specific locations on the map, detailing the surveillance operations currently in place. His fingers traced the routes Michael frequented, the known safe houses, and potential weak points.

"We've identified key IRA hotspots and set up comprehensive surveillance. Our goal is to track every move, every conversation. Michael's rise within the IRA presents us with an opportunity to gather critical intelligence."

Later, in his dimly lit office, the spook pored over the details provided by Liam. Maps of Belfast were spread across his desk, marked with key locations and notes on IRA activities. He understood the importance of this mission for Michael and his unit. It was a chance to prove themselves, and for the spook, it was a chance to ensnare them further.

As the night of the operation approached, the tension in the air was palpable. The spook double-checked every detail, ensuring that the surveillance teams were in place and the equipment was functioning perfectly. His mind raced through potential scenarios, anticipating Michael's moves and planning his counteractions.

When the night of the operation finally arrived, the spook watched the live feeds from the surveillance teams. Michael moved with the grace of someone well-trained, his movements deliberate and careful. The spook's eyes narrowed as he observed Michael approach the British military installation.

Through the eyes of the surveillance footage, he saw Michael slip through the perimeter, using the diversions created by his comrades. Explosions and shouts echoed in the distance, perfectly timed distractions that allowed Michael to advance unnoticed. The spook's admiration for the tactical execution was mingled with a cold resolve. Every step Michael took was another thread in the web the spook was weaving.

The spook leaned closer to the monitors as Michael entered the target office. His fingers deftly picked the lock, and he quickly began photographing the documents inside. The spook's mind raced, analyzing every move. Michael's efficiency was impressive, but it also revealed his patterns, his strengths, and his potential weaknesses.

"Interesting... this new recruit shows promise. His methods are precise, and he's clearly well-trained. But every step he takes further ensnares him in my web," the spook thought.

The spook watched as Michael completed his task and began his escape. The calculated movements, the seamless execution—it was all data to be stored, analyzed, and used. By the end of the mission, the spook had compiled a detailed dossier on Michael, complete with his strengths, weaknesses, and potential vulnerabilities.

Back in his office, the spook reviewed the footage again, meticulously noting every detail. Michael's successful mission had provided the IRA with critical intelligence, but it had also given the spook invaluable insights into their operations.

"Every move he makes, every success, only serves to tighten the web around him. Michael O'Connor may be a promising operative, but he is now firmly within my sights," the spook mused.

The spook knew that this was just the beginning. Michael's rising prominence within the IRA made him an even more valuable target. The spook's strategic mind began to formulate the next steps, planning how to use the gathered intelligence to further dismantle the IRA from within.

The spook's mind raced through the collected data. He instructed his team on the next steps, ensuring that each detail was meticulously planned.

"Moira's role is pivotal. She has gained Seán's trust, and through him, we can access deeper levels of the IRA's network. Her reports are crucial for understanding the inner workings and morale of their members," the spook explained.

"What about the risk of exposure, sir? If they discover Moira's true role, the entire operation could be compromised," a junior officer voiced, his concern evident.

"That's why we must be precise and cautious. Every piece of intelligence Moira gathers must be cross-verified. We cannot afford any mistakes. The Director's patience is running thin, but we are closer than ever to a significant breakthrough. We dismantle them from within, using their own operations against them."

The room buzzed with the intensity of the task ahead. The spook's strategic mind was evident in the way he orchestrated the operation, ensuring every angle was covered, every potential threat mitigated.

After the intense debrief session, the spook stepped back into the cold night air. His escort waited, the car's engine idling softly. He slid into the back seat, the door closing with a solid, reassuring thud. The car pulled away from the safe house, heading towards his home. The city lights blurred past the windows, casting fleeting shadows across his face. His mind, still consumed by the intricacies of his operations, began to drift over the key events that had led him to this moment.

The car pulled into the driveway of a modest, unassuming house. The spook stepped out, taking a deep breath of the cool night air. The quiet suburban street contrasted sharply with the tense environment of the safe house. He walked up to the front door, inserting his key into the lock with practiced precision. As the door swung open, he was greeted by the warm, inviting light of his home.

He hung up his keys on a small hook by the door and stepped inside, his shoes making a soft thud on the wooden floor. The housekeeper, an older woman with kind eyes and a gentle demeanor, greeted him.

"Good evening, sir. Dinner is ready," she said, her voice a soothing balm after the day's tensions.

The spook nodded in acknowledgment, offering a brief, but genuine smile. "Thank you, Margaret. I'll be in the dining room shortly."

He made his way to the dining room, the familiar surroundings providing a momentary sense of comfort and normalcy. The table was set, a simple but hearty meal waiting for him. He sat down, the weight of the day's events still heavy on his shoulders.

As he began to eat, his mind continued to replay the pivotal moments of his career and the current operation against the IRA.

"I was recruited because of my analytical skills

and my ability to think several steps ahead," he thought, recalling the rigorous training, the psychological conditioning, and the countless hours spent learning the intricacies of espionage. The early days at MI5, fresh out of university, were grueling but essential.

From the beginning, he demonstrated a keen analytical mind, excelling in strategic thinking. This foundation was critical in his ability to plan complex operations.

His thoughts shifted to his first significant operation, where he was tasked with infiltrating a suspected terrorist cell. "That operation taught me the importance of patience and precision. Every detail mattered, every move was calculated."

His success in that first major operation highlighted his patience and methodical approach, traits that had defined his career.

Liam's voice, filled with fear and urgency, still echoed in his mind. The information about Michael O'Connor's planned mission was invaluable. "Liam was a necessary risk. His fear made him compliant, and his information was crucial."

His ability to manipulate Liam into providing valuable intelligence showcased his skill in exploiting weaknesses and influencing others.

He recalled the meticulous setup of surveillance around key IRA hotspots. "Surveillance is an art form. It requires subtlety and skill. The slightest mistake can compromise the entire operation."

His effective use of surveillance technology and human intelligence (HUMINT) illustrated his resourcefulness and intelligence in leveraging available tools.

The ambush, using intelligence from Liam, was a turning point. "That night was critical. Capturing Seán alive gave us an edge. It was a calculated risk, but one that paid off."

His orchestration of the ambush, ensuring Seán's capture despite the dangers, underscored his cold and ruthless nature.

Moira's placement in the Maze prison was strategic. Her ability to gain Seán's trust and gather intelligence was pivotal. "Moira was a gamble, but a necessary one. Her position in the Maze allowed us to penetrate the IRA's defenses from the inside."

His decision to place Moira in the Maze and manage her role demonstrated his calm and composed nature, crucial for overseeing high-risk operations.

As he finished his meal, the spook stood up and walked over to the window. He looked out into the night, the city lights twinkling in the distance. His thoughts turned to Michael O'Connor, the rising star within the IRA who now occupied much of his strategic planning.

"Michael O'Connor, you're a formidable opponent," he mused. "Every step you take, every move you make, I have to anticipate and counter. Your first mission was a success, a testament to your capabilities and potential."

The spook acknowledged Michael's skills and potential, understanding that underestimating him could be a fatal mistake.

Exposure and Compromise: The spook knew that Michael was aware of the constant threat of surveillance and was likely taking measures to counteract it. Any slip-up could expose his operations.

Operational Failure: Each encounter with Michael was a high-stakes game of cat and mouse. Failure was not an option, but the risk was ever-present.

Political and Public Backlash: The spook was acutely aware that any misstep in handling Michael could lead to political fallout, especially if operations went public.

Psychological Toll: The constant mental chess game with Michael took a significant toll. The spook had to stay sharp, but the relentless pressure could be exhausting.

Operational Security Breaches: Maintaining the secrecy of his operations was critical. Michael's network was vast, and any breach could unravel months of work.

Legal and Ethical Dilemmas: The spook's tactics often skirted the boundaries of legality and ethics. Dealing with someone as capable as Michael required walking a fine line between necessary actions and moral compromises.

"This is only the beginning, Michael. The web is in place, and the pieces are set. Now, it's time to see who makes the next move. I must stay ahead, remain vigilant, and ensure that every decision tightens the net around you and your unit."

He turned away from the window, his resolve hardened. The battle against the IRA was far from over, and Michael O'Connor was a central figure in this ongoing conflict. The spook knew that every move had to be calculated, every risk weighed, as the intricate game of cat and mouse continued.

The spook stood by the window, looking out into the night. The lights of the city twinkled in the distance, but his mind was elsewhere. He contemplated the potential fallout if the political wing of the IRA, Sinn Féin, were to discover that MI5 had planted an agent within the Maze prison. His thoughts were a mix of strategic calculations and deep-seated concerns about the repercussions of such a revelation.

"If the truth about Moira ever comes out, the public outrage will be immense," he thought. "The nationalist and republican communities already view the British government with suspicion and hostility. This revelation would be seen as a gross betrayal of trust and a violation of civil rights."

The spook imagined the headlines: "MI5 Infiltrates Maze Prison," "Government Betrayal," "Spies Among Us." The media frenzy would be relentless, feeding off the public's anger and disillusionment.

"We would face severe political backlash. Sinn Féin would capitalize on this to rally their supporters, painting us as villains who stoop to any level to achieve our goals."

He knew that Sinn Féin's leadership, particularly figures like Gerry Adams and Martin McGuinness, would leverage this situation to their advantage, using it to strengthen their political position and undermine the British government.

"The peace process is already fragile. This could shatter any progress we've made. Trust is the foundation of these negotiations. Without it, we're back to square one."

The spook understood that the revelation would severely damage any trust built between the IRA's political representatives and the British government. Negotiations could stall, and the delicate balance of peace could be disrupted.

"If Sinn Féin pulls out of the talks, we could see a resurgence of violence. The streets of Belfast could once again become battlegrounds."

The thought of returning to the days of constant bombings and shootings weighed heavily on him. Every step towards peace was painstakingly slow, and any setback could be catastrophic.

"There will be legal challenges, no doubt about it," he considered. "Our methods will come under intense scrutiny. We could face inquiries, trials, and who knows what else."

The spook knew that exposing Moira's role would lead to a series of legal battles. The ethical and legal boundaries of MI5's operations would be questioned, potentially leading to significant reforms within the intelligence community.

"And then there's the operational security. If the IRA discovers Moira, they'll tighten their defenses. Every future operation will become exponentially more difficult."

He anticipated a brutal crackdown within the IRA, as they rooted out potential informants and spies. The paranoia would lead to increased security measures, making it harder for MI5 to gather intelligence.

"What would happen to Moira? She's in the lion's den. If they find out, her life is at risk," he worried. "And what about my own career? Will I be the scapegoat?"

The spook contemplated the personal risk to both Moira and himself. The potential fallout could see careers ruined, lives endangered, and the trust within MI5 itself eroded.

"Every move we make is a gamble. The higher the stakes, the greater the risk. But we must stay the course. The fight against the IRA is too important to back down now."

As he weighed all these considerations, a steely resolve hardened within him. "No matter the cost, Michael O'Connor and his unit must be destroyed. They represent a direct threat to everything we've worked for."

His mind raced through the strategies and tactics needed to dismantle Michael's team. "Moira's position must be protected at all costs. We'll double down on our efforts, increase surveillance, and tighten the noose."

He felt a cold determination settle over him. The moral and ethical dilemmas that once plagued him faded into the background. The mission was clear, and he would see it through to the end, regardless of the personal and professional risks.

The narrative shifts to a courtroom in the near future. The atmosphere is tense, filled with journalists, spectators, and high-profile figures. The spook sits in the defendant's chair, his face expressionless as the judge reads the verdict.

"For the actions taken under your directive, and the subsequent fallout, you are hereby sentenced to..." the judge's voice echoed through the courtroom.

The spook listened, unflinching, as the sentence was passed. His mind drifted back to the night by the window, the weight of his decisions, and the resolve that led him here.

The courtroom was a stark contrast to the shadowy world he operated in. Here, everything was laid bare, judged in the harsh light of day. The prosecution's arguments had painted a picture of a man who had crossed ethical boundaries, who had manipulated and coerced to achieve his goals. The defense had tried to justify his actions as necessary evils in the fight against terrorism, but the jury had seen through it.

As he was led away in handcuffs, he reflected on the sacrifices made and the mission that consumed his life. "I did what I had to. For the greater good."

The spook's thoughts drifted back to his interactions with Michael O'Connor, the countless hours of planning and executing operations, and the moments of doubt and resolve. He remembered the faces of those he manipulated, the lives he altered, and the legacy he left behind.

The courtroom faded, and with it, the story of the spook—an operative who gave everything in the shadowy world of intelligence, only to find himself judged in the harsh light of day.

The spook's journey was one of complexity, filled with moral ambiguity and relentless pursuit of his mission. His legacy was a tapestry of strategic brilliance and ethical compromises, a reminder of the high stakes

and harsh realities of the world he navigated.

As he was taken to his cell, the spook knew that the fight against the IRA would continue. New operatives would rise, new strategies would be devised, and the game of cat and mouse would persist. His role might have ended, but the struggle went on.

"Every move, every decision, it was all part of the game. And in this game, there are no clear winners, only survivors."

The door to his cell closed with a finality that echoed through his mind. The spook sat on the narrow bed, his thoughts a whirl of past deeds and future uncertainties. The lights dimmed, and he was left alone with his reflections, a man who played the game to the very end.

End of Part 1

www.ingramcontent.com/pod-product-compliance
Lightning Source LLC
Chambersburg PA
CBHW021930120726
47992CB00001B/3